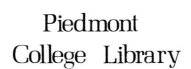

Philo C. Wasburn

PURDUE UNIVERSITY

POLITICAL SOCIOLOGY:
APPROACHES, CONCEPTS, HYPOTHESES

PRENTICE-HALL, INC. Englewood Cliffs, New Jersey 07632

Library of Congress Cataloging in Publication Data

WASBURN, PHILO C.
   Political sociology.

   Includes bibliographical references and
index.
   1. Political sociology. I. Title.
JA76.W36   306'.2   81-18260
ISBN 0-13-684860-5   AACR2

To Mara, Aaron, Leah and Hope

Editorial/production supervision: Richard Kilmartin
Cover design: Maureen Olsen
Manufacturing buyer: John Hall

Printed in the United States of America

10 9 8 7 6 5 4 3 2 1

Prentice-Hall International, Inc., *London*
Prentice-Hall of Australia Pty. Limited, *Sydney*
Prentice-Hall of Canada, Ltd., *Toronto*
Prentice-Hall of India Private Limited, *New Delhi*
Prentice-Hall of Japan, Inc., *Tokyo*
Prentice-Hall of Southeast Asia Pte. Ltd., *Singapore*
Whitehall Books Limited, Wellington, *New Zealand*

5/19/83 Berheart Tylr 2295

CONTENTS

PREFACE

In no known human society have all individuals or all groups been treated as equals. In all societies, to some extent, existing inequalities in social advantages, and often inequalities in social rights, are the results of the use of power and authority.

People are most likely to raise questions about the system of social inequality within which they have been living during periods of rapid and extensive social change. Because social inequality is tied to power and authority, it is during such times that political theory emerges. For example, Plato's political thought appeared during the breakdown of tribalism and the emergence of the urban community and the state. This transformation meant that the relatively simple choice of conformity with or deviation from received social rules was replaced by the more complex problem of deciding what social rules to live by. The Greeks of Plato's time began to ask: What is the right way? What is justice? Are there any limits to the rules we can make? Who should govern? How should social rewards be distributed?[1]

During the seventeenth and eighteenth centuries in Western Europe, the growth of science, the development of an industrial and commercial middle class, and the Protestant Reformation undermined the authority of the Catholic church, which had served as the cultural and social foundation of medieval society. Significant political theory was produced during this period. Philosophers raised questions about the validity of received opinion and about the long-existing structure of social inequality. They began to investigate empirically the physical and social spheres with a view to making them better places for human beings.[2]

The central ideas of late-nineteenth-century Western European political thought were forged as attempts to understand the major transformations that followed the French Revolution and the industrial revolution and to argue for the desirability of various alternative forms of social-political organization. Modern sociology has its origins within this body of thought.

The history of the United States also shows periods of vast social change during which prevailing structures of social inequality underwent the scrutiny of political theorists. The events of the first two decades of this century, when a rural and religious society was rapidly becoming urban, industrial, and secular, generated discussion of the social and political role of science. The Great Depression and the world wars raised questions about social inequalities associated with capitalism and economic individualism, about political responses to social and economic problems in the form of the New Deal, and about the stability and maintenance of Western industrial democracies. The investigation of these and related topics was the overriding concern of American sociologists from the mid-1930s to the early 1960s. To a considerable extent the analytic approaches of American sociologists to these problems were influenced by their late "discovery" and reinterpretation of the writings of Western European theorists of the preceding century.

Throughout the world, from the early 1960s and into the early 1970s, major challenges were made to systems of social inequality and to the uses of power and authority associated with them. Internationally, this was seen in the rise and continuing transformations of the nations of the Third World. In the United States the civil rights, student, antiwar, feminist, antinuclear, and other movements made an impact on society. These challenges influenced the subject matter of American sociology as topics such as the abuse of power, social conflict, and large-scale social change became widely discussed. The attention paid to these topics was highlighted by the Watergate scandals, public disclosures of various covert activities of the CIA, the FBI, and the military, and by growing public awareness of the role played by multinational corporations in domestic and international political affairs.

In this historical perspective, political concerns from the mid-1970s to the present appear to be rather parochial and nondramatic. Despite continuing violence in Northern Ireland, revolutions and wars in the Middle East, Africa, and Latin America, and shifting relationships among the United States, China, and the Soviet Union, the attention of most Americans, including many sociologists who study politics, has focused largely on matters of domestic political economy—determining the size and composition of the public budget, controlling inflation through regulatory mechanisms, distributing public goods and services, and redistributing income. Such relatively placid concerns are in fact linked to the more dramatic international political realities of the recent past. They are also linked to some major institutional changes that have occurred in the United States during the period, and they raise again some of the basic questions of political sociology. In one way or another, all of the concerns involve social inequalities and the uses of power and authority which created, have maintained, or can change them.

This book is an attempt to present some of what is known about power and authority. It seeks to offer a reasonably systematic interpretation of political sociology—a particular type of approach to understanding these topics. The basic thesis developed on the following pages is that political sociology can be identified as a set of intellectual concerns which originated in classical Greece, which were reintroduced during the Enlightenment, but which found their first widely influential modern expression in late-nineteenth-century political theory. These concerns center on relations of power and authority, particularly as these influence and are influenced by kinship, religion, class, interest groups of various kinds, and by shared beliefs and values. They involve questions about the ways in which family, church, class, and associations operate to create, maintain, and change the social distribution of rights and privileges through political activities.

Part One of this book identifies political sociology's central approaches and concepts. Chapter One identifies the major contributions of three of political sociology's theoretical forebears: Karl Marx, Max Weber, and Emile Durkheim. Chapter Two analyzes the ways in which the approaches, concepts, and hypotheses they introduced underwent certain modifications such that present-day formulations of their insights are quite different from those which were originally proposed. The chapter also discusses political sociology's future and its relationship to its origins and to its historical pattern of development. Chapter Three summarizes six well-known discussions of the subject matter, theoretical origins, and patterns of development of the field and compares and contrasts these with the viewpoint developed in this book.

Parts Two and Three describe some of political sociology's major substantive findings. Chapters Four, Five, and Six present the results of social-psychological research dealing with the question of who gets involved in political life and why. The chapters discuss both political support of and political challenge to systems of social inequality. Chapters Seven and Eight review findings on the structural and cultural conditions of democratic and nondemocratic political systems. Research in both of these sections is discussed in light of the view of political sociology and its history developed in section 1.

The Postscript sets forth a view of the analytic, practical, and moral significance of political sociology. Whatever one's position on these matters, it is clear that the topics of power, authority, and social inequality are far from irrelevant to most people.

I would like to offer my sincere thanks to several people who helped greatly in the long process of writing this book. My colleague Reece McGee helped keep the faith in the project even through the dark hours when there seemed to be no light at the end of any tunnel. Jeffrey Goldfarb of the New School For Social Research, Thomas Guterbock of the University of Virginia, and David Knoke of Indiana University all offered countless valuable suggestions for the organization of the manuscript and provided useful ideas for errors to eliminate, topics to include, and references to consider. Doris Fultz and Kay Solomon of Purdue's Social Research Institute always had the manuscript typed and ready when needed.

P.C.W.

NOTES TO THE PREFACE

1. Alvin W. Gouldner, *Enter Plato: Classical Greece and the Origins of Social Theory* (New York: The Free Press, 1965).

2. Reinhard Bendix, "The Age of Ideology: Persistent and Changing," in *Ideology and Discontent,* D. Apter, ed. (New York: The Free Press, 1964), pp. 294–328.

PART ONE
THE FIELD
OF POLITICAL SOCIOLOGY

CHAPTER ONE
THEORETICAL ORIGINS: THE CONTRIBUTIONS OF MARX, WEBER, AND DURKHEIM

LATE-NINETEENTH-CENTURY THOUGHT

The latter part of the eighteenth century was a period of vast social and intellectual change in Western Europe. The French Revolution and the beginnings of industrialization, both of which drastically disturbed existing social and political hierarchies, raised again many of the issues discussed earlier by the philosophers of the Enlightenment. One set of questions centers on the importance of tradition in the patterning of human affairs. What roles, if any, are kinship, religion, class, and other social relationships to play in the determination of the social rewards people receive and the part they take in making the decisions about the social rules under which they are to live? A second set of questions concerns social change. Since social structures are apparently so capable of drastic change, do past changes exhibit any regularities on the basis of which some future changes may be anticipated? To what extent is a single individual or group of individuals capable of initiating significant change in the structure of their society? What, if any, importance is to be attributed to people's ideas and ideals in the process of social and political change?

The writings of Karl Marx, Max Weber, and Emile Durkheim represent attempts to deal with these two related sets of questions. While similar questions had been raised by Plato, Aristotle, Aquinas, Machiavelli, Hobbes, and Locke, among many others, it was the ideas of the Enlightenment philosophers such as Montesquieu and Rousseau, rapidly followed by the sweeping social changes introduced by the French Revolution and the industrialization of Western Europe, that crystallized the issues with which these late-nineteenth-century analysts were to concern themselves.

In their writings Marx, Weber, and Durkheim introduced approaches, concepts, and hypotheses that remain central to political sociology. To cite some examples, Marx's discussion of *alienation*, Weber's characterization of *bureaucracy*, and Durkheim's consideration of *anomie* each continues to stimulate numerous studies of political phenomena. Researchers still investigate relationships, suggested by Marx, between aspects of economic systems and aspects of political systems; relationships between democracy and bureaucracy suggested by Weber; relationships between an increase in the degree of social interaction and political specialization suggested by Durkheim. Marx's view of social change as proceeding from contradictions inherent in economic structures, Weber's description of *rationalization*, and Durkheim's functional analysis of social institutions each provides an approach capable of yielding new insights into political stability and political change. These examples only begin to suggest the range of valuable analytic tools and insights that the three theorists have provided political sociologists. The remainder of this chapter will be devoted to an examination of their contributions.

Before proceeding, however, a number of common elements in their writings should be indicated. First, each theorist focuses primarily on macroanalytic problems; that is, each tends to concentrate on discussions of nation, class, or organization rather than on considerations of the individual or of the small face-to-face group. The concepts mentioned above can serve as illustrations. In his discussion of the alienation of the worker from the means of production, Marx is not considering the problems of separate individuals that stem from special features of their private experiences but the problem of a whole social class which derives from its location in social structure.[1] Weber's writings on bureaucracy are not primarily devoted to considerations of problems concerning the relationship between certain types of social roles and individual personalities but to analyses of the qualities of a historically unique authority system and the transformations this system has introduced in modern societies. For Durkheim, anomie refers to a state of social disorganization in which the social guides for conduct are unclear. The concept, as introduced by Durkheim, is explicitly not to be understood as referring to the acts of individuals or to a psychological state of individual persons.

A second similarity lies in their historical-comparative perspective. This refers simultaneously to the manner in which the theorists characteristically go about defining their concepts and to the process of explanation each commonly, though by no means exclusively, employs. Marx, Weber, and Durkheim often take considerable care to point out the historical specificity of the concepts they introduce. Modern alienation refers to a condition of a particular class of individuals in a historically unique type of society. Marx describes the alienated condition produced by capitalism by contrasting the situation of workers in capitalist societies with that of people living under the conditions of feudalism and primitive communism. Bureaucracy refers to a uniquely modern mode of the social relations of work developed in the West which, Weber thinks, can best be understood by contrast to that organization of work relationships found in traditional, non-Western societies such as India and China. Durkheim's discussions of anomie center on its description as a peculiarly modern social fact, most clearly comprehended by contrast to the social organization of traditional societies.

The three theorists tend to favor historical explanations. That is, they set out to explain why it is that a given subject of study has certain characteristics by describing how the subject evolved out of some earlier one. The objective of this pattern of explanation is to establish the sequence of major events through which some earlier system has been transformed into a later one. The same three concepts which are used above for illustrative purposes can serve here as well. Much of Marx's analysis of the alienation of the working class in capitalist societies consists in locating its historical sources in the breakdown of feudalism. Weber views bureaucracy as an administrative structure which arises subsequent to the disintegration of traditional or charismatic systems due to certain inherent incapacities of these systems. Durkheim's explanation of anomie consists of an analysis of the loosening of the social bonds which served to integrate premodern societies.

A third similarity in the interests of Marx, Weber, and Durkheim is implicit in the preceding—a basic concern with social change. Central to Marx's theory of social change is the notion that history proceeds from conflict between classes generated by contradictions inherent in the economic structures of all previously existing societies. While Weber does not present an explicit and elaborate theory of change comparable to that of Marx, his interest in this topic is nonetheless present. Bureaucracy, for example, is an expression of rationalization which has differentiated Western societies from non-Western societies and from their own traditional past. Central to Durkheim's sociology is his analysis of the transformation of traditional societies and an investigation of bases for the integration of the newly emerging industrial systems. Anomie refers to the state of social disorganization which accompanied this transformation prior to the development of a moral basis for the new industrial life.

Each of the three theorists also has as a major objective the elaboration of a set of hypotheses which are applicable across national boundaries. For example, certain relationships Marx notes between economy and polity are intended as assertions about processes operative in all societies at specific stages in their historical development. Weber's contentions concerning the democratizing implications of bureaucratic development are intended to hold for all Western societies. Durkheim's claims about the relationship between *dynamic density* and the development of the division of labor are clearly intended to be universally applicable.

While the interests of Marx, Weber, and Durkheim do exhibit these broad similarities, it must be recognized that even with respect to these, differences in approach are present. Even though the concerns of each are predominantly macroanalytic, Marx tends to focus on social classes, Weber on social institutions, and Durkheim on the division of labor and problems of normative order. Each theorist introduces many of his central concepts through the use of historical contrasts. However, they are far from showing an equal interest in presenting laws of social development. Marx's dialectic theory specifically centers on a discussion of societal change. Weber's discussion of rationalization focuses more on the differentiation of Western from non-Western societies than on the dynamics of change in Western societies. Durkheim concentrates on the bases of social stability and on establishing an appropriate moral foundation for the incipient order of Western Europe. These and other differences in approach, as well as the differences which divide them on many substantive questions, should be apparent in the following descriptions of some of the central ideas each has contributed to political sociology.

KARL MARX (1818-1883)

Karl Marx's interests were both in describing, explaining, and predicting aspects of the social world and in changing many of the contemporary social structures and processes about which he wrote. His importance to political sociology lies not only in the rich conceptual and theoretical materials he presents, but also in the fact that his writings continue to play an important role in the political lives of many nations. Any description and/or explanation of the political structures and processes of these nations requires at least some reference to his thought.

An Overview of Marx's Social Thought

People continuously modify and change the tools they use and the activities they perform in transforming the physical world to meet their needs. According to Marx, as people alter these tools and productive activities they also necessarily change their relationships to one another. The technological means of production determine the relationships which workers form to produce goods more effectively than they could if acting separately.

The relationships of individuals to each other with respect to the materials, the instruments, and the products of work determine the general character of their social, political, and intellectual life. For any given society at any point in its history, the basic features of its political and religious institutions, its laws, morality, science, philosophy, and art are determined by the kind of social relations of production that prevail. This is Marx's basic postulate of *historical materialism*. People's ideas and ideals, by themselves, have little impact on the social conditions under which they live. Rather, it is their social life or, more specifically, the social relationships they establish in the process of production which ultimately shape their beliefs and their goals.

Marx's phrase "social relations of production" refers to property relations—ownership or lack of ownership of the materials and tools of production. Marx directs attention to the relationships within and between sets of persons who own productive property and sets of persons who do not own the means of production. While the specific work people do may have some influence upon their beliefs, attitudes, and actions, it is their status as owners or nonowners of the means of production that is of fundamental importance.

Marx distinguishes four systems of relations of production which have existed up to the present: primitive communism, slavery, feudalism, and capitalism. While influential views on each of these are developed, it is Marx's analysis of capitalism which has had the greatest impact on political sociology. Capitalism, in Marx's view, is a system of production under which the direct producers own no portion of the raw materials or of the tools with which they work, or of the goods which they produce. They are makers of commodities, that is, objects for sale in a market to be purchased and consumed by others. These commodities are produced for purposes of profit of those who own the means of production. Workers are formally free to sell their services to anyone; labor itself is a commodity in the capitalist system.

During the first phase of capitalism, which prevailed in Western Europe roughly from the middle of the sixteenth to the last third of the eighteenth century, the owners of the means of production hired the services of a number of handicraft workers. Each worker carried out similar activities; each completed every stage in the manufacture of a product. Eventually, however, an elaborate division of labor emerged. Each worker became responsible for the manufacture of some one part of a commodity, and increasingly specialized tools were developed to facilitate the manufacture of each part. While at this historical state the worker was still a craftsman, he no longer shaped a product which reflected his talent alone. The worker thereby lost another kind of control over the products of his labor and the personal significance of his work again was reduced.

Marx maintains that the value of a commodity is determined by the amount of socially necessary labor time required for its production, that is, the amount of labor time required given the skills, technology, and intensity of effort on the part of workers that can be expected at a given time. Labor itself is a commodity the value of which is determined, like the value of any other commodity, by the amount of socially necessary labor time required to produce it. However, unlike other commodities, labor creates more value than it itself is worth. That is, the capitalist buys the worker's labor power for a wage which is less than the new value produced by this worker.

Capitalism is the modern form of exploitation. Under it the unjust treatment of the workers is simply more subtle than it was under slavery or feudalism. While the owners of the means of production appear to pay workers for their labor, in reality they pay them less than the value of that work. Whether under slavery, feudalism, or capitalism, the owners of the means of production take for themsleves the profit created by the exploitation of the direct producers.

Constantly increasing the profit of the bourgeoisie, the ownership class, is the aim of capitalist production. Because exploitation of workers is the source of their profit, capitalists are encouraged to get as much labor time from their workers as possible. When, at some point, a capitalist is no longer able to get still more labor time from his workers and thus is not able to increase production and profits and meet competition, he must make a proportionately greater investment in machines.

The second phase of capitalist production emerged at the end of the eighteenth century with the increasing use of mechanical means of production. Workers ceased to be craftsmen and became machine operators. With technological advances, a few comparatively unskilled laborers could manufacture in a short time what required considerable time of skilled artisans. Consequently, with the emergence of industrial capitalism and the factory, competition between workers for increasingly scarce and decreasingly skilled jobs became greater and greater.

Although in this second phase of capitalism workers are formally free to dispose of their labor, conditions are such that the choice is really between taking any available employment or starving. The workers' relation to the owners of the means of production is impersonal and indirect. Rather than cooperating as fellow workers, they are forced by industrial capitalism to compete with each other. Rather than directing the manufacture of a product, workers are limited to the operating requirements of the machines with which they work. In sum, under the conditions of industrial capitalism, workers control neither raw materials, nor tools, nor the making of products, nor their relations to others (whether owners or fellow laborers), nor the conditions of work, nor the manner in which they are to dispose of their own labor power.

Industrial capitalism results in the alienation of the workers. By this

Marx means more than that workers have no control over any aspect of their work activities. He means that workers also come to be dominated by the very objects they produce. They are dominated by forces of their own creation, which confront them as alien power. The more productive the workers are the greater the profit realized by the owners of the means of production and thus the greater the owners' resources available for dominating the workers. Marx also means that the workers, having lost control of their own products, which become used against them, alienated themselves. As Marx sums up: ". . . in his work he does not affirm himself but denies himself, does not feel content but unhappy, does not develop freely his mental and physical energy but mortifies his body and ruins his mind."[2]

Factory production leads to a greater output of commodities. However, the market for these is constantly dwindling due to the decrease in the number of available jobs and a decrease in wage levels resulting from the increased competition between workers for the few relatively unskilled jobs which are available. The ranks of unemployed workers vastly enlarge and eventually come to include small employers who fail to meet expanding competition. Industrial capitalism thus leads to the development of large monopolies as well as widespread unemployment. Society moves toward polarization, becoming composed of an increasingly large class of workers whose material conditions are relatively worsening and a class of property owners which is decreasing in membership but which is increasing the proportion of the society's surplus which it controls and perpetuating these inequalities through the institution of family inheritance. The objective opposition of social classes, found in all societies in which private property exists, is nowhere more pronounced in social history than under the second phase of capitalism.

The bourgeoisie uses a number of mechanisms to obscure this objective opposition and thereby reduce the revolutionary potential of the proletariat. According to Marx, the ruling ideas of each age have always been the ideas of its ruling class. The religious, moral, philosophical, and juridical ideas which are transmitted by the schools, churches, and various media of communication of capitalist societies are the ideas of the bourgeoisie and serve its economic interests by reducing the class consciousness of the proletariat—by producing its "false consciousness."

The legal codes of capitalist societies are another means whereby the bourgeoisie maintains its dominant economic position. The exploitation of workers is somewhat veiled under capitalism because it appears that workers are paid the full value of their labor. Similarly, the political domination of workers by the bourgeoisie is more subtle during the second period of capitalism. The transition from feudalism to capitalism brought about a change in the method of political rule. The unlimited power of the hereditary monarch was replaced either by a constitutional monarchy or by a parliamentary republic. Citizens were given certain political freedoms and were supposed to be equal before the law.

Such political changes are compatible with and, in fact, are required by a capitalist economy. Unregulated enterprise, free competition, and freedom of contract all work to the advantage of the bourgeoisie. Marx argues that, in reality, equality of rights in capitalist societies means nothing to the workers but the right to sell their labor power for less than it is worth—the right to be exploited.

Behind legal codes stands the state, viewed by Marx as those social agencies such as the police and the army with the power to compel compliance with the law and ultimately to settle economic disputes. While the state may appear to operate impartially in the interests of all members of a society, in all stable societies the state is actually the instrument of the dominant economic class. In capitalist societies the state is the means by which the bourgeoisie insures that its economic interests will be maintained. It is the agency which enforces the exploitation of the direct producers. According to Marx, it is only by overthrowing the state that the proletariat can free itself from exploitation by the bourgeoisie.

As capitalist societies mature, the population becomes more concentrated, the means of production become more centralized, and the class of owners narrows in size. A consequence of this is political centralization. Semiautonomous provinces with separate interests, laws, governments, and systems of taxation become organized into one nation with one code of laws and one government. Furthermore, control of the increasingly centralized and powerful state is in the hands of the bourgeoisie, whose numbers are diminishing. In sum, the development of an industrial capitalist society means that a small proportion of that society's population, the owners of the means of production, come to monopolize the society's wealth and power and will use that power to maintain and further advance those property relations from which they benefit. Concomitantly, the class of workers, whose material circumstances are relatively worsening, vastly increases its membership. Modern laborers in all societies, instead of rising with the progress of industry, are kept from realizing the full social benefits made possible by advanced technology.

The increasing size and relative impoverishment of the working class contribute to its members' growing awareness of their common interests.[3] Mature economic conditions produce a mature proletarian class. Once conscious of their common interests and vast numbers, workers begin to develop means of communication and begin to organize. They come to recognize that only by overthrowing the state can they free themselves from their subservience to the bourgeoisie. They realize that only revolution can end their alienation and exploitation. A self-conscious and organized proletariat can no longer be contained by the ideas, laws, and coercive apparatus of the bourgeois state. On the basis of this analysis Marx and Engels conclude the *Manifesto of the Communist Party*: "The proletarians have nothing to lose but their chains. They have a world to win. Working men of all countries unite!"

Marx believes that ultimately workers will seize power, vest ownership of the means of production in the community, and use them for the common good. The new economic system, socialism, will produce a society in which there are no social classes; the owner-worker distinction will no longer have validity. With the abolition of private property and after several transitionary phases will come the demise of the state, historically the tool used by the property class for the repression and exploitation of the direct producers. Finally, as the antagonism between classes within a nation vanishes, the hostility of one nation toward another will also come to an end.

Criticisms of Marx

Today few political sociologists either totally accept or totally reject Marx's analysis. A brief review of criticisms should begin to indicate how far and in what direction political sociology has traveled since Marx. The review should also reveal the lasting, genuine contributions Marx has made to political sociology.

Marx's concern with the "final" or "ultimate" cause of a given social phenomenon (for example, his claim that ideas are, *in the last analysis,* determined by the position of their holders in the relations of production) is at variance with contemporary notions of the objectives and capabilities of scientific investigation. Today social scientists are concerned with discovering empirically the interplay of a number of operationally defined variables. For example, while a political sociologist may be interested in which of a number of factors accounts for the most variance in voting behavior in a nation during a particular historical period (for example, class or region or religion), it is highly unlikely that he will raise a question such as "What factor determines *in the last analysis,* a person's economic attitudes, political attitudes, or voting behavior?" It should be noted that contemporary Marxists deny the validity of such criticism. They argue that Marx's assignment of primacy to one dimension of social life involved the recognition that social reality has many dimensions. It also involved the additional and crucial insight, not yet grasped by Western sociologists, that these dimensions have an inner, necessary relationship with one another. They influence one another in unequal ways with different weights and different effects. "The lack of such an idea as 'the inner bond of phenomena' cannot ... be substituted by a simple enumeration stringing together or demarcating single dimensions, factors or components of social life."[4]

A second set of criticisms concerns the validity of certain of Marx's assertions. First, while Marx claims that a society's economic system determines the form of its political system, no perfect correlation between type of economy and type of polity can be established. Capitalism, for example, has coexisted with a variety of political systems, including absolute monarchy and democracy. An important implication of this criticism for political sociology is that the degree of political democracy found in a society may be explained by other than factors attributable to its mode of production.

Marx contends that economic power is a sufficient and necessary condition for political power. Ralf Dahrendorf has commented on this point:

> . . . it was true in Marx's own time, and in English society, that the captains of industry or their relatives tended to monopolize many of the leading political positions. The same is still true in several countries, including the United States and Germany. But this particular observation does not legitimize the formulation of a general law. Should this law nevertheless be advanced as a general hypothesis, then it was refuted by the first government of a labor party in an industrial country. The political state and industrial production are two essentially independent associations in which power is exercised; and their interrelations are a subject for empirical research.[5]

Contrary to expectations based on Marxist theory, the will of those representing vast amounts of concentrated economic power can be resisted and manipulated by those with purely political resources. For example, hearings of the U.S. Senate subcommittee on multinational corporations revealed that in 1974 Gulf Oil Corporation had been "muscled into making $5 million in political contributions in South Korea and other countries." A Securities and Exchange Commission report indicated that, in that same year, United Brands Company was forced to pay $1.25 million in bribes in Honduras in exchange for a reduction of export taxes.[6] However, it must be added that resisting and manipulating are not the same as prevailing in the long run. In these and in similar examples, the corporations ultimately got what they wanted and paid for.

Many significant social and political changes that have been introduced in societies were not the result of the successful revolution of the exploited class. The introduction of welfare democracy in the United States did not follow the revolutionary victory of America's "proletariat" but was primarily the consequence of organized labor working through established political structures. Today it is certainly true, as Marxist thought predicts, that there are millions of people in advanced capitalist societies, such as the United States, who live well below the level of comfort and dignity that could be made available by existing means of production. The staggering costs of medical services, shortage of public housing, inadequate public transportation, massive military spending, environmental degradation, and the possible health threats of reliance on nuclear power, among other problems of the utmost seriousness, can largely be attributed to the operation of an economic system in which the importance accorded individual profit far outweighs the importance accorded social needs.[7] In light of such facts it is easy to overlook the political, social, and material gains made by the working class in Western industrial societies in the past decades. But to trivialize the significance of these changes is just as misleading as it is to exaggerate them. The extent to which, historically, the basic features of a nation's political institutions have been introduced by revolutionary action rather than by institutionalized means is an important variable accounting for many of the differences evident today between the political structures and cultures of nations.

A number of Marx's predictions, particularly those dealing with political developments within advanced, capitalist-industrial societies, have failed thus far to materialize. Factors such as the separation of ownership and management, social mobility, significant improvements in material standards of living, the dissemination by the mass media of a relatively uniform culture, widespread recognition of the social, political, and economic conditions within the Soviet Union, and the continuous though gradual enactment of legislation favorable to the working class facilitated the development of a "proletariat" committed to the nonrevolutionary change of a political-economic system whose basic features they support. It is possible, of course, that Marx's predictions will be realized within the next several decades. To project a future in which significant, class-based social, political, and ideological conflicts are absent represents more an act of faith or an expression of a wish than it represents social science.

While many of Marx's concepts have facilitated important insights into political phenomena, they have also proved at times to be misleading. In this connection his concepts of class, capitalism, socialism, political change, and ideology are discussed below.

Marx considers a *class* to be a conflict group comprised of persons having identical relations to the means of production of their society and consequently having identical objective interests. Owners of productive property are committed to the maintenance of the social order which operates to insure their advantages while those who own no productive property are committed to the destruction of the existing, exploiting institutions under which they live. Classes are most clearly visible in capitalist societies when the confrontation between the proletariat and the bourgeoisie fully emerges. Even if it is useful for some analytic purposes to define class solely in terms of property ownership, it does not follow that classes, so defined, necessarily constitute mutually antagonistic conflict groups. The implicit a priori assumption that property owners will always have identical political interests that are invariably opposed to those of nonowners is unwarranted. It always remains an empirical question in a given political system with respect to a given political issue whether there is political unity or conflict both within and between classes.

Writers from Max Weber to Ralf Dahrendorf have argued that Marx's conceptualization of class is too narrow. It disregards the fact that inequality possibly unrelated to property ownership may serve as an important basis for political cleavage. Differences in status, authority, religion, and ethnicity have each played an important role in the history of political conflict.[8]

Marx's typology of societies also embodies certain difficulties. His characterizations of capitalism and socialism, for example, do not correspond to the structures of modern societies generally regarded to be "capitalist" or "socialist." On this point Sidney Hook remarks:

> There are various (alternative forms of economic organization) which he ignored, like one which continues private ownership of the means of production with extensive social control of its operation or a mixed economy with private and public sectors of production. Both of these alternatives are equally removed from his conceptions of Capitalism and Socialism and closer to present-day realities in various countries.[9]

Marx considers political change to occur only with the revolutionary overthrow of an economic system and the state that supports it. This conceptualization of change is highly limiting, deflecting attention from such processes as changes of parties in power and the introduction of new legislation through parliamentary procedures. These latter types of change, rather than revolution, have been responsible for major developments within many modern "capitalist" societies.

Marx discusses an *ideology* as a set of beliefs about the political and economic structure of a society held and promoted by those in privileged positions as justification and support for the maintenance of the status quo. An ideology serves to mask the interests which are being served by the operation of a political-economic system and encourages the disadvantaged to contribute increasing effort on behalf of that system. This conceptualization contains two implicit assumptions. First, all of the belief components of a given ideology are functionally consistent. Second, the belief components of any given ideology are inherently false. Such matters cannot be assumed. However, the truth of each of these claims can be investigated empirically. Research described in Chapter 6 raises serious doubts concerning their validity.

Marx's Contributions to Political Sociology

The preceding criticisms might give the impression that Marx's writings, at best, have served as a resource of dubious value for political sociology. Such an impression would be false. The paragraphs immediately below only briefly suggest some of the areas in which Marx's thought has facilitated the development of political sociology. More detailed descriptions of each of these contributions will be found in the following chapters of this book.

The importance of class (as defined by Marx) as a determinant of political behavior may vary from society to society and from period to period. As will be seen in the following chapters, Marx's concept continues to stimulate new research and subsequent theoretical controversy concerning the "weight" of this factor in determining various kinds of political behavior in various societies. It also raises new questions concerning the importance this factor will have in the most advanced industrial nations, where ties of kinship, religion, and region still appear to be continually weakening. While the variable may not have the overriding significance which Marx attributed to it, numerous empirical studies of voting behavior, community power, national power, political participation, ideology, and the bases of cleavage in industrial nations suggest that class is indeed of considerable analytic utility. As Lipset and Bendix note:

> Every study of the social basis of political movements in the several countries of Western civilization indicates that the parties represent distinctive strata. Despite the great and complex diversity of historical conditions among the "Western" countries, three main political tendencies stand out in all of them: the left, based on the working class, and conservative right, based on the more privileged strata and institutions, and the center based on the middle classes, especially the self-employed.[10]

Some of Marx's earliest discussions of class in industrial, capitalist societies center around his concept *alienation*. The term alienation frequently appears in contemporary empirical studies of such political phenomena as voting behavior, community conflict, and extremist movements. In these research contexts the concept generally refers to individuals' feelings of isolation and powerlessness and not to a property of social structure. This social-psychological conceptualization, which is clearly derived from Marx even though it is theoretically quite different, has proven to be of considerable analytic utility. However, the importance of Marx's structural concept has yet to be adequately explored. As new means of measuring structural variables become available, political sociologists will be in a better position to assess the importance of alienation in political life. Investigations using structural measures might be productive of new insights into political conflict phenomena such as violence, protest, urban unrest, and revolution—events as yet poorly understood.

Marx argues that the interpretation of social reality prevailing in a society is always an interpretation which veils reality in the interests of the ruling class. Dominant ideas about society are tools used for the preservation of that social order and change only as a result of a new class gaining ascendancy. Ideas are weapons in the battle for maintenance and change of the social order and thus have a role to play in political life. However, according to Marx, their importance is never overriding. Dominant ideas change as social-political orders change, but never vice versa. Following chapters will show that Marx's writings on the role of political ideas in social life continue to serve as a fruitful point of departure for investigations of political socialization, voting behavior, and the uses of ideology by nations, corporations, parties, and candidates. Much research has shown that economic position is a good predictor of politically relevant beliefs. Social ideas are grounded in the economic circumstances of those who hold them. Other studies have suggested that certain economic conditions must be present before the cognitive and attitudinal preconditions for political democracy emerge. Still other inquiries have revealed that ideologies have been used in the manner Marx noted.

A widely discussed topic in political sociology has been the distribution and exercise of power within nations and within smaller political units such as communities. Until rather recently it was commonplace to categorize theories of power as either "elitist" or "pluralist." A discussion of the controversy between the advocates of these divergent positions will be presented in Chapter 7. However, here it must be noted that "elitists" share with Marx the view that authoritative political decisions are made to protect the interests of those in socially privileged positions. Such analysts, resting their case on a considerable amount of empirical data, agree with Marx that a few people in positions of power establish the social rules according to which all others in their society, to whom the decision makers are not formally responsible, must live. Furthermore, the development of huge multinational corporations has dramatically reemphasized the importance of economic factors in political life and suggests that policies of large and small nations alike can be influenced by economic interests that transcend their boundaries and ignore their political traditions.

For the most part, present-day political sociologists have avoided dealing with questions concerning large-scale historical processes. Primary concern has been with changes *within* rather than changes *of* political systems. For reasons presented in the following chapters it seems probable that, in the future, political sociologists will devote considerably more attention to noninstitutionalized conflict and change and will be more concerned with non-Western polities. A critical reconsideration of some of Marx's concepts such as "state" and "ideology," his model of structurally generated change, some of his propositions, such as those concerning the historical function of the state, the alienating features of social life in modern society, and the role of conflicting economic interests in political history, should provide some valuable analytic tools with which to advance the systematic, empirical investigation of such topics.

An adequate understanding of diverse political systems and of large-scale conflict and change will require the development of some totally new sociological approaches, concepts, and hypotheses. The search for these must be encouraged. However, the gains that have thus far been made should not be totally cast aside in the belief that a sociological Copernican revolution will somehow invalidate all previous work. The writings of Marx form an important part of the intellectual heritage of political sociology. They contain formulations of many questions, concepts, and claims which constitute the very core of the field. Political sociology has progressed and will continue to progress as earlier insights as well as failures are recognized. Errors can be instructive. So too can questions, even when the answers proposed to them are unsatisfactory. Where Marx was wrong, we have learned from the mistakes. On the other hand, many of his claims proved to be valid, and some of his concepts remain promising and await use in empirical research employing newly developed structural measures.

MAX WEBER (1864–1920)

Although he was far from being an uninvolved observer of his own society, Max Weber explicitly intended his writings to be nonevaluative investigations of the social world. Much of Weber's work can be seen as an attempt to extend and/or correct the analyses of Marx.

Weber's concern with precision rather than persuasion reduces the burden on the present-day interpreter of his writings. On the other hand, his work does not exhibit an obvious thematic unity. Weber does not present, as does Marx, an elaborate theory of history in relation to which his diverse concepts and propositions relevant to the understanding of politics can be neatly organized. He does, however, introduce a concept, *rationalization,* which underlies his discussions of such apparently diverse topics as Protestantism, the medieval city, and the Hindu social system. A discussion of rationalization will serve as the context within which Weber's numerous contributions to political sociology will be presented.

An Overview of Weber's Social Thought

In several senses Weber establishes a more limited set of objectives for social science than does Marx. He argues that any scientist can analyze only a limited segment of reality and do so from a selected perspective. The task of the social sciences is to develop precise, empirically relevant concepts with which to explore selected social relationships.

While social scientists have more modest aims than speculative and/or moral philosophers of history, their objectives are also quite different from those of historians who seek to empirically describe and explain that which is unique to a particular society. Social scientists are concerned with the description and explanation of social processes occurring in a number of societies which share certain historical, structural, or cultural attributes. They are concerned with the interpretative understanding of the subjective meaning actors attribute to given types of conduct in the context of these historical, structural, and cultural settings.

Much of Weber's work exhibits a general interest in the development of Western industrial civilization. Differences between various societies in dominant beliefs, practices, and social relationships in the area of religious, economic, intellectual, and political life, as well as differences in the bearing of these realms on each other, are seen by Weber as manifestations of the different degrees to which rationalization had proceeded. Weber conceptualizes rationalization as

> the product of the scientific specialization and technical differentiation peculiar to Western culture.... It might be defined as the organization of life through a division and coordination of activities on the basis of an exact study of men's relations with each other, with their tools and their environment, for the purpose of achieving greater efficiency and productivity. Hence it is a purely practical development brought about by man's technological genius.[11]

Rationalization in the political realm is manifested in the emergence of the modern state. Weber's discussion of the state and its differentiation from the organization of power in premodern societies is at the very heart of his political sociology. Like Marx, Weber is interested in delineating the various sets of political relationships under which, historically, people have lived. Unlike Marx, Weber does not contend that one social-political system necessarily gives rise to another in some sort of progressive series. Where he does analyze the historical development of a set of political relationships, he does not intend development to be interpreted as *progress*—either in the sense that historically more recent systems are somehow morally superior or in the sense that they represent a stage which must be passed through on the path toward some ideal social system. To Weber, the state is superior to other temporally prior political systems only in a technical sense; it is a more efficient and effective system for the organization of power.

The political aspect of social relations concerns the exercise of power. "He who is active in politics strives for power either as a means in serving other aims, ideal or egoistic, or as 'power for its own sake'; that is, in order to enjoy the prestige feelings that power gives."[12] *Power* is defined as "the possibility of imposing one's will upon the behavior of other persons even against their will." Weber realizes that it is necessary to specify additional qualities in order to differentiate political relationships from those which are more profitably analyzed as economic or religious or kin relationships. Political power, or *domination,* is power exercised within a group which occupies a relatively well defined territory by a person or set of persons responsible for maintaining the order and integrity of the group as a community and whose commands are supported by the use of legitimate force.

The notion of *legitimacy* is particularly important to Weber's conceptualization of domination. There is an element of reciprocity in legitimate political rule. The ability to exercise political power rests, in part, on the beliefs of those subject to that power. *Authority* exists where there is willing compliance of a group of people to the directives of a superior. The compliance is based to some extent upon their shared beliefs that it is illegitimate for them to refuse obedience. Weber's discussion of authority does not suggest that beliefs and values always are more important than other factors, such as the uses of coercion and the distribution of certain resources, for the maintenance of regimes. Rather, his position, as Randall Collins notes, is that

> ... physical resources do not automatically flow into power, and it makes all the difference in individual careers and in the long-run changes of human history just how men manipulate beliefs and emotions.[13]

In one of his most important contributions to political sociology, Weber distinguishes three systems of authority: the *traditional,* the *charismatic,* and the *legal*; each is an ideal type. His typology represents a parsimonious set of concepts in terms of which the major political systems under which human beings have lived can be systematically described and compared. His discussions of traditional, charismatic, and legal domination contain a number of hypotheses linking bases of legitimacy to forms of political organization. Weber's discussion of the typology also embodies his model of political change, which emphasizes that different forms of political organization embody some unique sources of tension and conflict.

Traditional domination is based on the belief that that which has "always existed" is valid. It is a system of rule which rests on "an established belief in the sanctity of immemorial tradition and the legitimacy of the statuses of those exercising authority under them."[14] Those living under traditional rule are subject to conventions but not to laws.

Rule according to custom rather than law affords rulers relatively great freedom in their behavior. The freedom of traditional rulers is also enhanced by the fact that they occupy office by virtue of inherited status and not by virtue of election or the possession of special, technical qualifications. It follows that under traditional domination rule is highly personal; obedience is owed to the person who occupies the position of authority and not to an abstract set of rules.

There are, of course, limits to the use of this personal power, even if these limits are not well defined. Commands must be legitimated in terms of tradition. Traditions themselves directly determine the content of the commands and the objects and extent of authority. Insofar as this is true, to overstep the traditional limitations would endanger the status of chiefs by undermining their legitimacy. In situations where there are no traditional guides for decision making, innovation must occur. However, new rules cannot be announced as such. Rather, chiefs claim that what is actually new has always been in force but only recently recognized by them. Finally, although no formal principles limit rulers, they must be sensitive, nevertheless, to the general notions of justice and ethical conduct held by their subjects.

Under traditional domination members of the rulers' administrative staffs are recruited on the basis of their personal loyalty. Often they are individuals who are economically dependent upon the rulers. Their rights and duties are personally determined by the rulers, who enjoy considerable freedom in making such specifications. The chiefs must take care, however, that such privileges and obligations as they do specify are not particularly well defined. Vagueness permits them to maintain the arbitrary nature of their command and keeps relationships with their staffs personal rather than contractual. Other aspects of the relationship between traditional rulers and their administrative staffs vary considerably between the two major historical forms of traditional domination: *patrimonialism* and *feudalism*. Reinhard Bendix has neatly summarized Weber's distinction between patrimonialism and feudalism in the following way:

> Patrimonial government is an extension of the ruler's household in which the relations between the ruler and his officials remain on the basis of paternal authority and filial dependence. Feudal government replaces the paternal relationship by a contractually fixed fealty on the basis of knightly militarism.[15]

Weber's characterization of traditional domination and his differentiation of its two major forms are carried out in primarily noneconomic terms. The defining quality of traditional domination is legitimation of rule by demonstrating its conformity with codes believed to be valid since time immemorial. Traditional rule is not inseparably linked to a particular type of productive system. Patrimonialism involves administration by a traditional ruler's personal dependents; under feudalism authority is delegated to a warrior-nobility. This distinction is based on the differences between the status and style of life of those who perform administrative services for the ruler. Weber's historical studies reveal that both patrimonialism and feudalism have occurred in conjunction with a variety of economic institutions.

Traditional rulers commonly confront the problem of political decentralization. According to Weber's analysis, although the struggle for power is inherent in patrimonial and feudal organization, it is not between "haves and have-nots"; it frequently involves the desire for prestige rather than material gain; it is not usually revolutionary, and the outcome of any given historical instance cannot be predicted a priori.

Whereas traditional domination involves historical continuity, *charis-*

matic rule introduces sharp changes. It is rule opposed to the restrictions of routine, custom, and law. It involves departure from the ordinary. Charismatic domination refers to rule to which the governed submit because of their belief in the extraordinary quality of a leader regardless of whether this quality is actual or presumed. The legitimacy of charismatic rulers rests on the belief in and devotion to the extraordinary. Charismatic rule has a "religious" quality. The relationship between charismatic rulers and those who recognize their legitimacy more closely resembles the relationship between prophets and disciples than that between rulers and subjects or between elected officials and citizens. Like prophets, charismatic leaders are regarded as having a mission. They lead in unconventional ways, breaking precedents and creating new ones. Thus they are revolutionary and are most likely to arise during periods of social instability.

Weber defines *charisma* as

> ... a certain quality of an individual personality by virtue of which he is set apart from ordinary men and treated as endowed with supernatural, superhuman, or at least specifically exceptional powers and qualities. These are such as are not accessible to the ordinary person, but are regarded as of divine origin or exemplary, and on the basis of them the individual concerned is treated as a leader.[16]

Charismatic leaders arise during periods of crisis or massive collective effort and establish their claims to leadership by dealing with problems in unconventional ways which appear to be successful. Charismatic rule is thus established by the performance of unconventional acts; it involves a break with tradition and routine. Charismatic domination means a rejection of all ties to any external order in favor of dictates, the legitimacy of which is based solely on the fact that they come personally from the leader. Charismatic leaders are free from tradition and from a system of formal, abstract rules. However, they must maintain legitimacy by continuing to demonstrate their unique capacity to deal with exceptional, collective problems. Because of this, charismatic rule is inherently unstable; legitimacy must constantly be proved.

Charismatic leaders have no administrative staffs—neither in the modern, bureaucratic sense nor in the sense in which traditional rulers had personal dependents or independent vassals on whom they relied for the performance of delegated tasks. Disciples who tend to live primarily in a communistic relationship with their leader and who possess some charisma of their own are called upon to serve as agents of the leader.

Problems of instability always accompany charismatic rule. Removal of a charismatic leader (by death or the inability to demonstrate exceptional qualities) leaves the community of followers without a clear successor to leadership and without an abstract set of principles by which to be governed. Therefore, it is in the interest of the followers to "depersonalize" charisma to some extent, that is, to make it compatible with some type of regularization. This can be done by treating charisma as an extraordinary quality which is transmitted through kinship ties ("familial charisma"— exemplified by royal dynasties) or by treating it as an attribute of a role or institution regardless of the person involved, which is transmitted through education and subsequent symbolic acts ("institutional charisma"— exemplified by the organization of the church).

The introduction of familial or institutional charisma as a means of dealing with the problem of succession and continuity represents the beginning of the transformation of a system of charismatic rule into a system of traditional or legal domination. While charismatic rule is commonly transformed into more stable forms of domination, it may again arise, in relatively pure form, in any historical period and in conjunction with any form of social and economic organization.

The third form of rule distinguished by Weber, *legal domination,* is based, in part, on the belief in the validity of commands given in accordance with a consistent system of abstract, impersonal rules. Such rules become established either by the voluntary agreement of all those concerned or by the imposition of what is held to be legitimate by some people over others.[17] The system of rules specifies the rights and obligations of both those who rule and those who are ruled. There is an obligation to obedience only under specified conditions. The persons subject to commands obey "the law" rather than the persons implementing it. Under legal domination, justice consists in the application of abstract rules to particular cases, and administrative processes are aimed at the protection of individuals' interests as these are specified in the social codes.

The purest type of exercise of legal authority is that which employs a bureaucratic administrative staff. Only the supreme chief of the organization occupies his position of authority by virtue of appropriation, of election, or of having been designated for succession. The whole administrative staff under the supreme authority consists, in its purest type, of individual officials who are appointed and function according to a set of criteria which Weber specifies.[18]

Weber discusses two politically significant social consequences of bureaucratic administration. First, the introduction of bureaucracy is "democratizing" in the sense that it tends to reduce social and economic differences between administrators and the governed and presents opportunities for members of all strata to hold administrative offices. Under bureaucratic principles authority is exercised according to abstract rules. Officials themselves are subject to these and are restricted from using their positions for personal gain. Furthermore, officials are recruited from all social strata on the basis of technical qualifications.

Weber also clearly indicates that the elaboration of a bureaucratic system of administration generates serious antidemocratic results. Most modern large-scale organizations such as industries, schools, armies, and political parties, in addition to the state, come to adopt bureaucratic techniques because of their technical superiority. Because administrative efficiency and accomplishment of organization goals are sometimes hampered by democratic freedom of dissent and majority rule, these are often set aside in these organizations.

As rationalization proceeds, bureaucratically structured organizations tend to grow larger and to become increasingly interrelated. A vast increase in the number and in the technical complexity of problems of coordination and control necessitates greater reliance of the leadership on its administrative bureaucracy whose training uniquely qualifies them to deal with these problems. More and more decisions come to be made by "experts." Concentrated social power then tends to slip from the hands of recognized leaders and into the hands of anonymous bureaucratic agents.

Rule according to rational-legal principles frees people from the bonds of tradition and from the arbitrarily imposed demands of traditional or charismatic rulers. Frequently, however, it does subject people to impersonal rules which they played little role in making. Seymour M. Lipset has pointed out the important implications of this analysis:

> The alienation inherent in bureaucracy is, for Weber, independent of the system of property relations. Socialism means more rather than less alienation, because it involves greater bureaucratization. There is little difference between capitalist and socialist societies in their class relations and their propensity to alienation. The source of alienation lies in bureaucracy, which is inherent in industrial society.[19]

Weber's discussions of bureaucracy also embody clear disagreements with Marx's analysis of power on a number of fundamental points. First, Marx contends that private ownership of productive property is the primary source of power in all societies. Weber's consideration of legal domination in general and bureaucratic organizations in particular suggests that within these systems, power resides in position and is independent of property relations. For Weber the relationship between the distribution of wealth and the distribution of power within a given social system is always an empirical question. He therefore treats Marx's postulate as a fundamental problem for social research.

Marx asserted that, following the destruction of capitalism, the state would perish, alienation would end, and all people would live together as equals. As noted above, Weber considered the extension of bureaucracy inevitable. Concomitant with this he foresaw the concentration of power in the hands of anonymous members of the political bureaucracy. The predictable future seemed to Weber to promise *greater* inequality.

No less important in Weber's political analysis than the distribution of wealth is the distribution of a society's social honor. Weber terms the way in which social honor or prestige is distributed in a community its "social order" and argues that the social order and the economic order are not identical. He comments that "the economic order is . . . merely the way in which economic goods and services are distributed and used. The social order is of course conditioned by the economic order to a high degree, and in its turn reacts upon it."[20] Economic advantage is not the sole reason people strive for power. They often seek the social honor or prestige the possession of power sometimes entails. In turn, prestige itself can serve as a source of economic advantage and power.

Weber, like Marx, conceptualizes social class in economic terms. A *class* refers to a set of persons who have in common a certain likelihood of obtaining goods and services due to their similar ability or lack of ability to dispose of other goods or skills for the sake of income in a given economic order. Classes, so defined, are frequent, though not universal, bases for collective action.

In contrast to a class, a *status group* refers to a set of persons who have in common life chances insofar as these are determined by a specific positive or negative social estimation of *honor*. Any quality or qualities shared by the set of persons can be a source of their social honor. "Property as such is not always recognized as a status qualification, but in the long run it is, and with extraordinary regularity. . . . (Nevertheless) both propertied and propertyless people can belong to the same status group and frequently they do with very tangible consequences."[21] Members of a status group exhibit a specific *style of life* and limit their social relations to those from whom this style of life can be expected. According to Weber, status groups, so characterized, are a frequent basis for collective political action.

> Whereas the genuine place of "classes" is within the economic order, the place of status groups is within the social order, that is, within the sphere of the distribution of "honor." From these spheres classes and status groups influence one another and they influence the legal order and are in turn influenced by it. But "parties" live in a house of "power." Their action is oriented toward the acquisition of social "power," that is to say, toward influencing a communal action no matter what its content may be.[22]

A political party is a formally voluntary association, the goal of which is to influence relations of authority within any corporate body or the state. The objective of planned party activity is to secure social power for its leaders in order to obtain material or ideal advantages for its members. The means by which a party can attain power range all the way from the use of physical violence to obstruction in parliamentary bodies to subtle attempts to influence voters.

According to Weber, parties are not necessarily pure class parties or pure status group associations. In most cases they are composed of a mixture of classes and status groups. In practice, any party may predominantly act in the interest of individual persons, classes, status groups, objective policies, or abstract principles. In all parties there is (a) a central group of individuals who assume the active direction of party affairs, including the formulation of programs and the selection of candidates; (b) a group of "members" whose role is considerably more passive; (c) the great mass of citizens whose only role is to choose between the various candidates and programs offered by the different parties. There is a tendency for the interests of the electorate to be taken into account only so far as their neglect would endanger electoral prospects. Weber notes that, given the voluntary character of party affiliation, this structure is inevitable.

Weber views a political democracy as a system in which there is universal suffrage and in which parties freely compete in appealing to the electorate for legitimation. In such a context parties seek *mass* support; they attempt to appeal to as many diverse groups as possible rather than solely and consistently relying on particular groups with fixed and differentiated statuses. Weber believes that political democracy, which encourages the emergence of leaders with wide personal appeal, has a considerable totalitarian potential. Heads of parties can take on some of the qualities of charismatic leaders. With wide enough support they can implicitly deny the legitimacy of the position of any rivals and can thus become dictators, thereby shifting the character of the authority system. Such a change will not necessarily be obvious, for a dictator can use the plebiscite as a symbol of democratic legitimation. "Bureaucratization becomes compatible with a system of legal domination only if the officials are prevented from usurping the political and legislative process. Weber believed, therefore, that bureaucratization would advance, but that it was an open question whether it would be bureaucratization under the rule of law."[23] Increasing *rationalization* did not mean increasing *democratization*.

Criticisms of Weber

As Peter Blau has noted, Weber's use of diverse patterns of explanation and his focus on conflicting social forces make him subject to criticisms from opposite perspectives. For example, he stressed the role of economic interests not enough for the Marxists and too much for the idealists.[24] His efforts toward developing a scientific study of politics drew criticism from supporters of the left, right, and center who refused to recognize any dividing line between ideology and sociology.[25] Nevertheless, some criticisms of Weber are widely accepted.

First, Peter Blau has noted an important omission in Weber's conceptual analysis of authority. Weber fails to discuss the origins of authority, that is, the processes through which other forms of power become transformed into legitimate rule. For example, Weber's writings contain no suggestion of the processes whereby the conqueror later becomes the king.

Weber's "focus on the types of legitimacy leads him to take the existence of legitimate authority for granted and never systematically to examine the structural conditions under which it emerges out of other forms of power."[26]

Karl Lowenstein has also criticized Weber for discussing only legitimate rule:

> ... since Weber dealt only with legitimate authority, his framework must be extended to include a new category of illegitimate violence, since this is no less a type of rule than the legitimate patterns ... the salient characteristic of present-day tyranny or revolutionary authority is not so much that the rulers have seized power by force as that they sustain their position by monopolizing the state apparatus of coercion and total propaganda.[27]

Blau is also particularly critical of Weber's discussion of charismatic domination. He argues that while Weber considers the processes that lead from charismatic rule to traditional or legal domination, he fails to mention the "historical conditions and social processes that give rise to charismatic eruptions in the social structure."[28] Consequently, Blau concludes, Weber has no theory of revolution.

Criticizing Weber's discussion of charismatic domination from an entirely different perspective, Edward Shils argues that the concept of charisma has a wider applicability than Weber's discussions indicate.[29] Weber focuses on the extraordinary disruptive exercise of authority by an individual and on the ways in which stability can be achieved through the transformation of charismatic rule into other forms of authority upon the absenting of the charismatic leader. As Shils sees it, Weber considers only the most intensive and concentrated forms of charisma and disregards the possibility of its dispersion. Shils claims there is in all societies a tendency for people to attribute charismatic qualities to ordinary roles, institutions, strata, or aggregates of persons which effectively exercise power on a large scale. Such a tendency, rather than being disruptive, tends to maintain or conserve a social order.

Serious omissions occur in Weber's analysis of rational-legal domination as exemplified by bureaucratic organization. First, Weber discusses only the formal aspects of bureaucratic structure and does not consider the ways in which these are modified by informal patterns of interaction.[30] Exchanges of power and privilege which are not regulated by the formal normative order occur within rational-legal systems and influence the outcomes of important decisions. To ignore such transactions is to miss much of what politics is all about. Second, Weber fails to analyze some important dysfunctions of the components of bureaucratic organization. "Thus, even if it is true that the hierarchy of authority promotes discipline and makes possible the coordination of activities, does it not also discourage subordinates from accepting responsibility?"[31] Third, Weber does not indicate that each of the components of bureaucratic structure can have different consequences in various organizational or cultural contexts. "It is highly unlikely that strict lines of authority in an organization have the same significance for effective administration in a hospital as in an army or in a country where an egalitarian ideology prevails as in Weber's imperial Germany."[32]

Weber's Contributions to Political Sociology

More than sixty years after his death, the influence of Max Weber on political sociology is still obvious. For reasons and in ways discussed in Chapter 3, it seems likely that the debt of political sociology to Weber will not diminish in the future but, on the contrary, will become greater. The paragraphs below consider only a sample of his lasting contributions.

Morris Janowitz credits Weber with providing the basic raison d'être for political sociology.

> In his essay "Class, Status, Party," Weber postulated that the emergence of modern society implied a historical process of separation of political institutions from economic and social structure. Political institutions thereby emerge as worthy of direct sociological inquiry because they are an independent source of societal change.[33]

Weber's distinction between classes and status groups and his realization that the latter can serve as bases for collective political action have provided an important key to understanding political alignments and political movements in modern industrial societies. For example, numerous American voting studies show that members of low-status religious and ethnic groups tend to support the Democratic party, while members of corresponding but comparatively high-status groups tend to support the Republican party. The status of such groups is attributable only in part to the modal economic position of their members and, in certain cases (for example, Jews), is even contrary to it. With respect to political movements, several studies have suggested that status deprivation rather than purely economic factors has accounted for much of the right-wing extremism recurrent in American political history.[34]

Weber's conceptualization of status calls attention to the fact that a number of variables simultaneously can play a role in determining the social honor of an individual or group. This presents the possibility that an individual or group may have some qualities which enhance its social honor and other qualities which detract. Research shows that status inconsistency has a number of important consequences for political attitudes and behavior.[35] For example, Gerhard Lenski argues that status inconsistency is a source of stress and that individuals will react to this by supporting political parties that favor social change.[36] Hence Weber's discussion of status has facilitated the identification of yet another analytically valuable concept for political sociology.

Weber's differentiation of parties, classes, and status groups emphasizes that the first of these is uniquely concerned with the acquistion of social power. This orientation has suggested numerous recent analyses which view political parties as bureaucratically structured organizations which struggle for power rather than primarily as ideologically committed conflict groups. According to Lowenstein,

> Max Weber repeatedly insisted that politics amounts to conflict and that political parties wage a struggle for political power. He has been proved perfectly right. Political parties today are merely bureaucratically administered and rationally conducted organizations fighting for power. The ideological infrastructure that once differentiated them has shrunk to campaign promises: each pledges that it will do better than others in improving the standard of living.[37]

Weber's discussion of rationalization and his typology of domination have significantly contributed to the development of parsimonious, empirically relevant, and theoretically useful means for comparing polities and for analyzing changes within them. Underlying Weber's typology is the assumption that there is an important connection between the beliefs and attitudes which are prevalent in a society concerning what constitutes legitimate rule and actual political structures which are likely to be found in that society. Although Weber should have treated this assumption as a hypothesis for empirical investigation, contemporary research does suggest its tenability. For example, in a comparative study of five nations, Almond and Verba indicate how the cognitions, feelings, and evaluation of a population toward political objects (what they term a nation's "political culture") form, sustain, and change the democratic potential of their political system. Sources of political conflict within these nations were traced to subgroup differences in political culture.[38]

Some contemporary efforts to systematically compare polities and to chart the probable course of their change have employed concepts similar to rationalization, suggesting anew the utility of Weber's discussions. For example, in a work related to the five-nation study, Almond and Powell view political "development" as a set of processes (which they term "structural differentiation" and "cultural secularization") whereby a political system increases its technical capabilities to extract resources, regulate behavior, allocate rewards, manipulate symbols, and respond to demands.[39] Like rationalization, these processes involve the development of pragmatic, empirical, functionally specific, and universalistic orientations.

Weber's interests in the democratic and antidemocratic consequences of bureaucratic organization are reflected in at least two related areas of research in contemporary political sociology. First, there are studies, such as that of Lipset, Trow, and Coleman, which are concerned with the internal government of voluntary associations.[40] Such works often investigate the conditions which give rise to oligarchic leadership and commonly focus on those which facilitate more democratic patterns of participation by organization members. Second, there are studies, like that of C. Wright Mills, which consider the disproportionate power possessed by those at the top of economic, military, and political hierarchies in putatively democratic societies,[41] and more recent investigations which question the political actions of multinational corporations whose budgets dwarf the economies of many nations.[42]

Today political sociologists tend to define their topics of investigation more narrowly than did Weber. Studies are commonly social-psychological, focusing on the attitudes and behavior of individuals. The data with which political sociologists work seldom resemble the encyclopedic variety of historical materials Weber characteristically gathered in the course of his inquiries. However, there is now apparent increasing interest in comparative politics and political change. Intellectual developments within the social sciences and further changes in international politics are likely to encourage even greater concern with these topics for some time to come. Discussions of comparative politics and political change require the use of concepts and data more closely resembling Weber's than do those presently in wide use.

With a return of interest in macroanalytic, historical-comparative, and developmental problems, political sociologists will continue to find much of value in Weber's writings. Weber's typology of authority, his discussion of classes, parties, and status groups, his conceptualization of bureaucracy, his claims concerning the political consequences of bureaucracy, and his model of change emphasizing conflict between various types of social units pursuing incompatible material and/or ideal interests all have served and continue to serve as valuable beginnings for the empirical study of such topics.

Weber's discussions of rationalization have been particularly influential in political sociology and warrant separate commentary. The concept calls attention to developments which increase efficiency and productivity in virtually all spheres of activity. While this concept has facilitated understanding of Western political and economic organizations, it has unavoidably diverted sociologists' attention from non-Western polities. The need to understand these extends far beyond political sociology.

The conceptual shortcomings and empirical errors present in Weber's works, as well as his clear insights, have been instructive for political sociologists. Methodological and technological developments within the social sciences have only recently made it possible to empirically investigate the tenability of many of his claims concerning social structures and processes and to determine the analytic utility of many of his concepts which refer to properties of social systems rather than to qualities of individuals.

Political sociology will advance not by an a priori rejection of the approaches, concepts, and hypotheses of its theoretical forebears, but by a systematic building upon their ground-breaking efforts.

EMILE DURKHEIM (1858–1917)

Emile Durkheim is universally recognized as a major figure in the history of sociology. His stature is equal to that of Marx and Weber. However, in most discussions of the history of political sociology Durkheim is mentioned only tangentially, if he is mentioned at all. Two lines of argument have diverted interest from considering the relevance of Durkheim's writings to the understanding of political phenomena. First, it is often contended that Durkheim was a "conservative" whose views on society led him to ignore the central topics of political power, conflict, and change.[43] Alternatively, it is commonly believed that Durkheim's own professional interests simply were quite removed from the realm of political affairs.

In the following pages an attempt will be made to demonstrate that these views are counterproductive and have discouraged most political sociologists from examining a potentially rich source of concepts and hypotheses. Political sociologists should no longer continue to ignore Durkheim's works on ideological grounds or dismiss them because of their presumed irrelevance. The discussion of Durkheim is intended to suggest something of the extent to which present-day political sociology actually embodies his concepts and hypotheses.

An Overview of Durkheim's Social Thought

Durkheim, like Marx, believes that a major defect exists in the order of industrial society and that steps to remedy this can be undertaken only after its cause or causes are "scientifically" understood. Each theorist sees his own work as uniquely providing that "scientific" understanding. Marx identifies the defect as alienation—the condition of the working class in which people have no control over any significant aspect of their lives and are dominated by the objects they themselves produce. On the basis of his analysis Marx concludes that only the revolution of the working class is capable of changing this situation. Durkheim identifies the most pressing problem of newly emerged industrial society as *anomie,* the state of social disorganization in which the social guides for conduct are unclear. For Durkheim the most troublesome feature of modern industrial society is not the development of a well-defined order in which the few clearly determine the fate of the many. On the contrary, he believes that industrialization introduced such extensive and rapid changes in social structure that people are uncertain of the rules by which they are to live. The once definite normative order has become poorly defined. Durkheim sees his task as the specification of a new moral order appropriate to modern industrial society. He aims not at plotting the course of revolutionary change but at scientifically discovering and recommending a new basis for social cohesion and stability.

Durkheim believes that only a genuinely *social* science is capable of uncovering a basis for the solidarity of the new industrial order. He argues that such a science must be distinguished from three other types of writing on human behavior: speculations about the nature of humankind and society which are not based on systematic observations, normative analyses in which observations are used to support a priori conclusions, and psychology. While Durkheim cites obvious reasons for excluding the first two of these from the domain of social science, the bases he sets forth to distinguish psychology from social science are considerably less prosaic.

Durkheim argues that sociology has a distinctive subject matter: "social facts."[44] These are the products of social interaction, such as group norms, which are qualitatively distinct from the characteristics of individual group members. Over time groups develop patterns of beliefs, expectations, and behavior which are external to their individual members and which constrain them. Such patterns, he believes, cannot be ascertained by psychological investigations. That is, social phenomena cannot be adequately explained by reference solely to the beliefs, values, and wants of individuals. While these indeed play a role in social causation, social phenomena are primarily the consequences of social processes and structures over which individuals have little control and which frequently run contrary to their desires. To a large extent individuals' beliefs, values, and wants are themselves shaped by these structures and processes. He thus asserts that causal explanations of social phenomena must link social fact to social fact rather than social fact to the intentions of individuals.

Durkheim recognizes an objective of sociological inquiry in addition to the assessment of the efficient causes of social facts. There is a need, he says, to account for the regularity with which certain social facts occur. He is impressed by his observation that "even the most minute and the most trivial practices recur with the most astonishing regularity."[45] Durkheim introduces the concept *function* in an attempt to account for the impressive similarity of certain social facts in different societies.

By the *function* of a social fact Durkheim means the correspondence between it and the needs of the society in which it occurs.[46] Because he rules out the explanation of social facts solely in terms of individuals' values, beliefs, and wants, Durkheim is not concerned with assessing whether or not such correspondence is intentional. Since function *can* refer to the consciously intended consequences of some social fact, this helps account, in part, for its maintenance over time. On the other hand, Durkheim wants to explore the possibility that any given social fact might have important unintended and unrecognized consequences.

Laws constitute a particularly important class of social facts for Durkheim. They are a clearly observable form of social constraint and reflect the most central values held by a group. Durkheim argues that the kind of law operative within a group (whether primarily penal or restitutive) is closely related to the basis of that group's solidarity. In his analysis of this association Durkheim presents many of his concepts which are valuable for the understanding of politics.

According to Durkheim, "primitive" societies are integrated on the basis of mechanical solidarity—deep commitment on the part of their members to a core of shared beliefs, values, and sentiments. Cohesion is the product of similarity. Political organization is little developed. There are tribal chiefs, whose decisions are absolutely binding and have a religious quality.[47] However, this quality is not derived from their being issued by persons who occupy well-defined, legitimate, and superordinate offices or from some special personal qualities which the leaders who issue them are thought to possess. Rather, it is the leaders' association with the group's collective conscience which gives their judgments this special religious quality.[48] Durkheim maintains that the character of leadership in any society reflects the basic features of that society's structure and culture.

> In the first place, whenever we find ourselves in the presence of a governmental system endowed with great authority, we must seek the reason for it, not in the particular situation of the governing, but in the nature of the societies they govern. We must observe the common beliefs, the common sentiments which, by incarnating themselves in a person or in a family, communicate such power to it. As for the personal superiority of the chief, it plays only a secondary role in this process. It explains why the collective force is concentrated in his hands rather than in some others, but does not explain its intensity.[49]

In dominating their societies tribal chiefs are no longer forced to follow all of its traditions. They are a source of initiative which has not existed before then. Contrary to Marx, Durkheim views tribal societies with their primitive communism as contexts within which individual freedom cannot be realized. The lack of the individuals' self-determination is due to the strength of the society's "collective conscience." Only the individual who personally represents that collective conscience is at least partially free from its direction. Weber discusses traditional domination as a "system of rule which rests on an established belief in the sanctity of immemorial tradition and the legitimacy of the statuses of those exercising authority under them." Durkheim also suggests something of the force of that tradition and the power of those who occupy such statuses.

In societies integrated on the basis of mechanical solidarity, behavior which significantly violates common sentiments is met in a severe and repressive manner. Social reactions, and their prescription in law, are aimed at punishment. This intensity of reaction is related to the strong and well-defined state of the common conscience. Behavior which is proscribed is that directed against collective objects (sentiments, practices, property) and has the character of sacrilege. Tribal laws governing what today would be considered "economic" and "political" activities are infused with this religious quality. Acts directed against constituted political authority are viewed as attacks on society and therefore upon religion itself and are not tolerated.

As the number and frequency of social contacts and the number of qualitatively different types of social relations that prevail in a given society increase over time, occupational organization becomes increasingly important. Societies with an advanced division of labor are no longer integrated on the basis of similarity of commitment to a core of beliefs and sentiments. Rather, they tend to exhibit *organic solidarity,* the functional interdependence of dissimilar individuals. As the division of labor progresses, individuals are less bound by long-held, widely shared beliefs and sentiments and are more free to pursue their own interests. The rules of social conduct lose their absolute, immutable quality.

When the way in which people are integrated is modified, the structure of societies changes as well. With a decrease in the significance of common beliefs and sentiments, consensus over rules begins to break down. Penal law tends to be replaced by civil and administrative law emphasizing the restoration of rights. Contractual relationships become increasingly important. Laws become more general and indeterminate, requiring more individual interpretation, and thus lose their appearance of finality. The character of leadership is similarly altered. Associated with mechanical solidarity is leadership that has a superhuman quality; authority is great because the common conscience itself is "highly developed." With organic solidarity everything about leadership becomes temporal and human. The preeminence of leaders is due to the nature of the role they fill.

Durkheim's description of such changes in the character of law and leadership resembles Weber's description of rationalization. As we saw earlier in this chapter, Weber continues his discussion of the process with an analysis of bureaucracy, which embodies all the principles of rational organization. In Weber's view the organization of work and government according to bureaucratic principles has the potential for subjecting individuals to abstract rules they themselves play little part in making and to the decisions of bureaucratic agents who are not formally responsible to them. Rationalization thus carries with it a serious political threat: loss of individual self-determination. Durkheim too believes that aspects of modern society potentially pose such a problem. However, in his view, individual self-determination is not threatened primarily because of the possible imposition of rules made by others. On the contrary, it is threatened by the *lack* of a clear-cut set of rules according to which individuals are to act. While both Durkheim and Weber are somewhat pessimistic about the fate of individuals under increasingly rational rule, some of their theoretical reasons for concern are altogether different.

According to Durkheim, when societies undergo rapid and extensive change they initially lack the ability to impose social norms upon their members. In such a state of social disorganization, or anomie, individuals commonly find that their wants exceed the means available for their realization. By imposing a normative structure on individuals, society creates the only situation in which they are capable of reaching personally meaningful goals. For Durkheim the most pressing political problem facing modern society is the threat of anarchy. When anarchy prevails, individual freedom is impossible.

Durkheim believes that the industrializing societies of his day had not yet developed mechanisms which could deal adequately with the problems of social disorder. His discussions of "political society" and the state are intended as specifications of the political structures and processes which would reduce the threat of anarchy and enhance individual liberty in industrial society.[50] Durkheim maintains that his political proposals are firmly grounded on a scientific understanding of modern society, particularly the basis of its solidarity.

As Durkheim sees it, modern societies as yet lack the functional equivalents of the collective conscience and the political authority found in mechanically integrated societies. In industrial societies, without sufficient external controls, the socially disruptive clash of individuals, each acting in self-interest, is inevitable. To avoid the development of this socially disastrous situation Durkheim advocates centralized control of economic life by the governing centers of society. In addition to such external controls modern society must also develop and inculcate a set of norms which define just economic exchanges. Durkheim assigns to the state not only the responsibility of economic regulation but also the moral task of ensuring that "each is treated as he deserves, that he is freed of all unjust and humiliating dependence, that he is joined to his fellows and to the group without abandoning his personality to them."[51] Hence, for Durkheim, individual well-being in industrial society cannot be achieved simply and immediately with the introduction of external economic controls. To believe that it can be so achieved is "unscientific," it is to ignore the basic role of moral norms in social life. Hence he concludes that "the state does not inevitably become either simply a spectator of social life . . . simply a cog in the economic machine. It is, above all, supremely the organ of moral discipline."[52]

To Durkheim social change must be gradual. Attempts at social engineering must proceed cautiously, taking account of those fundamental factors of social life—beliefs, values, and moral norms—which are resistant to change. This is one of the major points at which Durkheim's thought contrasts most sharply with that of Marx. As Anthony Giddens remarks,

> (Marxism maintains) that the capitalist division of labor is a system of power in which the only medium of change is the active struggles of the subordinate class, and that economic regulation can produce a just and equitable society only if the major institutions of society (including the division of labor itself) are thoroughly transformed. For Durkheim, the necessary changes were to come about by a process of social evolution assisted by the intervention of a beneficent state.[53]

Durkheim believes that as the division of labor advances, the state will assume an increasing number of social responsibilities.

> A multitude of functions which were diffuse become concentrated. The care of educating the young, of protecting the public health, of presiding over the ways of administering public aid, of administering the means of transport and communication, little by little move over into the sphere of the central organ. Accordingly, the central organ develops and, at the same time, it progressively extends a more compact system over the whole surface of the territory, a system more and more complex with ramifications which displace or assimilate pre-existing local organs.[54]

Such development is seen by Durkheim as the normal consequence of the growth of the division of labor. Only less advanced societies have less differentiated political institutions. While Marx envisions a postcapitalist future in which the state will wither away, such a development, to Durkheim, would represent not social progress but evolutionary regress. While Marx sees the state as an instrument of oppression, Durkheim argues that "far from its tyrannizing over the individual, it is the state that redeems the individual from the society."[55]

While Durkheim thus considers the growth of the state both normal and desirable, he recognizes that it also represents a potential threat to individual freedom and equality. Like Weber, he sees that in modern society the isolated individual is virtually powerless before the centralized authority of the state. Hence he argues that in addition to centralized control of economic activity and the promotion of individual well-being through the development of a structure of moral norms, it is also necessary that each modern society develop a rich pattern of occupational groups.

Such groups are appropriate for industrial society and will help secure individual freedom and equality in a number of ways. First, they will serve as contexts within which moral norms develop and are effectively transmitted. They will thus reduce anomie and thereby increase the possibility for individual freedom. Second, occupational groups will strive for increasing political, economic, and social rights for their members. No society, however great its wealth, will automatically distribute its scarce and valued resources in an equitable fashion. Only when workers are organized and thus have some power can they realistically hope to improve their social condition. A third contribution of occupational groups will be their ability to intervene between the individual and the state and restrain the state from infringing on the individual's rights. The possibility of tyrannical rule is reduced when there are countervailing forces pitted against the state. On the other hand, Durkheim also recognizes that occupational associations can be despotic. He therefore argues that while occupational groups should check the centralized power of the state, the state should insure that individual rights are not sacrificed in such organizations.

> (If the state) is to be the liberator of the individual, it has need of some counter-balance; it must be restrained by other collective forces, that is, by those secondary groups we shall discuss later on. . . . It is not a good thing for the groups to stand alone, nevertheless they have to exist. And it is out of this conflict of social forces that individual liberties are born.[56]

Criticisms of Durkheim

Fred Greenstein has pointed out that Durkheim's position that causal explanations of social phenomena must link social fact to social fact impedes empirical political research on at least two important topics:

1. the way in which personality types are distributed in political roles and with what consequences;
2. the circumstances under which the actions of single individuals are likely to have greater or lesser effect on the course of political events.[57]

Robert Merton has located additional problems in Durkheim's understanding of explanation in social science.[58] Unlike Weber, Durkheim does not clearly distinguish his abstract concepts, which are ideal constructions, from concrete, empirical situations in all their variety. In his descriptions of mechanical and organic solidarity, the incompatibility of these two principles of organization is emphasized. On the basis of the ethnographic data available to him, Durkheim concludes that primitive societies are held together through normative consensus and the prevalence of repressive laws. However, more recent field studies reveal that such societies have bodies of important, socially enforced regulations which are basically contractual in nature. Such findings indicate the need for treating mechanical and organic solidarity only as ideal constructs. They also call into question Durkheim's theory of unilinear social development. Furthermore, as Coser[59] has indicated, Durkheim believes that the major social norms of primitive societies reflect values and interests held in common by virtually all members of the societies. This must be recognized as an empirical assumption which does not allow for the real possibility that social norms can express the sentiments of only a specific stratum of the society which that stratum has imposed on others. Coser goes on to argue that Durkheim's discussions of modern societies have similar problems. The description of the importance of the division of labor and of restitutive law in modern society excludes consideration of the role that collective interests and concepts such as national honor can have—especially during periods of inter-societal conflict. His conceptualization of the modern state underemphasizes the possible role of governmental force, violence, and coercion in industrial society.

While these flaws in Durkheim's work are widely recognized, he is more commonly faulted for omissions in his writings. These lacunae supposedly are the result of his political conservatism. This is the thrust of Coser's discussion which contained the criticisms just noted. Coser argues that Durkheim is a "conservative" because it is his conviction that social change must be introduced gradually so that it will not endanger social order. This appears to underlie many of the criticisms of his sociology.

> It is said that Durkheim was so fascinated by the study of cohesion that he neglected to study the phenomenon of conflict; that he was so absorbed in the study of society as a whole that he did not deal adequately with the subgroups and subdivisions which make up the total society; that he neglected the individual and his claims because he concentrated on society and its claims; that he stressed the cohesive functions of religion without considering its divisive functions; that he did not duly appreciate the import of social innovation and social change because he was preoccupied with social order and equilibrium; and that he neglected to analyze power and violence in the body politic because he was overtly concerned with factors which make for agreement.[60]

There are two lines of argument which run counter to the implications of the characterization by Coser. First, it can be reasonably argued that Durkheim simply is not a conservative. This is the position taken by Melvin Richter.

> His perspective is dominated by his unquestioning faith in science, freedom of thought, and the reality of progress. His work, when read carefully, reveals no nostalgia for the past, he finds almost nothing commendable about that type of social cohesion characterized by traditionalism and an unquestioned religious authority. Its legal system imposed savage penalties; its members, because of excessive integration, were exposed to "altruistic" suicide. This condition could scarcely be preferred even to the *anomie* of modern society, which is but suffering from the pains of transition. Durkheim's contempt for the past is matched by his robust confidence that sociology can provide rational solutions to even the most profound problems revealed by his analysis.[61]

Taking a similar position, Anthony Giddens observes that classical sociology, as represented by both Weber and Durkheim, is primarily concerned with contrasts and continuities between traditional and modern societies. It is misleading, he contends, to suggest that such theorists generally view the traditional order as superior to the inchoate industrial order. And it is equally incorrect to maintain that they were conservative in terms of the concrete politics of their time and place.[62]

Second, and more important, if political sociology is to advance, it must assess earlier works, such as those reviewed in this chapter, on the basis of the validity of the hypotheses and the analytic utility of the approaches and concepts they contain and not, insofar as possible, in terms of their ideological acceptability.[63] The work of all scientists touches on only limited aspects of whatever empirical subject matter they may be investigating. In the political realm, Durkheim primarily deals with problems of stability. He raises and attempts to come to terms with legitimate empirical questions.

Durkheim's Contributions to Political Sociology

Much of Durkheim's effort is devoted to demonstrating that sociology is not an auxiliary of any other science but is itself distinct and autonomous. Clearly, he considers himself a pioneer whose own conceptual and empirical work will be supplanted when found deficient in the light of the findings of subsequent research. However, like the ground-breaking work of Marx and Weber, that of Durkheim contains much that remains of lasting value in contemporary empirical political research. For reasons presented in Chapter 3, it seems likely that these contributions will have increasing relevance for political sociology.

Durkheim's differentiation of sociology from psychology served to legitimate the former as a mode of scientific investigation. While Weber kept political events from being treated primarily as epiphenomena, Durkheim presented explicit methodological arguments which kept them from being explained in terms of the qualities of individual actors. The union of these two lines of thought provided the foundation for the development of political sociology.

By identifying the functional analysis of social items as a scientific objective, Durkheim provided the basis for what later became one of the major approaches in empirical political research. Clarification and elaboration of "functional analysis" by sociologists such as Talcott Parsons and Robert Merton yielded sets of concepts which have proved useful in such diverse tasks as explaining aspects of political machines, one-party systems, and nation-states and for comparing a number of national polities.

Like Marx and Weber, Durkheim incorporated historical materials in his sociological analysis. Robert Bellah has observed that his insistence on the importance of history was related to his belief that

> sociology as the science of human society involves a time span unlimited by the life duration of individuals or groups or even nations. It involves nothing less than the total life span of human society. For him there could be no opposition of history and science: the history of social forms is as central to sociology as is the history of life forms for biology, and for much the same reasons.[64]

Most contemporary sociologists do not subscribe to this belief. They tend to ignore history in their analyses of political phenomena. Alex Inkeles has pointed out the results of this ahistorical orientation and has argued that the writings of the founders of the sociological tradition are likely to receive greater attention in the future.

> One consequence of their neglect of history has been that sociologists played only a minor role in shaping the study of new forms of society, such as the totalitarian systems of Europe and the "new nations" emerging from tribal and colonial conditions in Asia and Africa. The growing interest of younger sociologists in the consequences of industrialism and in the resultant forms of industrial society may, however, be the path by which some types of work earlier fostered by the evolutionary perspective may be restored to a place of importance in contemporary sociology.[65]

Durkheim's discussion of the important roles to be played by occupational associations in the political life of modern industrial societies is a forerunner of studies which have dealt with the potential for tyranny in modern democracies. Such works note that political power has become highly concentrated and has weakened secondary associations which protect citizens from spontaneous and direct manipulation by government, and vice versa.[66]

Durkheim's distinction between mechanical and organic solidarity called attention to the important role which moral norms and the division of labor play in political life. Erik Allardt has argued that, with certain modifications, a theoretical scheme can be derived from Durkheim's discussions of social solidarity and the division of labor which permits the analysis within the same theoretical system of a wide range of political phenomena such as political movements, revolution, and political modernization.[67]

SUMMARY AND CONCLUSIONS

At the beginning of this chapter it was noted that the origins of modern sociology can be traced to Western European theorists of the late nineteenth century. These analysts, among whom Karl Marx, Max Weber, and Emile Durkheim were particularly influential, were attempting to describe, explain, and predict fundamental changes in their societies initiated by the French and industrial revolutions. Of central importance were questions concerning the role which traditional associations such as family, religion, and class were to play in the social-political life of industrial societies and questions dealing with the dynamics of social-political change.

Although the works of Marx, Weber, and Durkheim are clearly prescriptive, they do represent conscious attempts at "scientific" social-political analysis. They were to be distinguished from moral and political philosophy and from analyses which investigated formal structures such as legal rules and procedures and formal political ideologies but ignored the actual behavior of various social groupings. Their studies were also macroanalytic and historical-comparative. They were based, in part, on the assumptions that the properties of political systems cannot be ascertained through an analysis of the individual actors or small groups who constitute the systems considered in isolation and that an adequate explanation of modern political structures and processes entails reference to the historical contexts in which these occur.

The writings of Marx, Weber, and Durkheim introduced many of the topics, concepts, and hypotheses which remain central to contemporary political sociology. Throughout this chapter it was argued that it would be counterproductive to ignore these conceptually and theoretically rich origins of the field. By focusing on a limited set of topics and hypotheses found in their works and then indicating the character of the contemporary handling of these ideas, a first step is taken toward charting the historical continuity and cumulative development of the field. By locating a rather small set of concepts, developed in this literature, which have been widely and fruitfully used in contemporary empirical political research, relationships can be seen between apparently diverse studies.

Tables 1-1 and 1-2 briefly summarize some of the analytic approaches, concepts, and substantive discussions initiated by each of the theorists. Substantive discussions focused on the political significance of traditional groupings—family, religion, and class—in various types of societies. In addition to kinship, religion, and stratification (society's system of distributing scarce rewards), Marx, Weber, and Durkheim also discussed the political importance of economy (society's system for producing goods and services) and education (society's system of producing and disseminating ideas and information). The tables suggest topics in contemporary political sociology which have some relation to these discussions.

Discussions of the forebears of theoretical political sociology is but an introduction to the field. The next step is a description of major theoretical and methodological changes in the analysis of social life which have occurred since the writings of its founders and which have significantly influenced the empirical study of politics. Chapter 2 outlines these developments.

TABLE 1-1 Analytic Contributions of Classical Theorists

THEORIST	APPROACH (A) AND CONCEPTS (B)	DEFINITION	INCORPORATION IN POLITICAL SOCIOLOGY
Marx	A. Historical Materialism	Social life determined by prevailing social relations of production; emphasis on class conflict and social change.	As contemporary conflict analysis in studies of community and national power and in studies of political development; also as a modified technological determinism in studies of political development; in analyses of the social bases of ideological commitment; in studies of party alignment.
	B. 1. Class	Set of persons sharing position as owners or nonowners of social means of production; conflict group.	In studies of voting behavior, community and national power, political participation, and the bases of cleavage in industrial nations.
	2. Exploitation	Paying workers less than the value of their labor.	As social-psychological concept (feelings of "relative deprivation") in studies of nonroutine politics. As a macroanalytic concept in studies of relations between dominant and subordinate social units (social categories, corporate bodies, classes, nations).
	3. Alienation	Loss of control over one's own life—particularly over work activities; subordination to the objects one produces; self-denial.	As social-psychological concepts (feelings of normlessness, powerlessness, meaninglessness) in studies of political apathy, "deviant" political groups, and nonroutine political participation.
	4. State	Social agency with power to force compliance with	In studies of community, corporate, and national

(*continued*)

TABLE 1–1 (*Continued*)

ThEORIST	APPROACH (A) AND CONCEPTS (B)	DEFINITION	INCORPORATION IN POLITICAL SOCIOLOGY
		the law and ultimately to settle economic disputes; instrument of dominant class.	power; in analyses of nondemocratic political systems; in studies of regime opposition.
	5. Ideology	Ideas promoted by dominant class to obscure objective opposition of social classes and to reduce revolutionary potential of workers.	As point of departure for studies of political culture, political socialization, political development, and the functions and dysfunctions of ideology.
Weber	A. Ideal-type Analysis and Interpretative Sociology	Designation of categories of interaction (e.g., "feudalism," "bureaucracy") and the meaning actors assign to their behavior within these contexts.	In descriptive-comparative studies of polities and in analyses of political development based on survey data.
	B. 1. Rationalization	Scientific specialization and technical differentiation aimed at greater efficiency and productivity.	In descriptive-comparative studies of polities and in analyses of political development emphasizing structural differentiation and cultural secularization; in studies of the democratic and antidemocratic consequences of bureaucratization.
	2. Authority	Exists when there is willing compliance to the directives of a superior. Three bases of authority distinguished: traditional, charismatic, legal.	In studies of relationships between political structure and political culture; in analyses of regime opposition.
	3. Status Group	Set of persons having in common life chances insofar as these are determined by a specific positive or negative social estimation of honor.	In studies of political alignments and political movements in modern industrial societies; in analyses of the social bases of ideological commitment.

TABLE 1-1 (*Continued*)

THEORIST	APPROACH (A) AND CONCEPTS (B)	DEFINITION	INCORPORATION IN POLITICAL SOCIOLOGY
	4. Political Party	Voluntary association which seeks to influence power and authority within any corporate body	In studies of relations among party ideology, party policies, the political success of parties and the structure of party decision making.
Durkheim	A. Sociological Functionalism	Study of social facts (e.g., institutional arrangements) and their contribution to the maintenance of social order.	In contemporary functional analyses of polities and their components; in long-standing tendency to emphasize political consensus and the social and social-psychological sources of political stability.
	B. 1. Social Solidarity	Mechanical solidarity: society integrated on the basis of commitment to shared beliefs, values, and sentiments. Organic solidarity: society integrated on the basis of functional interdependence.	In studies of poltical culture and its bearing on political structure; in studies of the political relevance of the division of labor; in studies of political development.
	2. Anomie	State of social disorganization in which social guides for conduct are unclear.	A social-psychological concept (feelings of normlessness, powerlessness, meaninglessness) in studies of the ideologies of "deviant" political groups and non-routine political participation.
	3. Collective Conscience	Deeply inculcated beliefs and sentiments common to the average members of the same society.	In studies of public reactions to political events; in analyses of the political beliefs and attitudes of the mass public and their bearing on political structures and processes.

TABLE 1–2   Classic and Contemporary Discussions of Politics

TOPIC	THEORIST	HYPOTHESES	TOPICS IN POLITICAL SOCIOLOGY
Kinship	Marx	Family original source of private property and hence economic and political inequality and conflict. Systems of property inheritance perpetuate political inequalities.	Importance of kinship in authoritative decision making, conflict regulation, and the differentiation of political relationships in traditional societies; kinship systems as facilitating or hindering political-economic change; role of family in political socialization.
	Weber	Family organization basis of patriarchal and patrimonial rule; charisma sometimes transmitted through kinship ties; increasing rationalization reduces political significance of kinship.	
	Durkheim	Traditional societies organized on political-familial basis; increasing differentiation in division of labor reduces political significance of kinship.	
Religion	Marx	In all class societies religion source of values and beliefs facilitating maintenance of political-economic inequalities.	Importance of religion in legitimation of rule, as basis of political unity or conflict, as facilitating or hindering political economic change; religion and democracy; "religious" features of political institutions.
	Weber	Religion performs important legitimating functions, source of social power, can inhibit or facilitate political-economic rationalization.	
	Durkheim	In primitive societies central authority incarnates common conscience and has religious qualities; increasing differentiation in division of labor reduces absolute authority of centralized rule, increasing anomie and threat of anarchy.	
*Economy**	Marx	Dialectic economic change accounts for evolution from primitive communism to feudalism to capitalism to social-	Bearing of work-related experiences on political orientations; influence of economic technology (tools, methods),

TABLE 1-2 (*Continued*)

TOPIC	THEORIST	HYPOTHESES	TOPICS IN POLITICAL SOCIOLOGY
		ism; in all societies relations of production structure political relationships.	organization (ownership, control, exchange systems), and productivity (kinds and amounts of goods and services produced) on political organization.
	Weber	Forms of traditional rule not linked to types of productive systems; charismatic leader may arise during periods of economic crisis or massive economic effort; bureaucratization of economic organizations is related to political bureaucratization and has both democratic and anti-democratic consequences.	
	Durkheim	Lack of differentiated division of labor seen in political aspects of primitive societies; to avoid anarchy and loss of individual freedom modern societies require centralized control of economic activity and rich pattern of politically significant occupational groups.	
*Stratification**	Marx	Classes are economically based conflict groups; dominant economic class is dominant political class; political power used to maintain and enhance privilege of dominant economic class.	Importance of various status groups and classes as bearers of ideologies, as contenders for power and privilege, and as agents promoting or resisting political-economic change; relation of status groups, classes, and stratification variables (e.g., social mobility, status inconsistency) to party alignments and to social movements.
	Weber	Distribution of social honor and power as well as economic positions create potential conflict groups; conflict between certain social groupings over certain recurrent issues in part characterizes different systems of domination.	
	Durkheim	Degree of differentiation of social units and the bases of	

(*continued*)

TABLE 1-2 (*Continued*)

TOPIC	THEORIST	HYPOTHESES	TOPICS IN POLITICAL SOCIOLOGY
		the integration central to understanding different types of political unity and conflict.	
Shared Belief and Value Systems	Marx	In all class societies dominant ideas are ideas of ruling class used to facilitate maintenance of political-economic inequalities; development of class consciousness precondition for revolution.	The agencies, content, and processes of political socialization; the role of education in political development; control of information as source of social power; relation of political beliefs and attitudes of the mass public to political structures and processes.
	Weber	Distinctive belief systems legitimate different systems of domination; increasing rationalization concentrates power in hands of politically non-responsible experts.	
	Durkheim	In primitive societies transmission of collective conscience insures political stability and continuity; society's ability to impose a normative order reduces threat of anarchy and insures individual freedom.	

*The economy refers to a society's system for producing goods and services. It is closely tied to the class or stratification system, which refers to a society's system of distributing scarce rewards.

NOTES

1. This is not to say that Marx was unconcerned about the human individual. Adam Schaff has pointed out that Marx's early writings, in which his most extensive discussions of alienation appear, were humanistic and expressed a deep commitment to the happiness of the individual. Schaff demonstrates that this concern profoundly influenced Marx's subsequent work. See Adam Schaff, *Marxism and the Human Individual* (New York: McGraw-Hill, 1970).

2. Karl Marx, *Economic and Philosophical Manuscripts of 1844* (London: Lawrence and Wishart, 1959), p. 72.

3. Contrary to some critics, Marx never held that under the conditions of industrial capitalism the material standard of the working class would reach absolute impoverishment. In fact, he noted that their overall material well-being might be improved. However the absolute impoverishment thesis was intended to apply to the unemployed and to the unemployable in advanced industrial economies. For an exposition and documentation of this point, see Charles H. Anderson, *The Political Economy of Social Class* (Englewood Cliffs, N.J.: Prentice-Hall, 1974), p. 23.

4. Erich Hahn, "Contemporary Marxist Sociology," in Peter Berger (ed.), *Marxism and Sociology: Views from Eastern Europe* (New York: Appleton-Century-Crofts, 1969), pp. 78-79.

5. Ralf Dahrendorf, *Class and Class Conflict in Industrial Society* (Stanford, Calif.: Stanford University Press, 1959), pp. 141-142.

6. *Newsweek*, May 26, 1975, p. 65.

7. For a collection of empirical studies which support this thesis, see Jerome Skolnick and Elliot Currie, eds., *Crisis in American Institutions,* 3rd ed. (Boston: Little, Brown, 1976).

8. As a counterargument Marxists contend that the bourgeoisie has used differences in status, religion, ethnicity, and nationality to divide the proletariat. It has encouraged divisions within the proletariat to weaken its political power and to obscure the real source of political conflict. Marxists also maintain that individual differences in status and authority and differences in the status and power of various religious and ethnic groups within a nation are derived from their relative positions within the relations of production. Ownership of productive property is much more fundamental to status and power than status or power is to class status. Power in capitalist society is primarily economic ownership and control.

9. Sidney Hook, *Marx and the Marxists* (Princeton, N.J.: D. Van Nostrand, 1955), pp. 38-39.

10. Seymour Martin Lipset and Reinhard Bendix, "The Field of Political Sociology," in *Political Sociology: Selected Essays,* Lewis A. Coser, ed. (Evanston, Ill.: Harper & Row, 1967), p. 32.

11. Julien Freund, *The Sociology of Max Weber* (New York: Random House, Vintage Books edition, 1969), p. 18.

12. Max Weber, "Politics as a Vocation," in *From Max Weber: Essays in Sociology,* H. H. Gerth and C. W. Mills, eds. (New York: Oxford University Press, Galaxy Books edition, 1958), p. 78.

13. Randall Collins, *Conflict Sociology* (New York: Academic Press, 1975), p. 368.

14. Max Weber, *The Theory of Social and Economic Organization* (New York: Free Press Paperback edition, 1964), p. 328.

15. Reinhard Bendix, *Max Weber: An Intellectual Portrait* (Garden City: Doubleday, Anchor Books edition, 1962), p. 360.

16. Weber, *Theory of Social and Economic Organization,* pp. 358-359.

17. Weber notes that the distinction between a system of voluntarily agreed upon rules and one in which rules have been imposed is relative. There are political systems in which an authority is accepted by a majority of the members while the minority which holds different opinions merely acquiesces. In such cases the authority is actually imposed by the majority on the minority. It is also not uncommon to find political systems in which an organized and active minority imposes an authority which eventually comes to be regarded as legitimate by those who originally opposed it. It also frequently happens that, where voting is the legal method of creating or changing rules or rulers, the will of the minority achieves a formal majority to which the real majority acquiesces. In this case, as Weber sees it, "majority rule" becomes mere sham.

18. They are personally free and subject to authority only with respect to their impersonal official obligations. They are organized in a clearly defined hierarchy of offices. Each office has a clearly defined sphere of competence in the legal sense. The office is filled by a free contractual relationship. Thus, in principle, there is a free selection. Candidates are selected on the basis of technical qualifications. In the most rational case, this is tested by examination or guaranteed by diplomas certifying technical training, or both. They are appointed, not elected. They are remunerated by fixed salaries in money, for the most part with a right to pensions. Only under certain circumstances does the employing authority, especially in private organizations, have the right to terminate the appointment, but the official is always free to resign. The salary scale is primarily graded according to rank in the hierarchy, but in addition to this criterion, the responsibility of the position and the requirements of the incumbent's social status may be taken into account. The office is treated as the sole, or at least the primary occupation of the incumbent. It constitutes a career. There is a system of "promotion"

according to seniority or to achievement, or both. Promotion is dependent on the judgment of superiors. The official works entirely separated from ownership of the means of administration and without appropriation of his position. He is subject to strict and systematic discipline and control in the conduct of the office.

19. Seymour Martin Lipset, *Revolution and Counterrevolution: Change and Persistence in Social Structures* (New York: Basic Books, 1968), p. 137.

20. Gerth and Mills, eds., *From Max Weber,* p. 181.

21. Ibid, p. 187.

22. Ibid, p. 194.

23. Bendix, *Max Weber,* p. 465.

24. Peter M. Blau, "Critical Remarks on Weber's Theory of Authority," *American Political Science Review,* 57, no. 2 (June 1963), 305–316.

25. For a discussion of these criticisms, see Gunther Roth, "Political Critiques of Max Weber," *American Sociological Review,* 30, no. 2 (April 1965), 213–223.

26. Blau, "Critical Remarks," p. 307.

27. Karl Lowenstein, *Max Weber's Political Ideas in the Perspective of our Time,* R. and C. Winston, trans. (Amherst: University of Massachusetts Press, 1966), p. 90.

28. Blau, "Critical Remarks," p. 309.

29. Edward Shils, "Charisma, Order and Status," *American Sociological Review,* 30, no. 2 (April 1965), 119–213.

30. Peter M. Blau and W. Richard Scott, *Formal Organizations* (San Francisco: Chandler, 1962), p. 35.

31. Ibid.

32. Blau, "Critical Remarks," p. 311.

33. Morris Janowitz, *Political Conflict* (Chicago: Quandrangle Books, 1970), p. 8.

34. See Seymour Martin Lipset and Earl Raab, *The Politics of Unreason* (New York: Harper & Row, 1970).

35. For the seminal discussion of status inconsistency, see Gerhard Lenski, "Status Crystallization: A Non-Vertical Dimension of Social Status," *American Sociological Review,* 19, no. 4 (August 1954), 405–413.

36. For a critical review of research relating status inconsistency to political behavior, see David R. Segal, "Status Inconsistency, Cross Pressures and American Political Behavior," *American Sociological Review,* 34, no. 3 (June 1969), 353–359.

37. Lowenstein, *Max Weber's Political Ideas,* p. 61.

38. Gabriel Almond and Sidney Verba, *The Civic Culture* (Boston: Little, Brown, 1965).

39. Gabriel Almond and G. B. Powell, *Comparative Politics: A Developmental Approach* (Boston: Little, Brown, 1966).

40. Seymour Martin Lipset, Martin Trow, and James Coleman, *Union Democracy* (New York: The Free Press, 1956).

41. C. Wright Mills, *The Power Elite* (New York: Oxford University Press, 1956).

42. See, for example, George W. Ball, ed., *Global Companies: The Political Economy of World Business* (Englewood Cliffs, N.J.: Prentice-Hall, 1975); C. Fred Bergsten, Thomas Horst, and Theodore H. Moran, *American Multinationals and American Interests* (Washington, D.C.: The Brookings Institution, 1978); United Nations Economic and Social Council, *Transnational Corporations in World Development: A Re-examination* (New York: United Nations, 1978); Raymond Vernon, *Storm over the Multinational: The Real Issues* (Cambridge, Mass.: Harvard University Press, 1977).

43. See Lewis A. Coser, "Durkheim's Conservatism and Its Implications for Political Sociology," in *Emile Durkheim: A Collection of Essays,* Kurt H. Wolff, ed. (Columbus: Ohio State University Press, 1960), pp. 211–232.

44. There are a number of interpretations of what Durkheim meant by a "social fact." The discussion presented here follows Harry Alpert's characterization of Durkheim's position as "Relational Social Realism." See Harry Alpert, *Emile Durkheim and His Sociology* (New York: Columbia University Press, 1939), pp. 156–157.

45. Emile Durkheim, *The Rules of Sociological Method* (New York: The Free Press, 1950), p. 94.

46. The concept "needs of society" itself requires clarification. Anthropologist A. R. Radcliffe-Browne suggested that by "needs" Durkheim intended "necessary conditions for existence." A. R. Radcliffe-Browne, "On the concept of Function in Social Science, *American Anthropoligist,* XXXVII (1935), 394–402.

47. The presence of tribal chiefs capable of making authoritative decisions seems to contradict the claim that political organization in primitive societies was little advanced. Durkheim comments on this point, " . . . a power can be at once absolute and very simple. Nothing is less complex than the despotic government of a barbarian chief. The functions he fills are rudimentary and not very numerous." Emile Durkheim, *The Division of Labor in Society,* George Simpson, trans. (New York: Free Press Paperback edition, 1964), p. 220.

48. "The totality of beliefs and sentiments common to the average citizens of the same society forms a determinant system which has its own life; one may call it collective or common conscience . . . it is, by definition diffuse in every reach of society. . . . It is, in effect, independent of the particular conditions in which individuals are placed; they pass on and it remains . . . . Moreover, it does not change with each generation, but on the contrary, it connects successive generations with one another." Ibid., pp. 79–80.

49. Ibid, p. 196. This analysis has been interpreted as presenting Durkheim's theory of charisma and the nearest he came to developing a theory of totalitarianism. See Stephen Lukes, *Emile Durkheim* (New York: Peregrine Books, 1975), p. 262.

50. For a comparison of differences between Durkheim's and Weber's conceptualizations of the state, see Anthony Giddens, *Emile Durkheim* (New York: Penguin Books, 1979), pp. 61–66.

51. Emile Durkheim, *Professional Ethics and Civic Morals,* Cornelia Brookfield, trans. (New York: The Free Press, 1958),p. 72.

52. Ibid.

53. Giddens, *Emile Durkheim,* p. 61.

54. Durkheim, *Division of Labor,* pp. 221–222.

55. Durkheim, *Professional Ethics,* p. 69.

56. Ibid. p. 63.

57. Fred I. Greenstein, "Personality and Politics: Problems of Evidence, Inference and Conceptualization," in Seymour Martin Lipset, ed., *Politics and the Social Sciences* (New York: Oxford University Press, 1969), pp. 163–206.

58. Robert K. Merton, "Durkheim's Division of Labor in Society," *American Journal of Sociology,* XL, no. 2 (November 1934), 319–328.

59. Coser, "Durkheim's Conservatism,"

60. Ibid., p. 211.

61. Melvin Richter, "Durkheim's Politics and Political Theory," in Wolff, *Emile Durkheim,* pp. 201–202.

62. Anthony Giddens, "Classical Social Theory and the Origins of Modern Sociology," *American Journal of Sociology,* 81, no. 4 (January 1976), 703–729.

63. Like everyone else, a sociologist's personal beliefs and attitudes intrude, to some extent, in his assessment of concepts, propositions, and theories. For a discussion of the sources and consequences of the modal political attitudes of American sociologists, see Alvin W. Gouldner, *The Coming Crisis of Western Sociology* (New York: Basic Books, 1970).

64. Robert N. Bellah, "Durkheim and History," *American Sociological Review,* 24, no. 4 (August 1959), 459.

65. Alex Inkeles, *What Is Sociology?* (Englewood Cliffs, N.J.: Prentice-Hall, 1964), p. 34.

66. See William Kornhauser, *The Politics of Mass Society* (New York: Free Press, 1959).

67. Allardt's analysis is developed in two papers: "Emile Durkheim—Deductions for Political Sociology," prepared for the Second Conference on Comparative Political Sociology, Cambridge, 1965; "Types of Protest and Alienation," in *Mass Politics,* Erik Allardt and Stein Rokkan, eds., (New York: The Free Press, 1970), pp. 45–63.

CHAPTER TWO
HISTORICAL DEVELOPMENT: POLITICAL SOCIOLOGY IN THE UNITED STATES

THE NEW SOCIAL CONTEXT OF POLITICAL SOCIOLOGY

We have just considered the central concerns of political sociology that were formulated in Western Europe at the end of the nineteenth century. Many subsequent developments relevant to the sociological study of politics occurred in the United States.

American social theorists modified the approaches, concepts, and hypotheses which Marx, Weber, and Durkheim provided. In part, some changes were prompted by the findings of empirical research and by observations of contemporary social history, both of which indicated inadequacies in the earlier work. However, equally as important to the understanding of political sociology's development in the United States is the recognition that methods, research techniques, and theories of political sociology reflect American history, social structure, and culture. American political sociology developed in the context of a nation which originated in political revolution, which initially had an open frontier, which never had a hereditary aristocracy or an established church. It developed in a society which endured two world wars and an economic depression but only one civil war in its more than two-hundred-year process of becoming the most industrialized and materially productive nation in history. It developed in a society which has as some of its major value orientations "achievement and success," "activity and work," "efficiency and practicality," "equality of opportunity," "freedom and progress"—all understood in basically economic terms.[1] It continues to develop in a society which increasingly takes on the charateristics of a welfare democracy while more and more of its citizens challenge long-standing value orientations, institutions, and political policies.

In this chapter some of the major methodological and theoretical contributions of American sociology to the understanding of politics will be considered. Discussion will focus on those methodological and theoretical developments which are related to the changing ways in which analysts have treated the approaches, concepts, and hypotheses introduced by Marx, Weber, and Durkheim. Brief references will be made to the changing social conditions in America under which these intellectual changes took place. The aims of such references are to make the pattern of methodological and theoretical development more intelligible, to suggest why certain late-nineteenth-century theoretical work has remained important in American studies of political phenomena, and to present reasons for the claim, presented in Chapter 1, that in the foreseeable future the work of Marx, Weber, and Durkheim will have increasing importance.

STAGES IN THE GROWTH OF
AMERICAN SOCIOLOGY

From the beginning of this century sociology has undergone continuous growth in the United States. Nevertheless, its history does reveal patterns of changing interests and emphases. Hinkle and Hinkle have suggested that between roughly 1900 and 1950 there were three relatively distinct stages in sociology's development: (1) the period of the founding of American sociology (1905–1918), which was dominated by men with rural and religious backgrounds who were particularly interested in the condition and problems of urban industrial life; (2) the period between 1918 and 1935, during which efforts were devoted to making sociology increasingly "scientific"; (3) the period shaped by the Great Depression and World War II (1935–1954), in which there was increased reciprocity of theory, research, and applications.[2] The more recent history of American sociology can be roughly divided into three periods: (4) the period between 1954 and 1966, during which considerable social-psychological research was conducted, new methodological approaches and techniques were advanced, and a major bifurcation of general social theory occurred; (5) the period extending from 1966 to about 1975, in which both domestic and international political turmoil focused attention on social, economic, and political inequality, conflict, the illegitimate uses of power and large-scale social change; (6) the period from 1975 to the present, in which unresolved theoretical issues of the preceding period and the reemergence of problems of confidence in political leadership and of long-standing problems of political economy have renewed interest in the questions which were of central concern to the Western European founders of the sociological tradition and to America's earliest sociologists.

Each of these six "eras" will be briefly described in this chapter. Obviously the descriptions will be highly selective and incomplete. As in the discussions of Chapter 1, attention will be given only to some developments which have had a rather direct bearing on the way in which sociologists deal with political phenomena.

THE PERIOD OF THE FOUNDING
OF AMERICAN SOCIOLOGY
(1905–1918)

Any date specifying the "beginning" or "founding" of American sociology is rather arbitrary. Whatever the choice, in the period from about the beginning of this century to the end of World War I there developed in American sociology a number of theoretical and methodological tendencies which have persisted to the present and which have had a clear influence on political sociology.

By 1900, Marx, Weber, and Durkheim had published many of their major works. Some of their most central concerns were also expressed in the writings of the pioneers of American sociology. However, the correspondence between certain themes appearing in classical Western European sociology and in the writings of early American sociologists was not the result of Americans' detailed reading of Marx, Weber, and Durkheim. The direct and extensive influence of these theorists on American sociology did not develop until the 1930s. Rather, it was the result of independent theorists attempting to understand similar, though by no means identical, social situations.

At the end of the nineteenth century social and political hierarchies were undergoing significant changes in the United States. Such changes lacked the drama of the social upheavals which occurred in Western Europe during the second half of the eighteenth century. Americans had no established church, no hereditary aristocracy, and no monarchy to overthrow. The social transformations they were experiencing were, nonetheless, significant. Rapidly increasing secularization, urbanization, and industrialization were forcing the reconstruction of a predominantly puritanical, rural, and small-town society of small merchants and farmers. America's family, religious, economic, stratification, and education systems were becoming parts of a technologically advanced, materially productive society. Such changes naturally raised questions about the roles which family, church, business, class, and school were to continue to play in the patterning of American political life.

Increasing productivity and prosperity led many Americans to view their society as evolving in a positive direction. Americans were optimistic about their ability to solve problems technologically. They were well aware of the very serious difficulties which accompanied rapid industrialization and urbanization: unemployment, child labor, juvenile delinquency, vice, mental disorders, crime, family instability, suicide, minority relations, and so on. However, many Americans believed that these were capable of control, once principles which governed their occurrence were understood. They were interested in understanding social change, for they believed that understanding is a first step toward control. It is not surprising, then, that early American sociologists directed their efforts toward understanding the social problems which seemed inevitably to accompany "progress." Two influential sociologists whose works exhibit many qualities characteristic of the pioneers of American sociology are briefly discussed below.

No figure in the history of American sociology has been more devoted to the application of the knowledge of social laws to the operation of government than Lester Frank Ward (1841–1913). He was convinced that the major social problems facing American society in his day stemmed from widespread ignorance of social laws and from the associated prevailing belief in the desirability of governmental laissez-faire.[3] Against the "Social Darwinists" such as Herbert Spencer and William Graham Sumner (both of whom were exceptionally influential at the time of Ward's writing) Ward argued that social development could and should be controlled. While social laws, like the laws of physics and biology, are unalterable, people can use them to achieve social goals in the same manner in which they use physical laws to alter the physical environment to meet their needs.[4]

Ward saw the state as the most important instrument people have developed for the conscious control of society. In his view the state originated as a tool of exploitation, and many governments continued to be conducted so that power and authority were used to continue inequalities in the distribution of social rewards. Nevertheless, the state still represented the chief instrument for the amelioration of society's ills. Ward believed that government could fulfill its function of social amelioration when an extensive system of education was established which made as widely available as possible the understanding of individuals' relation to society. There could be no genuinely democratic government until legislators and citizens had some knowledge of the nature and means of controlling social forces for social improvement.

Ward believed that the wealthy in America still governed in their own interest. However, he foresaw a future in which the dynamics of a competitive multiparty system and an expanded educational system which disseminated social information would produce a state dedicated to the general welfare.

Ward and another influential founder of sociology in the United

States, Franklin Giddings (1855–1931), maintained that the laws of social behavior were psychological laws which could be determined by the inductive procedures used by the natural sciences. Giddings went on to specify that "scientific" description must include measurement and that statistics should be applied to the analysis of social life.

Giddens also presented some explicitly normative views. He expressed concern for individual liberty and for the development of society with policies of equality and assistance. These views exemplify the interest in progress and meliorism he also shared with Ward.[5]

Giddings and Ward had a basic interest in social change in common with Marx, Weber, and Durkheim. American society was undergoing important structural alterations at the time they wrote. They sought to determine fundamental principles of human behavior on the basis of which certain future changes, particularly political changes, might be anticipated. They raised questions about the ways and the extent to which individuals and groups might bring about alterations in the structure of their society. They also inquired into the role of ideas and ideals in the process of social-political change.

In their discussions of change, Giddings and Ward focused on psychological principles rather than on the role of traditional groupings such as kinship, religion, class, and community. This psychological orientation, together with the emphasis on natural law and progress, constitutes a configuration of attitudes and assumptions which have had a lasting impression on American political sociology. The concern with meliorism has arisen intermittently and is presently receiving some renewed interest.

As the works of Marx, Weber, and Durkheim became an integral part of American sociology, the understanding of the concepts and hypotheses they contained was influenced by the intellectual tradition initiated by theorists such as Ward and Giddings. The writings of the three late-nineteenth-century European analysts were incorporated into an existing set of theoretical orientations. These orientations themselves reflected a culture in which individualism, concern with practicality, equality of economic opportunity and freedom, and belief in progress were central components.

Discussions of processes such as class conflict, increasing division of labor, and rationalization would come to be of particular interest to those who believe that sociology seeks to establish general laws similar to those of the physical sciences. Structural concepts such as alienation, anomie, and bureaucracy would prove to be valuable analytic tools for those trying to understand the social consequences of the rapid industrialization and urbanization which American society was undergoing.

Leon Bramson has pointed out that the response of American sociologists to these changes was influenced by their compassion for the social and economic difficulties of the small farmer and businessman and more generally by their frontier values of rural simplicity and neighborliness and of a religious concern for the individual.

The American treatment of the consequences of urbanization and industrialization differed in some important respects from the European reaction to these social changes, which were discussed in Chapter 1.

> (American sociologists) did not, by and large, see America as another vaster Europe, with a class struggle and an exploiting bourgeoisie oppressing the proletarian masses. If they sometimes wrote as if a collectivist society were the answer to American social problems they did not often write as revolutionaries or even as Socialists. They were engaged in a search for (small, close knit, middle class) community, but they were the products of a liberal milieu. Though their key concepts were often expressions of a demand for a new social order, the individual was often the vehicle for their reform idealism, and here they were quite inconsistent.[6]

The psychological orientation of the early American sociologists and their hope for the development of a society concerned with the general welfare of its members provided an intellectual climate in which social structural concepts such as alienation and anomie would later come to be treated as psychological characteristics of individuals and in which the increasing size and activity of the federal government would be seen as necessary to guarantee citizens some degree of individual liberty and equality of economic opportunity. Historical conditions as well as theoretical and methodological developments within sociology contributed to the continuation and elaboration of these orientations.

THE HEGEMONY OF THE CHICAGO SCHOOL (1918-1935)

American sociology developed primarily within the context of colleges and universities. In this setting sociologists had considerable interest in differentiating their field from social philosophy. To this end they argued that sociology was to be evaluated solely on cognitive grounds—that ideological evaluations were inappropriate since they proceeded from an initial and fundamental misunderstanding of the character of the field. They contended that sociological principles were established on the basis of logically ordered empirical evidence and that such principles were always open to revision in the light of new empirical findings.

It is not surprising, then, that many substantive theories, such as those of Ward and Giddings, were abandoned during the second period of American sociology's history. One stated reason for discontent was the increasing concern with the empirical bases of the truth claims such theories contained. Speculation, a priori reasoning, and extrapolation from meager data no longer were considered adequate components for constructing social theories. New acquisitions of ethnographic data made it increasingly difficult to maintain unilinear evolutionary doctrines. New psychological investigations seriously challenged assumptions about human nature upon which many social theories were based.

The dogmatic manner in which early American social theories frequently were presented was a second source of discontent. The growing beliefs that sociology dealt with probabilities rather than with certainties and that social phenomena generally were the result of the interplay of a number of factors rather than the result of some single variable were often at variance with the orientation of earlier theoretical work.

The explicit meliorism of the pioneers of American sociology also fell into disfavor during the second period. There was a growing feeling that sociology should be a "pure science" and, as such, must maintain a disinterested approach to all social structures and events. Interest in the construction of empirically sound theories gradually replaced interest in the reconstruction of society guided by sociological speculations and egalitarian values.

Theory and research of the second period did exhibit a number of important continuities with that of the first. The belief continued that sociology is concerned with inductively discovering natural laws of society. Gidding's further specification that establishing social laws requires the use of statistics was not only accepted but was considerably elaborated. While a priori psychological principles were given up, American sociologists persisted in the analytic emphasis on the individual person and his or her relation to society.

During the second period, the question of how individual character shapes social institutions was converted into the question of how social institutions shape individual personality. This reformulation led to the consideration of the roles of family, religion, class, and politics in the life of the individual. While explicit social reformism was given up in favor of a value-free conception of sociology, analysts of the second period chose to investigate collective behavior of the type commonly labeled "social problems," such as crime, vice, political corruption, and poverty.

These characteristics of the second period of American sociology are not best illustrated by reference to the writings of a few sociologists but rather by a brief description of the type of work done by a number of sociologists in a single university department.

From the time of its founding by Albion W. Small to the present, the sociology department of the University of Chicago has been one of the most influential in the United States. During the second period, the influence of the Chicago department was unusually great. The department's strong emphasis on *objectivity* and its advancement of the substantive areas of *social psychology* and *urban sociology* attracted the attention and channeled the interests of many American sociologists during this period. The relationship between the methodological and substantive concerns of the members of the Chicago department and their location in the most rapidly growing major city in the United States exemplifies the way in which social change of the period influenced American sociological thought.

The Emphasis on "Objectivity"

At Chicago, the position that sociology ought to be objective had at least two independent components. Each of these has remained controversial, particularly with respect to the analysis of political life. The first component was the position that sociologists should not be concerned primarily with evaluation. Rather, their professional responsibility lay in providing explanations.[7]

The second normative component asserted that sociology should deal only with observable and measurable phenomena. This restriction was the source of considerable controversy. First, it initially appeared to exclude from sociology all studies which were concerned with subjective aspects of social life, such as values, beliefs, and sentiments. Second, it called into question the worth of numerous empirical descriptive studies which aimed at *qualitatively* understanding social behavior. While no specific date can be set, it does appear that by 1930 challenges to the second normative component had become infrequent. Misunderstandings had been cleared up and questions had received relatively satisfactory answers. The particular resolution of those questions continues to give American political sociology some of its most characteristic features.

It is not difficult to identify some persons at the University of Chicago who were involved in resolving the issues. William F. Ogburn, a student of Giddings while he attended Columbia University, became a member of the Chicago department in 1927. Ogburn shared Giddings's belief that scientific understanding of social phenomena required the use of descriptive and analytic statistics. One of the research projects in which Ogburn demonstrated the capabilities of statistical analysis concerned the 1928 Hoover-Smith election. In that contest at least two issues were thought to be important: Smith's catholicism and his opposition to the prohibition of alcoholic beverages. Ogburn's use of partial correlational analysis made it possible to determine the relative importance of each of these factors in the vote. One of Ogburn's students, Samuel A. Stouffer, who later became a prominent sociologist and joined the Chicago department, completed his dissertation in 1930. In it he demonstrated that attitude scales could yield information comparable to that obtained through the use of long and extensive interviews. His study made it clear that descriptive case studies and investigations that employed scales and statistical analysis were not competitive approaches but were complementary methodologies. Case studies could serve as a rich source of hypotheses which subsequently could be investigated through the use of attitude measures and then the statistical manipulation of the data which they provided.

At the University of Chicago, interest in attitude measurement and analytic statistics was not limited to members of the sociology department. Early in the 1920s psychologist L. L. Thurstone attempted to devise a technique that would represent the attitudes of a group on a specific issue in the form of a frequency distribution. More important than Thurstone's specific technique were the discussions he had with many political scientists. He argued convincingly that many aspects of political life were amenable to the application of precise, quantitative measurement. In connection with this point he suggested that the attitude be the basic unit of political analysis. He felt that not only could attitudes be measured but they could also be studied experimentally. Thurstone contended that the results of such experiments could be causally interpreted and the conclusions be stated in semimathematical form.

Charles Merriam, head of Chicago's political science department, was convinced that improved understanding of politics required greater precision in the description of political life. He thought that this could be achieved through the use of statistics. This belief, coupled with his interest in the irrational determinants of politics, led him to a position resembling that of Ogburn and Thurstone. Merriam's importance rests on his influential statement of this position in several books, his training of a number of students who later became leaders of the "behavioral persuasion" in political science,[8] and on the fact that his "odyssey from historical progressivism to psychological behaviorism paralleled that of (political science) as a whole, with a short lead."[9]

A number of historical, structural, and cultural factors help to account for the concern with objectivity and for the expression of this concern through an emphasis on psychology and statistics. During this period sociology was still very new to American universities. It lacked the status of the humanities and the biological and physical sciences. Increasing academic acceptance entailed emulating what were thought to be some of the basic features either of the humanities or of the "harder" sciences. The first path was unpromising because social commentary and criticism were already well within the established and defended domains of literature, history, and philosophy. It was also less promising in the context of a utilitarian, technologically oriented society.

At least two factors contributed to the emphasis on the study of attitudes. First, the concern with attitudes suggested an interest in the subjective aspects of social life. This implied a nonmechanistic model of individual and society which would not be thoroughly unacceptable to those in the humanities. On the other hand, since attitudes were treated as measurable phenomena, physical and biological scientists could not dismiss sociology as metaphysics. Second, and more important, the trauma of World War I led to a rejection of the widely held views that human beings are essentially rational and that social change is inevitably in the direction of "progress." The war generated great interest in the irrational determinants of social behavior. This concern with the relationship between the psychological and the social is seen in the work of several Chicago sociologists discussed in the following subsection.

The Development of Social Psychology

If its emphasis on the measurable attitudes of individuals served to differentiate sociology from the various humanities, it also generated the problem of distinguishing sociology from psychology. This problem was partially solved by a number of scholars at the University of Chicago. Although their writings probably were not intended as direct responses to the challenge of making sociology neither metaphysics nor psychology, they did have that effect.

Ellsworth Faris and George Herbert Mead, among others, urged the investigation of the role of social interaction in personality formation. Much of Mead's writing in particular was concerned with the way in which individuals come to internalize socially shared prescriptions for behavior in commonly encountered situations. In particular he focused on the development of the self-concept and on the relation between self and society. Mead argued that the way in which an individual conceives himself is conditioned by the roles which he takes and that these roles are defined by others' treatment of him.

Such studies established an important type of inquiry that was not a part of psychology as that field was defined during this period. Later social psychologists would also include in their field the study of the ways in which social structures are influenced by the personalities of those who operate within them, thus asking anew questions discussed by Ward and Giddings. As we shall see in the following chapters, much empirical research in contemporary political sociology deals with the ways in which certain personality characteristics associated with a person's class position influence his or her political attitudes and behavior. Another large body of empirical research is concerned with the ways in which the political institutions of a society are affected by the distribution of individuals with certain personality characteristics in its population. Such investigations are not within the domain of either political philosophy or psychology.

In addition to firmly establishing a field of investigation within American universities, the Chicago social psychologists also encouraged the tendency of American sociologists to treat structural variables in psychological terms. The work of W. I. Thomas is important in this regard. Like his associates, Thomas focused on the behavior of the individual and on the importance of attitudes in accounting for actions. He contended that the explanation of an individual's social behavior must take into account three interrelated elements: (1) objective conditions (which include norms, socially shared values, and institutions) confronting the actor, (2) the preexisting attitudes of the actor, (3) the definition of the situation by the actor. This third element was crucial for Thomas, who noted that "if men define situations as real they are real in their consequences." This argument supported the already existing tendency to focus on individuals' reactions to social structure rather than on social structure itself.

The Advancement of Urban Sociology

It is not surprising that sociologists living in what was at the time the "world's newest large city" would consider the city itself a topic for sociological investigation. Chicago was a site of almost unparalleled urbanization and industrialization. Its population was growing at an extraordinary rate, due primarily to the immigration of various ethnic groups.

Unlike most of his American contemporaries and successors, Chicago sociologist Robert E. Park was well aware of and interested in the writings of Marx, Weber, and Durkheim. Park was a macroanalyst; he was not primarily concerned with the behavior of individuals. Rather, within the context of the city, he focused his attention on the movement and spatial distribution of peoples with similar economic and cultural traits, on the spatial distribution of functional areas (manufacturing, commerce, rooming house, working-class residences), and on the distribution of various cultural and social phenomena (such as crime, suicide, and mental abnormalities) within these regions. Park contended that the areas he identified and studied were "natural" in the sense that they were the unplanned consequence of competition between various social groups. To him they represented the results of social forces rather than the intentions of individuals and thus were truly sociological phenomena.

Park and other Chicago sociologists had particular interest in the concentration of social problems in the slum areas of the city. From their studies they concluded that the source of these problems was not the genetic qualities of the inhabitants of such areas. Rather, it was the lack of social organization. The population of such areas was typically made up of immigrant groups from societies whose culture and social organization were maladapted to the demands of urban industrial life. The traditional family, religion, class, and educational systems which had served the needs of the immigrants in their native lands hindered their integration and social advancement within the rationalized social order. Social disorganization was the result of the subsequent weakening of the traditional social bonds of new groups and their failure to rapidly develop patterns more appropriate for their environment. Park believed that over time an immigrant group would develop adaptive modes of behavior, would improve its social position, and move out of the slum areas of the city. It would be replaced by newer groups, which would, in their turn, undergo the same processes.

The emphases of the early Chicago urban sociologists have an important and interesting place in the history of American sociology. Understanding that place should enhance understanding certain theoretical and methodological concerns of contemporary political sociology. One of the most central theoretical problems in American sociology is the stability and instability of urban-industrial society, particularly urban-industrial society as found in North America and Western Europe. Park's discussion exhibited a greater interest in the adjustment of immigrant groups to the demands of urbanization and industrialization than in the ways in which urban-industrial society might meet some of the needs of its new minority groups. He paid attention to the possibilities of fitting immigrant groups into an organized way of life but not to the possibility that such groups might want to resist integration and might want to change basic aspects of the society to which they immigrated. This orientation toward integration and stability, which Park shared with Durkheim, has remained a rather conspicuous feature of American sociology in general. In political sociology it is manifested in the vast body of research literature on the conditions which support and maintain the political systems of the industrial nations of North America and Western Europe.

Park's macroanalytic, historical, and comparative orientations were not shared by the majority of his contemporaries. Nor are they now shared by his successors. With the exception of demographic and ecological analysis, somewhat resembling that initiated by Park, American sociology has remained primarily microanalytic. Some reasons for this orientation have already been suggested. Research techniques developed since the second period of American sociology further encouraged microanalysis. It was not until the late 1950s that there was widespread expression of interest in advancing sociology along macroanalytic, historical, and comparative lines. Even today sociological research is predominantly microanalytic. Some of the technical, methodological bases for this orientation are discussed in the following section.

ADVANCES IN ABSTRACT THEORY AND IN SOCIAL-PSYCHOLOGICAL RESEARCH (1935–1954)

American sociology developed along two lines during the next two decades. First, in the area of sociological theory, increasing attention was paid to the

Western European founders of the sociological tradition and to integrating the vast amount of empirical research data that had been and was being acquired. Second, the tools, techniques, and statistics used in sociological research and theory construction became, in and of themselves, the central concerns of many sociologists. Each of these thrusts has made a lasting impression on political sociology, reinforcing the previously established emphasis on the individual actor and directing attention to the stability of Western "democratic" political systems.

Interest in Theoretical Integration

Until the 1930s the writings of Marx, Durkheim, Weber, and other Western European social theorists were ignored by most American sociologists. Historical factors such as America's lack of a feudal past and its origin in political revolution led American theorists to formulate their analytic problems in terms which made them appear to be quite different from the problems that concerned European scholars. As it developed in academic settings, America's widely shared social-psychological orientation was contrary to the approaches of these European theorists. Furthermore, sociologists still lacked the technical means of appropriately conducting empirical, macroanalytic investigations. Certain sampling procedures, data-processing techniques, aggregative statistics, and social indicators had yet to be developed. These limitations discouraged interest in macroanalysis among Americans, who characteristically tend to require that techniques of empirical research for dealing with an intellectual problem be present before the problem is seriously discussed. American pragmatism and egalitarianism also led sociologists to deemphasize the kind of scholarship they associated with studying works such as those of Marx, Weber, and Durkheim. "Classical scholarship" might be an acceptable activity for leisured, hereditary aristocrats but it was not really acceptable to a group of social scientists living in a highly utilitarian culture.

The Great Depression, which severely affected virtually all areas of American life, forced sociologists to realize that they had no theoretical perspective with which they might begin to understand systematically such a phenomenon. Although possibly most sociologists supported the New Deal, none had recourse to a solid theoretical structure which helped him to anticipate many of the unintended social consequences of this far-reaching set of political policies. Sociologists had collected enormous amounts of empirical data, but these remained to be theoretically codified. Large numbers of European sociologists who immigrated to the United States in the 1930s communicated to their new colleagues their shared feeling that American sociology seriously lacked the conceptual sophistication and the logical rigor that characterized European work. All of these factors set the stage for some attempts to provide sociology with an integrating theoretical structure.

Two books by Talcott Parsons of Harvard University, one written at the beginning and one written at the end of the third period, introduced a theoretical scheme which, many sociologists contend, has had an enormous influence on American sociology. Recent discussions of Parsons's work, while frequently critical, concede to him, if implicitly and reluctantly, a paramount place among American social theorists. Whatever judgment future historians of sociology may render of his work, the claim that it influenced the analysis of a large number of sociologists for a period extending well over three decades is unlikely to be seriously contested. While other scholars writing from the mid-1930s to the mid-1950s helped advance sociological theory, none had the influence of Parsons. Given this situation, this subsection will be limited to a discussion of his two major books written during this period: *The Structure of Social Action* (1937) and *The Social System* (1951).

Since the significance of Parsons's theoretical work has been so great, it is important to relate it to that of the classical European writers discussed in the first chapter and to the writings of the early American sociologists just considered.

Marx, Weber, and Durkheim all were concerned with problematic aspects of the social and economic order which was still in the process of developing in Western Europe long after the French and industrial revolutions. As they were writing, social disorganization and exploitation were widespread. Marx believed that people would experience their greatest alienation under industrial capitalism. However, he was optimistic about the future once the revolutionary destruction of that system of production had occurred. Weber feared the alienation produced by increasing rationalization as embodied in bureaucratic organization. According to Weber's analysis, alienation inevitably accompanied the bureaucratic organization that was likely to be a component of all modern economic systems—capitalist and noncapitalist alike. Durkheim concluded that by the early twentieth century Western Europe had yet to develop a moral order appropriate for industrialism.

Early American sociologists also were concerned with problems of the modern socioeconomic order. Coming from rural and religious backgrounds, they sought ways of bettering their society, in which the traditional ties of family, class, religion, and community were weakening under the impact of urbanization and industrialization. As they were writing, widespread support for governmental laissez-faire coupled with mass immigration had produced economic and political crises. Ward argued that the rapid and unregulated growth of industrial capitalism had produced a plutocracy whose power could be curtailed only by extensive government limitation of industry and by the introduction of an elaborate system of social education. Giddings discussed America's need of voluntary and private associations which could insure minority rights and equality of economic and cultural opportunities. Neither Giddings nor Ward advocated anything resembling revolution. Neither was opposed to all forms of industrial capitalism. Rather, both supported a gradualist meliorism emphasizing the development of new structures of government and private associations.

The urban sociologists at the University of Chicago eschewed explicit meliorism in favor of a sociology which was nonevaluative and which would deal solely with measurable phenomena. Nevertheless, the central problem to which they addressed themselves was that of the order of the industrial city. As they were writing they read daily reports of vice and political corruption in their city. They personally saw the grim conditions of Chicago's ghettos. They focused on the social problems concentrated in these slum areas occupied by immigrant groups whose culture and social organization did not facilitate adaptation to urban-industrial living. However, they were remarkably optimistic that, over time, the lot of such groups would naturally improve.

Given this stream of social thought, the basic orientation and concerns of Parsons's *The Structure of Social Action* are not surprising.[10] The book involves a critical review of the writings of four major social theorists, most of whose works were published during the first quarter of this century: economist Alfred Marshall, Italian social analyst Vilfredo Pareto, Max Weber, and Emile Durkheim. Each of these writers was concerned with a range of empirical problems involving modern capitalism or economic individualism. Parsons did not intend the book to be a history of social thought but rather an attempt to take stock of the theoretical resources which were at the disposal of sociologists. He further sought to formulate the analytically promising aspects of their writings in such a way as to make them useful tools for empirical research. Parsons believed that the result of such formulation would represent a new development of theory and not merely a restatement and a synthesis of an established intellectual tradition.

In his examination of the four writers, Parsons claims to have empirically discovered the development of a single system of generalized social theory. He describes a theoretical convergence of writers who started from different points of view.[11] Parsons terms this system of generalized theory the "voluntaristic theory of action."

According to Parsons, Marshall's major contribution to the theoretical system is his rejection of the position that wants vary randomly from actor to actor within a society. Marshall attributes this lack of randomness neither to heredity nor to environment but to the "fact" that the wants pursued in a society are expressions of a single ethic—of a self-consistent ideal of conduct. Marshall further maintains that a system of shared ideals plays an important part as a variable in the determination of human conduct. Such a position contrasts sharply with that of Marx, who held that societal values have little causal significance except as tools for manipulating the property-less class.

Parsons identifies Pareto's primary contribution as his differentiation of logical and nonlogical action and his discussion of societal goals. Pareto points out that the ultimate ends of action must be distinguished from the ultimate means and conditions of rational action. He makes the further important distinction between those ultimate ends held in common by members of a society and those held distributively by individuals and groups within the society. With respect to the latter, the problem of distributive justice in the allocation of means, particularly power and wealth, arises. Pareto praises Marx for his attention to the importance of differences in power for the distribution of scarce rewards in a society. However, Marx does not consider ultimate goals held in common by members of a society, for he asserts that societal goals are always the goals of the dominant class—and only that class. To Marx's observation that power is a resource used by individuals and groups in a society to achieve their own goals, Pareto adds that power can be viewed as a societal resource that can be used in the pursuit of ultimate ends held in common by members of a society. This fact is one of the essential conditions for the equilibrium of societies.

Parsons's discussion of Durkheim's contribution to the general social theory centers on the importance Durkheim attributes to moral norms. Like Pareto, Durkheim emphasizes the importance of a common value system. He came to see that the maintenance of a system of rules rests on a set of common values. He contends that fear of sanctions constitutes only the secondary motive for adherence to social norms; the primary motive is the sense of moral obligation. Durkheim criticizes theories that interpret social phenomena exclusively in terms of the external environment and heredity. His analysis of moral norms contrasts sharply with the view of Marx that the prevailing moral norms of a society are always those of the ruling class, which uses them to control the class of nonowners in their own interests. Moral norms are tools used by one class against another. For Durkheim, moral norms serve to integrate society and provide a necessary context within which the orderly and mutually beneficial exchange of differentiated goods and services is possible.

Finally, Parsons credits Weber with attributing appropriate importance to the role of ideas in the determination of economic life. Parsons claims that Weber's main attack was on Marxian historical materialism. He discusses at length Weber's analysis of the role which Calvinism played in the advancement of Western capitalism. This theme in Weber's writing, perhaps more than any other, conflicts with Marx's interpretation of the development of capitalism. For Marx, capitalism emerged from social conflicts inherent in the feudal order. The ideas which prevail under capitalism, like those which prevailed under feudalism, are those which serve the economic interests (and hence the political interests) of the ruling class. Changes in belief systems merely reflect changes in economic systems. While Weber does not claim that Calvinism caused the emergence of capitalism, he does argue that that configuration of beliefs and values provided a context highly congenial to its development.

This review led Parsons to conclude that on the most general level the explanation of social phenomena necessarily involves categories referring to heredity and to the external environment as the ultimate conditions of action, to the ends actors pursue, to the means they employ in the pursuit of these ends, to the ultimate values of the society within which these ends are sought, and to the effort people spend in their goal-directed action.

From the preceding it should be clear that the general theory of action described by Parsons contains a number of elements opposed to Marx's social doctrines. For Marx, prior to the appearance of socialism, the dominant ideas, norms, and values of a society are always those of its dominant class. They are tools in the struggle for power and privilege. In *The Structure of Social Action* there is an emphasis on shared ideas, norms, and values. There is a concern with factors that make possible and preserve the orderly exchanges of social life.

Marx sees social life as composed of the actions of contending classes. Parsons, in keeping with the established orientation of American sociology, sees society as composed of the normatively guided actions of individuals. These points are more fully developed in *The Social System*, where their implications for political analysis are more clearly present.[12]

The Social System represents a shift in theoretical level from the structure of social action as such to the "structural-functional" analysis of social systems. Durkheim discusses the *functions* of *social facts*. *Social facts* are products of social interaction, such as group norms, which are qualitatively distinct from the characteristics of individual group members. The function of a social fact refers to the correspondence between it and the needs of the society in which it occurs. Parsons intends something similar. A *structure* is a relatively persistent and stable feature of a social system. The *function* of a structure refers to its consequences in terms of maintenance of stability or production of change, of integration or disruption of the system in which it occurs. The social processes with which Parsons is most concerned are those which maintain social order. The two processes he discusses in this regard are *socialization,* whereby individuals come to incorporate the standards of society in their personalities, and *social control,* whereby the behavior of persons who have undergone socialization but are still motivated to nonconformity is regulated.

Attention is focused on conformity to and deviation from a relatively stable and well-integrated set of culturally structured and shared expectations. Parsons, like Durkheim, emphasizes the normative aspects of social life. He assigns considerable importance to the maintenance and stability of normative order. The position is taken that any social phenomenon is better understood when viewed in the broad normative context in which it occurs, and in terms of its bearing on the stability of that normative context.

Although Parsons does not present a detailed discussion of the nature of political institutions in *The Social System,* his analysis does suggest that they are patterns of interdependent status roles involved in setting and attaining collective goals. Such activities involve power that is diffuse and hierarchically organized. Following Weber, Parsons comments that the ability to use force in relation to territoriality is one ultimate focus of power and that the control of the use and organization of force relative to territory is always a crucial focus of the political power system. It is this which gives the state its central position in the power system of a complex society.

It is no doubt true that a large proportion of American sociologists have selectively adopted a number of theoretical concepts specified by Parsons. However, today it is probably true that most, or at least a large proportion, of American sociologists would not identify themselves as "structural-functional analysts." Many have found that the conceptual scheme has undesirable consequences for research and theory construction. At this point, then, there is a need to specify some of the merits of the kind of approach developed in Parsons's two books of this period, to indicate the criticisms commonly directed against it, and to indicate the significance of this discussion of highly abstract sociological theory for the understanding of political life.

Parsons's position that the ultimate values of a society tend to eliminate randomness of the goals which its members pursue is congruent with the vast amount of empirical data that clearly show that the goals people seek in a society are not random and that members of different societies do pursue certain goals with significantly greater frequency than members of certain other societies. It thereby encourages research into such differences and carries a suggestion of where such research should begin.[13]

Parsons's insistence on the importance of shared moral values and norms has had a number of important consequences for American political sociology. Political institutions are now generally seen as shaped by such factors. It is generally accepted that political institutions must be understood in the context of the societal values and norms in which they occur. Partially as a result of Parsons's work, many sociological studies of politically relevant values did not proceed from the assumption that these values are mere artifacts of the structural location of those who hold them and are without independent causal significance. Parsons's discussions have encouraged inquiry into the way in which shared value orientations, or configurations of divergent value orientations in heterogeneous societies, influence political structures.

While it is undoubtedly true that a society's political institutions reflect its moral norms to some degree, it is also equally true that moral norms do change as a result of changing political structures, as, for example, in the case of legislative action.[14] An emphasis on the primacy of moral norms deflects the attention of researchers from normative change initiated by the operation of political institutions. It also can lead researchers to underestimate the extent to which moral norms are manipulated by those in positions of power and privilege to maintain the existing system of social inequality.

Interest in shared values and norms encourages research into the processes by which these are acquired and maintained. In keeping with Parsons's suggestion that socialization is the prime mechanism of social control, political analysts initiated studies of the intergenerational congruence of political orientations. To date, most political socialization studies have investigated the continuity of political orientations, the acquisition of loyalty, and the desire to support the political institutions of American society, particularly through participation in routine politics such as voting and writing to elected officials.[15]

Parsons's work directs attention to values held in common by members of a society rather than to scarce values that are the objects of competition between various subgroups of society. It therefore suggests a view of power as a societal resource used for the achievement of collective goals rather than the conceptualization of power as an unevenly distributed resource used by various subgroups in their competitive struggles for scarce values. The importance attributed to common values also suggests the conceptualization of politics as being concerned with the ways in which societal goals are established and resources are mobilized for their realization.[16]

Parsons's approach to functional analysis has provided a systematic basis for describing and comparing the relatively stable features of different political systems.[17] It has also encouraged research into the ways in which institutionalized features of various political systems contribute to the stability of and/or to the disruption of the broader social order of which they are a part.

Despite its analytic utility in the past decade Parsons's explanatory framework has been the object of considerable criticism. Objections in addition to those already noted will be discussed later in this chapter.

Advances Facilitating Empirical Research

To this point only two features of American sociology which have encouraged empirical understanding of political phenomena have been noted. First, arguments to the effect that sociology is, or at least should become, a "science" were described. Second, various approaches, concepts, and hypotheses intended to identify and to aid in the explanation of various observable aspects of the social-political world were discussed. Neither of these features involves "methods," except in the broadest sense of the term. However, some of the most important contributions American scholars have made to the understanding of social life are methods in the narrower sense of the term, that is, specific means for gathering, processing, and interpreting data which are compatible with those common to all physical and life sciences. Americans' development and use of various tools, processes, and techniques has been a major source of many differences between their work and that of their Western European counterparts. Findings about any objects of study are influenced by the methods used for ascertaining answers to questions about those objects.

The questions American sociologists have asked and the concepts they have used in treating these questions often have been influenced by their awareness of the possibilities presented by, and the limitations imposed by, the methodological equipment available to them. This section illustrates some of the "equipment" developed and used during the third period. Only a very limited number of innovations will be considered. Those selected for discussion have been particularly important in political studies.

American sociologists of the third period were certainly not the first people to be concerned with tools and techniques appropriate for empirically understanding the social-political world. As noted in Chapter 1, Marx, Weber, and Durkheim each employed new approaches which he thought considerably elevated his substantive work over the claims of previous moralists, political philosophers, and practical politicians. The use of the dialectic, ideal-type analysis, and functional explanations each was expected to yield "scientific" results.

Some of the methods mentioned below were developed prior to 1935. The general methodological concerns which served as a major impetus to innovation also predate this period. The mid-1920s is often cited as the time during which the first significant advances in empirical methodology and techniques directly useful in political investigations were produced. In particular, faculty members at the University of Chicago are credited with major contributions, often achieved by struggling to legitimate efforts to develop empirical theories of political behavior. Whatever the origin of explicit interest in developing tools and techniques with which to understand observable political phenomena, it was during the third period of American sociology that rapidly accelerating progress in this area really began. Advances in two areas are noted below: techniques of sampling and measuring instruments. Additional developments will be described later in this chapter and in the context of discussions of research in Parts 2 and 3 of this book.

Enhanced empirical understanding of politics requires the quantitative expression of claims concerning attitudes and behavior. Empirical researchers in America, unlike others who have been interested in political life, are particularly concerned with questions about how much and how many. They ask of any relationship they investigate: "What is its form?" and "What is its magnitude?" Their aims in raising such questions are fivefold: to replace the vagueness and ambiguity of assertions expressed in the language of ordinary discourse with the precision of mathematical notation; to reduce individual bias; to permit others to verify, falsify, or present alternatives to specified claims; to reduce yet make explicit the margin of one's errors; and to provide others with an objective basis for determining how much confidence they wish to place in one's claims (this enhances the likelihood of cumulative theoretical development).

There seems to be consensus among historians of empirical political analysis in the United States that voting studies afford the best example of an area in which researchers readily adopted new methods when they became available with the result that their empirical theory was continually improved.[18] This aspect of the history of voting studies is traced briefly below. It will serve as the context for viewing developments in sampling techniques, measuring techniques, and patterns of explanation which occurred between roughly 1935 and 1954.

The first major voting study, *The People's Choice*,[19] appeared in 1944. The investigators used a probability sample (one in which the researcher can specify for each element of the population the probability that it will be included in the sample) of three thousand adults (every fourth household) in Erie County, Ohio. From these, four groups of six hundred were selected by stratified sampling. Three of these groups were interviewed only once during the election. However, the remaining group was interviewed seven times from May through election day in November, 1940. The technique of repeatedly interviewing the same respondents, known as the "panel design," was developed and used for the first time in this study. The sampling technique eliminated a systematically biased selection of respondents which would have affected significantly the findings. The panel design made it possible to investigate numerous aspects of the development of political attitudes leading to the voting decision.

Use of new methods increased confidence in the important substantive conclusion of the volume. The study demonstrated that American voters are not relatively rational individuals advancing their own self-interest by voting for the candidate or party which they believe, on the basis of the best information available to them, to be most likely to realize the goals they consider most important. Because *The People's Choice* began with the assumption that voting was a rational act, this refutation of initial assumptions was "mute testimony of the self-correcting nature of the design."[20] A carefully planned piece of empirical research had prevented authors from finding what they expected to find. This self-correcting aspect of properly designed empirical inquiry represented a considerable advance over other previous modes of political investigation.

A major limitation of *The People's Choice* is rather characteristic of voting studies and of much research in political sociology generally. By focusing on individuals little attention was paid to the political aspects of the environment that enter into the determination of political behavior. In this particular study nothing was said about the possible influence on voting decisions of a party machine in Erie County.

Voting[21] also employed a probability sample and a panel design in studying the residents of a single community—this time Elmira, New York, and the 1948 election. The study illustrated the cumulative development of voting research—extending the findings and techniques of *The People's Choice*. The authors themselves saw *Voting* "as one phase in a cumulative enterprise."[22] Since the earlier research indicated that rational processes are far from all that is involved in voting decisions, *Voting* focused on such factors as peer group influence, community political climate, and the hereditary nature of party affiliations.

The Voter Decides[23] presented an analysis of the 1952 election based on data gathered from a probability sample of the national electorate interviewed before and after the election. One of the key criticisms of *Voting* was that in reaching conclusions the authors went well beyond the limits of their data. *The Voter Decides* began with the claim that the data on which it was based were gathered through the use of advanced sampling methods that afforded the possibility of making inferences about the total population from characteristics of a relatively few cases.

The study approached voting from a social-psychological perspective, emphasizing the intervening variables of attitudes, perceptions, and group loyalties. "The basic assumption of the study (is) that a major portion of the total motivation of the individual citizen in the election situation can be reduced to a manageable number of variables, and that these variables can be adequately measured."[24]

A number of important measuring instruments were developed in the study. One, an "Index of Political Participation," was designed as a "crude but serviceable" index of the level of political activity in the national electorate. The index was found to be closely related to three attitudinal measures developed in the study: "sense of political efficacy," "sense of citizen duty," and "issue involvement." The development of each of these measures made use of "scale analysis," a technique developed by Louis Guttman and his associates in the War Department during World War II.[25] In a perfect Guttman scale, items have a cumulative property which justifies the assumption of an ordinal scale. Items may be arranged from least to most extreme so that the exact response pattern of an individual can be reproduced from his total score.

Each of the three attitude scales mentioned above met Guttman criteria. Hence, on the basis of response patterns, the authors could legitimately talk about some individuals having a greater sense of political efficacy than others or as having less of a sense of citizen duty than others, and so on. This represented a major advance over the use of single-item indicators and over the use of partially ordered scales which made it possible to say that in some respects A is more something (informed, motivated to perform citizen duties, etc.) than B but in other respects less, because the individuals have endorsed different sets of items. It also represented an advance in that improved levels of measurement made possible the use of more powerful mathematical techniques for the manipulation of data. The introduction of completely ordered scales in empirical political research thus made possible an increasing precision in the statements that political sociologists were able to make.

The American Voter,[26] the final voting study to be considered, is a product of the fourth rather than the third period in the history of American sociology. The methodological and theoretical advances it represents suggest that it does belong to a later historical segment. However, for purposes of continuity, it is discussed here.

The American Voter used a nationwide probability sample to investigate the 1956 presidential election. Like its predecessors, the study involved a social-psychological perspective, with emphasis on the individual's perception of political stimuli. However, data on beliefs and attitudes were treated within a perspective which took into account election laws, the social and economic context of voting, the role of social class, agrarian political behavior, and population movement, and which included a broad discussion of the electoral decision and the political system.

The pattern of explanation employed in *The American Voter* emphasized the interplay of a number of variables over a period of time. Taken together these variables structure voting behavior in a particular election. The intention of the authors in using such a pattern was to provide some understanding of the multivariate nature of the determination of the vote.

Concerns with the relative importance of a large number of variables at different points in time preceding the vote and with developing an analytic scheme which encompasses factors ranging from personality characteristics of voters to formal voting requirements are all apparent in *The American Voter*. Drawing on and extending existing sampling and scaling techniques, *The American Voter* took many topics in voting analysis as far as they could be developed. Further advances in such areas as the structure of political belief systems and in causally interpreting the sequence of variables preceding the vote awaited further development in psychology, mathematics, statistics, and cybernetics.

In the course of the four voting studies, respondent-selection techniques advanced from contacting a member of every fourth household in a single county to conducting national probability samples. Measuring instruments advanced from single-item indicators to fully ordered scales. The investigation of relationships advanced from two-variable to multivariable analysis. One set of intended consequences of such changes already has been mentioned: reducing investigator bias, increasing precision of claims, increasing the possibility of verification or falsification, and encouraging cumulative development.

A second set of consequences, possibly unintended, also accompanied these changes. Voting studies exemplified and reinforced the microanalytic tendencies of American political research. Primary concern was always with the individual who votes. Voting studies also diverted analysts from a consideration of historical materials. Investigators did not use data more than twenty years old and avoided confronting historical problems. The voter who decided and the person who chose was always the American voter. Even within brief discussions of "democracy" there was not even speculation concerning how American voters might compare in certain ways with their peers in other nations.

Voting is one of the most routine and uninvolved forms of participation in most political systems. Concentration on voting behavior may lead some to forget that politics often involves coercion, conflict, violence, rapid and extensive societal change. Politics is not always a series of peaceful battles between competing private interests which are carried on within a set of mutually acceptable rules.[27]

Voting studies have been discussed because they serve as a convenient context for viewing some general advances in the area of methods which occurred between 1935 and 1954. Now it can be seen that such studies also serve to illustrate orientations in American sociology which have their origin in American culture and, more specifically, in the history of American universities.

During the third period in the history of American sociology Parsons's work on the one hand and advances in methods on the other both served to reinforce long-established analytic tendencies. Empirical studies, such as those dealing with party identification and voting behavior, were social-psychological and directed attention to such variables as individuals' interest in and concern about political affairs, level of political information, sense of political efficacy, reaction to cross pressures, and so on. In such investigations, family, religion, and class were viewed almost exclusively in their roles as socializing agents, instilling in the individual beliefs, values, and behavioral tendencies relevant to performing institutionalized roles in the ongoing political system. Social classes were viewed as different social-cultural settings rather than as potential political conflict groups differentially oriented to the stability or change of the political order. Furthermore, studies tended to be ahistorical and noncomparative.[28]

CONCERN WITH CONSENSUS
AND CONFLICT (1954-1966)

The discussion of the third period proceeded from a consideration of theory to a description of some new methods used in one substantive area of political research. This subsection will follow the opposite course. Several areas of research will be briefly described. This will be followed by short characterizations of some new methods of social research developed between 1954 and 1966. Finally, changes in general theory will be considered. There is a reason for this choice of order. During the third period general theory and methods developed more or less independently, though both embodied the same analytic emphases. However, in the fourth period major developments in theory represented a definite reaction to trends in research and research methods. Fundamental questions about the microanalytic, ahistorical, and stability orientations of American sociology were explicitly raised and widely discussed. To understand these questions it is first necessary to see the research and a few of the research methods and techniques that prompted them. Like most general questions about the conduct of inquiry, the questions about the basic orientations of American sociology did not represent merely intellectual responses to intellectual problems. They were also prompted by changing social realities.

Continuing Empirical Research
on Politics

By the mid-1950s America had experienced the Great Depression, had taken steps toward becoming an advanced industrial welfare democracy, had had some time to assess the causes and consequences of World War II, and had seen some of the effects of considering "internal communism" and the "international communist movement" as the threat to freedom and democracy that fascism once represented.

These events focused attention on a number of related questions. Why do some men become fascists, others fight and die under the banner of communism, others struggle in the name of political democracy, while still others remain totally indifferent to political ideas, ideals, and processes? What are the appeals of fascism, communism, and democracy? What factors politicize people or encourage political apathy? Why are some people tolerant of those who have radically different political opinions while others actively condemn those whose views are only slightly divergent from their own?

It is possible to approach such questions from macroanalytic, historical, and comparative perspectives. It is a theoretically reasonable endeavor to seek cross-societally applicable propositions dealing with the cultural and structural sources of communism, fascism, and democracy. Theoretically significant questions can be raised about the way or ways in which changes in family, religion, class, and cultural systems bring about changes in political systems, and vice versa. Typically, American political sociology did not proceed along these lines.

Like *voting* studies, social-psychological and stability concerns also predominated in empirical studies of other varieties of *political participation* such as joining political organizations, petitioning public offices, campaigning, discussing politics, and attending to the political content of the mass media. In a major review of the research literature on this topic, Robert Lane devotes much of his discussion to the role of personality ("conscious needs," "unconscious needs," and "social attitudes") as a determinant of participation rather than to structural factors.[29] Lester Milbrath's first review of this body of research literature also reveals a heavily social-psychological orientation.[30]

Most studies of *public opinion* and *ideology* conducted from the mid-1950s to the mid-1960s made use of the sample survey. Attitudes were the primary objects of investigation. Findings indicating that different segments of the population have highly divergent political opinions were seldom interpreted as indicators of the potentiality of serious political conflict and change. Rather, the nonmodal opinions were often attributed to social-psychological characteristics shared by those who maintain them.[31] Individuals with nonmodal political attitudes were not seen as posing a threat to routine political processes since their social-psychological attributes were positively associated with political apathy and withdrawal rather than with organized participation. Studies of supporters of nonmodal ideologies (for example, Communist party members in non-Communist nations)[32] or of individuals who express "antidemocratic attitudes"[33] were also carried out in social-psychological terms and viewed the phenomenon as nonthreatening to institutionalized politics. More general studies of popular ideologies often concluded that the importance of ideology was rapidly diminishing in industrial societies[34] or that it is misleading in the first place to even speak of most people as having an ideology.[35]

During the 1950s and 1960s the study of *political movements* in American sociology was dominated by the "mass society" thesis.[36] The thesis maintained that advanced industrial societies, like the United States, lacked a network of psychologically significant and politically effective kinship, class, or religious associations; they are societies particularly prone to mass movements of the left or right. Such a position saw mass movements as resulting from structurally induced psychological problems (often called *alienation*) and as representing a "crisis" in relatively stable political systems.

Investigations of *community power* tended to be noncomparative and ahistorical and to ignore changes in the distribution of power over time.[37] However, such studies did appear to be macroanalytic. Between the 1950s and the mid-1960s two antithetical views of the distribution of power in

American communities received wide attention. Both views took the position that power is institutional rather than personal and that it is differentially available to individuals and to groups according to their place in the larger social subsystems of which they are a part. However, each view emphasized a different research procedure. One measured the frequency with which persons are reputed to be powerful. The other measured the repeated involvement of the same persons in influencing community decisions. Yet each of these methods assumed that some aspect of the individuals, their desire for involvement or their primary institutional affiliation (for example, banker, lawyer, industrialist) is sufficient to explain the extent of their actual or reputed power in community affairs. Hence both views, despite their references to power as a system of social relationships and to power as residing in institutions rather than in persons, used the individual as the unit of analysis.[38]

Between the mid-1950s and the early 1960s most studies of voting, political participation, ideologies, political movements, and community power were based exclusively on data gathered in America and lacked a research design which would make possible the testing of hypotheses across several nations. Works exhibiting some of the four characteristics of the sociological tradition, described in Chapter 1, were conducted by anthropologists studying the politics of historical and traditional societies, by economists studying systems of allocation of societal resources, or by political scientists studying the formal structures of governments. However, these works were ignored by most sociologists and by most political scientists "of the behavioral persuasion." Anthropological topics appeared too exotic and irrelevant, economic topics too narrow, and descriptions of formal structure too far removed from actual behavior to merit serious consideration.

With the eruption of the political drama of the 1960s political sociologists began to recognize that anthropological studies provided needed insight into the politics of the developing nations of Asia, Africa, and Latin America. Such studies contained information on the role that traditional kinship, religious, and class bonds and traditional cognitive and evaluative orientations would have on the scope, direction, and rapidity of political change. Political sociologists began to recognize the extent to which economic studies facilitated understanding of the origins, course, intensity, and probable outcomes of political conflicts over the distribution of scarce goods and services such as food, housing, education, access to jobs, medical care, security. Political sociologists also began to see that formal political structures themselves produce, channel, and resolve social cleavages and conflicts and are not mere reflections of the stratification system. Such realizations enhanced understanding of many differences between the groups, issues, and outcomes of political struggles in various nations and encouraged further investigations into comparative politics.

These vastly expanded interests of political sociologists, triggered by worldwide political change, placed them in a position similar to that which all American sociologists had faced approximately two decades earlier. They lacked a theoretical scheme in terms of which they might systematically investigate and explain a mass of new and uncodified facts which confronted them. The first steps they took toward understanding new patterns of change, occurring in highly diverse regions throughout the world, covered familiar ground.

In the face of rising anti-Western feelings in Asia, Africa, and Latin America and with the apparently increasing strength of communism throughout these regions, political sociologists focused their attention on those social forces which might move political changes in these areas in a direction more compatible with the political interests of the United States. Lipset argues that "one of political sociology's prime concerns is the analysis of the social conditions making for democracy."[39] The study of political change in Third World nations came to be the study of "political development." However, political development tended to be equated with taking on the characteristics of the "most developed" political system in the world—which happened to be the United States.[40] Such an approach to political development was obviously normative. There is nothing wrong with using a given empirical political system as a model and then raising the question of how political development might or might not move in the desired direction. However, preoccupation with a particular model seriously deflects analytic efforts to understand other potential and perhaps even more probable courses of political change. Of paramount importance to most leaders and citizens of Third World nations is economic development, which might actually be hindered by democratic participation in political affairs.[41]

The bias of American sociology in its emphasis on social order has thus been detrimental to the analysis of political change in the Third World. The bias, as Leon Bramson observes, is not one that appropriately can be labeled "left" or "right."[42] It favors a political order in which there are constitutional opportunities for changing government officials and in which there is a social mechanism which permits the largest possible part of the population to influence decisions by choosing among contenders for political office. Sometimes the nature of the preferred order is made even more specific. Lipset, for example, expresses his feeling that a two-party system rather than a multiparty system, elections on a territorial rather than a proportional representation basis, and federal rather than unitary states are most conducive to political democracy.[43] A sociology of factors that contribute to the development and maintenance of American political forms is but a part of a sociology of political change.

While, in American sociology, the study of political change in the Third World became the study of "political development" in the sense just indicated, the study of vehement protests and conflict became the social psychology of violent behavior. Concepts such as *frustration* and *relative deprivation* took their place alongside *alienation* and *anomie* (in their psychological as opposed to their structural meanings) as the most commonly used explanatory variables in accounts of such phenomena.[44] There is nothing wrong with such basically psychological studies. However, preoccupation with such variables deflects attention from objective structural conditions which might precipitate violence and from the social organization and social-political consequences of protest movements. A social psychology of violent behavior is but a portion of a sociology of vehement political protest and conflict.

With the increasing political and economic importance of Third World nations, political sociology is challenged to develop more complete and adequate explanations of political change. With the newly obvious potential of mass political actions to occur anywhere from the streets of Londonderry to the gold mines of South Africa to the campuses of American universities, political sociology was challenged to develop more complete and adequate explanations of vehement protest. A major future thrust of political sociology still lies in meeting these challenges.

New Contexts and Tools of Research

For the most part, the studies discussed above employed refinements of well-established methods and techniques of research. For example, sample surveys and attitude scales were used extensively in these investigations. However, during this period, other research was undertaken which introduced new research contexts, new models of social behavior, and new techniques for storing, retrieving, and manipulating data.

Small-group research: During the 1950s laboratory studies of artificially created task-oriented groups became increasingly popular. Such investigations offered sociologists one of their few opportunities for controlled experimentation.

Sidney Verba, in an extensive review of the research literature, points out that small face-to-face groups are politically significant in at least two ways.[45] First, they are the locus of most political decision making. Decisions of political leaders and justices of high courts as well as decisions of ordinary citizens concerning how to vote usually take place within small face-to-face groups. Small groups are also key contexts in all societies for the transmission of political communications. Groups that involve face-to-face contact exercise a major influence on the political beliefs and attitudes of their members.

Verba isolates three topics extensively studied in experimental settings which have clear implications for political analysis. The first is the relationship between affective and instrumental leadership. Investigations of this topic suggest that it is not enough for a political system to be instrumentally effective. It must also gain and keep the allegiance of its citizens. A system that does not have such loyalty may be stable for a time, but it will be hard pressed to survive the breakdown of its instrumental effectiveness. A second topic frequently studied is the relationship between stability and conformity on the one hand, both needed in any political system, and nonconformity and change, which are also needed. Third, much experimental research has been conducted on participatory leadership, that is, on the effect of participation in decision making on willingness to accept the decision that is reached.

An emphasis on stability and democracy is present in the vast majority of studies reviewed by Verba. In fact, the two are related, for research indicates that if leaders inculcate in followers the belief that they are participating in setting group norms—whether or not they actually are—they are more likely to accept decisions. Verba points out that in much of the small-group literature participatory leadership refers not to a technique of decision making but to a technique of persuasion. This is not surprising because in the United States interest in the small group began in the 1930s with studies of factory worker productivity. Presenting workers with the appearance of democracy was a way to exercise control—control that is needed in industrial society.

Verba notes that small-group studies often involve a "no-conflict" assumption—an assumption that there is a single group goal or a single method for attaining a group goal that is in the best interests of all concerned, both leaders and followers. If this single goal or means for attaining a goal is properly presented to the members of a group by its leaders, they will recognize that it is in their best interests. Verba comments on this assumption:

> This approach to decision-making ignores the myriad of complex social situations in which the goals of some members of the system may not be the same as that of others, and the best solution for some participants will not be the best for others. There are numerous cases where the goal of an organization is congruent with the goal of the small groups and individuals of which it is composed. But there are also situations in which these goals are in conflict.[46]

The small-group laboratory represented a new context within which empirical political research might be carried out. However, while such a research context was new, the theoretical orientations of investigators using the setting were not. An approach emphasizing democracy and social stability and de-emphasizing social conflict was hardly new to American sociology. The small-group laboratory was designed explicitly to investigate social relations under controlled conditions. The preceding indicates that controls did not eliminate the long-established biases of American researchers.

Data processing: It is far beyond the scope of this book even to list the advances in the technology of storing, recalling, copying, transmitting, and statistically manipulating information that occurred between 1954 and 1966. Nevertheless, the basic impetus to and aims of such technological progress can be simply sketched.

In an increasingly complex and competitive world, organizations of all sorts, political and nonpolitical, find it necessary to gather information about themselves, about their competitors, and about factors in their environment likely to affect the nature and outcomes of their struggles.

Any collection of information is valuable only if it can be used—that is, only if each of the items or sets of items of which it is composed can be located and brought to bear on questions of interest to the collector. Vast collections of data, such as those possessed by governments and industrial corporations, require sophisticated techniques of organizing, storing, retrieving, copying, transmitting, and displaying in succinct and intelligible form all available data which are to be of any use. Prior to the invention of new data-processing methods some data were almost inevitably lost and had to be recollected. Some data-gathering projects also were duplicated since, without the methods, organizations sometimes were unaware that the information they sought had already been ascertained. Hence there was interest in developing information-processing technology.

New methods of processing data do more than reduce the necessity of regathering information. Electronic data storage and retrieval systems make it possible to bring to bear on analytic problems a greater quantity of data and more diverse data. Under certain conditions findings of independent investigations can be brought together and used in the study of relationships. This not only can increase confidence in findings but possibly can also increase their generalizability. Such a procedure, if successful, enhances the theoretical and practical significance of the original independent analyses by indicating that they can be viewed as case studies of more general uniformities. If properly stored data are made widely available, the likelihood both of replication and of secondary analyses generating new insights is also increased.

Technological advances introduced the possibility of two major developments in empirical theory. First, genuine comparative analysis might be undertaken once international agreement had been reached on matters such as categorizing variables, establishing widely applicable social indicators, and making data available. In 1960, the Committee on Political Sociology of the International Sociological Association was established to achieve such ends.[47] Second, new technology made it possible to systematically accumulate over time vast amounts of data. Even after relatively short periods of time such data could be retrieved for investigations of changes in beliefs, attitudes, and social structure. As yet neither of these two possibilities has been fully explored by social scientists. New data-processing technology can facilitate comparative analysis and the study of social change. With their use social scientists might begin to provide empirically grounded answers to questions of the sort raised by Marx, Weber, and Durkheim—macroanalytic questions about the role of kinship, religion, class, and community in political life and questions about broad patterns of social-political change. Some work carried out during this period, such as that of Deutsch,[48] Russett,[49] Banks and Textor,[50] and Marsh,[51] can be interpreted as steps in this direction.

The hardware embodying the technological advances in processing information is exceedingly expensive. Mostly it is owned by organizations of government or by large private corporations. Academic research using such hardware requires funding, which, when it is available, usually comes from federal agencies or from private foundations. Since each of these has interests of its own, research topics and the ways in which such topics are treated are often not entirely determined by academic investigators. It is at this point that researchers must ask themselves serious questions about their own basic political beliefs and attitudes.

The Bifurcation of General Theory

Those engaged in small-group research and those developing and utilizing advanced data-processing technology had a common concern with the precision and accuracy of empirical sociological theory. Progress in sociological theory was equated with its exactness. Such an interest, which became increasingly popular, often led investigators to limit the scope of their studies. Many opted for small-scope problems which could be studied using experimental or quasi-experimental designs.

Other sociologists, largely influenced by Parsons's work, did not equate progress in sociological theory with increasing exactness so much as with increasing comprehensiveness. That is, they felt that sociology would advance as interrelated sets of broad concepts and generalizations were developed which would theoretically integrate numerous central findings of the various social sciences.

In 1959 C. Wright Mills attacked works representing each of these views of the proper course of sociological theory.[52] In an influential book he argued that sociologists had become absorbed by matters of little or no concern to the real problems that beset human society.

As Mills saw it, the work of "grand theorists," exemplified by Parsons, involved an endless elaboration of distinctions which neither facilitated our understanding of social life nor made our own social experiences more sensible. When we descend from the level of grand theory to historical realities, Mills said, we immediately realize the irrelevance of highly abstract concepts. For example, Parsons's approach assumes the operation of a normative structure insuring a minimum amount of social conflict and rule by *authority* (power justified by the beliefs of the voluntary obedient) rather than rule by *manipulation* (power wielded unbeknown to the powerless) or rule by *coercion*. Such a theoretical orientation removes the sociologist from any concern with power, with economic and political institutions, and with political change.

According to Mills, then, "grand theory" is concerned with remote abstractions which divert attention from genuine questions about social and political structure. On the other hand, Mills also attacks "abstract empiricism," the attempt to restate and adopt methodologies of natural science in such a way as to form a program and a canon for work in social science. It too lacks a firm connection with substantive sociological problems.

In the area of political investigations "abstract empiricism" is most clearly seen in voting studies. In those, Mills argues, there is great emphasis on method but little of substantive content. For example, from such studies we learn that rich, rural, and Protestant persons tend to vote Republican and that people of the opposite type are inclined to be Democrats; and so on. But we learn little about the dynamics of American politics. Important questions involving concepts of social structure and depth psychology and requiring historical knowledge are raised neither to formulate problems nor to explain findings since these concerns are outside the accredited style of such empiricists. As a result numerous details about scattered topics are compiled. Researchers of this sort have not selected problems in such a way as to allow a true accumulation of results—that is, one that would add up to systematic development of theory.[53]

Mills's own work, *The Power Elite*,[54] written three years before *The Sociological Imagination*, apparently represented that kind of analysis which, Mills believed, had the shortcomings neither of grand theory nor of abstract empiricism. In that study of power in America, Mills draws on data from government publications, newspapers, magazines, and journals of political opinion as well as from conventional academic sources. His conclusions are not about the attitudes and behavior of individuals but about the institutional locus of power. His concern is not only with the distribution of power at the time of his writing, but also with historical changes in the American structure of power. He specifically addresses the questions of the roles kinship, religion, and class play in the political life of industrial society—questions of the sort raised by Marx, Durkheim, and Weber.[55]

Mills's critique of American theory and methods, both of which he felt represented "abdications of classic social science," as well as his substantive discussions in *The Power Elite*, created an intellectual atmosphere for American social scientists which enhanced the influence of German sociologist Ralf Dahrendorf's *Class and Class Conflict in Industrial Society*,[56] written in 1957 and translated and published in the United States in 1959. This book, probably more than any other by a contemporary social scientist, encouraged American sociologists to reconsider the analytic utility of Marx's discussions of industrial society. It also generated concern about the emphasis on social order and stability which characterized American sociology.

Dahrendorf's book led many to think that American sociologists had to choose between two models of society to guide their analyses—one emphasizing order and stability, the other focusing on conflict and change.[57] Dahrendorf prefaces his book with the following observation:

> ... There is today considerable need for reorienting sociological analysis to problems of change, conflict and coercion in social structures, and especially in those of total societies. The interest in total societies, as well as in their historical dimension, is of course as old as sociology itself. Yet their neglect in recent decades makes a study like this a venture into unmapped areas of inquiry.[58]

Dahrendorf says that there are two different images which pervade political thought and sociological theory. One is concerned with problems of stability and displays a bias in favor of analysis in terms of values and norms. The other is concerned with problems of conflict and tends to emphasize not the normative but the institutional aspects of social structure.

Dahrendorf proceeds to develop his own theory of conflict in industrial society. He argues that in every social organization, including total societies, there are some positions with the right to exercise control over others. This differential distribution of authority becomes the determining factor of politically significant social conflict. Dahrendorf asserts that it is not property relations per se, as Marx argued, but more generally relations of authority that constitute the structural origin of social conflict. That is, politically important social conflict originates in the arrangement of social roles endowed with expectations of domination or subjection. Whenever there are such roles, group conflicts are to be expected. In any given social organization, a clear line at least in theory can be drawn between those who exercise authority and those who are subject to the authoritative commands of others. Dahrendorf maintains that in the sociological analysis of group conflict the unit of analysis is always a specific association and this particular dichotomy of positions within it.

"Power," a concept closely related to "authority," is also central to Dahrendorf's theory. His treatment of this term places him in the tradition of Marx and Mills and sets off this tradition from that represented by Parsons. Power, unlike authority, is not always associated with social positions or roles; it is a "factual" relation rather than a legitimate relation of domination and subjection; it may be a relation of generalized control over others.

The conceptualization of power and authority used by Dahrendorf represents the position Parsons criticizes in his review of Mills's *The Power Elite*. "The essential point," Parsons says, "is that to Mills (and to Dahrendorf) power is not a facility for the performance of function in and on behalf of the society as a system, but is interpreted exclusively as a facility for getting what one group, the holders of power, wants by preventing another group, the 'outs,' from getting what it wants."[59]

The work of Mills and Dahrendorf presented contemporary theoretical alternatives to Parsons's approach. Sociologists seemed to face a choice between operating within the framework of "conflict analysis" or within the framework of "structural-functional analysis." Although Dahrendorf himself, along with others, argued that sociologists "have to choose between them only for the explanation of specific problems; but in the conceptual arsenal of sociological analysis they exist side by side,"[60] their arguments were not widely heeded.

Gerhard Lenski's *Power and Privilege*,[61] published in 1966, represents one major attempt to demonstrate that "theories as contradictory as those of Marx and Mosca, Dahrendorf and Parsons, can be understood within a single framework."[62] In an effort to determine the causes of the differential distribution of power and privilege within societies at various levels of technological development, Lenski selects analytically useful aspects of social thought from antagonistic intellectual traditions, which he labels "conservative" (of which, presumably, Parsons is a contemporary representative) and "radical" (of which, presumably, Mills and Dahrendorf are representatives). After reviewing extensive literature on the distributive systems of hunting and gathering, horticultural, agrarian, and industrial societies, Lenski reaches certain tentative conclusions about the validity of each of the alternative positions on a number of issues.[63] Details of Lenski's synthesis will not be reviewed here. However, three general features of his work should be indicated. First, it clearly locates some of the points of division between theorists which were so clearly drawn during the 1955–65 period. All of these points bear directly on the ways in which specifically political relationships are to be understood. Second, the very attempt at synthesis showed that sociologists did not have to choose between conflicting, exclusive ideological guides to theory construction. They could empirically investigate theoretically significant, individual hypotheses about the distribution of power and privilege. Third, Lenski's synthesis points the way toward future theoretical development in American sociology. His study is macroanalytic, historical-comparative, and concerned with social change as well as stability. It has, in short, the basic features of the work of the founders of the sociological tradition that was characterized in Chapter 1.

The work of Dahrendorf and Lenski suggests that toward the end of the 1955–65 period American sociology was beginning to move full circle—toward some adoption of the concerns and general approaches of such authors as Marx, Weber, and Durkheim. Social and political events from 1966 to the early 1970s further urged American sociology in this direction, even though they did not encourage further attempts at integrating the two general perspectives represented by Parsons and Mills.

AMERICAN SOCIOLOGY IN A CONTEXT OF TURMOIL (1966–1975)

Lenski's book might have served as a prototype for future attempts at theoretical synthesis. However, political and social events that erupted shortly after its publication diverted attention away from such theoretical efforts. Violence in black ghettos, mass rallies demanding greater social, economic, and political equality for various minorities, demonstrations in major cities in opposition to the Vietnam War, protest and sometimes violent confrontations on American campuses centering around American involvement in Vietnam and also around the political rights of students at their colleges and universities—all of these events at least temporarily consumed the attention of many sociologists.

Naturally, then, much of the social research which was initiated during this period dealt with the political and social upheavals of the immediate environment. Studies of student protesters and surveys of the American public's reaction to the war and to civil disobedience were particularly numerous. To some extent this was beneficial to American sociology, which had exhibited a clear tendency to overlook conflict and change in favor of analyzing consensus and stability. On the other hand, many of the studies had limitations which came to be widely recognized. Such limitations raised some fundamental questions about the research activities in which many sociologists routinely engaged and about the theoretical perspectives which many sociologists routinely assumed.

Contemporary Political Movements as Subjects of Research

Two features of many of these studies reduced their potential value. First, the investigations seldom were guided by theoretical interests. They were not commonly undertaken to test sets of interrelated hypotheses but to describe the drama of the present in apparently more valid and precise terms than the mass media had used. When sociological explanations were offered, they were often presented in a post hoc fashion. Investigations were not cumulative in the sense that later studies refined and extended earlier research.

The atheoretical, nonabstractive character of this line of empirical research on politics was apparent to most sociologists with the publication of some of the first studies. In fact, this was one of the most common bases of their criticism. The general importance of the criticism was not only that it applied to ongoing studies of political movements but that it seemed to apply to a considerable proportion of all of the empirical research which American political sociologists had conducted. The specific criticism encouraged a general critical reevaluation of political sociology. (This will be seen in several of the overviews of the field that are reviewed in Chapter 3.)

A second, related problem was also present in the studies. Those theories which were set forth to deal with certain types of behavior, such as student protest, commonly more resembled attempts to defend or to criticize the behavior than to explain it. For example, student protesters were treated both as young intelligentsia seeking personal autonomy and individuality within a restrictive social order[64] and as a spoiled and rebellious generation dangerously devoid of historical awareness.[65]

Whatever its negative consequences, interest in ongoing social movements did have the positive effect of producing some research concerned with conflict and change—with the confrontation of various social groups and with the uses of power and authority to maintain or change existing inequalities in social advantages—the very phenomena which lie at the heart of political sociology. (Chapter 5 reviews the substantive findings of a number of these studies.)

The Influence of Social Movements on the Theoretical Perspectives of Sociologists

A second beneficial result of the period of political turbulence was that it forced sociologists to again ask some very basic questions about the nature of their work (specifically, what role do values play in the conduct of inquiry?), about the purposes of sociology (specifically, whose ends are served by sociological studies and what are these ends?), and about the future of sociology (specifically, on what analytic problems would it focus and what approaches would be employed in the investigation of these problems?). Such questions also invited normative responses: What role *should* values play in sociological inquiry? Whose values *should be* considered? What perspective or perspectives *ought to be* pursued? What problems *ought to be* considered? What perspective or perspectives *ought to be* used? Asking such questions was extremely beneficial for it encouraged sociologists to be sensitive to possible biases in their work and to guide the changes in their field, rather than to permit the speed and direction of change to be entirely dictated by social and political forces.

The book that most clearly embodies sociology's self-reflective stance during this period is Alvin Gouldner's *The Coming Crisis of Western Sociology*, published in 1970.[66] The book also specifically aimed at unveiling the structural sources of biases in American sociology and sketching a course for its future development. The study has particular relevance for political sociology because the biases that Gouldner discovers are more likely to influence the sociological study of political institutions than the study of any other social institutions.

The first section of *The Coming Crisis* locates the sources of, and criticizes the character of some unquestioned fundamental assumptions upon which American sociology operates. One of the most important of these is the assumption that the only important question to be asked about a social theory concerns its empirical validity. Gouldner argues that other equally important questions can be asked as well. These include: "What are the social and political consequences of the intellectual system under examination? Do they liberate or repress men? Do they bind men into the social world that now exists, or do they enable him to transcend it?"[67] To limit evaluation of social theories solely to technical criteria, he contends, "is in effect not only to allow but to require men to be moral cretins in their technical roles."[68] The function of such a norm, Gouldner argues, is to sever the moral sensibilities of social scientists and to enable them to be used by private corporations and government as deployables, willing to pursue practically any objective.

A second central, yet unquestioned assumption of American sociology concerns the desirability of cumulative research and theoretical convergence. Such an ideal, Gouldner asserts, arose as part of the drive to professionalize sociology and to recruit to sociology men who saw themselves as technicians rather than as intellectuals. One consequence of this, he argues, is to smother intellectual and political criticism and innovation.

Gouldner observes that, while modern sociology was conceived in nineteenth-century Western Europe, its major growth has taken place in Eastern Europe and in the United States. Both Eastern European and American sociology were concerned with the problems of modern society. Sociology, developed in the United States, tended to assume that problems of maturing industrial society would be worked out in time by a social system that it regarded as fundamentally sound. Eastern European or Marxist sociology, on the other hand, tended to assume that there are conflicts inherent in modern society which would be solved only through its radical restructuring.

The movement toward increasing professionalism in American sociology and the widespread assumption concerning the basic viability of American social structure were both compatible with liberal (as opposed to conservative or radical) political views. This political stance, Gouldner argues, permits sociologists to seek remedies for the problems of contemporary American society without challenging its basic institutional structure. This obviously affects what they have to say about political matters.

America's dominant utilitarianism also leaves its mark on sociology. A demand is placed on social theory for practical application. Gouldner asserts that the social science of a utilitarian culture always tends toward a theoryless empiricism. The concerns of sociologists are supplied by the practical interests of clients, sponsors, and research funders who make sociology useful to their interests. In a highly utilitarian culture the state's contribution to the well-being of individuals becomes the standard of political legitimacy. Utilitarianism encourages the development of the welfare state. In turn it is the welfare state which exerts the greatest pressure on social science to be practical and applicable.

According to Gouldner, there is a "crisis" in sociology precisely because of its inability to meet the demands of the welfare state. Gouldner equates Western sociology with the functionalism of Parsons, which, he maintains, has a number of features that inhibit the development of socially useful sociological theory, i.e., theory which can facilitate decision making and planned social intervention and which can persuade the population of the existence of important problems with which the state is ready to deal.

Gouldner goes on to argue for the development of a "reflexive" sociology. This is characterized neither by the analytic problems to which it is addressed nor by the use of particular techniques and instruments. Rather, it is characterized by the relationship it establishes between sociologists and their work. It involves the sociologists' recognition that the self plays an important role in processing information—not only a distorting role but also as a source of valid insight and motivation.

There is little doubt that American sociologists do make the unquestioned assumptions Gouldner attributes to them. However, questions can be raised about the consequences that Gouldner claims are the inevitable results of maintaining such beliefs and attitudes. While American sociologists have particularly emphasized "technical" assessments of theories and have tended not to publicly discuss the social consequences of theories, there appear to be no data conclusively demonstrating or even strongly suggesting that this has seriously dulled their moral sensitivities and reduced them to the status of "deployables." The moral judgments of many sociologists are made privately and before they engage in research projects. It seems unlikely that most sociologists are either unaware that, or totally insensitive to the fact that, social research has social consequences. It also seems unlikely that they systematically fail to take them into account when considering participation in various projects. In sociology, as anywhere else, there will always be some whose concerns with personal rewards of income and status invariably will outweigh other factors bearing on the decision to participate. There will always be others who are particularly sensitive to the political and ideological significance of their work and take this into account in their decision making. Furthermore, because the consequences of most social-research projects are numerous and are sometimes difficult to assess, usually it should be possible to view any research project in terms reasonably compatible with one's own political and ideological orientations. Sociologists, like all people, seek to reduce dissonance. There is no reason to believe they fail in their efforts more frequently than do others. Following Gouldner's suggestion that sociologists stress other than technical criteria in their assessments of social theories is unlikely to reduce the proportion among them who are "deployables" or "moral cretins." Such changes as Gouldner desires can be achieved only through basic changes in the presently institutionalized reward system of social science. At present, just as when Gouldner wrote his book, this appears to be far beyond the power of social scientists.

It has yet to be conclusively demonstrated that an emphasis on cumulative research and theoretical convergence stifles innovation and criticism. While such norms are clearly operative, in American sociology today there are a number of alternative approaches and sets of hypotheses for the analysis of any given social phenomenon. These are given short shrift by Gouldner, who treats Parsons as the sole representative of all of American sociology.

It is not the canons of empirical research that are detrimental to creativity and criticism. Rather, it is those who play either of two roles within university social science departments. The first are the "intellectual imperialists"—those who claim exclusive validity for a particular approach or set of research procedures and are in a position to professionally reward or punish others in accordance with the extent to which they adopt their position. The second are the "economic imperialists"—those whose concern is not so much with abstract ideas as with acquiring research funds and who are in a position to professionally reward or punish others in accordance with the extent to which they bring such funds into their department. The "intellectual imperialists" assume that the quality of their department improves as others adopt their view of what constitutes "important" research or as others who hold this view are recruited. The "economic imperialists" assume that the quality of their department improves as more research grants make possible an increase in the size of its graduate enrollment, the size of its faculty, and the size of its nonacademic staff. While Gouldner's criticisms apply to both of these roles, it is the "economic imperialists" who are more clearly the "deployables."

It is conceivable that content analyses of university courses and texts dealing with social problems and social stratification might call into question Gouldner's contention that sociologists assume that Western industrial societies are basically "sound." However, as noted earlier in this chapter, this assumption does seem to influence much of the work of political sociologists. It is certainly true that, in general, American political sociologists do not seek "remedies" to political problems by "challenging" the basic political structure of America.

Gouldner sets forth a view of the sociologist as social-political critic who advocates far-reaching institutional changes aimed at removing the burdens of many types of social repression. Certainly most will sympathize with the apparent humaneness of this view. However, many will raise the usual questions that constitute the chronic controversy over the social scientist's rights and obligations. Consideration of this topic will be deferred until the end of this book, where it will be presented as a postscript discussing the analytic, moral, and practical applications of political sociology. Discussion of what sociology *is for* and of what political sociology *should be* must be preceded by an evaluation of what sociologists "know" at present and what they are likely to "know" in the future. It should also be preceded by a related description of the positions that sociologists occupy within universities, corporate bureaucracies, government bureaucracies, and private research organizations. Discussions of what sociologists should do must be related to discussions of what they know and what they can do given the social positions they occupy.

Gouldner, and Mills before him,[69] correctly argue that the demand of corporate and government bureaucracies and American utilitarianism generally, that sociologists deal with fragmentary problems has encouraged theoryless empiricism. Their further argument that *practical* has come to mean that which serves the purposes of the established economic, political, and military orders is also plausible. It may be that the "economic imperialists" referred to above are rather directly responsible for the situation. However, if piecemeal approaches to various social problems obviously fail or continue to prove inadequate, and serious economic and political crises develop, this will serve as a strong impetus to the development of integrated empirical social theory.[70]

Several criticisms which Gouldner directs toward Parsons's work require some tempering. First, it is not the case that multivariate approaches cannot provide direction for those concerned with transforming society. Multivariate models encourage research which determines the relative importance of various factors in the process of social change rather than assuring the overriding significance of one variable. Multivariate models also indicate the difficulties of planned social intervention by calling attention to many possible unintended consequences of proposed actions. Second, while Parsons does strongly emphasize socialization and the internalization of moral norms in his social theory, he certainly recognizes that few members of any society thoroughly internalize all the society's dominant values and institutionalized norms. Parsons recognizes that heterogeneous societies require formal agencies of social control because they cannot rely solely on socialization to insure conformity. Furthermore, he certainly understands that the formal control agencies sometimes do not perform on behalf of the society as a whole but in the interests of its more privileged strata. Third, the assumption of stability is an analytic device used to generate sets of empirical questions concerning the recurring patterns of interaction which tend to maintain a society in relatively good working order over a period of time. This set of questions is simply different from the set of questions Gouldner wishes to address. He himself may be practicing "intellectual imperialism."

The discussions of American sociology's drift toward Marxism are at once too broad and too narrow. They are too broad in the sense that they suggest American sociology will adopt a number of the distinctive points of Marxist theory rather than some of its most general features. While broad concepts such as *vested interests* and *alienation* and discussions of topics such as structurally generated social conflict may be appearing with greater frequency in American sociology, there is little evidence that there has been an increase in the frequency with which American sociologists write about the specific inherent contradictions in capitalism that concerned Marx or about the proletarian revolution. The discussions are too narrow in the sense that changes in American sociology can be seen not so much as a drift toward Marxism per se but as a drift toward the general analytic concerns shared by the late-nineteenth-century founders of the sociological tradition.

The discussion of "reflexive" sociology is too brief to warrant critical response. The idea of such a sociology arose naturally during the political turmoil of the late 1960s when old discussions of the role of values in social research were rejuvenated and when any lines that might be drawn between empirical social theory and ideology were at least temporarily blurred. A "reflexive" sociology of politics merely might be one in which the investigator is particularly alert to the ways in which his values and the values of others, related in a variety of ways to his research, influence his theoretical conclusions about the interplay of family, class, education, and religion with politics. Alternatively, a "reflexive" sociology of politics might be one in which an author either explicitly advocates a set of political values and policies (given a body of theory and research suggesting the probable outcomes of such policies) or explicitly evaluates an existing set of political structures and policies (given data about those structures and policies and given a specified set of empirical observations on the basis of which such evaluations can be made—e.g., operational definitions of "democratic" and "totalitarian"). An evaluation of these two kinds of political discussion will constitute part of the postscript of this book.

Despite the preceding criticisms a number of valuable points are made in Gouldner's *The Coming Crisis of Western Sociology*. American sociologists do make unquestioned assumptions of the sort Gouldner indicates. It is certainly true that these assumptions are not without significant consequences for the construction of empirical political theory. Many of the assumptions are undoubtedly related in a number of ways to the penchant of American sociologists to study the social-psychological conditions which contribute to the stability of Western industrial democracies. There also appear to be bases for claiming that Parsonian functionalism offered a theoretical alternative to Marxism and further encouraged the longstanding tendencies of American political sociologists to study political consensus more frequently than political conflict and to discuss political stability more frequently than political change. Some of the general changes discussed under the heading "The Drift Toward Marxism" also seem to have taken place in American sociology. A further consideration of the general character of this "drift" should suggest some future changes in American political sociology.

Gouldner refers to two relatively recent developments in American sociology as "symptoms of the crisis": the "dramaturgy" of Erving Goffman and the "ethnomethodology" of Harold Garfinkle.[71] Both of these merit some consideration because each suggests an approach useful for understanding certain political phenomena in a way quite different from previous theoretical schemes. Also, they should be mentioned because they have influenced other politically relevant theoretical work published since *The Coming Crisis*.

Erving Goffman's point of departure is the introduction of the metaphor of theatrical performance for understanding the routine actions of everyday social life. His studies center on the ways in which individuals present themselves and their activities to others. He is concerned with the technique people employ for manipulating impressions in the manner of actors presenting characters to an audience. Hence, the basic thrust of Goffman's analysis is that any social structure may be studied profitably from the point of view of impression management. Such a view clearly is applicable to political life. One obvious example is its use in studying the activities of government agencies and officials. Other applications involve its use in studies of routine political participation, such as attending to the political content of the mass media and voting, and in studies of nonroutine activity, such as participating in political demonstrations. Here future research might investigate the conditions under which and the extent to which people engage in primarily expressive (as opposed to instrumental) political activity in order to appear to their significant others to have certain qualities. At this point a dramaturgical approach to politics might be linked up with reference-group theory.

Harold Garfinkle's "ethnomethodology" is an effort to understand the conditions under which members of a group construct the taken-for-granted rules that influence the ways in which they conduct their everyday world of practical activities. It focuses on the aspects of social life that are

"just there" and on the ways these are continuously constructed and recon-
structed in daily, commonplace interactions. Garfinkle observes that one
way to achieve some understanding of society's tacit assumptions is to
violate them and to observe the reactions to such acts. This style of research
is a response to ethnomethodology's distinctive subject matter. It is a significant departure from most previous social research methods, which are
based on subject-investigator cooperation and on the use of unobtrusive
measures.

There are a number of possible applications of Garfinkle's approach
to political life. One would involve investigating the conditions under which
individuals will resort to force or to the threat of force in an effort to insure
that certain tacit assumptions of various social relationships are not violated. For example, in a political demonstration, what actions of the participants generally prompt the use of force by political authorities? Another
application, suggested by Young, involves establishing an adversary relationship between researcher and subject.[72] This can produce information
otherwise unavailable. For example, a sociologist's request for information
can be ignored by government or by private organizations, but a court
order for documents cannot be dismissed so easily. Hence the lawsuit,
based on partisanship and conflict, can be superior to conventional
methodologies based on consensus and cooperation. Data gathered for
congressional hearings regularly underscore the validity of the point. Such
data serve as valuable supplements to our understanding of routine political life. A related use would involve investigating the tacit rules limiting or
encouraging the production and flow of "cynical knowledge" in organizations. "Cynical knowledge" refers to the understanding by members of an
organization that presumably altruistic actions of that organization actually
serve the purpose of maintaining the legitimacy of existing authority or preserving institutional structure.[73]

Both Goffman's and Garfinkle's approaches fail to attend to the importance of the power and reward systems within which interactions occur.[74] Goffman does not specify the ways in which power and wealth influence the ability to present the self in various ways. Garfinkle does not
consider the ways in which tacit understandings get established in the conflict between opposing social groups. The perspective of both theorists is
microanalytic, ahistorical, and noncomparative. This might account for
their failure to consider institutional contexts. Both are concerned, though
in somewhat different manners, with the ways in which social order is
created and preserved. Goffman deals with how people manipulate images
in order to give the impression that established social standards are being
met. They are not discussed as people actively attempting to realize social
norms and values—let alone change them. Garfinkle primarily deals with
how people reaffirm tacit understandings in their behavior and thereby
contribute to the stability of the everyday world. They are not discussed as

actors whose social identities enhance or diminish their abilities to establish such taken-for-granted rules. Nevertheless, despite the fact that the explanation of social order is the objective of their theoretical efforts, both Goffman and Garfinkle do suggest that the routine world we see every day rests on appearances and tacit assumptions that are susceptible to disruption.

Such insights provide a link between microanalysis and macroanalysis and serve as a point from which to begin the study of political and social change. Randall Collins's *Conflict Sociology* extensively explores this suggestion.[75] The work represents a major development in American sociology because it is one of the few full-scale contemporary efforts to develop a sociological approach that is macroanalytic, historical-comparative, and primarily and explicitly concerned with change.

In developing his approach, Collins draws heavily on microanalysis, the value of which is seen in its capacity to provide explanations for macroanalytic propositions. The propositions of greatest interest to Collins are contained in the writings of Marx and Weber on stratification and organizations and in Durkheim's study of ritual. Underlying the interest is Collins's judgment that the areas of stratification and organizations serve as the explanatory foundations of sociology. The two areas are related. Occupational position, which is a unit of an organization, is a major determinant of position within the social stratification system. The distribution of power, authority, and wealth can be seen, at least in part, as the result of the struggles for occupational position. From this perspective, political sociology is simply an area of stratification theory which deals with the causes and effects of the distribution of power and authority and which is particularly concerned with political organizations.

Collins's conflict approach presents social structure as the transactions that occur between individuals who are pursuing their own self-interests according to the resources available to them and to their competitors. People's social views are derived from such experiences in the past and are the subjective side of their future intentions. Following Goffman and Garfinkle, Collins argues that in their interactions people are continually re-creating social organization. Social change in general and political change in particular result when the balance of resources changes so that the relations people continually negotiate come out in changed form.

Like Lenski's theory, Collins's work seeks integration around the topic of stratification. In his effort at pulling together the apparently diverse findings of sociology, Lenski selected what he saw as the major insights provided by functionalism and by conflict analysis. Collins, however, argues that functionalism contains no real insights. Rather, it fails to set forth specific causal statements and instead consists of after-the-fact rationalizations for existing social and political institutions. On the other hand, he believes, the explanatory potential of conflict analysis, much of which can be found in Marx and Weber as well as in the extensive research literature on stratification and organizations, has yet to be developed. This is the task he set for himself. Collins agrees with Gouldner about the ideological bias of functionalism. His work does represent something of the drift toward Marxism that Gouldner predicted. His is also a "reflexive" sociology in the sense that he is concerned explicitly with the intrusion of values in the construction of social theory.[76] Collins moves beyond Gouldner in actually attempting to produce such theory.

As suggested above, the value of Collins's work for political sociology consists in its effort to reorient theoretical development in American sociology and stimulate the production of macroanalytic, historical-comparative studies and the investigation of social and political change. A second contribution is its identification and synthesis of the approaches, concepts and hypotheses of Marx and Weber which can inform further study of the distribution of power and power-related resources within organizations and within the broader social order. Third, the book is valuable for its identification and theoretical codification of contemporary empirical research findings on these topics. Finally, Collins's critique of the idealogical bias of American sociology has considerable merit.

Collins's study is not without its troublesome aspects. The view that stratification and organization theory constitute the core of sociology is certainly open to question. So too is his claim that conflict sociology is relatively free of the type of ideological commitments that plagued functionalism. In fact, it could be argued that his critique of functionalism is more an ideological assessment than a consideration of analytic utility. Whatever the case, the full impact of Collins's work is yet to be seen.

A RETURN TO TRADITIONAL CONCERNS? (1975–Present)

By the early to mid-1970s domestic turmoil had largely ceased. In several ways 1975 was a benchmark year. In 1975 the Vietnam War ended as Cambodia and South Vietnam fell before Communist military offensives. In that year the trial of the last major figure in the Watergate scandal was concluded. Also by 1975 data indicated that, despite the continuation of some major political, economic, and social inequalities of minorities, the overall status of American minorities had improved steadily for a decade.[77] In 1975 were recorded the highest unemployment rate since 1941 and the deepest drop in industrial production since 1937—factors that immediately began to erode the gains made by minorities. And during 1975 there were new revelations of illegitimate government activity: illegal wiretaps, testing drugs on unsuspecting subjects, compiling secret dossiers on American citizens, and plotting assassinations of foreign leaders. The net effect of all of these occurrences was the growth of widespread lack of confidence in American institutions in general and the political system in particular.[78] This was enforced in the following years by, among other things, foreign-policy setbacks in Ethiopia, Iran, Nicaragua, and Chile, by inept government handling of the worst commercial nuclear accident in U.S. history, by apparently uncontrollable inflation, and by the dramatic decline in the international value of the dollar.

A second outcome of the political events of the 1970's was a general increase in the conservatism of the American public. This was exemplified by, among other things, the tax revolt, gains in the 1978 and 1980 elections by conservative candidates, and by sample survey data indicating attitude shifts in conservative directions, coupled with continuing expressions of faith in the "free enterprise" economic system. Lipset explains this configuration of attitudes:

> The seeming contradiction between a low level of confidence in major American institutions, and considerable support for the American political, social and economic systems may be related to the fact that all through the tension-filled years of the late sixties and seventies, Americans, though worried about what was happening to their institutions and highly critical of most of their leaders, have felt positively about their own personal situation.[79]

This political history and the widely shared pattern of political attitudes which it produced constitute the social context in which present-day political sociology is developing. The intellectual context consists not only of the large set of substantive empirical questions which the political history and reactions to it raise, but also of the continuation of unresolved theoretical issues which remain from the preceding period. As it happens, these diverse influences all encourage the same set of responses from political sociologists.

In terms of general theory, what remains from the preceding period is the existence of a rather wide range and large number of diverse approaches to social and political phenomena: the possibility of a "reflexive" sociology, dramaturgical sociology, ethnomethodology, conflict sociology, some continuing interest in functionalism, and so on.[80] In terms of general topics for analysis, what remains from the preceding period includes the illegitimate uses of power and authority; the sources, patterns, and outcomes of political conflict—particularly conflict occurring outside institutionalized channels; and social change—particularly change in patterns of inequality brought about in response to new, more rigorous enforcement of legislation (in particular the 1964 Civil Rights Act; new policies of enforcement themselves were a response to the nonroutine political activities of disadvantaged minorities).

American political history since 1975 has reemphasized the importance of each of these topics. In particular it has focused attention on the formation of social policy bearing on social, political, and economic inequalities—the social forces that channel its thrust and the role which social science can play in forming its content. Sociological studies of such topics as criminal justice, income-maintenance programs, and health-care delivery systems illustrate this interest.

In political sociology specifically, questions centering around the uses of power and authority in determining social policy and its applications are likely to receive considerable attention. Such questions may appear to be considerably less dramatic than those raised during the preceding period of political turmoil. However, it was that turmoil which finally forced such problems to be considered. And the personal terms in which some sections of the population experience problems of injustice, inadequate income, unemployment, poor housing, lack of access to quality medical care, and so on, are anything but undramatic.

The diversity of general theoretical approaches developed during the preceding period represents a potentially rich conceptual arsenal which political sociology might employ in attacking these topics. The diversity of approaches might also prove useful in helping to explain the complex pattern of political attitudes which seems to characterize the present-day political thinking of the American public. However, if any general theoretical approach does achieve some degree of dominance, it is likely to be the one which has been demonstrated to have the greatest utility for understanding the ways in which power and authority are used to create, administer, and transform social policy. Correlatively, it would be the approach which most clearly suggested policy likely to achieve certain social goals.

The results of empirical research that was explicitly and systematically guided by such an approach would not be atheoretical. While resulting theories would be "ideologically biased" in the sense that their application was intended to realize one set of political objectives as against or in preference to others, such "bias" would be explicitly stated.

Throughout this chapter it has been argued that, historically, American political sociologists have tended to deal with contemporary political phenomena in social-psychological terms—most studies concerned beliefs about and attitudes toward various political elites, groups, movements, events, and structures. In such studies, the family, the church, and the school were seen as agents of political socialization, instilling in individuals more or less democratic beliefs and attitudes and predisposing them to express their ideas and ideals through participation in routine politics, particularly through voting. Investigations of the role of the economy in political life often were formulated as studies of individuals' adjustments to work roles and the ways in which such adjustments or lack of adjustments are related to political beliefs and attitudes. Studies of the bearing of social stratification on politics often involved consideration of the association of class self-identification with political beliefs, attitudes, and patterns of behavior or with modal political opinions and participation patterns of various income or occupational status categories.

Many of the limitations of the type of research conducted by most American sociologists (i.e., microanalytic, ahistorical, noncomparative, stability-oriented) became evident in efforts to deal with the turbulence of the late 1960s—civil rights protest, racial conflict, student protest, and Third World changes. The more recent events and situations in the United States noted above also are likely to encourage political sociology to develop theoretical orientations which are quite different from those which have prevailed for so long.

Future studies of the uses of power and authority which bear on social, economic, and political inequalities might well resemble, in several ways, the writings of the founders of the sociological tradition such as Marx, Weber, and Durkheim, as well as the works of America's earliest sociologists.[81] Such studies would require macroanalysis. Questions would focus on the operations of institutions and not on the beliefs, values, and behaviors of individuals. They would involve consideration of structurally generated conflict between social units such as social classes, status groups, corporate and occupational groups, political parties, and so on. They would be concerned with collective action aimed at changing institutional structures.[82] Many studies might employ historical-comparative designs to produce suggestive insights into the probable consequences of adopting certain social policies.[83]

An inability to deal in a satisfactory manner with major present-day topics such as the formation and application of social policy, the illegitimate uses of power and authority, patterns of noninstitutionalized political conflict and widespread political dissatisfaction, and political distrust might well create a "crisis" in American political sociology. It may also be that in response to such a "crisis" political sociology will develop new approaches and thus experience a "scientific revolution." Perhaps the results of such a "revolution" would appear remarkably familiar.

NOTES

1. Robin M. William, Jr., *American Society: A Sociological Interpretation* (New York: Alfred A. Knopf, 1970), pp. 438–504.

2. Roscoe C. Hinkle, Jr. and Gisela J. Hinkle, *The Development of Modern Sociology: Its Nature and Growth in the United States* (New York: Random House, 1954).

3. For a discussion of the crises which faced American society at the time Ward reached these conclusions, see Henry Steele Commager, *Lester Ward and the Welfare State* (Indianapolis, Ind.: Bobbs-Merrill, 1967).

4. See Lester Frank Ward, *Psychic Factors of Civilization* (Boston: Ginn & Company, 1893).

5. See Franklin Giddings, *Descriptive and Historical Sociology* (New York: Macmillan, 1906).

6. Leon Bramson, *The Political Context of Sociology* (Princeton: Princeton University Press, 1961, paperback edition), p. 78.

7. The emphasis on developing empirically grounded explanations made the concern of earlier American sociologists with the application of sociological knowledge to human welfare seem premature. It was argued that attempts at social change which were based on inadequate information about human behavior were unlikely to succeed. All programs for social reform which were present at the time were "unscientific." Programs for political revolution which, by definition, advocated more rapid and extensive alterations of social structure and required an even greater quantity of information if they were to be successful, had an even more questionable scientific status. Such a perspective led sociologists to ignore works such as Ward's *Applied Sociology* and would later serve as a basis for rejecting a priori many of the discussions of Marx.

8. Merriam's students included Gabriel Almond, Harold Gosnell, V. O. Key, Harold Lasswell, Avery Leiserson, Herbert Simon, and David Truman.

9. Richard Jensen, "History and the Political Scientist," *Politics and the Social Sciences,* Seymour M. Lipset, ed. (New York: Oxford University Press, 1969), pp. 1–28.

10. Talcott Parsons, *The Structure of Social Action* (New York: The Free Press, 1949).

11. For a critical review of Parsons's account see Whitney Pope, et al., "On the Divergence of Weber and Durkheim: a Critique of Parsons' Convergence Thesis," *American Sociological Review,* 40, no. 4 (August 1975), 417–427. For purposes of this chapter it is not essential whether or not Parsons was right but that his thesis was highly influential.

12. Talcott Parsons, *The Social System* (New York: The Free Press, 1951). Parsons presents extensive considerations of specifically political phenomena neither in *The Structure of Social Action* nor in *The Social System.* His numerous individual papers on politics have been collected and are presented in his *Politics and Social Structure* (New York: The Free Press, 1969).

13. In such comparative research the operational definition of the values must be independent of the behavior which is to be explained. If values are inferred from the behavior to be explained, the claim that differences in behavior are due to differences in values is merely tautological.

14. In the United States a continuing difference between political scientists and sociologists who study politics is that the former tend to stress the causal importance of formal institutional arrangements while the work of the latter tends to reflect Parsons's orientation.

15. For an overview of the scope and limits of political socialization research see Jack Dennis, "Major Problems of Political Socialization Research," *Midwest Journal of Political Science,* 12, no. 1 (1968), 85–114; David C. Schwartz and Sandra K. Schwartz, (eds.), *New Directions in Political Socialization* (New York: The Free Press, 1975); Richard G. Niemi, "Political Socialization," in *Handbook of Political Psychology,* Jeanne N. Knutson, ed. (San Francisco: Jossey-Bass, 1973), pp. 117–138.

16. These conceptualizations of power and politics are explicated neither in *The Structure of Social Action* nor in *The Social System.* However, Parsons does elaborate such a position in later articles. See "The Distribution of Power in American Society," *World Politics,* 10 (October 1957), 123–143, and "The Political Aspect of Social Structure and Process," in *Varieties of Political Theory,* David Easton, ed. (Englewood Cliffs, N.J.: Prentice-Hall, 1966), Chapter 4.

17. For an example of the use of Parsons's concepts to describe a single political system see William C. Mitchell, *The American Polity* (New York: The Free Press, 1962). Although not strictly derived from Parsons's work, Gabriel A. Almond and G. Bingham Powell, Jr., *Comparative Politics: A Developmental Approach* (Boston: Little, Brown, 1966) illustrates the application of such a mode of analysis to comparative politics.

18. See Robert A. Dahl, "The Behavioral Approach in Political Science: Epitaph for a Monument to a Successful Protest," *American Political Science Review,* 55 (December 1961), 763–772; Richard Jensen, "History and the Political Scientist," in *Politics and the Social Sciences,* Seymour Martin Lipset, ed. (New York: Oxford University Press, 1969), pp. 10–28.

19. Paul Lazarsfeld, Bernard Berelson, and Hazel Gaudet, *The People's Choice* (New York: Columbia University Press, 1944).

20. Robert T. Golembiewski, William A. Welsh, and William J. Crotty, *A Methodological Primer for Political Scientists* (Chicago: Rand McNally, 1969), p. 398.

21. Bernard Berelson, Paul Lazarsfeld, William McPhee, *Voting* (Chicago: University of Chicago Press, 1954), p. ix.

22. Ibid., p. ix.

23. Angus Campbell, Gerald Gurin, and Warren Miller, *The Voter Decides* (Evanston, Ill.: Row, Peterson, 1954).

24. Ibid., p. 182.

25. See Samuel A. Stouffer, et al., *Measurement and Prediction,* Volume IV of *Studies in Social Psychology in World War II* (Princeton, N.J.: Princeton University Press, 1950).

26. Angus Campbell, Philip Converse, Warren Miller, and Donald Stokes, *The American Voter* (New York: John Wiley & Sons, 1964).

27. For an elaboration of this criticism, see Christian Bay, "Politics and Pseudopolitics: A Critical Evaluation of Some Behavior Literature," *American Political Science Review,* 59 (March 1965), 39–51.

28. The final chapters of *The American Voter* shifted attention away from the individual voter and his decision-making processes toward aggregate properties of the electorate and the party system. This macroanalytic orientation is further developed by Campbell, Converse, Miller, and Stokes in their later volume, *Elections and the Political Order* (New York: John Wiley & Sons, 1966). While this shift in level of analysis is desirable, this particular effort has been criticized on two grounds. First, it contains no information on the social structure of the flow of information and influence. It tells us nothing about *how* information and influence get to the individual. Second, it fails to view voting from a historical perspective. It tells us nothing about how the dynamics of voting can vary from one election to another. See Carl A. Sheigold, "Social Networks and Voting: The Resurrection of a Research Agenda," *American Sociological Review,* 38, no. 6 (December 1973), 712–720.

29. Robert E. Lane, *Political Life* (New York: The Free Press, 1959).

30. Lester W. Milbrath, *Political Participation* (Chicago: Rand McNally, 1965). A second edition of this book was published in 1977. It contains reference to a considerably larger number of macroanalytic studies.

31. For example, see the discussion of "working-class authoritarianism" in Seymour Martin Lipset, *Political Man* (Garden City, New York: Anchor Books, Doubleday & Co., Inc., 1963): 87–126.

32. Gabriel A. Almond, *The Appeal of Communism* (Princeton, N.J.: Princeton University Press, 1954).

33. Robert E. Lane, *Political Ideology* (New York: The Free Press, 1962).

34. Daniel Bell, *The End of Ideology* (New York: The Free Press, 1960); Seymour Martin Lipset, "The Changing Class Structure and Contemporary European Politics," *Daedalus,* XCIII (Winter 1964), 271–303; Robert E. Lane, "The Politics of Consensus in an Age of Affluence," *American Political Science Review,* CIX (December 1965), 875–895.

35. Philip Converse, "The Nature of Belief Systems in Mass Publics," in *Ideology and Discontent,* David Apter, ed. (New York: The Free Press, 1964), pp. 206–261.

36. For the most influential statement of the position, see William Kornhauser, *The Politics of Mass Society* (New York: The Free Press, 1959).

37. An important exception to this generalization is Robert A. Dahl, *Who Governs?* (New Haven, Conn.: Yale University Press, 1961).

38. This perspective on community power studies is based on Robert Perrucci and Marc Pilisuk, "Leaders and Ruling Elites: The Interorganizational Bases of Community Power," *American Sociological Review,* 35 no. 6 (December 1970), 1040–1057.

39. Lipset, *Political Man,* p. 1.

40. The position that the American polity represented the "most developed" political

system was clearly taken by Daniel Lerner, *The Passing of Traditional Society* (New York: The Free Press, 1958); Gabriel Almond and James Coleman, *The Politics of the Developing Areas* (Princeton: Princeton University Press, 1960); Lipset, *Political Man*; Gabriel Almond and G. Bingham Powell, *Comparative Politics: A Developmental Approach* (Boston: Little, Brown, 1966); and Robert Marsh, *Comparative Sociology* (New York: Harcourt, Brace and World, 1967) among numerous others.

41. See Karl DeSchweinitz, *Industrialization and Democracy* (New York: The Free Press, 1964); Samuel P. Huntington and Joan M. Nelson, *No Easy Choice: Political Participation in Developing Countries* (Cambridge, Mass.: Harvard University Press, 1976).

42. Bramson, *Political Context*, p. 16.

43. Lipset, *Political Man*, p. 80.

44. See, for example, James C. Davies, "Toward a Theory of Revolution," *American Sociological Review*, 27 (February 1962), 5–19; Ted Robert Gurr, *Why Men Rebel* (Princeton, N.J.: Princeton University Press, 1970); Leonard Berkowitz, "The Study of Urban Violence: Some Implications of Laboratory Studies of Frustration and Aggression," in *When Men Revolt and Why*, James C. Davies, ed. (New York: The Free Press, 1971), pp. 182–197.

This statement will be amended in Chapters 5 and 6, which deal with nonroutine politics and ideology. There it will be argued that in many studies psychological variables have been used in an attempt to discredit those whose politics are disagreeable to social scientists. Political adversaries frequently seem to suffer from some psychopathology.

45. Sidney Verba, *Small Groups and Political Behavior* (Princeton, N.J.: Princeton University Press, 1961).

46. Ibid., p. 223. Verba notes that early small-group studies seemed to aim at proving the advantages of democracy over alternative forms of governing. He also observes that many of the definitions of "democracy" used in small-group research really are definitions of American democratic leadership. See pp. 118–119.

47. See Stein Rokkan, "International Cooperation in Political Sociology: Current Efforts and Future Possibilities," in *Mass Politics*, Erik Allardt and Stein Rokkan, eds. (New York: The Free Press, 1970), pp. 1–20.

48. Karl W. Deutsch, *The Nerves of Government, Models of Political Communication and Control* (New York: The Free Press, 1963).

49. Bruce M. Russett, et al., *World Handbook of Political and Social Indicators* (New Haven, Conn.: Yale University Press, 1964).

50. Arthur S. Banks and Robert B. Textor, *A Cross Polity Survey* (Cambridge, Mass.: M.I.T. Press, 1963).

51. Robert M. Marsh, *Comparative Sociology*.

52. C. Wright Mills, *The Sociological Imagination* (New York: Oxford University Press, 1959).

53. Mills points out that microscopic empirical studies are usually quite expensive and are shaped by those who have paid for them. Since funding agents have diverse concerns, the result has been the accumulation of information bearing on largely unrelated problems.

54. C. Wright Mills, *The Power Elite* (New York: Oxford University Press, 1956).

55. Mills contends that "families and churches and schools adapt to modern life, governments and armies and corporations shape it; and, as they do so, they turn these lesser institutions into means for their ends." Ibid., p. 6.

56. Ralf Dahrendorf, *Class and Class Conflict in Industrial Society* (Stanford, Calif.: Stanford University Press, 1959).

57. Dahrendorf explicitly states that the two models stress complementary rather than alternative aspects of social structure. Both models are useful and necessary for sociological analysis. Exclusive validity cannot be claimed for either model. For a collection of the major articles dealing with the debate over functionalism, see N. J. Demerath III and Richard A. Peterson, eds., *System, Change and Conflict* (New York: The Free Press, 1967).

58. Dahrendorf, *Class and Class Conflict*, p. xi.

59. Talcott Parsons, "The Distribution of Power in American Society," *World Politics,* X, no. 1 (October 1957), 139.

60. Dahrendorf, *Class and Class Conflict,* p. 163.

61. Gerhard E. Lenski, *Power and Privilege* (New York: McGraw-Hill, 1966).

62. Ibid., p. vii.

63. The issues involve the nature of man, the nature of society, the importance of coercion in social life, the sources of social conflict, the inevitability in inequality, and the nature of the state and the law.

64. Richard Flacks, "Young Intelligentsia in Revolt," *Trans-action,* 7, no. 8 (June 1970), 49–55.

65. Raymond Aron, "Student Rebellion: Vision of the Future or Echo from the Past?," *Political Science Quarterly,* 84, no. 2 (June 1969), 289–310.

66. Alvin W. Gouldner, *The Coming Crisis of Western Sociology* (New York: Basic Books, 1970).

67. Ibid., p. 12.

68. Ibid., p. 13.

69. C. Wright Mills, *The Sociological Imagination* (Evergreen Edition, 1961) pp. 76–99.

70. Gouldner himself notes that continuing social problems of America, such as in-equality of economic, cultural, and political opportunities, have encouraged sociologists to begin mending the long-severed connection between sociology and economics. Such impulses for change, while limited, are distinctly different from the order-oriented assumptions of functionalism.

71. See Erving Goffman, *The Presentation of Self in Everyday Life* (Garden City, N.Y.: Doubleday, 1959) and Harold Garfinkle, *Studies in Ethnomethodology* (Englewood Cliffs, N.J.: Prentice-Hall, 1967).

72. See T. R. Young, "The Politics of Sociology: Gouldner, Goffman and Garfinkle," *The American Sociologist,* 6 (November 1971), 276–281.

73. See Fred H. Goldner, R. Richard Ritti, and Thomas P. Ference, "The Production of Cynical Knowledge in Organizations," *American Sociological Review,* 42, no. 4 (August 1977), 539–551.

74. Goffman does refer to Durkheim's insight that when a performance expresses dominant social values it serves to reinforce them. See *Presentation of Self,* pp. 35.

75. Randall Collins, *Conflict Sociology* (New York: Academic Press, 1975).

76. These points of agreement between Gouldner and Collins are not noted in *Conflict Sociology,* in which there is but one passing reference to *The Coming Crisis.*

77. See, for example, Stanley H. Masters, *Black-White Income Differentials* (New York: Academic Press, 1975).

78. For data supporting this contention, see Seymour M. Lipset and William Schreider, *The Evaluation of Basic American Institutions, with Special Reference to Business* (New York: Macmillan, 1980); Arthur H. Miller, "Public Support for Political Institutions Erodes," *ISR Newsletter* (Ann Arbor: Institute for Social Research, University of Michigan, Autumn 1979), pp. 4–5.

79. Seymour M. Lipset, *The First New Nation* (New York: W. W. Norton, 1979), "Introduction to the Norton edition," p. ix. Of particular interest is Lipset's observation that "young people (18 to 29), the age group which contributed most to the protest waves of the late 60's and early 70's, turned out in 1976 to be the most optimistic for their personal futures." For an alternative to Lipset's explanation of Americans' continuing support of the "free-enterprise economy," see Charles E. Lindblom, *Politics and Markets* (New York: Basic Books, 1977), pp. 161–236. Lindblom's analysis will be discussed in Chapter 7.

80. For a discussion of the lack of a dominant paradigm in American sociology, see George Ritzer, *Sociology: A Multiple Paradigm Science* (Boston: Allyn & Bacon, 1975).

81. There are also several ways in which their writings would not resemble those of several of the early authors. The qualitative spirit of many of the earlier works would be replaced by quantification and the statistical manipulation of data. Hypotheses would be

tested rather than generalizations asserted. Probabilistic accounts would replace certainties. Multivariable analyses would often be substituted for single-variable explanations.

82. Structural concepts such as *alienation* and *anomie* and concepts referring to processes such as class conflict, rationalization, and increasing division of labor might prove to have analytic utility once they are understood in the context of advanced industrial economies and once social indicators for them are developed.

83. For example, sociological analyses of future uses of power and authority to alter the prevailing patterns of political, economic, and social inequalities in the United States might involve considerations of nations which have institutionalized much broader conceptions of social rights, such as Norway, and nations which have relied primarily on nonmarket mechanisms for regulating their distributive systems, such as Cuba or China.

CHAPTER THREE
PRESENT CHARACTERISTICS: CONTEMPORARY DISCUSSIONS OF POLITICAL SOCIOLOGY

ALTERNATIVE VIEWS OF POLITICAL SOCIOLOGY

Chapter 1 identified the origins of political sociology with the beginnings of modern sociology itself. Basic questions about relations of power and authority were generated by the French and industrial revolutions. Theorists such as Marx, Weber, and Durkheim concerned themselves to varying degrees with the roles which kinship, class, religion, interest groups of various sorts, and shifting belief and value systems were to play in the political life of the rising industrial societies of Western Europe. The approach of each theorist to these topics was characteristically macroanalytic- and historical-comparative and dealt extensively with change.

Chapter 2 sketched the development of sociology in the United States. Early American sociologists raised questions about the changing political roles of traditional structures in a democracy under conditions of increasing industrialization and urbanization. The social and cultural setting which gave rise to their questions differed in a number of ways from the conditions of Western Europe in the nineteenth century. Certain features of American history, social structure, dominant values, and the position of sociology within American colleges and universities encouraged theorists to conduct their inquiries in microanalytic, ahistorical, noncomparative terms and to concentrate on conditions facilitating the stability and continuation of their society and its political institutions rather than on dissension, instability, conflict, and change.

Since the turn of the century the major social and political events of American history shaped the different eras of American sociology and presented the specific political topics that were raised in each period. Problems of developing urban industrial life, the Depression, the threat of Fascism, the fear of Communism, the quest for equality of opportunity, the emergence of the Third World, the eruption of vehement domestic protest, the involvement in an unpopular war, the continuation of social, political, and economic inequalities into an advanced industrial age, and the apparent decrease of American influence in world affairs—each in its turn presented the subject matter for political sociologists.

The specific political questions addressed by American political sociologists obviously are not identical to those considered by Marx, Weber, and Durkheim. The basic theoretical approach widely used by present-day American sociologists is opposite that most often seen in the writings of sociology's founders. Nevertheless, a set of intellectual concerns does continue from the time of Marx, Weber, and Durkheim to the present. It is this set of concerns which defines political sociology. The concerns center around relations of power and authority as these are organized at relatively inclusive levels of social organization, such as in large formal organizations, communities, regions, and nation-states. Questions deal with the reciprocal influence of power and authority relations on the one hand and the social ties of kinship, religion, class, interest groups, and shared belief and value systems on the other.

From Marx to the present it has been maintained that kinship and politics have important links which warrant consideration. Marx was concerned with the family as a perpetuator of political inequality. Weber discussed the varying political significance of kinship within different systems of domination. Durkheim was interested in changes in the political role of kinship associated with changes in the division of labor in society. Present-day political sociologists are primarily interested in the family as an agent of socialization. Particular attention is paid to its role in developing ideological predispositions, in establishing loyalty to the nation-state, and in transmitting party identification.

From Marx to the present it has been maintained that religion and politics have important links which warrant consideration. Marx was concerned with religion's role in maintaining political and economic inequalities. Weber investigated the role of religion in political legitimation and in political-economic rationalization. Durkheim was concerned with the reduction in the religious quality of centralized rule which accompanied increasing differentiation of the division of labor and the increasing threat of anarchy. Contemporary political sociologists are interested in churches as political interest groups and as agents of political socialization. With the election of Pope John Paul II from Poland, interest increased in the political role of religion in Communist nations. With the Iranian revolution led by Ayatollah Khomeini, interest was regenerated in the political importance of pursuing religious values in the contemporary world. Before these events interest in such topics may have seemed antique to many sociologists.

From Marx to the present it has been maintained that economic life and political life have important links. Marx asserted that all aspects of political life were a function of the social relations of production. Weber was particularly interested in the political consequences of the bureaucratization of economic organizations. Durkheim wrote on the importance of centralized control of the economy and on the political significance of occupational groups. Present-day political sociologists investigate relationships between work roles and ideological predispositions. Some macroanalysis considers the bearing of technological development and form of economic organization and control on political institutions. In the light of recent high levels of inflation, considerable unemployment, and a possible "energy crisis," studies have begun exploring new and complex relations between political systems and market systems.

From Marx to the present it has been maintained that stratification systems and political institutions have important links. For Marx all political history had been determined by struggles between economically determined conflict groups. For Weber inequalities in economic resource and in social honor created political conflict groups which engaged in political struggles over different issues under differing systems of domination. Durkheim was interested in social differentiation both as a source of unity and as a source of conflict. Contemporary political sociologists often consider classes as social-cultural settings in which political loyalties are established and in which politically relevant beliefs, values, and behavior patterns are acquired. The apparent decline of family, church, and other traditional ties (such as that to region) in the most technologically advanced industrial societies has renewed interest in the political significance of social classes.[1]

From Marx to the present it has been maintained that interest groups of various sorts play a variety of important political roles. For Marx social classes were the only politically influential interest groups. Weber broadened Marx's concerns, adding discussions of the political roles of numerous types of status groups. Durkheim argued that important political functions might be performed by occupational groups that would develop with the increasing division of labor. Contemporary political sociologists consider interest groups important not only as potentially effective sources of power but also as important contexts for the aggregation and articulation of political goals, for the acquisition of political information and the development of political skills, and as a necessary component for democratic societies.

Finally, from Marx to the present it has been maintained that political belief and value systems as well as belief and value systems which are not manifestly political (e.g., sets of religious beliefs) have important consequences for political life. Marx wrote about ideologies as the tools of those in positions of power and privilege and about the functions of class consciousness in political revolution. Weber's typology of domination rested in part on a discussion of distinctive belief and value systems. His concern with rationalization also directed attention to a particular set of beliefs and values—those that find expression in bureaucratic organization. Durkheim was concerned with the integrative function of shared beliefs and values and with the threat of anarchy which accompanied dissensus on basic values. Contemporary political sociologists investigate political socialization, control of information as a source of power, political ideologies, and the relationship between political culture and political structure.

The continuing set of concerns noted in the preceding paragraphs constitutes the core of political sociology. In each of the chapters of Parts 2 and 3 of this book there will be consideration of the political importance of kinship, religion, economy, stratification, interest groups, and shared belief and value systems. The definition of political sociology set forth in the first two chapters thus determines the contents of the remainder of this book. Before turning to the substantive materials in these chapters, it is reasonable to raise an important question about the definition of political sociology which is so central here. How does this definition differ from other well-known discussions of the field? If differences are great, then the following sections, which report research findings, represent a highly idiosyncratic interpretation of what political sociology is all about. If differences between the preceding discussion and the views of other authors about the nature of the field are not great, then readers can have some confidence that the impression of political sociology they have gained from this book is such that they are not likely to be surprised at the contents of other texts, books of readings, and monographs that purport to deal with matters of political sociology.

A question must also be raised about the degree to which there is consensus over the particular view of the history of political sociology in the United States which was sketched in Chapter 2. Central to that interpretation was the position that sociology in general and political sociology in particular have moved from a macroanalytic, historical-comparative, change-oriented past to a microanalytic, ahistorical, noncomparative, stability-oriented period and now are likely to reassume their original qualities. Since this view influences the organization of the following sections of this book one should see what others have to say about these matters. A view of others' positions will provide a baseline for judging how controversial was the discussion in Chapter 2. It will also aid in assessing the likelihood that other political sociologists who would write a book such as this would include such topics as are selected here, would organize them in a roughly similar manner, and would devote roughly equivalent amounts of space to each of the topics as are allotted here.

Six well-known discussions of political sociology are reviewed below. They are presented in chronological order. Comparisons will be made between the views set forth by each of the authors and the views developed in Chapters 1 and 2.

LIPSET: THE STUDY OF
CLEAVAGE AND CONSENSUS

Of the discussions of political sociology Seymour Martin Lipset's is undoubtedly the best known.[2] It appears in a volume published in association with the American Sociological Society. The book was intended as an authoritative, comprehensive presentation of the trends, unsolved problems, and future prospects of contemporary sociology.

Lipset identifies the origin of political sociology with the Reformation and the industrial revolution. Both promoted the breakdown of traditional society and its traditional authority structure. The disruption of the old social order raised the central problem of political sociology: "How can a society incorporate continuous conflict among its members and social groups and yet maintain social cohesion and legitimacy of state and authority?"[3]

The nineteenth-century founders of political sociology took opposite positions on the proper relations between state and society. Some, like Marx, argued that social bonds had to be strengthened while the state had to be limited or abolished. Others, like Hegel, argued that society must be subordinate to the sovereign state. Contemporary political sociologists now argue that the state is just one of many institutions and that the relation between political institutions and other social institutions is the special province of their field.

While, according to Lipset, the ideological debates over state versus society have subsided, the question that was basic to the debate—that of the proper balance between conflict and consensus within a society—remains and constitutes political sociology's central problem of analysis. However, at least until the late 1950s political sociologists directed considerably more attention to the conditions facilitating cleavage than to the social conditions which promote political consensus. This tendency is seen in studies of electoral behavior, extremist movements, bureaucracy, the internal government of voluntary associations, and power. Its theoretical significance becomes clear when considering the work of four European sociologists whose ideas, as Lipset sees them, are more or less the basis of political sociology: Karl Marx, Alexis de Tocqueville, Max Weber, and Robert Michels.

Marx and Tocqueville maintained opposing views of the roles which conflict and consensus play in society. According to Marx, any society with a complex division of labor will experience constant conflict. Consensus is possible only through the elimination of differentiated economic roles. Marx was concerned with but two mutually exclusive social types: a society of conflict and a society of harmony. A democracy is neither of these. Democracies require some cleavages so that there will be struggle over ruling positions, challenges to parties in power, and shifts of parties in office. They also require some consensus—some agreement on the basic rules of the political game allowing for the peaceful "play" of power. Because Marx did not consider the sources of solidarity and shared societal values in societies with complex divisions of labor, he had no interest in democracy or in democratic mechanisms such as safeguards against state power.

Tocqueville, unlike Marx, emphasized that societies which are internally differentiated can incorporate a balance of political conflict and political consensus. Tocqueville stressed local communities and voluntary associations rather than classes as society's politically significant units. Such units could contribute to political cleavage and to political consensus at the same time. Private associations, for example, are sources of restrictions on the government, serve as major channels for involving people in politics, and also help train political opposition leaders in politically relevant skills. By performing such functions they serve to check the increasing centralized power of the state which accompanies industrialization and bureaucratization.

Lipset goes on to note that while Marx and Tocqueville dealt with problems of political conflict and political consensus, Weber and Michels considered the related problems of bureaucracy and democracy. Weber discussed the integrative aspects of bureaucratization in democratic society such as the transfer to the entire society of the bureaucratic norms of equality of treatment before the law and authority. However, he also maintained that bureaucracies represented the single most important source of institutional change and hence constituted a threat to existing forces of social cohesion.

Michels was particularly interested in antidemocratic tendencies inherent in large-scale bureaucratic associations such as political parties and labor unions. Michels isolated those elements in such organizations which make control by their mass membership virtually impossible.

Lipset concludes his discussion of the founders of political sociology with an argument that a focus on cleavage has led American political sociologists to neglect a number of theoretically significant questions. He argues that this limitation can be seen through a brief survey of some of the most important areas of empirical research in political sociology.

Voting studies have been concerned most typically with the relation between one type of cleavage, political parties, and other sources of cleavage such as classes, occupational groups, and religion. The focus on cleavage has encouraged social-psychological approaches to voting which investigate how various structural cleavages affect the decisions of the individual. Future research, he suggests, might emphasize the integrative aspects of electoral behavior and investigate the structural requirements for a stable democracy.

Studies of political movements, Lipset asserts, also display the penchant of American political sociologists to emphasize aspects of conflict and change. Historically, there has been much more interest in reform movements than in conventional and conservative parties. Studies of right-wing movements such as fascism and McCarthyism focused on the strains such movements introduced into the polity rather than on the factors which caused their decline. Some theory was developed to explain extremist political movements in modern societies. However, such theories emphasized social disintegration and did not look for possible resolutions of the problem. Future research, Lipset feels, might aim at developing empirical theory which explains how new mechanisms are developed by some societies to fulfill the political functions no longer satisfied by older, preindustrial social institutions.

Studies of political bureaucracy have been little influenced by Weber's analysis of the social consequences of bureaucratization. Studies have focused on the ways in which bureaucratic procedures create conflicts, block channels of communication, prevent initiative, and so on. Future work might develop the view of bureaucracy as a source of stability for democratic processes. Research on the politics of the new nations in which bureaucratic values and behavior patterns are not fully accepted indicates the utility of such a theoretical perspective.

Studies of the internal government of voluntary associations have focused on the factors which create and maintain nonrepresentative government. Few comparative studies have investigated variations in structures that might encourage democracy, retard oligarchy, and increase solidarity. Little research has been concerned with the question of the extent to which the democracy or lack of democracy of a society's voluntary associations affects the operation of its larger political order.

Discussions of power in American political sociology center on political conflict. Power is viewed as power over others. It is usually held that an increase in the power of one group always occurs at the expense of another. Future theoretical discussions, according to Lipset, might view power as a resource to be used for the benefit of the entire society. Such a position would exhibit an interest in political consensus, serve as a needed supplement to the existing literature, and provide insight into the processes by which collective goals are sought.

Finally, if the study of the social conditions of democracy is to be the main task of political sociology, there are other topics which require further inquiry. Among the most important of these are the comparative study of the nature of political integration and legitimacy, the changing functions of the intellectual elite in political life, the role of multiple group affiliations and deviations from normal cleavage patterns in contributing to political stability, the measurement and comparison of the relative cohesion of political structures, the ways in which organizations handle conflict and create consensus, and the role of family, religion, and secular culture in political systems. Lipset concludes that an attempt to deal adequately with such problems will force political sociology to reassert a concern with consensus as well as with cleavage.

Comparison with Lipset's View

Lipset's identification of the modern origins of political sociology coincides with the view developed in Chapter 1. Although he discusses the contributions of Marx and Weber, Lipset chooses to consider the work of Tocqueville and Michels rather than that of Durkheim. Undoubtedly these theorists have been of considerable importance, as have many others such as Mosca and Pareto, for example. Nevertheless, the exclusion of Durkheim merits brief comment.

Durkheim, like Tocqueville, was concerned about the relative absence in modern society of the social ties which provide the individual with a social identity, with a set of distinctive norms and values by which and for which to live, and with a set of other persons with whom to pursue collective goals or resist the will of antagonists. Durkheim, like Michels, was concerned with enhancing individual liberty in industrial society. While Durkheim emphasized the potential contribution of occupational groups in reducing the possibility of tyrannical rule of the state, he, like Michels, saw that occupational associations could themselves become despotic.

The failure of American sociologists to attribute greater importance to the political implications of Durkheim's writings was discussed in Chapter 1. Durkheim was primarily concerned with the problem of social order, that is, with the threat of anomie and the avoidance of anarchy. In Lipset's terms, Durkheim was a theorist who placed great emphasis on consensus and social stability. Acknowledging Durkheim's importance to American political sociology involves admitting evidence contrary to the thesis that the overwhelming concern of American political sociologists (up to the time of the publication of Lipset's article in 1959) has been with cleavage and conflict.

Lipset's paper was published during the period of the bifurcation of general theory described in Chapter 2. It clearly reflects the tendency to view authors in terms of the perceived location of their work as "conflict theory" or "consensus theory" or occasionally, as in the case of Tocqueville, as theory which attempts some synthesis. For additional reasons presented below, Lipset's position that American sociology up to 1959 primarily focused on conflict and instability is rejected here. However, during subsequent periods of American sociology, the topics of conflict, instability, and change were given some consideration. This was particularly true during the turbulent period of the late 1960s and early 1970s. Such topics are receiving considerable attention today as basically uncontrolled inflation threatens to erode gains made by minorities during the past two decades, as American world influence seems to have significantly decreased, and as confidence in American political leaders and institutions is at a very low point. In the early to mid-1980s the continuation of a series of unresolved social issues that serve as the basis for potential conflict (e.g., energy, school busing, "reverse discrimination," abortion, social rights for minorities) maintains interest in conflict and change.

Political democracy can be viewed as a political system in which conflict between social aggregates of various sorts is carried on within the framework of a particular set of "rules of the game" accepted by all parties involved in the conflict. The investigation of the social conditions which foster this balance of conflict and consensus does constitute a very important topic in political sociology. It can be argued that, historically, this has been the central interest of American political analysts. It also can be pointed out that, historically, the strong emphasis on the social conditions of democracy, which has often been confined to an emphasis on the conditions of existing Western industrial political systems, has diverted attention from other important political topics. These include varieties of noninstitutionalized political behavior, the politics of the Third World, and the vast variety of nondemocratic political systems under which people have lived.

Lipset's position that most contemporary political research has focused on cleavage and has neglected the study of consensus is in direct opposition to the view developed in Chapter 2. Lipset illustrates his claim with references to studies in five important substantive areas. However, the studies he cites can be viewed in such a way as to call his generalization about the basic thrust of American political sociology into question.

Voting studies do constitute a large portion of the empirical research conducted by political sociologists. Such studies have indeed been conducted in social-psychological terms. Most commonly they investigated the ways in which the differential identifications of individuals are associated with differences in their political attitudes and voting patterns. Voting, however, is a highly routine political act. Research indicates that those who are most likely to vote are little alienated, believe that they are being offered some genuine choice between parties and candidates, believe that their vote will have some impact, believe that they have a duty to participate, and believe that their participation is relatively important. The act of voting is an act of support for the regime. It expresses belief in the legitimacy of the general rules of the political game and in the legitimacy of opposing parties, candidates, and principles. Hence it can be argued that the amount of attention devoted to the study of voting suggests an interest in consensus rather than an interest in conflict. It can also be argued that the belief that participation is to be preferred to apathy rests on the assumption that an increase in the proportion of those who vote represents a decrease in social alienation and a general increase in regime support. It rests upon the assumption that democracy, widespread participation, and a high level of political consensus all go hand in hand. If American political sociologists have failed to attribute proper importance to Tocqueville, as Lipset claims, it may be because Tocqueville's warnings about the "tyranny of the majority" are contrary to the high value they place on political consensus.

It can be argued that the focus on the individual in voting studies does not reflect real concern with conflict and change. Those differences which are most relevant to social-political conflict and change are not differences in attitudes between individuals who have varying self-identities. Rather, they are between relatively organized and self-conscious social aggregates which have apparently incompatible material and ideological interests. A microanalytic perspective does not facilitate understanding this kind of opposition.

If American political sociologists had favored the investigation of conflict and change, then the empirical work on *political movements* should have generally been extensive and sophisticated. By 1959 there were a number of studies on the temperance movement, feminism, McCarthyism, right-wing extremism, and student politics. Yet the fact remains that Joseph Gusfield could claim as late as 1970 that:

> The study of social change through collective action has been one of the great *terrae incognitae* of sociology. Introductory texts usually have devoted one or two chapters to "social change" and consequently have given the illusion that society was a largely static and unchanging system of relationships, norms and values. Certainly social scientists have recognized this as illusory, but we have been far less able to develop the analytic tools to study change.[4]

The literature on student politics, which subsequently developed and which remains the most extensive in the area of social movements, is comprised, in a large part, of descriptions of student attitudes. General explanations of student activism that were offered more often referred to students' socialization experiences in their homes or on their campuses than to students as a self-conscious conflict group in pursuit of a relatively well defined set of political goals. As in the analysis of participants in other movements, students tended to be treated in one of two ways. Some viewed them as admirable idealists in pursuit of democratic values who were likely to be thwarted by the realities of the American power structure. Alternatively, they were seen as individuals whose social position and personality structure predisposed them to antidemocratic appeals. Such characteristics, however, are also associated with alienation and withdrawal from long-term active involvement in politics. In short, in neither view were participants treated as members of persisting organized groups which were likely to bring about significant changes in the structure of the American polity. In neither view was there an emphasis on social conflict and social change.[5]

Studies of *political bureaucracy* have directed considerable attention to the defects of bureaucratic organization. However, at least since Lipset's article was published, much research has also reflected Weber's concern with the antidemocratic consequences of bureaucracy as well as with its integrative functions. For example, studies of modern totalitarian political systems indicate that some, such as Nazi Germany and Fascist Italy, emphasized the idea of the corporate state. This involved the incorporation of the national economy and polity within a single bureaucratic framework. In such a system all organizations, whether business corporations or labor unions, were made part of one hierarchical structure with the supreme political leader at the head. In this system the functionaries of almost all organizations do in fact become public bureaucrats.[6] The integrative functions of bureaucracy have been considered in, among other places, the study of the politics of modernization. Apter, for example, pointed out that in Turkey modernization came in the nineteenth century, in part through the efforts of various dissident groups in the bureaucracy of the Ottoman Empire and in part through the identification of bureaucracy with innovation and modernization.[7] Other studies of these types also evidence a commitment to the stability of Western democratic political institutions by analyzing the structural conditions which undermine them (and can lead to "totalitarianism") or which encourage their development (and can facilitate "modernization").

There still appears to be little research on the *internal government of voluntary associations* that is macroanalytic and comparative. Important questions about structural factors which facilitate or impede democracy and about the links between organizational structures and the structure of the more inclusive political systems of which they are a part remain to be answered.[8] Success in dealing with the five analytic problems specified at the end of Chapter 2 should facilitate the research process by which answers to such questions are found.

Throughout Chapters 1 and 2 it was argued that a commitment to the basic features of Western industrial welfare democracies and the influence of Parsons have led American sociologists to consider *power* a resource for the achievement of collective goals rather than a resource unequally distributed among various social subgroups and used by them in their conflicts with each other over scarce resources. Lipset's statement flatly contradicts this view.

It is, of course, an empirical question as to which description of the analytic tendencies of American political sociologists is more accurate. Answering this question would involve extensive content analysis of a representative sample of their writings. Such a study was beyond the possibilities of Lipset's paper and is beyond the limitations of this book. While the question cannot be settled except through empirical research, at least one additional argument in support of the position taken in Chapters 1 and 2 can be presented.

A case can be made for the contention that, in the United States, all of the major areas of sociology have emphasized social order rather than social change. For example, texts, courses, and research in "marriage and the family" stress the psychological and social needs met by the nuclear family under the stressful conditions of urban industrial life. The sociology of religion most commonly deals with the ways in which religious organizations serve the needs of individuals under social conditions encouraging competition, anomie, and alienation. The sociology of occupations and professions commonly investigates problems of individuals in adjusting to the demands of various work roles. The sociology of economic life tends to concentrate on the ways in which production, distribution, exchange, and consumption are structured, legitimized, and regulated so as to facilitate the achievement of social goals. And so on. In each of these areas attention is directed toward meeting individual needs, which in turn helps insure the stability and continuity of society. Whether areas emphasize the ways in which tensions, alienation, and anomie are reduced, socially useful skills and motives are acquired, or goods and services are made, distributed, and consumed, primary concern is with social stability and continuity—not with conflict and change.

The view developed in Chapter 2 suggests that the characteristic emphases of American political sociology are not significantly different from those of the rest of American sociology. Lipset's position suggests that major differences do exist. If Lipset's position is correct, then these differences should be accounted for. The alternative is that American sociology in general, like political sociology, has focused on conflict and change. If this view is correct, then the misperceptions of commentators on the state of American sociology such as Mills, Dahrendorf, Bramson, and Gouldner, among others, should be accounted for.

GREER AND ORLEANS: THE EXPLANATION OF THE STATE[9]

Scott Greer and Peter Orleans see the major empirical problem of political sociology as "the description, analysis and sociological explanation of the peculiar structure called the state."[10] The importance of the state lies in the fact that it is the contemporary locus of power and authority. It is the largest and most inclusive social unit within which control is exercised.

Three sets of related topics are basic to the empirical understanding of the state. First, a number of problems center around consensus and legitimacy. Here the basic question is this: How is it possible, given the vast proliferation of subgroups within modern society, to maintain a viable polity based on consensus? Second, several major areas of investigation deal with participation and representation. Here questions concern the constraining power of traditional social cleavages such as race, religion, and class on the behavior of elected representatives. The third major problem area deals with the relation between economic development and political change. Here questions concern the process by which various social groups become eligibile for positions of political control under the conditions of increasing economic complexity.

Relevant to the analysis of *consensus and legitimacy* are studies investigating the role which public agencies, the family, and parapolitical structures play in the process of political socialization. Public agencies such as the mass media and public schools perform an integrating function in heterogeneous society by transmitting generally agreed upon definitions of legitimate authority. The mass media facilitate democratic processes by providing feedback from citizens to the polity in the form of public opinion. The family adds an element of stability by transmitting party identification and orientations supportive of the ongoing political system from one generation to the next. The network of manifestly nonpolitical relationships which transmit politically relevant information (the parapolitical structure) tends to discourage political extremism.

A number of problems dealing with consensus and legitimacy require further inquiry. Research is needed to determine more precisely what politically relevant information the mass media communicate and what they fail to communicate to the public. The bearing of formal education on politically relevant beliefs and attitudes also needs further exploration, particularly the bearing of education on those beliefs and attitudes which support democratic principles. Adult socialization, the process by which the individual's allegiances are altered or reinforced, has yet to receive extensive consideration.

Empirical studies dealing with *participation and representation* include investigations of voting behavior, research on elite decision making, analyses of the behavior of representatives, and inquiries into the determinants of political involvement.

Voting studies have aimed at understanding the determinants of individual electoral choice. To some extent voting represents participation in a ritual. Elections can be seen as a ceremonial affirmation of solidarity. The population coheres first around its own leaders and then, after the ceremonial battle, around the resulting unified leadership. Further studies are needed of variations in the voting of different segments of the electorate. Analyses of decision making have yet to fully address the general question of the difference that the franchise makes to the fortunes of various groups and to the operation of the state. A related problem concerns the relative weight to assign to different interest groups in predicting the response of representatives. Numerous descriptions of the behavior of representatives emphasize that to a considerable degree their actions are structured by stable, largely unwritten rules of the game. The conditions under which an assembly develops and maintains controlling norms that cross lines of party, race, religion, and other social differences are as yet poorly understood. The manner in which such agreed-upon rules bear on the role of political heads of state also needs further study. Investigations of political participation and interest show that persons more educated, highly paid, and with more highly regarded jobs are more likely to be better informed and interested in politics and are more likely to participate. This raises the question of the minimal rights and duties of membership in the polity and how these vary by categories of citizens.

Studies of political elites, that is, of those who occupy positions of political control, are central to understanding *economic development and political change.* There are a number of basic questions concerning elites. What social groups have access to various command posts? What other elites are significant for political elites? What are the relations among elites in general? How are the organizations which they head structured? How are the organizations which they head linked?

Meeting increasing public demand for economic prosperity and external safety requires increasingly efficient and effective political and economic organization and control; it necessitates increasing bureaucratization. Elites become organizational commanders and staff members recruited on the basis of technical competence. Political problems such as inflation of currency, the nature of armament requisites for military safety, the balance of trade and payments, among others, are questions of policy in all contemporary states. Each requires a decision of "experts." Much of the operation of the modern state is contingent on successfully solving technical problems. However, technical efficiency is unlikely to be enough to guarantee the stability and continuity of the political regime. The polity must have available a reservoir of the general trust and confidence of its members. Without this general commitment to its legitimacy, a political system will face an uncertain future each time it confronts problems not obviously amenable to rapid technical solution. A major continuing problem in political sociology consists in understanding the ways in which the resource of legitimacy is created, maintained, and used in all political systems.

Finally, the study of the state requires some consideration of ideology. Early-twentieth-century utopian theories and deterministic evolutionary models have little influence today. However, some of the major social changes which gave rise to such intellectual schemes continue to this day. Less privileged groups in many societies still struggle for first-class citizenship and for the guarantee of new rights by the state. Other more privileged strata in the same societies endeavor to protect against threats to their positions of power and privilege which often accompany modernization. Groups such as these exhibit norms which may change into fighting ideologies.

Comparison with Greer and Orleans's View

The authors do not present a separate discussion of political sociology's intellectual origins. However, at various points references are made to the writings of late-nineteenth-century European theorists. For example, Vilfredo Pareto's contention that the circulation of elites alone accounts for a substantial degree of variation in the character and policy of the state is presented as a central provocative hypothesis in political sociology which remains to be adequately subjected to empirical investigation. Max Weber's discussions of the nature of bureaucratic organization and consequences of the widespread adoption of bureaucratic norms to economic and political life are credited with providing important guides to understanding the delicate and precarious balance struck in some political systems between efficiency, democracy, and legitimacy. Karl Marx is credited with greatly advancing the important discussion of the relation between economic interests and government. References such as these are in keeping with the view developed in Chapter 1 and with Lipset's view outlined above.

What is rather unique about Greer and Orleans's discussion is the importance they attribute to Durkheim. The authors argue that American sociology has largely adopted Durkheim's view of modern, complex society as composed of a vast number of subgroups which mediate between the individual and the state. Each of these groups generates politically relevant action which is tolerated or reinforced or resisted by other subgroups within the society. Such subgroups can, and on occasion do, exercise a veto power over the state. These principles are embodied in Federalism, a major feature of the American polity. The American system allocates considerable legal autonomy to the states and through these to local communities. The effort to keep legally separate the economy and the polity is also in accordance with Durkheim's principles. This is the setting within which American political sociology is written. It is the pluralism to which many political sociologists are committed. This value orientation is often seen in their work.

Dispersed political control restrains the centralized power of the state from infringing on the rights of the isolated individual. The possibility of tyrannical rule is reduced when there are countervailing forces pitted against the state. However, decentralized control presents its own problems. The multiplication of necessary parties to an agreement is positively correlated with legitimacy, but negatively correlated with efficiency. The ways in which contemporary urban crises are treated afford an example of this problem. Federal agencies, which operate on a national scale and which work independently of one another, are commonly consulted. Such agencies have no desire to coordinate their actions and take into account the effects of their work on the local community. Increasing fragmentation of policy takes control out of the hands of the community most affected.

Greer and Orleans refer to this tension between representativeness and effectiveness as "Durkheim's dilemma." It is the central problem of consensus and legitimacy, participation and representation, economic development and political change. The problem is quite similar to that which Lipset sets forth as the central problem of political sociology—the social conditions of democracy—the problem of conflict and consensus.

The view of political sociology developed in this book is broader than that maintained either by Lipset or by Greer and Orleans. Undoubtedly the social conditions which encourage democracy have been the topic to which most political sociologists have devoted most attention. But efforts have also been made toward understanding nondemocratic systems which are as much a part of political reality as are democratic systems. Including these studies in the domain of political sociology may not facilitate understanding the modal tendencies of contemporary American political sociologists. However, the broader definition does direct attention to the continuing set of analytic problems which stem from Marx, Weber, and Durkheim to the present. It also includes studies of the political systems of Eastern Europe and the nations of Asia, Africa, and Latin America, which are likely to receive increasing attention in the near future. Erosion of American prestige and power since the end of World War II—beginning with the Soviet Union's subjugation of Eastern Europe and Mao Tse-tung's takeover of China, and more recently illustrated by Cuban military actions in Africa, the revolutions in Nicaragua and Iran, and the inability to influence economic actions taken by the petroleum producing and exporting nations—clearly indicates the need to develop the sociological understanding such studies are capable of producing.

Many of the topics singled out by Greer and Orleans for new research are macroanalytic. Examples of such topics include the political role of the mass media in contemporary societies, the importance of the franchise for various groups in different societies, and the linkages between the manifestly nonpolitical organizations headed by those who have considerable political power. Understanding some of these topics could be facilitated by comparative and historical approaches. If such topics do receive considerable attention in the future, political sociology will again have the analytic thrust found in the writings of those who first formulated its central concepts and problems. In short, Greer and Orleans's discussion is compatible with the position taken in Chapters 1 and 2.

The research literature reviewed by Greer and Orleans suggests that political sociologists have tended to investigate political harmony and stability rather than political conflict and change. Research exemplifying this orientation includes studies of the ways in which political stability is achieved, the social means by which representatives are kept responsive to their constituents, and the processes by which access to elite political positions becomes more open. On the other hand, the problems which are suggested for future investigation (important problems which still remain to be investigated in the 1980s) deal more with conflict and change. These include studies of the ways in which political allegiances are altered and interest groups compete to influence the decisions of representatives, potential threats to the legitimacy of the political systems of technologically advanced societies, and the possible emergence of new ideologically oriented conflict groups in modernizing societies. Such concerns with conflict would also move political sociology to a position more in line with the intellectual tradition in which it originated.

JANOWITZ: THE STUDY OF THE PRECONDITIONS OF POLITICAL DEMOCRACY[11]

Janowitz's discussion of political sociology, like that of Lipset, appears in a highly prestigious context. The article is an entry in *The International Encyclopedia of the Social Sciences,* an authoritative reference source on the basic concepts, models, theories, and methodological approaches in all the social sciences.

Janowitz maintains that there are two distinct but converging views of political sociology. The broader view, deriving from the writings of Marx, sees political sociology as concerned with the social basis of power in all institutional sectors of society. More specifically, it takes the position that a society's political institutions are shaped by its system of social stratification. The more narrow view of political sociology draws on Weber's works. It focuses on the organizational analysis of political groups and political leadership.

The vastly increased division of labor found in contemporary industrial societies has made it necessary to reformulate each of these general approaches. The social stratification position has been modified as interest-group theory. That is, politics is now seen as derived from the conflicts between highly differentiated economic, professional (including political professions), ethnic, religious, and other associations. The organizational approach has been reformulated as a theory of social strain. The theory focuses on political parties, which are seen as central mechanisms for accommodating the strains that exist in modern societies.

Most of the empirical research in political sociology derives from the interest-group theory. Studies of the bearing of such variables as occupation, income, status, ethnicity, and religion on voting behavior, party affiliation, membership in voluntary associations, and exposure to the media serve as examples. Empirical investigations of these topics most commonly rely on the sample survey. This approach does not produce data bearing directly on questions of the political behavior of social subgroups or on questions of political change. Furthermore, due to the difficulty of developing standardized indices, comparisons between nations which rely on sample survey data are extremely difficult. Hence the basic problem with most of the empirical work in political sociology is its lack of relevance to basic theoretical issues.

Sample surveys dealing with the social correlates of party identification and voting have been supplemented by research on public opinion and ideology. These investigate the extent to which political attitudes not only reflect social structure but also are influenced by party organization and the mass media.

The theory of social strain has been expanded to include not only the analysis of party organization but also its relation to the proliferation of professional and voluntary associations which act as pressure groups. Specific topics studied include the recruitment, career development, and patterns of interaction among political elites, the maintenance of linkages between the electorate and the government bureaucracy, the mobilization of mass political participation, and the formulation of consent. There have been numerous studies of local-community, regional, and national elite systems. Comparative studies related to the societal strain theory have focused on models for describing the dilemmas facing similar groups of nations, such as the developing nations.

In political sociology macroanalytic studies and studies of change have tended to focus on two related topics: (1) the impact of modernization on representative institutions and (2) the significance of differing political institutions in accounting for various patterns of national development. Tocqueville's analysis of prerevolutionary and postrevolutionary France, Veblen's study of Imperial Germany and the industrial revolution, and Thomas's study of the Polish peasant in Europe and America are among the most important classic theoretical sources on the interplay of political institutions and social and economic development.[12] However, interest in these topics derives less from intellectual history than from modern political history—particularly the rise and transformation of totalitarianism and the rapid process of decolonization after World War II.

Regardless of particular subject matter, the central focus of political sociology is on the sources of political conflict and on the processes by which political consensus is created. More work has been done on routine and ongoing processes than on crisis and conflict situations. This, however, is not the expression of a theoretical bias. Rather, it is simply the result of the difficulty of getting the relevant data.

There is a clear basic value commitment on the part of most political sociologists. This is their commitment to explore the conditions under which political democracy would be most fully realized. Janowitz concludes:

> If economic analysis is designed to maximize the use of economic resources, then political sociology has the goal of formulating social psychological and economic conditions under which political democracy would be maximized.[13]

Comparison with Janowitz's View

Janowitz makes a number of points also made by Lipset and by Greer and Orleans: (1) the writings of Marx and Weber are major theoretical sources of contemporary political sociology; (2) the social conditions of political conflict and consensus are the central topics of political sociology; (3) political sociologists are committed to the maintenance and development of democratic political institutions.

With respect to points 1 and 2, it has already been argued that Durkheim's contributions to modern political sociology are seldom noted and that political sociologists study political consensus much more frequently than political conflict. (Lipset does not agree with this generalization. Janowitz does not deny it but attributes the emphasis on consensus merely to the technical difficulties of acquiring data on conflict.) Point 3 is quite different from the explanation developed in Chapter 2, namely, that an explicit statement of value commitments is desirable because it alerts an analyst and his audience alike to the most likely direction of any distortion in his theory and research. An individual's values help determine those aspects of the world he will attempt to understand—what he will focus on and what he will ignore. When value commitments are widely shared within a group of social scientists, they will tend to "over-study" some topics at the price of "under-studying" others. The commitment to the general features of Western industrial democracies has led political sociologists to pay comparatively little attention to nondemocratic political systems and political relations in nonindustrial societies.

Janowitz does not consider the magnitude of the changes that are involved in the shift from Marx's stratification theory to interest-group theory and from Weber's organizational approach to the theory of social strain. Marx was concerned with the conflict of groups with irreconcilable opposing objective interests. Such conflicts would forever change the character of the societies in which they occurred. Interest-group theory, on the other hand, investigates the ways social conflict is handled within a stable political framework to which all parties are more or less committed. Weber considered at length inherent sources of conflict and antidemocratic development in all bureaucracies. It is not clear that the social strain approach, as characterized by Janowitz, treats such problems.

Janowitz offers no explicit hypotheses concerning the course of political sociology's future. Nevertheless, he does argue that excessive reliance on sample survey data has prompted atheoretical empiricism. He does suggest that the development of structural, as opposed to social-psychological, measuring instruments should facilitate comparative studies and reduce the gap between theory and research. This is similar to the position taken in Chapter 2.

SARTORI: FROM THE SOCIOLOGY OF POLITICS TO POLITICAL SOCIOLOGY[14]

Giovanni Sartori's essay is one of a collection of ten discussions exploring the influence upon political analysis of economics, history, anthropology, psychology and psychiatry, sociology and statistics. It neither traces the intellectual origins of political sociology nor describes the primary areas of empirical research. However, the essay does discuss three important, related topics that bear directly on this chapter: the relationship between political science and political sociology, the state of theory and research in contemporary political sociology, and the future course of political sociology's development.

According to Sartori, most of what is called "political sociology" is more appropriately termed "the sociology of politics." Sociological studies of political phenomena generally have proceeded from the assumption that political sociology is a subfield of sociology. From this perspective, sociologists' objective was to explain political phenomena in terms of non-political variables such as social class and stratifcation. Hence what has passed for political sociology really has been the sociological reduction of politics. Political science, on the other hand, has tended to explain political phenomena, such as voting behavior, in terms of explicitly political factors, such as parties and party systems. A genuine political sociology would be an interdisciplinary hybrid that would "combine social and political explanatory variables, i.e., the inputs suggested by the sociologist with the inputs suggested by the political scientists."[15]

The characteristic features of the sociology of politics (as opposed to political sociology) can be seen in existing studies of the bearing of social class and stratification upon political behavior such as voting. Such studies are based on a broad theory according to which politics is ultimately a struggle between social classes pursuing incompatible interests. The theory is widely supported because it provides sociologists with a central independent variable that is quantifiable and "objective" (as opposed to religion, for example, which is a "subjective" variable). The need to have an objective "prime mover" is a function of sociologists' desire to emulate and thereby somehow to achieve the status of the physical sciences. Following this path has been dysfunctional for both theory and research.

The theory that significant social conflict in political democracies is expressed through political parties which represent the interests of different classes has serious flaws. All of the components of the theory are, at best, ambiguous. First, no distinction is made between the kind of social conflict considered by Marx (according to which social conflict is a temporary necessity until social inequality, alienation, and exploitation have ended) and the kind of social conflict considered by many American writers (according to which conflict is positively valued because all parties stand to gain and because conflict results from social diversity, which is valued in itself). Second, discussions of class and class interest are often unclear. "Class" can refer to an individual's self-perception of status, to a self-conscious social aggregate, or to a set of individuals sharing some attribute (e.g., level of income). These are analytically and empirically distinct phenomena although they are often treated as though they were not. The notion of "interest" is similarly unclear. The distinction between self-perceived interests and objective interests is seldom recognized. Little attention is paid to the important point made by Weber that collectivities often pursue noneconomic goals. Finally, in light of the assumption of self-interest, the discussion of representation is puzzling. The more individuals pursue their self-interest, and the more numerous these individuals, the less their interests can be represented by large-scale organizations such as political parties.

According to Sartori, research prompted by the desire to demonstrate the importance of sociology's objective prime mover, social class, exhibits similar flaws. Voting studies employing the sample survey have established correlation between class position (most often measured by occupation) and voting behavior. Such findings are taken to reflect the class basis of political cleavage in a society. However, the best comparative evidence, such as that offered by Alford,[16] warrants only the hypothesis that class is the major determinant of voting behavior only if no other cleavages happen to be salient. There exist no data which demonstrate that, given multiple social cleavages in societies, the division of social class is the one which invariably has greatest political significance. The commonly reported finding that individuals vote in ways they believe to be in their own economic self-interest is trivial. It reveals nothing about class structure, class consciousness, the likelihood of class action, or about party alignments. Even on the level of individuals, a far more interesting question which the sociology of politics does not consider is why, as in England, France, and Italy, so many working-class people do not vote for working-class parties.

Inattention to political factors as independent variables has caused most sociologists to miss the point that class is an *ideology*. Whenever ideologies seem to be important in politics, they have a firm organizational basis. Political parties persuade social aggregates that they have common interests which can be realized through party support. Whenever parties reflect social classes, this signifies more about the parties than about the classes. The class receives its identity from the party rather than vice versa. In a society where social class is found to have greater political significance than religion, for example, it is not because class is an "objective" reality while religion is "subjective." Rather, it is because mass party organization proved to be more effective than church organization.

As Sartori sees it, a genuine political sociology will emerge as those engaged in empirical research conduct studies which take into account the following points:[17] (1) Cleavages such as race, religion, locality, culture, tradition, and ideology can have as great a political significance as social class. (2) Cleavages do not automatically translate themselves into party oppositions. Some divisions (e.g., racial cleavages in the United States) are not translated at all. (3) Explanations of voter alignments behind particular parties in single nations sometimes require reference to historical factors. (These may help account for cases in which the economic self-interest hypothesis is not applicable.) (4) Cross-national studies of voter alignments between political parties always necessitate considerations of national histories. Variations in alignments cannot be fully explained without data on differences in the sequences of party formation. (5) While present party systems and alignments in part can be understood by reference to historical factors, party systems themselves operate as independent variables. Much of political life can be understood in terms of the operation of explicitly political structures. (6) The assumption that party systems reflect socioeconomic cleavages leads to a study of past, not emerging, cleavages. The assumption leads to static, retrospective analysis. (7) Just as party systems at times may reflect social cleavages, so, at times, political structures such as parties can manipulate social cleavages.

Comparison with Sartori's View

The position that political sociology is an "interdisciplinary hybrid" rather than a subfield of sociology has already been adopted in this book. Sartori's article focuses on the interplay of sociology and political science. Again, it must be noted that other fields such as anthropology, economics, and history also contribute to political sociology.

Political sociology has been defined as the study of power and authority relations as these are structured at relatively inclusive levels of social organization and as these influence and are influenced by the social bonds of kinship, religion, class, interest groups of various kinds, and by shared beliefs and values. This definition takes into account many of Sartori's points. First, it recognizes that not only are political relationships structured by social factors but also that all social institutions can be affected by political structures and processes. Second, the definition explicitly mentions a variety of social cleavages in addition to social class which can be politically relevant. Third, the definition does not reflect the "objective bias." Shared belief and value systems as well as religion are identified as important to the empirical understanding of political life.

Sartori's description of the atheoretical empiricism fostered by the objectivist bias of the sociology of politics is compatible with arguments presented in Chapter 2. His suggestion that a genuine political sociology will develop as interdisciplinary, macroanalytic, and historical-comparative studies dealing with change are initiated was developed as a major theme in Chapters 1 and 2.

There are several points of difference between Sartori's assessment of the present state of political sociology and the view developed in this book.[18] Sartori argues that empirical research dealing with the bearing of social class on party systems and voter alignments has produced, with very few exceptions, trivial results. However, it can be argued that data indicating the relative importance of social class in the political life of a number of countries as well as the political influence of social class in societies in which traditional ties are generally losing their significance are far from trivial findings.

The sociology of politics has intellectual roots that stem from Weber and Durkheim as well as from Marx. The hypothesis that on occasion status factors can be of primary importance in the explanation of party alignments or social movements is commonly encountered.[19] Another frequently encountered theme is that during periods of crisis in modern industrial societies, mass, as opposed to class-based, political action is probable.[20] Despite the flaws which Sartori accurately identifies, at the time he wrote his article and certainly today, the sociology of politics is neither as devoid of theoretical substance nor as monolithic in thoughts as he suggests.

EISENSTADT: RESOLVING THE STATE-SOCIETY DICHOTOMY

S. N. Eisenstadt's discussion serves as a general introduction to his comprehensive reader *Political Sociology*.[21] His broad view of the field is suggested by listing the topics he includes: the political systems of preliterate societies, patrimonialism, tribal federations, city-states, feudal systems, bureaucratic empires, political modernization, and the major types of the modern political regime.

Eisenstadt's introductory remarks are aimed at describing in very general terms the intellectual origins of political sociology, the concerns of contemporary analysts which reflect these intellectual origins, and the most general interests which also express long-standing topics and which are likely to occupy political sociologists in the foreseeable future. Little attention is directed toward locating the major contributions of particular theorists or to describing in any detail the history of the development of political sociology.

According to Eisenstadt, political sociology originated in nineteenth-century French and German ideological, historiographic, and social-political thought concerning the conditions and mechanisms of the continuity, disruption, and change of different types of societies. Central to such considerations was a dichotomy between state and society. The dichotomy raised an empirical question: Is the state or is society more important in human affairs? It also raised a normative question: Should the state or society be more important in human affairs? At one pole of the empirical question were those who believed that political institutions were but mere reflections of other social forces such as economy, environment, or technology. At the other pole were those who argued that political institutions played a determining role in social life—they are the master institutions.

The dichotomy of state and society also brought into focus two related major political issues: How is it possible to maintain social order and stability while simultaneously permitting individual liberties? and How is it possible to combine social development and progress with institutional continuity and stability? These questions were at the heart of most discussions of bureaucracy and rationalization.

Bureaucracy is the most efficient and effective organization of power. It represents a means of implementing social reforms and promoting desired change while at the same time insuring a stable structure of authority. On the other hand, bureaucracy has the potential of enveloping all areas of social life and stifling the liberties of the relatively powerless individual.

Like bureaucracies, social classes are also a constant feature of modern societies. And, like bureaucracies, social classes have been seen to have both desirable and undesirable aspects. On the one hand, individual freedom within a society has been thought to be dependent on the existence of a variety of different hierarchies in class and status. On the other hand, classes are at least in part the result of the exploitation of some of society's members by other members and are an embodiment of the distinction between state and society which must be overcome. Similar ambivalent attitudes also developed with regard to other concepts referring to components of modern social life, such as *mass* and *elite*.

Modern political analysis has not yet entirely freed itself from the tendency to take opposing ideological stances with respect to concepts which are related to the state-society dichotomy and which refer to components of the modern social order. However, a major step has been taken by the widely accepted conceptualization of political institutions as but one of several institutions, including the family, economy, and religion, which together make up society. It is now recognized that in any given society the character of the relations among these institutions is always a matter for empirical inquiry. However, despite these advances the dichotomy between state and society continues to influence the central analytic problems and assumptions of political sociology.

In modern political sociology studies of single nations have centered around two topic areas: (1) *political elites* (recruitment, composition, changes, relations with nonelite groups, patterns of political organization and mobilization they employ) and (2) *types of political organization* (political parties, rules of the political game, political participation of different groups and strata—including voting, informal processes of influence, and private ideologies). Comparative studies have developed their own tradition of research which is not closely connected with single-nation investigations. Contemporary comparative research has been prompted by the emergence of the new nations of the Third World. Analyses of these nations have been conducted within the perspectives of anthropology, history, some traditions of comparative constitutions and legal history, as well as political science and sociology. Particular attention has been paid to the social conditions for the emergence of stability and continuity of the modern democratic regime.

In recent decades considerable consensus appears to have developed concerning the defining characteristics and functions of political systems. It seems to be generally agreed that the political system (1) is the organization of a society having the legitimate monopoly over the authorized use and regulation of force in the society, (2) has defined responsibilities of maintaining the society of which it is a part, (3) imposes severe secular sanctions in order to maintain collective goals, maintain the society's internal order, and regulate its foreign relations. It also seems to be generally accepted that the political system of every society (4) determines the society's primary goals and general rules for the maintenance or changing of the existing order of the society, (5) carries out administrative activity to provide various goods, services, prestige, and influence to various groups and to extract resources necessary to the operation of the political system itself—including mobilizing support for the regime in general as well as support for particular policies and role incumbents, and (6) tests and authorizes the validity of applying the basic rules to particular concrete cases arising in the society. Finally, there appears to be general agreement that political institutions are dependent on the other institutions of society for resources, services, and support needed for the implementation of collective goals, for the maintenance of the polity's position in society, and for the fulfillment of its integrative functions.

Eisenstadt argues that such theoretical agreement is desirable because it moves political analysis away from the continuing influence of the state-society dichotomy and away from the ideological disputes which are related to it. Unfortunately, similar agreement has not been achieved on many aspects of comparative studies and on aspects of investigations concerning political change. In particular, patterns of protest, rebellion, and revolution require further study. The relatively recent investigation of these topics was prompted by the emergence of the new nations. Early studies of these nations often employed the state-society dichotomy. For example, some studies sought to determine the nonpolitical conditions for the development of different types of regimes or the importance of the one-party state for the creation of national integration. Again the dichotomy proved to be dysfunctional. Many of the developing nations were not "states" in the European sense of being strong autonomous units with identifiable, effective political centers. Many were not really "societies" in the sense of being a relatively homogeneous, integrated national community.

A review of studies of new nations reveals an important variable virtually ignored by sociologists—the international political environment. The structure and operation of a society's political system are undoubtedly influenced to some extent by the set of external political-economic relations in which it is involved. In the case of a new nation, such relations may be the most important determinant of the central features of its political system. Such an oversight is a result of the fact that modern sociology has always focused on Western industrial nations, which have been relatively autonomous and which were not colonies or peripheries of other cultural centers.

Sociology's Western bias can also be seen in its ambivalent attitude toward the concepts of force and power. These concepts are particularly basic to understanding societies which are attempting to establish centralized authority. Such societies typically do not have relatively homogeneous populations which are likely to achieve consensus on the basic rules of the political system or about its legitimation.

According to Eisenstadt, the most important breakthrough in recent political sociology has been the realization that participation in political life represents something in addition to the desire to influence the distribution of power and to affect authoritative decisions about the allocation of values and facilities in a society. It also represents a quest for participation in a broader meaningful order. Similarly, the selection of elites is important not only because they have the ability to redistribute scarce values to different social subgroups but also because they have the ability to change the symbols and the meaning of the political system in which they operate. In this perspective, processes of legitimation, so important to the understanding of both political stability and political development, are related to the quest for the "good society" itself. The political system of any society is never fully accepted or accepted to the same degree by all of that society's subgroups. The quest by different social subgroups with different ideas about what constitutes the "good" political order and the "good" citizen, ruler, and subject can produce conflict and change. Hence previous theory that has assumed that the stability and continuity of a political system are dependent on consensus about its legitimation is in need of reformulation. Questions must be raised not only about the character of legitimacy itself but also about the extent to which a political system, if it is to function and endure, must be viewed as acceptable, and by whom. Finding answers to such questions will constitute central problems for further research by political sociologists. It will involve moving beyond the legacy of the state-society dichotomy.

Comparison with Eisenstadt's View

Eisenstadt's broad interdisciplinary approach, like that of Sartori, is compatible with the view of political sociology developed in Chapters 1 and 2. Anthropologists, historians, economists, students of comparative constitutions, as well as sociologists and political scientists, all play an important role in understanding the mutual interplay of political and other social organizations and institutions.

Like Sartori, Eisenstadt emphasizes the promise of future empirical comparative political studies. He has little to say, except by way of passing criticism, of the immense body of existing studies on the social psychology of politics in contemporary industrial democracies. Such studies all too often have been atheoretical. They have been overly concerned with consensus and stability. They do represent a tradition of research quite unlike the historical studies of the theoretical forebears of modern sociology. However, to ignore such studies is to miss a vast amount of empirical information about the political life of many modern societies—particularly as it is actually experienced by most of the members of these societies. The second section of this book presents a sample of this tradition of research. It should give some indication of what most of political sociology, at least as it has been conducted in the United States, has been all about. It should also convey a feeling that what has been discovered is of considerable value for understanding the political world which confronts us daily.

Western European social thought of the nineteenth century did bequeath to modern political investigations a host of analytically useful concepts and hypotheses. However, many of the concepts, such as state and society, mass and elite, appeared as dichotomies which encouraged analysts more in the direction of taking ideological stances than in the direction of exploring empirical questions. The elitist-pluralist controversy described in Chapters 2, 6, and 7 serves as an example of this.

The state-society dichotomy in particular is probably the source of the major difference between political science as an academic field and the sociology of politics. Bendix and Lipset have characterized this difference:

> Like political science, political sociology is concerned with the distribution and exercise of power in society. Unlike political science, it is not concerned with the institutional provisions for the distribution and exercise, but takes these as given. Thus, political science starts with the state and examines how it affects society, while political sociology starts with society and examines how it affects the distribution and exercise of power.[22]

Political sociology, as conceptualized in this book, involves the view of political institutions as both dependent and independent variables. Its growth does require overcoming the state-society dichotomy.

Political sociologists often do assume that all societies have operative political centers and that such centers have some legitimacy expressing the consensus of the majority of the members of the society who share a relatively homogeneous political culture. They also have tended to assume that the development of political systems entails assuming the general structural and cultural characteristics of the polities of Western industrial societies. None of these assumptions facilitates understanding the politics of premodern and newly developing societies.

It is probably true that sociologists who have conducted multination macroanalytic studies have tended to pay inadequate attention to internal features of the polities they were investigating. It is not the case that social-psychological studies have ignored international politics. Individuals' attitudes toward international events have been studied extensively. Particular attention has been given to the relationship between individuals' orientations toward domestic politics and their orientations toward international affairs.

It is important to recognize that political participation can have considerable symbolic and psychological significance as well as importance for the distribution of power and privilege. This point becomes increasingly important as the populations of modern societies become larger and more urbanized, as the division of labor increases, as government becomes more centralized, powerful, and remote, and as traditional ties weaken. If recognition of this point represents a "breakthrough of recent sociology" it is because sociologists have paid little attention to their theoretical tradition. Marx's discussions of *alienation,* Weber's writing on *rationalization,* and, above all, Durkheim's analyses of *anomie* all specify that modern industrial life in the West involves individuals' loss of control of important areas of their lives. These studies point out that modern social life also involves an absence of social ties from which individuals once derived security and identity. They further recognized that, faced with this situation, people will seek to regain, in some sense, what has been lost through social participation—sometimes in the form of revolution, sometimes in the form of supporting charismatically led social movements, and sometimes by involvement in politically relevant voluntary associations. What Eisenstadt terms a breakthrough is better characterized as a "rediscovery." As suggested in the preceding chapters, the future of political sociology is likely to witness other such valuable rediscoveries.

HOROWITZ: FROM POLITICAL ECONOMY TO POLITICAL SOCIOLOGY[23]

Irving L. Horowitz locates the origins of political sociology in two distinctive bodies of social thought—that which developed primarily in France in the eighteenth century, and the social philosophy which developed primarily in Germany in the nineteenth century. Eighteenth-century thought was ideologically liberal. Emphasis was on the individual and on democracy. Democracy was conceived as a form of government which liberated the individual from imposed obligations. Society was to have responsibilities to its citizens. Democracy was freedom from tyranny and the realization of universal brotherhood. However, this liberalism involved an element of compromise: the existence of different social and economic classes bringing about change and progress in a consensual way. By way of contrast, nineteenth-century thought was ideologically egalitarian. Emphasis was on class struggle, race, and group conflict. The necessity of doing one's duty replaced freedom from obligation as a primary theme.

While there are important differences between these two systems of social-political philosophy, they did express a number of important common themes. First, they both supported the replacement of custom and tradition by reason in structuring the affairs of people. Second, they both stressed the value of political democracy. Third, to insure a reasonable and democratic social order they argued that prime attention must be directed toward economic factors.

Though there remain important traces of this thought in contemporary social analyses, the facts of social history seriously challenged the tenability of many of its underlying suppositions. The rise of the bourgeoisie, industrialism, and urbanism produced new social inequalities and led to a breakdown of faith in democracy. Industrialism did not produce revolution but led away from it. Class consciousness was converted into nationalism and the working class was coopted by the bourgeoisie, who encouraged them to join the government and participate in political organizations. The rise of nationalism in the nineteenth century destroyed hope in the possibility of universal brotherhood. National identities became more important than class identities.

By far the most important fact of modern political history according to Horowitz is the shift in the locus of power in the twentieth century from Central Europe or Southern Europe and England to the United States, the Soviet Union, and the Third World. While totally new political and intellectual problems did not develop in these locations, the old explanatory schemes did not prove to be entirely applicable to the political structures and processes which were emerging.

The primary shortcoming in using eighteenth- and nineteenth-century intellectual schemes to account for twentieth-century politics is their emphasis on political economy—on the principle that economic factors determine political life. In the twentieth century the relationship between economy and polity is an inverse one from that which existed in the eighteenth and nineteenth centuries. Economics and the division of labor have given way to the primacy of management and regulation—particularly regulation by "experts." "(S)ociological and political aspects have conspired to determine at least as often as they are determined by economic factors and thus to shape the substance of our social world."[24] Weber reduced the major analytic elements of political life to three: class, status, and party. Horowitz notes that "if reduction is necessary, I prefer the formulation of economy, polity and military. How the 'big three' as a whole then in parts intersect and interact with problems of social stratification and social structure is the essence of (political sociology)."[25]

Sociology's repudiation of economic determinism and its recognition of the importance of political factors in social affairs raises the question of the difference between political sociology and political science. Horowitz answers, as do most of the authors considered in this chapter, that existing differences stem from differences in the view of the extent to which the state or society has greater importance in human life. Political science takes the state as the central object of study. Political scientists are concerned with relatively well defined legal structures, particularly as they bear on the distribution of power. They argue that the polity can create and change social cleavages. They are concerned with who has power and how much. They focus on *interests*. Political sociology takes society as the central object of study. Rather than investigating laws, sociologists have greater interest in the norms of everyday behavior. They are concerned with the ways in which informal, normative, culturally bound phenomena influence political structures and processes. They focus on *values* rather than on interests. They argue that the polity reflects social cleavages. Like Sartori and Janowitz, Horowitz argues that to develop a true political sociology "the need is to arrive at an interactionist framework in which questions of causal primacy are precisely what is left open, and not prematurely settled by professional fiat."[26]

More is required for the growth of political sociology than taking into account the insights produced by the political science perspective on the state. American political sociology has developed from two sources: the grand European theorists and survey researchers exploring electoral and opinion data. Neither of these sources provides an adequate basis for understanding the new political realities of the twentieth century: the international political importance of the United States, the Soviet Union, and the nations of the Third World, and the concomitant ascendance of social management and control. Americans remain uncomfortable with self-definitions of colonialism, imperialism, and explanation systems based on raw power. They continue to treat politics as if it has to do exclusively with parties and party voting. Political sociology must deal with twentieth-century realities in terms of a perspective which recognizes that the distance between the polity and the rest of society has vastly narrowed in the contemporary world. It must develop a perspective which is neither too abstract to have political meaning nor too ambiguous to serve as a guide for social policy.

Comparison with Horowitz's View

Before comparing Horowitz's view of political sociology with that developed in this book, the controversial character of his position should be pointed out. Few would disagree with Sartori that political sociology must move from sociological reductionism to analyses which take account of the fact that political life is influenced by formal political structures and processes as well as by sociological forces. However, many would disagree with Horowitz's contention that in the twentieth century economic factors have lost their primacy in the determination of political life. Particularly today, in the light of a high rate of inflation, high unemployment, decline productivity, and an "energy crisis," it is difficult to de-emphasize in any way the social and political impact of the economy. Perhaps the best way to view the relative importance of economic and political factors in modern social life is in a comparative perspective which emphasizes their mutual interactions. Such a position was developed by Charles Lindblom:

> Aside from the great differences between despotic and libertarian governments, the great distinction between one government and another is the degree to which market replaces government or government replaces market. . . . Hence, certain questions about the governmental-market relation are at the core of both political science and economics, no less for planned systems than for market systems.[27]

Even accepting Horowitz's strong thesis (which does not seem to be amenable to empirical verification or falsification) does not necessitate accepting his conclusion that in the twentieth century political economy is no longer a viable subject. In the preface to his book, Horowitz argues:

Today our realities are dictated by problems of allocation as much as by problems of production. They are guided by the articulation of interests as much as by the stampeding of masses or the sullen alienation of individuals. In whatever direction one looks, the increase in the role of political life with respect to economic life becomes clear.[28]

Another political analyst, William Mitchell, makes a similar point, only to conclude that political sociology's future lies in its developing into a new political economy.[29] Mitchell, like Horowitz, argues that, at present, the major domestic issues facing the polity involve decisions concerning how to allocate resources. However, for Mitchell, this formulation of the problems makes them conducive to economic-model analysis. The use of economic models, he argues, will overcome the reluctance of many political sociologists to develop normative theory and polity prescriptions.[30]

According to Mitchell there are four basic questions of political economy.[31]

1. What is the size of the public budget, or the volume of public goods and services?
2. What is the composition of the public budget, or what goods are produced, in what quantities?
3. How is the political division of labor organized?
4. How are public goods and services distributed and income redistributed?

He contends that how political systems arrive at their answers to each of these questions through nonmarket institutions is the central problem of the new political economy. The plausibility of this argument indicates that Horowitz's thesis concerning the future of the relation between political sociology and political economy is certainly debatable.

Horowitz's identification of the origins of political sociology with eighteenth- and nineteenth-century western European thought involves a broader discussion than that presented in Chapter 1, though in no way is it incompatible with it. As political sociology developed in the United States it expressed, at various points in time, many of the components of the social doctrines Horowitz describes. For example, in the mid-1950s eighteenth-century assumptions seem to have been predominant while in the late 1960s, the egalitarianism of nineteenth-century thought seemed to be more prominent. The set of politically relevant problems, concepts, and hypotheses provided by Marx, Weber, and Durkheim form a more readily identifiable and constant theoretical core of political sociology from the beginning of the twentieth century to the present.

The discussion of the basic features of contemporary American political sociology is completely compatible with the characterization developed in Chapter 2. The use of opinion data and the emphasis on parties and voting has encouraged the development of a political-social psychology which concentrates on routine, democratic processes. There has been little emphasis on the uses of power—shared values play a considerably more central role in most analytic schemes. There has been relatively little concern with macrophenomena and with political change. There have been very few studies of colonialism and imperialism. Finally, Horowitz's positions that political sociology must develop an "interactionist framework" and that political and other social phenomena now are more inseparably linked than ever before both support the interdisciplinary view of political sociology maintained throughout this book.

SUMMARY AND CONCLUSIONS

Two questions were raised at the beginning of this chapter. One concerned the extent of difference between the conceptualization of political sociology developed in Chapters 1 and 2 and other statements about the nature of the field. The second question concerned the extent of difference between the history of political sociology as depicted in the second chapter and others' views of the course of political sociology's development. Answers to these questions reveal what is unusual and what is not with respect to the topics which have been selected for consideration in the following sections of this book. They also reveal what is unusual and what is not with respect to the manner in which these topics are organized for presentation. Table 3-1 summarizes each of the six discussions of political sociology and makes it possible to compare them with one another as well as with the position taken in this book.

All authors at least implicitly accepted the position, maintained in Chapter 1, that political sociology involves the study of power and authority relations as they are organized and exercised at relatively inclusive levels of social organization. All authors who addressed the topic also noted that enhanced empirical understanding of political structures and processes requires an explanatory framework which incorporates the "inputs" of many of the social sciences. All discussions encouraged interdisciplinary work. This too was a position maintained in Chapters 1 and 2.

Lipset, Greer and Orleans, Janowitz, and Sartori identified political sociology as the investigation of the social conditions of democracy. While this is a central analytic problem, its investigation is not coextensive with political sociology itself. The subject matter of political sociology as viewed here corresponds rather closely with the range of topics listed by Eisenstadt. It is possible that the view of political sociology maintained in this book is somewhat broader than the view of the field held by many other political sociologists.

There is full agreement that eighteenth- and nineteenth-century Western European social-political thought constitutes the modern theoretical origins of political sociology. Marx and Weber are the theorists most commonly cited as major figures.

There is also agreement that theory and research, which once had a structural focus in modern American political sociology, are more psychological and social-psychological in character. Related to this view is the commonly encountered criticism, described and elaborated in Chapter 2, that empirical research as it has been conducted over the past several decades is not providing answers to fundamental questions about important structural phenomena such as social conflict, political development, stability, management, and change.

All the discussions indicate that, in general, political sociologists have tended to study routine, ongoing political processes—typically those occurring in Western industrial democracies. This, too, agrees with the position developed in previous chapters. However, there is no clear agreement concerning how these routine events are usually treated. Lipset and Sartori explicitly argue that processes such as voting are characteristically viewed as expressions of antagonisms between various social strata—they are expressions of conflict. This approach, they contend, reflects political sociology's Marxist heritage. The views of the other authors on this point are not perfectly clear. However, the others do note the frequency with which political sociologists discuss legitimacy, stability, and continuity. Institutionalized phenomena are more often seen as manifestations of consensus than as expressions of conflict. In Chapter 2 it was argued that the political action political sociologists study takes place within the framework of a generally agreed upon set of rules of the game. The action they study helps perpetuate that normative order. More often then not, political sociologists have focused on the functions of political structures and processes—i.e., on the contributions they make to the goal attainment, integration, and therefore to the stability of the social system of which they are a part. Whether political sociologists have emphasized and continue to emphasize stability more than conflict or vice versa is ultimately an empirical question. Until research is conducted on it, it is only fair to conclude that the question must be regarded as unsettled.

There is consensus that the future of political sociology should involve more interdisciplinary effort directed toward understanding politically relevant aspects of social structure. Lipset, Janowitz, and Horowitz go on to argue that such studies should produce theory relevant to the formulation of social policy—particularly policy encouraging the maximization of democracy. This important line of argument will be discussed in a postscript to this book.

In sum, there appear to be but two points at which some controversy might arise concerning the conceptualization of political sociology and the view of its history maintained in this book:

TABLE 3-1 Alternative Views of Political Sociology

	PRIMARY SUBJECT MATTER	THEORETICAL ORIGINS	PATTERN OF DEVELOPMENT	PRESENT MAJOR EMPHASES	CRITICISMS OF PRESENT STATUS	FUTURE DEVELOPMENT
Chapters 1 and 2	Role of kinship, class, religion, interest groups, belief, and value systems in political life of historical, traditional, modernizing, and industrial societies	Late-nineteenth-century Western social theory, particularly that of Marx, Weber, and Durkheim	From macro-historical comparative studies emphasizing change to micro- ahistorical studies focusing on stability	Routine processes like voting. Stability of Western political democracies	Political systems of nonindustrial and non-Western societies under-studied. Conflict, change, and noninstitutionalized politics under-studied	Renewal of interest in the type of questions raised by Marx, Weber, Durkheim; greater attention to conflict and change
Lipset	The social conditions of democracy	Late-nineteenth-century Western social theory, particularly that of Marx, Tocqueville, Weber, and Michels	Continuing concern with the social bases of conflict. Change from structural to psychological approaches	Relationship between politics and various cleavages such as class, occupational groups, religion	Inattention to ways in which political systems resolve problems and encourage social democracy	Research on the integrative aspects of political behavior and on the structural requirements for a stable democracy
Greer and Orleans	The explanation of the state; the social conditions of democracy	Not discussed; but references to Pareto, Marx, Weber, and Durkheim	Not discussed	Political consensus and legitimacy, participation and representation, economic development and political change	Not discussed	Macroanalytic research on alteration of group alliances, interest-group competition, threats to legitimacy, new ideological conflict groups

Janowitz	The social conditions of democracy	Two major traditions of work: one stems from Marx, the other from Weber	Marxist position reformulated as interest-group theory. Weberian position modified as theory of societal strain	Sources of political conflict and creation of political consensus. Most research on routine, ongoing processes in political democracies	Research often not relevant to basic theoretical issues	Formulating conditions under which democracy would be maximized
Sartori	Not discussed. Studies of party systems and voter alignments used for illustrative purposes	Not discussed	Not discussed	Political phenomena as expression of class antagonisms	Sociological reductionism, atheoretical empiricism	Interdisciplinary macroanalytic historical-comparative studies
Eisenstadt	The political systems of preliterate societies, patrimonialism, tribal federations, feudalism, empires, modernization, modern political regimes	Nineteenth-century French and German ideological historiographic social-political thought	Increasing consensus on the defining qualities and functions of the political system. Continuing influence of state-society dichotomy in comparative studies	Political elites, types of political organization, social conditions for the emergence, stability, and continuity of the modern democratic regime	Continuing influence of state-society dichotomy encouraging ideological disputes rather than empirical inquiry and hindering studies of new nations	Comparative macroanalytic studies, research on new questions concerning stability legitimacy and consensus
Horowitz	How the economy, polity, and military interact with problems of social stratification and social structure	Eighteenth- and nineteenth-century Western European social theory	Continuing influence of European grand theorists. New impetus from survey researchers studying electoral and opinion data	Political parties and voting behavior	Present analytic schemes inadequate for understanding social management and control, colonialism and imperialism	Development of analytic schemes recognizing interrelatedness of politics with all other social institutions which facilitate prediction and can guide social policy

1. The field is more broadly conceived than usual.
2. The argument that the field focuses on stability and consensus rather than on conflict and change is a matter of some debate.

Neither of these points, however, would suggest that the content and organization of the following sections of this book are highly idiosyncratic. The review of six well-known discussions of political sociology indicates that this book will not give an unusual impression of what political sociology is all about.

NOTES

1. See Robert R. Alford, *Party and Society* (Chicago: Rand McNally, 1963); Morris Janowitz and David R. Segal, "Social Cleavage and Party Affiliation: Germany, Great Britain and the United States," *American Journal of Sociology*, 72, No. 6 (May 1967), 601–618; Richard F. Hamilton, *Class and Politics in the United States* (New York: John Wiley & Sons, 1972).

2. Seymour M. Lipset, "Political Sociology," in *Sociology Today*, Robert K. Merton, Leonard Broom, and Leonard S. Cottrell, Jr., eds. (New York: Basic Books, 1959), pp. 81–114.

3. Ibid. p. 81.

4. Joseph R. Gusfield, *Protest, Reform and Revolt: A Reader in Social Movements* (New York: John Wiley & Sons, 1970), p. vii.

5. For an example of the favorable view of student protesters see Richard Flacks, "Young Intelligentsia in Revolt," *Trans-action* 8 (June 1970), 49–58. An unfavorable picture is painted by Raymond Aron, "Student Rebellion: Vision of the Future or Echo from the Past?," *Political Science Quarterly* 84 (June 1969), 289–310.

6. For a description of totalitarian bureaucracy see Carl J. Frederich and Zbigniew K. Brzezinski, *Totalitarian Dictatorship and Autocracy*, 2nd ed. (New York: Praeger, 1966), pp. 205–218.

7. David E. Apter, *The Politics of Modernization* (Chicago: University of Chicago Press, 1965).

8. For an interesting attempt to deal theoretically with the links between the structures and activities of organizations and the structures and activities of the larger social order of which they are a part, see Odd Ramsöy, *Social Group as System and Subsystem* (New York: The Free Press, 1963). The related question of the relationship between individual and collective political behavior is treated in Heinz Eulau, *Micro-Macro Political Analysis* (Chicago: Aldine, 1969).

9. Scott Greer and Peter Orleans, "Political Sociology," in *Handbook of Modern Sociology*, E. L. Faris, ed. (Chicago, Rand McNally, 1964), pp. 808–851.

10. Ibid. p. 180.

11. Morris Janowitz, "Political Sociology," in *International Encyclopedia of the Social Sciences*, ed. David L. Sills (New York: Macmillan and The Free Press, 1968), vol. 12, pp. 298–307.

12. Alexis de Tocqueville, *The Old Regime and The Revolution* (New York: Doubleday Anchor, 1955). Originally published 1856. Thorstein Veblen, *Imperial Germany and the Revolution* (New York: Macmillan, 1915). W. I. Thomas with F. Znaniecki, *The Polish Peasant in Europe and America*, 5 vols. (Chicago: University of Chicago Press, 1918–1920).

13. Janowitz, "Political Sociology," p. 306.

14. Giovanni Sartori, "From the Sociology of Politics to Political Sociology," in *Politics and the Social Sciences*, Seymour M. Lipset, ed. (New York: Oxford University Press, 1969), pp. 65–100.

15. Ibid., p. 96.

16. Alford, *Party and Society.*

17. Sartori does believe that a genuine political sociology is already developing. He cites the introductory chapter of Seymour M. Lipset and Stein Rokkan, eds., *Party Systems and Voter Alignments—Cross National Perspectives* (New York: The Free Press, 1967) as a landmark which does deal with the problems of how conflict and changes are translated into a party system.

18. One major difference is related to Sartori's choice of the research literature on party systems and voter alignments to represent all of political sociology. Such a choice excludes from discussion all studies of nonmodern and nondemocratic political systems. While less work has been done on these topics than on other topics in political sociology, some important studies do exist. Considerably more research in these areas does seem likely in the future. Nevertheless, the differences which are discussed below proceed from the assumption that the literature chosen by Sartori does illustrate basic features of political sociology as it presently exists.

19. See, for example, Talcott Parsons, "Social Strains in America," in *The Radical Right,* Daniel Bell, ed. (New York: Doubleday, 1963), pp. 209–238; Seymour M. Lipset and Earl Raab, *The Politics of Unreason* (New York: Harper & Row, 1970).

20. For the most influential statement of this position, see William Kornhauser, *The Politics of Mass Society,* (New York: The Free Press, 1959).

21. S. N. Eisenstadt, *Political Sociology* (New York: Basic Books, 1971).

22. Reinhard Bendix and Seymour M. Lipset, "The Field of Political Sociology," in *Political Sociology: Selected Essays,* Lewis A. Coser, ed. (New York: Harper Torchbooks, 1967), p. 26.

23. Irving Louis Horowitz, *Foundations of Political Sociology* (New York: Harper & Row, 1972).

24. Ibid. p. xviii.

25. Ibid. p. xvii.

26. Ibid. p. 17.

27. Charles E. Lindblom, *Politics and Markets* (New York: Basic Books, 1977), p. ix.

28. Horowitz, *Foundations of Political Sociology,* p. xxi.

29. William C. Mitchell, "The Shape of Political Theory to Come—From Political Sociology to Political Economy," in *Politics and the Social Sciences,* Seymour M. Lipset, ed., pp. 101–136.

30. It is interesting that Horowitz also wants to encourage the development of policy-relevant theory and research.

31. Mitchell, "The Shape of Political Theory to Come," p. 104. Since Mitchell's article was published, the importance of economic factors in political life has become much more apparent. One reason for this is that the prices Americans pay for goods and services more than doubled between December 1969 and December 1979. The previous doubling of prices took twenty-four years, from 1945 to 1969. Prices have not doubled that fast since the decade of 1910–1920, when World War I caused widespread shortages of goods. In the 1980s political officials, parties, and candidates must present policies aimed at slowing the rate of inflation. Continued enjoyment of a high standard of material living, which such inflation threatens, is one of the cornerstones of the continuing legitimacy citizens attribute to the American political-economic system.

PART TWO
MICROANALYTIC STUDIES

CHAPTER FOUR
PARTICIPATION IN ROUTINE POLITICAL ACTIVITIES

THE CHARACTER OF ROUTINE PARTICIPATION

In the broadest sense *political* acts are those which are oriented toward the acquisition and use of power and authority within a specified social system. Since all social systems—tribes, families, churches, clubs, schools, hospitals, unions, nations, etc., have at least intermittent power structures, at times they all have going on within them some political activity. That is, in every tribe, in every family, in every church, and so on, at some time or other, binding decisions potentially affecting all the members of the system are made. (Binding decisions are those with which decision makers can compel compliance because they maintain a monopoly over the use of legitimate force within the system.)

Making binding decisions or attempting to influence the content of such decisions are acts of political participation.[1] Acts directed toward influencing the way in which binding decisions are made and toward determining who shall make such decisions within the system are also acts of political participation. So too are the comparatively passive acts of gathering information about binding decisions which have been made. Obeying binding decisions, however, does not constitute political participation but rather political compliance. Resisting binding decisions does constitute an act of political participation, but of a nonroutine kind.

While all social systems on occasion are scenes of political activity, political sociologists usually focus their attention on relatively large systems such as formal organizations, communities, and nations. This focus does not deny that politics go on within individual homes, churches, schools, clubs, and so on. It merely reflects a decision to study processes related to the making of binding decisions which have broader social significance.

Routine acts of political participation are those which are encouraged (as opposed to merely permitted) though not required within a social system. One is "doing one's duty" by routine participation. One is being a good citizen, a loyal organization member, a concerned student, by routine participation. Such participation expresses a belief in the legitimacy of the structure of power and authority of the social system. Voting and attending to the political content of the mass media serve as examples of routine participation.

Various acts of routine political participation obviously differ with respect to the amount of time, effort, and economic expense they require. For example, in the United States voting in national elections requires little time, effort, or personal expense, while running for public office, even at the local level, is usually quite costly in all those regards. There are several other related differences between forms of routine political participation. Lester Milbrath has distinguished the following:

1. *Overt versus covert.* Some political acts are relatively private, such as discussing politics within a family. Others are relatively public, such as discussing politics before the mass media. In most cases the overt acts are more costly.

2. *Approaching versus avoiding.* Some political acts are attractive to individuals while they may seek to avoid others. Avoiding behavior is probably the result of anticipating high costs while approaching behavior is probably associated with anticipation of high rewards.

3. *Episodic versus continuous.* Some forms of routine participation, like voting, take place at specified times. Such action involves a conscious decision to participate. Other forms, like contacting a political official, can be undertaken at any time and also involve a conscious decision to participate. Other forms of participation, such as holding a political office, can extend for periods of time. Actions that are continuous often become a part of one's routine pattern of living and involve little conscious decision to act or not to act. Continuous action generally is more costly than episodic action and requires a stable reward structure like a salary to insure performance of the action.

4. *Inputs versus outtakes.* Some political activities involve providing resources for the political system. Voting, for example, provides the political system with symbolic support. Other acts involve drawing on the resources of the political system. Seeking justice serves as an example. Some individuals tend to emphasize outtakes in their orientation to the political system and others tend to emphasize inputs.

5. *Expressive versus instrumental.* Expressive political acts are those which have primarily symbolic significance for the participant. Activity in itself is satisfying. Instrumental acts are oriented toward manipulating or changing things. The distinction is a motivational one. Any given act may be either primarily expressive or instrumental for any given actor.

6. *Verbal versus nonverbal.* Political acts vary in the extent to which they require

the use of verbal skills. Lacking such skills is a barrier to certain kinds of participation.

7. *Social versus nonsocial.* Political acts vary in the amount of social interaction they require. Campaigning door to door is a highly social act while contributing money to a campaign clearly is not. Lacking social skills and general sociability increases the costs of participating in acts requiring considerable interaction.[2]

Until the late 1960s it was generally assumed that routine forms of political participation could be arranged from those which are engaged in most frequently because they are not costly, to those which are relatively rare because they are costly. However, subsequent studies have shown that political participation is not a unidimensional phenomenon.

Using national sample survey data Verba and Nie found that the American public is not divided simply into more or less active citizens.[3] Rather, their data indicate that there are many types of participants engaging in different acts with different motives and different consequences. According to their analysis, political acts differ with respect to the type of influence they exert (i.e., how much pressure they put on political elites and how much information they convey), whether the activity is likely to bring the individual into open conflict with others, whether the outcome of the activity has individual or collective consequences, and with respect to the amount of initiative they require (i.e., how much they demand of one's time, resources, and skills). Data reveal four distinctive modes of participation:

1. *Voting:* puts high pressure on political figures but conveys relatively little information, involves the individual in conflict, has collective results, and requires little initiative.
2. *Campaign activity:* exerts high to low pressure and conveys little to much information, involves the individual in conflict, has collective results, and requires some initiative.
3. *Citizen-initiated contacts:* exert low to high pressure on elites and convey considerable information, do not usually involve the individual in conflict, have individual results, and require some to considerable initiative.
4. *Cooperative participation:* exerts low pressure but conveys considerable information, does not involve the individual in conflict, has both collective and particularized outcomes, and requires considerable initiative.

Citizens who are generally active or generally inactive can be identified, but analysis reveals that others tend to concentrate their activities by modes. Data suggest the following typology of political participants and indicate their proportion among the American citizenry:

1. *Inactives:* initiate no political activity (22%).
2. *Voting specialists:* vote rather regularly but do not try to influence the actions of government in any other way (21%).

3. *Parochial participants:* make particularized contacts with political officials on matters they themselves define as important; they also vote but do not engage in communal or campaign activity (4%).

4. *Communalists:* combine the willingness to be quite active in the affairs of their community while staying out of the relatively conflictful realm of campaigning (20%).

5. *Campaigners:* partisans who are most active in political campaigns but engage in almost no community activity (15%).

6. *Complete activists:* participate in all types of activity with great frequency (11%).

A study by Zipp and Smith based on Canadian data underscores the point that political participation is not a unidimensional phenomenon.[4] Specifically, their data revealed that voting and campaign participation are qualitatively different forms of activity. Voting is largely influenced by a variety of individual attributes (e.g., feelings of political efficacy, amount of political information). Campaign activity is largely influenced by social-interactive factors external to the individual (i.e., being contacted). Those whose social networks connect them to government functionaries, party officials, and so on are more likely to have the information and access needed for becoming involved in political activities beyond voting.

PRECONDITIONS FOR ROUTINE PARTICIPATION

There are a number of preconditions for participation in routine political activities. Unless these conditions are met it is unlikely that an individual will participate at all politically—even through acts which involve minimal costs. Using Maslow's hierarchy of needs,[5] James Davies organized sets of data suggesting several types of needs which, if left unfulfilled, will destroy politics for an individual.[6]

First and most basically, there are *physical needs.* Depoliticization follows physical deprivation. Data from laboratory studies of food deprivation, interviews with people from economically depressed villages and people in wartime detention camps all show that individuals who become preoccupied with meeting their physical needs are highly unlikely to participate in politics. (This has considerable importance for understanding levels of political participation in societies with marginal economies.) Closely related to physical needs is the *need for a relatively ordered, predictable, dependable environment.* Interviews with individuals who lived under police terror in the Soviet Union and with former prisoners who survived indoctrination of the Chinese during the Korean War showed that government efforts did not produce active support but rather induced political apathy.

Social needs are usually subsequent to physical needs. However, these too must be met if an individual is likely to become involved in politics. One sort of social need is the basic *need to associate*—the need for a sense of belonging and solidarity with others. People who are so lonely, so bereft of human contact that they are preoccupied with meeting this particular need will probably have to meet it first by interaction with others in nonpolitical groups. And before they can do even this, people must have acquired a minimal sense of belonging in the family itself. (The family is necessary for the individual to become social and thereafter political.) Isolation is negatively associated with political involvement. Furthermore, political participation cannot become nationwide until people develop a sense of community, i.e., a sense of common identity that makes possible collective political action.

The need for association is closely related to the *need for self-esteem and respect*. Social isolation destroys, among other things, the sense of having worth in the eyes of others. On the other hand, complete submission to others also destroys one's sense of self-worth. Individuals who are alone or who are completely absorbed are likely to be involved with the self and withdrawn from politics.

And finally, according to Maslow and Davies there is the need for *self-actualization*. People generally tend to pursue inherently satisfying activities in nonpolitical ways. Unless they find political activity rewarding in itself they will not participate, except in the case where their securing of some valued objectives is threatened. When people's achievement of personally significant goals becomes problematic or is interfered with, they turn to government.

This chapter concerns the behavior of those who do participate in routine politics—if only minimally. Hence, it is about individuals (1) who are not likely to be very poor, (2) who are not likely to be socially or psychologically isolated, (3) who are not likely to be politically harassed and, (4) (by way of contrast) who are not entirely satisfied with the order of their society, i.e., who perceive some threat to their self-actualization. In all societies there is some limitation on elegibility for participation in a variety of political acts. Age, sex, nativity, property ownership, and literacy generally have been important in this regard. Hence, this chapter is about people who not only meet social-psychological preconditions but who meet legal ones as well. It must be recognized that such individuals constitute a comparatively small segment of the world's population.

NATIONAL LEVELS OF ROUTINE PARTICIPATION

While data on levels of participation in the United States were presented above, questions must be raised about the amount of routine participation typical in other nations. The United States probably ranks first among the

TABLE 4-1 Frequency of Routine Political Participation*

	OFTEN	SOMETIMES	RARELY	NEVER	MISSING DATA** (=100%)
The Netherlands					
Read about politics in papers	35%	29%	20%	16%	(0)%
Discuss politics with friends	17	35	27	21	(0)
Convince friends to vote as self	3	7	12	77	(1)
Work to solve community problems	5	13	16	66	(1)
Attend political meetings	1	5	8	85	(1)
Contact officials or politicians	5	8	13	73	(1)
Campaign for candidate	1	2	6	90	(1)
Britain					
Read about politics in papers	36	30	19	15	(1)
Discuss politics with friends	16	30	23	30	(1)
Convince friends to vote as self	3	6	8	82	(1)
Work to solve community problems	4	13	13	69	(2)
Attend political meetings	2	7	12	78	(2)
Contact officials or politicians	2	9	13	74	(2)
Campaign for candidate	1	3	3	91	(2)
United States					
Read about politics in papers	47	27	17	8	(1)
Discuss politics with friends	27	37	24	11	(1)
Convince friends to vote as self	6	13	21	59	(1)
Work to solve community problems	8	28	25	38	(1)
Attend political meetings	3	15	25	57	(1)

Contact officials or politicians	4%	23%	24%	48%	(1)%
Campaign for candidate	2	12	15	70	(0)
Germany					
Read about politics in papers	46	27	19	8	(0)
Discuss politics with friends	13	30	31	26	(1)
Convince friends to vote as self	7	16	23	54	(1)
Work to solve community problems	4	10	21	64	(1)
Attend political meetings	5	17	24	52	(1)
Contact officials or politicians	3	8	16	72	(1)
Campaign for candidate	2	6	13	78	(1)
Austria					
Read about politics in papers	30	28	22	19	(0)
Discuss politics with friends	13	32	31	25	(0)
Convince friends to vote as self	5	12	14	69	(1)
Work to solve community problems	4	10	12	73	(1)
Attend political meetings	5	13	20	61	(1)
Contact officials or politicians	2	10	16	72	(1)
Campaign for candidate	2	3	7	87	(1)

*Percentages in this table add row-wise to 100 percent. Rounding errors are possible. The percentages are based on the full samples in each country. Ns are: The Netherlands: 1201; Britain: 1483; United States: 1719; Germany: 2307; Austria: 1584.

**Missing data includes don't know and not ascertained.

Source: Samuel H. Barnes, Max Kaase, *et al., Political Action: Mass Participation in Five Western Democracies* (Beverley Hills, CA: Sage, 1979), pp. 541–542.

nations of the world with respect to the proportion of its population meeting all of the first three social-psychological preconditions for participation. The United States has, by world comparison, a highly educated population. It has a diversified mass media system which penetrates virtually all levels of the social structure. It has a profuse number of voluntary associations. It also has social norms encouraging political participation. All of the factors should work to increase the amount of routine political activity found in the United States beyond what is found elsewhere in the world.[7]

Several points must be kept in mind while reading multinational data on participation. First, the meaning of a given political action varies within and among nations. For example, for American blacks, registering and voting in a strongly intolerant political climate involves a willingness to take significant risks that such participation does not involve in a supportive political climate.[8] Similarly, engaging in political discussions in the United States is not the same thing as engaging in public discussion in several Latin American or Eastern European nations. And so on. Second, some data are derived from government sources. The governments of many nations have vested interests in presenting certain images of their levels of citizen participation to the world community. The images they present may not be accurate. Third, other data are derived from sample surveys in which individuals are asked about their political behavior. Their responses may reflect their perceptions of social norms rather than their actual behavior.[9]

The most readily available and relatively comparable multinational data on routine political participation are voting data. Although one cannot make inferences about level of participation in other forms of routine politics from voting data, such information at least provides a first clue to similarities of and differences between nations with respect to their general level of citizen participation in routine activities.

Russett and his colleagues report that voting turnout ranges from a low of 1.9 percent in Rhodesia (now Zimbabwe) to a high of 99.6 percent in the Soviet Union.[10] Their data show that higher levels of voting are found in more industrialized societies.[11] Comparison of levels of voting participation between nations at similar levels of industrialization does not reveal so vast a range of participation rates as the Rhodesia-Soviet Union comparison suggests.

The study by Barnes, Kaase, and their colleagues of mass participation in five Western democracies (Austria, the Netherlands, the United States, Great Britain, and West Germany) provides data on seven other forms of routine participation. See Table 4-1.

ORGANIZATION OF FINDINGS

In this chapter data will be presented on the bearing of experiences in the family, in the church, and in various other settings—specifically work and the school—on the likelihood of individuals participating in the routine politics of their community and nation. Data on the impact of class-linked belief and value systems will also be discussed.

Within the context of empirical microanalysis of routine politics, families, churches, social classes, schools, and work organizations are seen as settings within which ideas, feelings, and motives are acquired which influence a person's pattern of political participation. That is, the family, the church, social class, the school, and the occupational group are viewed as agents of political socialization. Families, churches, social classes, schools, and work organizations are also primary loci for establishing social networks. The social relationships formed in and through these social units which are of particular importance for routine political participation are those which directly or indirectly connect individuals with political officials and organizations. Research dealing with the importance of parties and the role of mobilization in political participation will be discussed in Chapters 7 and 8.

The beliefs, values, norms, sentiments, and motives which are transmitted in these contexts which affect the likelihood of an individual's participation in routine politics include those concerning:

1. *political participation itself* (Is politics important? Is participation worthwhile?)
2. *the self as a political actor* (Am I personally capable of manipulating aspects of my political environment?)
3. *the political behavior of others* (Do others participate who are like me in certain salient respects? Do others expect me to participate? Are political officials responsive to citizen demands? Are others trustworthy?)
4. *government* (Who are the political officials? What are some of their more salient personal and professional qualities? How do I feel about these particular officials?)
5. *the regime* (What are the general norms which govern the operation of the political system? How do I feel about these norms?)
6. *the political community* (How do I feel about being a member of the political system [local community, state, region, nation]?)[12]
7. *other political systems* (How do I feel about other social systems whose politics I perceive to affect the social systems to which I belong?)

Descriptions of research dealing with the bearing of experience in the family, in the church, in the school, and at work on the answers individuals give to such questions constitute the remainder of this chapter. At the end of each section dealing with the influence of one of the agents of political socialization on routine participation, some consideration will be given to the relation of the research to discussions initiated by Marx, Weber, and Durkheim.

There are two primary sources of detailed information on the role which family, religion, social class, school, work, and work-related associations each plays in determining individuals' patterns of participation in routine politics: voting studies and studies of political socialization. The vast majority of these investigations have been conducted in the United States. They tend to focus on the development of the political orientations of youth. There are also other sources of such information, though the detail they provide is considerably less. These include social-psychological studies comparing the political orientations of the citizens of two or more nations and descriptions of politically relevant socialization practices in individual nations.

KINSHIP

Introduction

The very meaning of "family" and the political role this social unit plays in nonindustrial societies is vastly different from its meaning and its political role in industrial societies. The structure and political functions of families in societies undergoing industrialization is different from both of these. And among industrial societies the political significance of the family in democratic systems is not the same as in totalitarian systems. Such variety makes it necessary to limit discussion in this section, which will deal with the bearing of the nuclear family on routine participation in contemporary Western industrial democracies. More specifically it will consider the family as a context within which children acquire beliefs, values, norms, sentiments, and motives which are likely to affect the pattern of their routine political participation as adults.

Although there is little research on exactly how children acquire their politically relevant orientations, it does seem clear that many are learned in unplanned ways. Much political learning on the part of children is not the result of conscious efforts at political indoctrination. Furthermore, many of the beliefs and attitudes acquired in the family which later influence political behavior are not manifestly political. For example, the very general belief that, for most part, others are trustworthy, or the feeling that, on occasion, you can manipulate your environment in ways you desire, both are positively associated with routine political participation.

Several factors contribute to the great importance of the family as an agent of political socialization. The family is a social system within which there is a considerable amount of interaction and to which generally there is deep emotional attachment. It is the first agent of socialization children experience. During the initial period of their physical, intellectual, and moral development it has virtually exclusive control over them. For a long period it is the sole source to which they can turn for the satisfaction of all basic needs. Children identify with, act, and think like those who are regularly relevant to the satisfaction of their needs.[13] The family is hierarchically structured and serves as the first setting in which children can observe and participate in processes of making social decisions. Finally, it is through the family that individuals acquire many of their politically relevant social identities such as religion and ethnicity.

There is a major reason to believe that the family into which one is born will have limited impact on one's adult political behavior. This is the fact that once one leaves one's family home, the school, peer group, and later work and other associational contacts and experiences will produce orientations which are less remote from and more directly relevant to one's adult political activities. Research described below identifies some politically relevant orientations acquired early in one's life within the family. Studies are also presented which consider the enduring character of these orientations and which assess the relative importance of the family as an agent of political socialization.

Strength of Family Influence

A number of factors determine the extent of the influence which children's families will have on their later patterns of routine political participation. These include:

1. the relative attractiveness of the family to the child
2. parental agreement on politics
3. cohesiveness of the family
4. parental interest in politics

The more attractive a group is to a person the more likely he or she is to adopt its norms. The question of strength of attraction arises when an individual is drawn to a number of groups which have incompatible norms. For example, a young person can have parents who are staunch Republicans and highly attractive peers who are equally staunch Democrats. In such a situation where, for some reason or other, a choice must be made, all things being equal, an individual will choose the norms of the group which is more attractive to him.[14] However, most political situations do not involve forced choices. In most contexts, such as voting for example, one can avoid making a choice by withdrawing from the situation. In the case of voting, one can consciously choose not to vote, can "forget" to vote, or can fail to vote because one has lost interest. This so-called withdrawal effect is a common reaction to such a decision-making situation. The child with Republican parents and Democratic friends is not likely to have strong partisan feelings or to maintain a high level of interest in politics. If such weakened political orientations persist into adulthood, he is not likely to be active in routine political affairs.[15]

Children face another situation of conflicting norms if parents disagree politically. Data indicate that, in general, family influence tends to be stronger when the members' viewpoints are homogeneous.[16] Individuals with parents who support different parties are less likely to have a strong party preference than are those from families in which both parents support the same party.[17] In turn, weak party identification tends to be negatively associated with routine participation. According to Niemi, the ability of parents to instill partisan orientations is so influenced by parental agreement that "whether . . . parents agree with each other seems to be more important than the family's degree of interest in politics, the compatibility of family members, demographic factors such as region or personal characteristics such as race and sex."[18]

The more cohesive a family is the more likely it is that its young members will adopt the political orientations of their parents. McClosky and Dahlgren show that, with respect to orientations toward political parties, the higher the rate of interaction and the stronger the emotional ties between child and parents, the greater the impact of the family.[19] However, where families do not establish clear partisan orientations in their children, the children are less likely to be politically involved when they reach maturity. In addition, Maccoby, Mathews, and Morton found that cohesive families tend to try to resolve political conflicts which arise within them through discussion.[20] This makes politics more salient for the family. Where politics remains salient to children, they are more likely to participate in political life.

A number of studies indicate a positive association between the level of children's interest in politics and the level of their parents' interest. Politically interested parents tend to communicate political information to their children and tend to transmit a positive party identification. Having a party identification and being politically informed are positively associated with routine participation. Marvick and Nixon conclude that politically involved persons tend to be the products of politically interested families.[21] Langton notes that children reared in families where parents are interested in politics, discuss politics among themselves, and also participate in political activities are more likely to develop a sense of being politically effective than children from less politically interested families.[22] For adults, a feeling that one can have an impact on political affairs through one's own action encourages routine participation.

In sum, the politically interested, politically homogeneous, cohesive family which the child finds attractive is most likely to have a great impact as an agent of political socialization. We now turn to consider family socialization practices which tend to produce orientations related to routine participation.

Family Socialization Practices

Within the family children observe, sometimes participate in, and continually are subject to social desion-making processes. They are sheltered within the family while being prepared for participation in the broader society. Family socialization practices differ in a number of ways which have some bearing on children's development of orientations relevant to their subsequent patterns of routine political participation. These include:

1. the structure of parental decision making
2. the participation of children in making family decisions
3. modes of establishing discipline and responsibility
4. parental protectiveness

It is commonly noted that men are more interested in, informed about, and generally active in politics than are women. This observation promotes the belief that within families husbands rather than wives set the political tone—i.e., establish party identification for the entire family, are the primary personal source of political information, establish views on issues, and so on. It is the essence of this assumption that, when political questions arise in the family, it is the male who decides them.

There are several explanations for these views. Lane notes that the association of polities with power and domination tends to discourage women from participating in many kinds of political activities in Western culture. The culture emphasizes a dependent and politically less competent image of women which tends to reduce their partisanship and sense of political effectiveness and defines a less active political role for them.[23] Greenstein reviewed literature revealing that adult sex differences in political behavior have their sources in early preadolescent differences.[24] His own data showed that whenever questionnaire responses differentiated between boys and girls the former were invariably "more political." He further found that children of both sexes were more likely to choose their father than their mother as an appropriate source of voting advice.[25]

Despite such observations and findings, additional studies demonstrate that the father is not as clearly the sole source of family political decision making as the preceding suggests. On the basis of a national sample of high school students and their parents, Jennings and Niemi report that, though differences are slight, mothers rather than fathers tend to be more influential politically within the family. In a comparison of student-mother and student-father correlations in families in which the parents disagree, the student-mother correlation was higher than the student-father correlation 13 of 20 times with 3 being ties and 4 showing minimal advantage for the fathers.[26] In a study of college-age students, Thomas also found greater congruence of political attitudes between mothers and their children than between fathers and their children.[27] In France, where there is evidence of widespread absence of party loyalties, many persons do not even know their father's party identification.[28] Such studies run counter to the thesis of the political omnipotence of the father.

While the father does not appear to have as great a political impact on the family as might be expected, the lack of a dominant male head of household does significantly alter political socialization within the family and does have important effects on children's later patterns of political participation. In a study of some 12,000 elementary school children in 8 large and medium-sized American cities, Hess and Torney found that boys who perceived their mother "was boss" in the family tended to have lower senses of efficiency and lower levels of political interest, participated less frequently in political discussions, engaged in fewer political activities, and had less concern about political issues than boys who believed their father "was boss."[29] They also found that, for children of both sexes, those who believed that their father could not "make people do what he wants" also were lower in sense of efficacy, participated less frequently in political discussions, engaged in fewer political activities, and had less concern about political issues than children who believed that their father was high in power. Three studies conducted by Langton using a sample of Jamaican families and a national survey of high school students in the United States showed that boys from nuclear families in which the mother was dominant were less politically efficacious, less politically interested, and less likely to engage in political activity than those from father-dominant families. This is particularly true among the least educated families. Langton also found that, in general, the structure of parental decision making had little politically relevant impact upon girls.[30]

Another study by Lane dealing with the consequences of patterns of parental decision making in the United States and Germany involved asking adult respondents how much influence they remember having in their family decisions when they were around sixteen years old.[31] The respondents were also asked how satisfied they remembered being with that amount of influence. Those who remembered having had at least some influence in their family during adolescence and who were not dissatisfied with the amount of influence they had had tended more than others to feel that people care about you and had a sense of understanding complex affairs and of having some influence over them. These feelings were found to be positively associated with participation in routine politics such as voting, discussing politics, and following accounts of political and governmental affairs. In an earlier study Almond and Verba found that in five countries (the United Kingdom, Germany, Italy, Mexico, and the United States) family participation was positively associated with political participation among those with primary school education.[32] However, among those with higher education there was very little connection between family participation and political participation. They suggest that for the better educated political participation receives support outside the family sphere and thus family participation becomes less crucial as a determinant of political involvement.

Merelman has identified three additional dimensions of child-rearing practices which are politically relevant: mode of punishing children, warmth of relationship between parents and children, and the age at which children are first expected to be responsible for their own behavior.[33] Each of these is related to children's identification with their parents and to their cognitive and moral development. Identification and cognitive and moral development in turn affect political participation.[34] According to Merelman, the optimal pattern for the intellectual and moral growth of children combines rapid shouldering of responsibility, the use of psychological rather than physical discipline, and continuing warmth. However, this pattern is not frequently found. Many parents believe that warmth, affection, and "permissiveness" are incompatible with early assumption of responsibilities. Many who do attempt early training find it difficult to remain affectionate toward their children when errors occur and resort to physical punishment. This often produces anxiety on the part of both parents and children and establishes a relatively cold relationship between them.

Merelman reports on experimental evidence suggesting that frustration and excessive physical punishment make behavior rigid and retard cognitive development. Specifically, they hinder development of the capacity to think temporally, i.e., to link present trends to desired future states or to past experiences. Frustration and physical punishment also reduce responsiveness and alertness to new information and retard language ability.[35] These effects persist after the cessation of frustration and physical punishment. Severe discipline of children and lack of warmth in their parents' relationship to them seems likely to interfere with cognitive development and the acquisition of language abilities and thereby to inhibit inclination to participate in routine polities. An earlier study by Mussen and Wyssinski also suggests that rigid and severely punitive parents are likely to have politically apathetic children. Their explanation is somewhat different from that of Merelman. Punitiveness is seen as discouraging independence of thought and action and as encouraging passive acceptance of authority.

While subjecting children rather regularly to severe punishment may lead to their later political apathy, so too may the effort to protect children from many aspects of their "hostile and threatening" environment. Pinner's study of Belgian, Dutch, and French high school and university students found that parents who attempted to restrict or control many of their children's contacts outside the home and to guide their intellectual and emotional growth with "much anxious care" tended to produce in their children distrust of political processes and institutions.[36]

In sum, the family in which the father and mother share decision making or in which the father is dominant, in which children take part in family decision making, in which children shoulder responsibility at an early age, in which psychological rather than physical discipline is used, in which there are warm parent-child relations, and in which parents do not overprotect their children is the ideal family context for producing orientations positively associated with routine political participation. We now turn to consider historical and institutional factors which affect the role of the family as an agent of political socialization.

Historical and Institutional Factors

It has already been pointed out that the political significance of the family varies from one nation to another and from time to time within nations. Past and present historical experiences and modal differences in the nature of parent-child relationships help account for such diversity. For example, Lane has observed that in the United States adolescent rebellion against one's father is not an important source of political orientations. The permissive family structure and the relatively low salience of politics in the United States makes other forms of rebellion such as quitting school or delinquency more likely.[37] In reviewing Lane's argument, Dawson and Prewitt suggest that adolescent rebellion may be more common and more politically significant in societies in which family structure is more authoritarian and in which rapid social and political change cause tension between generations.[38]

Jaros draws attention to the fact that agents of early political socialization cannot possibly prepare anyone for unforeseen political, economic, and military crises. These often require the acquisition of new standards for evaluating political objects and the development of new patterns of social and political participation. The Great Depression of the 1930s, the postwar period in Japan, the American civil rights movement of the 1950s and 1960s, and the American crisis over the Vietnam War in the late 1960s and early 1970s serve as examples of events which significantly changed the political orientations of entire generations.[39]

Inglehart's comparative study of political socialization in the Netherlands, Belgium, Italy, France, West Germany, and Great Britain notes that in the 1960s many of those acting as personal agents of political socialization—parents, teachers, organization advisers, and others—grew up during periods of great political and economic insecurity and instability.[40] During those times needs centered around subsistence, economic security, and symbols of affluence to enhance status. Such needs were tied to a high evaluation of economic security and domestic order. These values, formed during youth, were retained. Political socialization in the industrialized West in the 1960s and early 1970s proceeded in the context of an unprecedentedly long period of affluence. Children grew up with values that had no direct relation to the need for economic security. Rather, younger cohorts of the middle classes of that period pursued a set of "post-bourgeois" values related to associational, aesthetic, and intellectual needs. These were expressed in Ingelhart's study by their choice of "giving the people more say in making important political decisions" and of "protecting freedom of speech" over "maintaining order in the nation" and "fighting rising prices." Inglehart hypothesizes that these value differences produced by differing historical experiences were likely to be a source of intergenerational political conflict. Such conflict could generate interest in and concern about political affairs and lead to increasing levels of political participation of both routine and nonroutine types.[41]

Early Theories and Contemporary
Micro-Research: Kinship

Contemporary empirical studies of the political role of the family seem far removed from the interests of the founders of the sociological tradition. The writings of Marx, Weber, and Durkheim do contain discussions of the political significance of kinship. For the most part their discussions are macroanalytic, historical-comparative, and concerned with change. The studies described above are microanalytic, deal almost exclusively with contemporary Western industrial societies, and concern the acquisition of beliefs and values which encourage participation supporting at least the basic features of an ongoing political system. Despite such differences, present-day research does represent an extension and elaboration of earlier themes. Many findings are relevant to questions raised by the earlier writers.

Microprocesses have a direct bearing on the structure, functioning, stability, and change of political systems at all levels of social organization. Easton and Dennis have identified four ways in which political socialization within the family can affect the polity.[42] First, the family can help assure acceptance of authoritative decisions. It can promote beliefs and attitudes supporting the legitimacy of the ongoing system. Second, the family can transmit beliefs about what is and what is not appropriate to demand of the polity. The development of a sense of political self-restraint limits the volume and variety of demands with which a polity is called upon to deal. This prevents the polity from being so overloaded with demands that it is incapable of processing any but a few. A third contribution of the family is the transmission of knowledge, skills, and motivation to take some active part in politics. The persistence of political systems requires trained and motivated persons to perform formal political roles. Finally, the family can generate diffuse positive support for the polity. The presence of such support becomes crucial during periods of social stress.

Marx saw the family as a social structure which perpetuated inequalities through the mechanism of property inheritance. Contemporary research also focuses on the ways in which the family contributes to the maintenance and stability of the political systems of class societies—and thereby to the perpetuation of the basic features of their distributive systems. However, the family's conservative function is seen as being performed primarily through its activities as an agent of political socialization. Contemporary microanalytic research on the political role of the family does not contradict Marx. Rather, it extends his discussions and brings to mind his analyses of ideology. Research indicates that political orientations promoted by the family do tend to justify and support the maintenance of the status quo.

The family generally does play a conservative role in political life, but three points must be kept in mind. First, not all subgroups in a complex society transmit orientations highly supportive of the ongoing political system. For example, Greenberg's study of American black children reveals that they are less supportive of the political system than are comparable white children. They also become increasingly less supportive as they grow older.[43] Second, family political socialization is immune from direct government control. Within the family orientations critical of or even hostile toward the ongoing system can be inculcated. Third, family socialization can support, rather than oppose, even revolutionary political changes once they have occurred. For example Inkeles's interviews of Russian immigrants suggest that parents who had grown up in Russia prior to the revolution and whose own personal political orientations reflected this fact nevertheless tried to make their children into loyal Soviet citizens by having them accept the principles of the new revolutionary government.[44]

Weber pointed out the diminished role which kinship plays in Western rationalized societies in comparison to the role it plays in the non-Western, less rationalized world. Rationalization was seen as reducing the political significance of kinship. Nevertheless, the contrasts Weber presented were never intended to suggest that kinship plays no important political role in rationalized societies. In fact, his discussion of legitimation suggests a point at which the impact of the family can be most significant.

According to Weber, rule in rationalized society rests in part on belief in the validity of commands given in accordance with a consistent set of abstract, impersonal rules. Establishing positive orientations toward "the law" therefore is a crucial function for the political system of rationalized societies. The family is the major context in which this can be accomplished. A study by Easton and Hess does show that, at least in the United States, by age nine or ten children are aware of and more of less committed to legalistic concepts such as democracy and civil liberties.[45] It seems quite likely that some information about and feeling toward such abstract concepts were acquired within their homes. It also seems likely that beliefs and attitudes concerning legal rights and obligations and social responsibilities will affect patterns of routine political participation. Weber's writings can serve as a guide to empirical research by encouraging further work on the social-psychological processes by which beliefs necessary for the legitimation of various systems of domination become established. Such research would be of particular interest to the leaders of contemporary nations in Eastern Europe and the Third World.

Durkheim postulated an inverse relationship between the political significance of the family in a society and the degree of differentiation of the society's division of labor. He believed that in highly differentiated societies occupational associations would be the only structured units other than the state itself with genuine political importance. Only they could effectively intervene between the individual and the state and restrain it from infringing on individual rights. Only they could effectively generate moral norms which defined legitimate and realizable objectives for masses of individuals and thus reduce anomie.

While the occupational association does have considerable importance in modern political life, so too does the family. While economic exchanges serve to integrate a modern nation both socially and politically, so too do values, beliefs, and feelings. The critical role of the family in establishing political identities, party loyalties, and patterns of routine participation is missed by Durkheim's analysis. Contemporary microanalytic research on the political significance of the family reveals the limitations of Durkheim's understanding of the industrial order which was only beginning to develop during his lifetime. His positive contributions to political sociology lie elsewhere.

RELIGION

Introduction

Like the family, the religious organization is not manifestly an agent of political socialization. On occasion churches do take public stands on political issues—as, for example, did many churches in the United States in the 1960s with respect to civil rights and the Vietnam War. However, the basic thrust of church activity is not directed toward influencing political life. The beliefs, values, and sentiments transmitted by the church which do have some impact on political behavior most commonly are not overtly political. For example, many churches, particularly those of the poor, emphasize the relative unimportance of a person's brief period here on earth in contrast to the significance of an existence in an eternal hereafter. Such a devaluation of the temporal world is often coupled with the belief that the physical and social world are parts of God's order and, as such, cannot be significantly altered by the activities of people. An otherworldly orientation and a belief in one's inability to alter the social world through one's own action or through participation in collective action will certainly discourage involvement in even routine politics.

The family tends to be an auxiliary of the church—for the most part reasserting its tenets and establishing a firmer commitment to them than the church could establish on its own. In the United States, church and family together tend to reinforce the political orientations encouraged by other major socializing agents such as the school. However, Dawson and Prewitt point out that this is not true in all countries. For example, "In diversified political cultures, like those of France and Italy, the differences in political orientations taught by a conservative Catholic family, the governmental school system, a socialist oriented labor union and proletarian parties are great. It is not uncommon for individuals in these nations to have contact with each of these types of socializing agents."[46] The experience of such discontinuities may increase political withdrawal tendencies. However, conflicts are more likely to be dealt with not by withdrawal, but by accepting the political norms of the preferred socializing agent.[47]

Religious groups tend to coincide with socioeconomic, ethnic, and racial grouping. This makes it difficult to determine the extent to which religion per se affects the political behavior of individuals. Data do show that in the United States white Protestants are from two to four times as likely to become Republicans as their Catholic counterparts even when controlling for class level of father and father's political preference.[48] This suggests the existence of an independent "religious factor." Other findings also support the conclusion that religion operates as an independent variable apart from the influence of other factors such as social class. For example, in industrial societies lower classes tend to support welfare state activities of the government and tend to favor government regulation of the economy. However, one study found middle-class Jews more likely to express the view that the government is doing too little than were working-class members of either white Protestant or Catholic groups. The study also found that an extremely low percentage of working-class white Protestants were favorably disposed to the idea of nationalizing basic industries. This idea found even less favor with them than it did with members of other religious groups who were predominantly middle class.[49]

When turning from issue orientation to routine participation, the impact of the religious factor can also be seen. In the United States, Jews tend to be somewhat more active than Catholics, who, in turn, tend to be somewhat more active than Protestants.[50] The source of these differences appears to be more organizational than theological. (This will be discussed below.) The relation of religion to nonroutine participation and to mass political movements will be discussed in later chapters.

Religion and Early Political Socialization

In the family children have their first encounters with authority. Here they learn that they do not have unchallenged command of the social world. However, early on they perceive their parents as having this power. Parents seem to be omniscient and omnipotent and are taken to be the source of immutable social rules. Children often believe that their parents have control even over natural phenomena such as the weather. At some point such views give way to the realization that parents are not omnipotent but are themselves subject to rules not of their own making. The sources of such rules are vaguely understood to be religion and, to a lesser extent, politics. In fact, many children confuse religious and political authority. Jaros observed that

> there is some evidence that young children confuse religious ritual with patriotic observance. The similarity between hymns and national anthems, between flags and crosses, is obvious. Great sanctity can surround both realms. It is not at all surprising that U.S. children regard the pledge of allegiance as a prayer, and indeed a request to God for aid and protection.[51]

Hess and Torney noted:

> One striking aspect of young children's comments about the President (whether Eisenhower or Kennedy) was the similarity of the image of the President to images usually associated with religious authority or even the Deity. The President was described as "about the best person in the world" as having absolute power over the nation, as being personally interested in the needs of each individual citizen.[52]

The authors felt that such findings suggested the hypothesis that "the teachings of the church which induce respect for religious authority and law (possibly) generalize to non-religious authority systems, particularly ones in which the image of supreme authority has certain features common to religious figures."[53] It seems likely that certain features of early religious training encourage later attribution of legitimacy to the political system. In turn such sentiments tend to encourage support of the political system through routine participation.

Religious Organizations and Political Activity

Religious organizations can influence routine participation by:

1. bestowing legitimacy on the political system
2. providing experience with democratic procedures
3. providing a context for developing politically relevant skills

Factors affecting the impact of an individual's church on routine participation include its:

1. social history of acceptance or rejection
2. cohesiveness
3. degree of organization
4. significance as a status group

Lenski found in his study of 750 residents of Detroit that religion plays an important role in supporting the Western principle of "government by law, not by men." Respondents were asked whether they preferred a president who adheres to the rules or one who ignores the rules in the interest of efficiency. Persons who were relatively inactive in their churches were found to be roughly half again as likely to prefer the man who ignores the rules. Here again religious involvement seems to encourage the feeling that the political order is legitimate and deserves support through routine participation.

Active involvement in the church is not only positively associated with support for the rule of law among American Protestants (but not among Catholics) it is also negatively associated with maintaining highly critical attitudes toward public officials. Lenski explains this relationship in this way:

> ... The democratic character of the Protestant churches provides valuable experience in, and stimulates commitment to democratic procedures especially for those who are active in the churches. This experience and commitment later become translated into more frequent and effective political action in the secular realm, and ultimately provide the basis for a greater sense of satisfaction with democratic institutions.[54]

There are additional historical and organizational factors linking religious commitment and political behavior. Milbrath has hypothesized that religious groups, such as Jews, which have historically suffered extreme persecution and discrimination are likely to participate more heavily in routine politics to forstall use of the machinery of the state for oppression. Groups without such fears have less motive for political activity.[55]

The cohesiveness of a religious group, a factor not unrelated to its social history of acceptance or rejection, is also positively associated with the level of its members' political participation. Group cohesiveness may in part account for the fact that, as we have seen, in the United States Jews generally are more active in routine politics than Catholics, who are generally more active than Protestants.[56] Also related to group cohesiveness, partly as cause and partly as effect, is the extent of group organization. Members of more highly organized religious groups such as Jews and Catholics participate more than persons who acknowledge other religious affiliations. The existence of some degree of organization itself may tend to increase a feeling of mutual interest and raise the salience of belonging to the group. Participation in the organized social life of the church heightens these feelings.[57]

Research indicates that religious groups are accorded differing amounts of social honor and prestige. In the United States, for example, Catholics enjoy higher social status than Jews. This occurs in spite of the fact that Jews generally tend to be employed in more prestigious occupations and tend to have higher incomes and higher levels of education than Catholics. Religious groups are thus status groups whose relative positions are not entirely determined by the class composition of their membership. Such groups have considerable importance in contemporary politics. According to Lenski:

> . . . Political controversy in modern industrial societies has a tendency to change in character from one decade to the next. Sometimes the basic controversies are between classes; other times they are between status groups. Class-based controversies normally dominate politics in periods of economic crisis, while controversies involving status groups tend to dominate in periods of prosperity.[58]

Individuals often seek to enhance the standing of the status groups with which they identify. A status gain or loss for their group is a gain or loss for them as well: ". . . The denial of equal honor and respect to all socio-religious groups may be as powerful a factor in stimulating political discontent as the denial of economic advantages and political authority."[59] When the occasions arise it may be that the desire to enhance the status of one's religious group (and thus one's own status) operates as an important stimulus to political activity. This may account for such occurrences as heavy Catholic turnout at the polls in support of Catholic candidates and on occasions when social policies of interest to the church (e.g., abortion, divorce) are voted on.[60] The election of a member of one's religious group may give one a feeling that the group, and therefore oneself, is more powerful and thus deserving of enhanced status. The outcome of a referendum desired by one's church may have the same effect. Similarly, an attack on a coreligionist who holds public office may be seen as a status threat. A defeat on a referendum may be viewed as an expression of public hostility to the social objectives of the church and its members.

Early Theories and Contemporary Micro-Research: Religion

Much of the empirical research on the political role of the church in contemporary industrial societies has many points in common with equivalent research on the family. It too is microanalytic and focuses on the transmission of beliefs, values, and feelings which encourage participation supporting the basic features of ongoing political systems. The one major exception to this is the study of the political role of the churches of the poor. Such investigations show that their otherworldly emphasis encourages political apathy and withdrawal. However, it can be argued that these orientations of the poor support the status quo by depoliticizing those who should have the greatest interest in changing the political and stratification system of their society.

Microanalysis of the political functions of the church reveals three contributions it makes to political stability in common with the family: bolstering acceptance of authoritative political decisions by promoting beliefs, attitudes and feelings supporting the exercise of authority; motivating individuals to take part in routine politics by providing them with the experience of democratic participation and thereby also helping them to develop relevant skills; and generating diffuse positive support—in the case of religion, for "God and country."

Marx contended that in all societies in which there are social classes, religion is a source of values and beliefs which help maintain political-economic inequalities. To the extent that supporting an ongoing political system constitutes supporting the perpetuation of political and economic inequalities, the research just reviewed supports Marx in two instances. Early religious training and later church involvement do motivate routine participation. The theology of the churches of the poor does tend to depoliticize those most likely to want change in the political-economic order.

These facts have only indirect bearing on the major thrust of Marx's discussion of religion—that it is the opiate of the masses. Description of research more directly related to this hypothesis will be presented in Chapter 5, which deals with nonroutine participation. There, discussion will focus on the relationship between religiosity and militancy.

The major theoretical shortcoming in Marx's analysis of religion is his failure to recognize the importance of status groups in political life. As Weber argued, within any society the distribution of social honor can be independent of the relations of production. Status groups do not always correspond to social classes. In advanced industrial societies much of the political activity of individuals with strong religious identification may be understood better as motivated by status concerns than by economic interests. Politically active American Catholics and politically active American Jews are likely to be seeking social recognition rather than economic redistribution through their routine political participation.

Two major hypotheses which have been investigated within the framework of empirical microanalysis and which were discussed above are present in the writing of Weber. The first is that religion performs important legitimating functions. Religion has this function even in rational-legal systems. Effective and continuing rule of law requires supporting social attitudes. The maintenance of a rational order is dependent on the presence of nonrational factors. Weber noted that charismatic rule has a "religious quality." In a sense, so too does rational-legal rule. Without some shared feeling that any given structure of authority is something over and above a set of socially useful conventions, support for that structure in the form of routine participation is likely to be considerably diminished. We shall return to this topic in Chapter 7.

The second major hypothesis suggested by Weber is that a status group—a set of persons who have in common life chances determined by their social honor—can serve as a base for collective political action. According to Weber, any quality or qualities shared by a set of persons can be a source of their social honor. Clearly, religion is one of the most important of such qualities. On the individual level, pursuit of enhanced social status through support of the political fortunes of coreligionists or through supporting church-sponsored social policies does not seem to be a rare or unlikely motive for routine participation.

Durkheim provides both a pattern of explanation and a key hypothesis with which contemporary micro-research can explore the bearing of religious beliefs, attitudes, and feelings on political participation. The pattern of explanation directs attention to possible links between the presence of various religious orientations in a society and the stability and maintenance of that society, including the stability and maintenance of its political institutions. This pattern certainly guided much of the research described above. Its major limitation is that it deflects attention away from the ways in which religion can divide groups, alienate individuals, and thus foster socially disruptive political conflict.

Durkheim held that in societies in which there is little division of labor central authority embodies the "common conscience" and has a religious quality. Studies reviewed in this subsection and in Chapter 7 suggest that political life in highly differentiated societies is not quite as far removed from political life in less differentiated societies as Durkheim thought.

ECONOMY

Introduction

Microanalysis of the linkage of economy and polity centers on the ways in which individuals' work roles influence their political attitudes and behavior. Research has dealt with politically relevant qualities of jobs themselves and with politically relevant reactions to certain types of jobs. It has also been concerned with the ways in which individuals are influenced by their involvement in work associations such as trade unions and professional organizations. The political implications of the fact that occupations constitute status groups have also been studied.

Assessing the bearing of work and work-related factors on the politics of individuals is difficult. Different occupations recruit from different segments of a population. Hence, care must be taken to distinguish the influence of job and job-related factors from variables such as race and ethnicity. Another complication stems from the informal and unintended character of much political socialization. Employers and employee associations alike often have formal educational programs intended to inculcate certain attitudes toward work and (sometimes directly and sometimes indirectly) toward politics. Undoubtedly many of these programs have their intended effects. However, much of the individual's politically relevant learning that takes place in work-related contexts occurs in the form of casual interchanges with peers and associates. This learning can either reinforce or counteract the goals of the formal programs. Finally, analysis is complicated by the fact that different persons can react quite differently to the same work situation. For example, while factory labor may seem dehumanizing and alienate one individual, it may represent upward social mobility and thus seem desirable to another. Such work-related feelings find very different forms of political expression.

Work Roles and Political Activity

The ways in which work roles vary that are related to the development of orientations affecting political involvement include:

1. the extent to which they are alienating or integrating (in the several senses of the terms identified below)
2. the extent to which and the way in which they are socially isolating
3. the extent to which they are perceived as being affected by political affairs
4. the extent to which they require and/or produce politically relevant skills.[61]

Alienation from work has a number of meanings. It has been used to refer to engagement in work that is not intrinsically rewarding; feelings of powerlessness in the work setting; the perception that decisions regarding one's work (for example, what constitutes the specific rights and responsibilities of one's job) are made by others in a random, unpredictable, and unintelligible manner; the perception that the norms or rules intended to govern work relations have broken down and that departures from prescribed behaviors are common; and the rejection of work norms and goals that are widely held and shared by other members of the work organization.

Work and work-related activity consume a good deal of most people's time and energy and serve as a major source of their social identity. Hence, work-related social attitudes and perceptions might be expected to generalize to other areas of social life. For example, it seems reasonable to hypothesize that persons who feel powerless in their work situations are also likely to feel that they cannot affect the actions of government. It also seems plausible to extend this line of reasoning to political behavior: Individuals who feel powerless at work are likely to feel politically powerless and therefore are likely to be politically apathetic and to refrain from routine political participation.[62]

Much of the research investigating possible links between alienation and political participation exhibits a number of problems which stem from uncritical acceptance of this line of reasoning. Yinger has pointed out that while there is probably some connection in many cases between feelings of political powerlessness and other forms of perceived powerlessness, it is not difficult to imagine situations in which the relationship does not hold. "Some persons who have strong feelings of efficacy in one setting—owners of a small business, for example—may experience feelings of powerlessness in politics precisely because they cannot match the degree of control there that they have in their occupations."[63]

Finifter has noted several additional points to consider when attempting to understand the bearing of alienation (whatever its source) on routine political participation.[64] First, it may be that varying levels of alienation tend to be associated with different forms of participation rather than with different amounts of participation. Second, alienation has several dimensions. Not all of these are highly correlated. For example, many persons might feel politically powerless while at the same time accepting the political norms and goals that are widely held and shared by other members of the society. Finifter hypothesizes that combinations of different dimensions of political alienation will be associated with different forms of political involvement. For example, considering the dimensions of perceived political powerlessness and perceived political normlessness, she speculates that (a) high powerlessness and high normlessness will be associated with complete political withdrawal,[65] (b) low powerlessness and high normlessness will be associated with reform tendencies manifested in involvement with protest groups working within the existing political framework, (c) high powerlessness and low normlessness with political apathy and a very low level of political involvement, (d) low powerlessness and low normlessness will be associated with conformative (i.e., routine) participation.

Finifter's own empirical investigation, based on American data from Almond and Verba's five-nation study, dealt with two dimensions of alienation: feelings of political powerlessness (exemplified by the feeling that one is affected by political decisions made independent or in spite of one's judgment or wishes) and perceptions of political normlessness (exemplified by the belief that officials violate legal procedures in dealing with the public or in arriving at policy decisions). She inquired into both the sources of (i.e., the social contexts and experiences which are conducive to the development of) each dimension of alienation and into the bearing of each dimension of alienation on political participation. Finifter's zero-order Pearsonian correlations between two dimensions of alienation and twenty-three predictor variables showed that occupation accounts for a comparatively large amount of the variance in powerlessness scores but for a substantially smaller amount of the variance in normlessness scores. A high negative correlation was found between powerlessness and political participation but no significant relationship was found between perceived normlessness and participation.

Finifter's occupation variable dealt only with occupational prestige. Her data tell us nothing directly about links between work alienation and political behavior. Nevertheless, her findings are helpful in beginning to understand the relative importance of work life as a determinant of political alienation. The two factors which accounted for significantly larger proportion of the variation in powerlessness than did occupation were political participation and education—both of which have negative associations. This suggests that political knowledge and experiences rather than manifestly nonpolitical factors play the paramount role in producing feelings of political alienation—an important variable negatively associated with routine participation.[66]

An earlier study supports this interpretation.[67] Using a random sample of the male work force in a Swedish community, Seeman found that those with strong feelings of political powerlessness were less likely to have knowledge of political affairs and were less likely to be interested in discussing politics or in keeping up with public affairs. While Seeman argues that powerlessness inhibits the learning of political information and interest in political affairs, he goes on to hypothesize that a cyclic pattern may be involved—from powerlessness to low levels of knowledge and interest back to powerlessness. His findings indicated that alienation toward work was unrelated to political engagement and powerlessness.

Factors associated with the social isolation of certain occupations also can have political importance.[68] Work can isolate single individuals (e.g., housewives) or isolate communities of workers (e.g., miners). Workers can be isolated from contact with those with whom they share political, social, and economic circumstances while engaging in extensive interaction with others whose social position they do not share (e.g., domestic servants). They can be isolated from contact with those in different circumstances while interacting intensively with those like themselves (e.g., lumbermen). Vast improvements in transportation and the enormous growth of the mass media in the past several decades have reduced the political significance of occupational isolation. Nevertheless, it remains a relatively important variable.

The isolation of single individuals from contact with others who have political interest, information, and skills tends to reduce their political involvement. This may account in part for the often observed low levels of voting among housewives and farmers.

Those experiencing the combination of isolation from other members of their own social class and relatively extensive interaction with individuals of higher status tend to have little political interest and commitment. When social structure exposes lower-class groups to cross-pressures, their rates of participation decline. This is particularly true in societies with relatively open class structures. The desire to be like and to be accepted by others of higher status often involves adoption of their norms, values, and patterns of behavior. When these differ significantly from those of one's more usual associates, the individual receives incompatible cues for action. A common response to such a situation is apathy and withdrawal. Hence Lipset comments that "White collar workers' well known lack of organization and class consciousness may . . . be partially due to the small units in which they work and their scattering among higher-level management personnel."[69]

Occupational isolation, which intensifies intraclass communication while simultaneously reducing or cutting off cross-class communication, tends to heighten political involvement. Occupationally homogeneous communities usually provide individuals with a congruent set of mutually reinforcing political cues. In such a setting individuals are more likely to be aware of the political interests they share with others and to have a stronger sense of partisanship. The more extensively organized such a community, the greater the opportunity for individuals to participate in organizations in which they can acquire politically relevant information and skills and the more likely they are to participate in politics. However, in times of political-economic crisis such communities often engage in nonroutine participation in the form of support for political extremists. These patterns have been illustrated by the behavior of workers in several isolated industries in a number of nations: miners, sailors, fishermen, sheepshearers, longshoremen, and farmers.[70] They also have been illustrated by peasant revolutions.[71]

In modern industrial societies no occupational roles are completely immune from the influence of political decisions. Licensing and certification requirements, minimum wage laws, child-labor laws, laws governing working hours and conditions all illustrate public policies affecting work. Government decisions to fund or to discontinue funding various programs and projects affect the employment or unemployment of thousands. Government itself, at all levels, is a major direct employer in all industrial societies. While every worker is affected in one way or another, those who believe that their occupational group is particularly influenced by political affairs are more likely than others to participate in routine politics. Such persons are likely to be in occupations requiring or facilitating the acquisition of politically relevant information and intellectual and social skills. An exception to this generalization occurs in cases where members of certain occupations believe that their political involvement may threaten their job status and security (e.g., teachers in public institutions).

It has already been noted at several points that occupations which require the possession of politically relevant intellectual and social skills and those which lead to their development or refinement are likely to have politically active members. Such skills include the ability to understand, interpret, and effectively communicate social, economic, and political information; the ability to formulate and express the political goals one desires as well as the possible means for their attainment; and some ability to work satisfactorily with others in both leader and follower roles. In general, high-status occupations such as most professions and executive and managerial positions require the education and later involve the performance of tasks which make likely the possession of such skills. Most manual and clerical jobs, on the other hand, have neither the educational requirements nor provide the experiences which are associated with their possession or development. This, in part, accounts for the fact that persons of higher occupational status are more likely to participate in routine politics.[72]

Occupational Associations and Political Activity

The fact that a particular occupation neither requires nor develops skills that can be used in politics does not rule out their acquisition in voluntary associations formed by members of the occupation. These associations include not only formal organizations, such as trade unions through which workers act collectively in their relations with employers and in their relations with government, but also informal, manifestly nonpolitical organizations such as social clubs, athletic teams, and lodges.

A study of the International Typographical Union (I.T.U.) by Lipset, Trow, and Coleman extensively analyzed the relationship between participation in these latter types of organizations and participation in union politics.[73] Their data, though dealing with intraorganization politics, served as basis for the general theory of the political significance of secondary associations.

The authors introduce their study by noting two unusual features of the I.T.U.: a democratic, two-party political system, and a vast network of voluntary associations independently organized by its members to satisfy their social and recreational needs. Their research explored the possible relationships between these two structures.

Findings indicated that the manifestly nonpolitical associations within the I.T.U. served as contexts within which new ideas on union politics were developed, served as communications centers in which people learned about and formed attitudes about politics, served as contexts in which potential leaders could acquire training in the skills of politics, and served as contexts in which persons could attain the status necessary to become political leaders. In general those men who were active, whether formally or informally, in its occupational community—in its social clubs, veterans groups, benevolent associations, and so forth—were those who were politically involved and active in the union.

The authors go to considerable length to point out that the I.T.U. had an unusually elaborate occupational community and that this community developed and remained independent of union control. Most unions lack so elaborate an infrastructure and, where some exists, it is frequently controlled by the union.[74] Hence they comment:

> It is perhaps paradoxical that the very organizations which allow workers to act collectively in their relations with employers are ordinarily so constructed that within them members are usually unable to act collectively in dealing with their leaders.[75]

Early theories and Contemporary Micro-Research: Economy

While most of Marx's work bears, in one way or another, on the interplay of polity and economy (he argued in fact that these cannot be meaningfully separated), two specific topics which he explored have stimulated considerable amounts of micro-research: alienation and political involvement; relations between workers and their politicization.

Marx was particularly interested in the relation between work alienation in industrial, capitalist society—the workers' lack of control over virtually all aspects of their lives—and political revolution. Discussion of this topic will be taken up in the next chapter, which deals with nonroutine politics. Nevertheless, some materials reviewed above do shed some light on the validity of Marx's contention that work alienation fosters political revolution. The study by Horton and Thompson does indicate that under certain conditions the alienated (at least in the attitudinal sense of the term) will become involved in politics with the aim of thwarting the objectives of those in positions of power and privilege.

Lipset, Trow, and Coleman's analysis of the consequences of participation in an independent occupational community as well as Lipset's discussion of the results of extensive involvement in an occupational community separated from interclass communications are consistent with Marx's discussions of the preconditions for effective collective political action.

While more work is needed, existing empirical data do call into question several of Marx's claims concerning these subjects. For example, at least in the United States, alienation—feelings of powerlessness, normlessness, and meaninglessness—are associated with political withdrawal rather than with political involvement. Those political situations in which the alienated do appear to participate are provided by the normal operation of the established political order. Opportunities to vote no in a local referendum or to cast a ballot for a maverick political candidate serve as examples. In his discussions of modern alienation Marx is writing about the structural situation of the workers under industrial capitalism and not about the feelings and attitudes of individuals. Nevertheless, if those who feel powerless tend toward political withdrawal, it may be that effective collective action must begin by overcoming such feelings. Psychological alienation may be politically dysfunctional for those who are alienated in Marx's structural interpretation of the concept.

A Marxist might respond to the preceding by arguing that the reduction of psychological alienation is part of what is involved in the process of creating what Marx termed "class consciousness." However, he might not have as ready an interpretation of data indicating that work experience is not a primary source of feelings of political alienation. Perhaps creating class consciousness in the Marxist sense involves not only reducing alienation but also convincing workers that the sources of any feelings of powerlessness, normlessness, and meaninglessness are other than they experience them to be.

Weber's concepts of status groups and bureaucratization provide points from which to understand the linkage of work life and political participation. The realization that occupation groups have interest in their social honor as well as in their economic well-being broadens understanding of the ways in which occupational groups can be affected by political processes. It helps explain increased routine participation by members of an occupation on occasion when their material interests do not appear to be particularly threatened by ongoing political affairs.

Weber saw the inevitable presence of bureaucracy in modern society as the major source of alienation. The incorporation of its principles of organization by government meant that political issues were becoming increasingly complex and, with increasing frequency, would be dealt with by anonymous "experts" remote from the individual citizen. It is hardly surprising that many, faced by highly complex issues and by concentrated centralized power both at work and in the state, withdraw from participation in the political life of modern industrial societies. The finding reported above, that alienation is negatively associated with political participation, could have been anticipated on the basis of Weber's discussions of rationalization and bureaucracy.

A central theme in Durkheim's politically relevant work concerns the importance of a rich pattern of occupational groups as a necessary structural condition for avoiding the related threats of anomie, anarchy, and loss of individual freedom which he believed were inherent in all societies with advanced divisions of labor. The I.T.U. study does show that independent voluntary associations of workers can and do operate as centers in which workers learn and form attitudes about politics, in which they acquire political skills, and in which they are encouraged to participate in the larger political arena. The authors of the study acknowledge the insights of Durkheim by citing this passage from *The Division of Labor in Society:*

> A [democratic] nation can be maintained only if, between the states and the individual, there is intercalated a whole series of secondary groups near enough to individuals to attract them strongly in the sphere of action and drag them, in this way, into the general torrent of social life.[76]

An apparent flaw in Durkheim's analysis, similar to one of Marx's major analytic problems, involves the political importance assigned to social relations specifically in the sphere of work. Data indicate that, while work life does affect political life, experiences outside of work, particularly with political participation itself, are the primary sources of feelings of alienation and anomie which find expression in political behavior.

STRATIFICATION

Introduction

The stratification or class system of a society refers to the way in which its scarce rewards are distributed. These rewards include material privileges (e.g., wealth), social privileges (e.g., authority), and social-psychological privileges (e.g., prestige). All societies rank order their members in terms of the distribution of these privileges. A social class is an aggregate of individuals within a particular society who have a relatively similar share in the distribution of that society's material, social, and social-psychological privileges. Members of such aggregates tend to be relatively "acceptable to one another for social interaction that is culturally regarded as more or less symbolic of equality,"[77] to share beliefs concerning the desirability or undesirability of the social order of their system, and to have similar value orientations. Such aggregates also tend to be relatively endogamous.

Considerable research shows that within societies members of different social classes often have quite different beliefs and patterns of behavior in various areas of social life. The areas most frequently studied include child-rearing and socialization practices and religious affiliation. The relation of such differences to differences in patterns of routine political participation is discussed below.

Class Differences in Attitudes and Personality Structure

In a seminal article Lipset drew the attention of many contemporary political researchers to certain political consequences of apparent class differences in socialization practices, cultural emphases, and social experiences.[78] With respect to differential socialization practices he cited studies which showed that, while the gap between the social classes shows signs of narrowing, these uniformities have persisted: (1) in matters of discipline working-class parents are consistently more likely to employ physical punishment while middle-class families rely more on reasoning, isolation, appeals to guilt, and other methods involving threat of loss of love; (2) working-class parents are consistently less permissive toward their children's expressive needs and wishes; (3) working-class parents have low expectations of their children in terms of taking care of themselves at an earlier age, accepting more responsibilities around the home, and progressing further in school; (4) parent-child relationships in the middle class are more acceptant and egalitarian while those in the working class are oriented toward maintaining order and obedience.

Noting these basic characteristics of working-class socialization practices, Lipset goes on to point out five additional features of working-class life: (1) little education, (2) infrequent participation in voluntary associations of any type, (3) little reading, (4) a homogeneous environment resulting in a highly restricted view of the world and simplistic thinking, (5) economic insecurity. The combination of these qualities of working-class life produces what Lipset terms "working-class authoritarianism." This is the observed tendency of many working-class persons to oppose civil rights and liberties for minority groups and to be generally prejudiced, to be chauvinistic, to engage in black-and-white thinking, and to engage in extremist thinking in which multiparty political systems and the politics of compromise and gradualist change have no place.

Lipset notes that the authoritarianism of members of a social class in any country is highly relative and that its influence on actual behavior can be modified or overridden by strong commitment to democratic procedures and ideals which are dominant in the larger society and operative in the organizations to which the class members belong. Nevertheless, all things being equal, the authoritarian tendencies of working-class individuals are hypothesized to encourage their support of social movements which suggest easy and quick solutions to social problems and have a rigid outlook. This hypothesis was suggested by sample survey data indicating that workers are less likely than others to see the need for a number of political parties, by studies of racial and ethnic prejudice indicating that workers are more intolerant and tough-minded than others, by studies showing workers' emotionally intense and fundamentalist approach to religion, and by voting studies illustrating workers' support for extremist political groups.

Antidemocratic tendencies and nonroutine participation will be discussed in later chapters. Here two of Lipset's claims that bear on the routine participation of working-class persons will be discussed. First, are workers relatively more authoritarian than other members of their society?

Second, is authoritarianism negatively associated with routine democratic participation?

Miller and Riessman have challenged the contention that workers are relatively more authoritarian.[79] They argue that much of Lipset's analysis is based on faulty conceptualizations of authoritarianism on the one hand and democracy on the other. These lead to an overestimation of workers' authoritarian tendencies. Criticism of a specific democratic practice such as the multiparty system, they note, may not imply embracing a totally anti-democratic position. Multiparty systems are only one means of achieving political democracy. Workers' less tolerant racial and ethnic attitudes may reflect a general acceptance of punitive measures against deviance rather than a disavowal of civil liberties. While workers do show some tendency in attitude studies to engage in black-and-white thinking, they also frequently respond to questions with "don't know" or "uncertain." These are not authoritarian responses. And if workers really did consistently think in black-and-white terms, this would encourage, not discourage, their political participation. If one "knows" what is right and wrong, decision making is easy and action is important.[80]

Miller and Riessman also point out two major empirical problems in Lipset's discussion of working-class authoritarianism. First, more recent studies of working-class socialization practices reveal that working-class parents use both physical and psychological forms of discipline. This mixed form produces more "realistic" orientations to authority and facilitates the development of children who are neither uncontrolled nor overly constricted and who are not excessively aggressive. Second, workers are exposed to the views of the upper classes in schools, in churches, and through exposure to the mass media. They are often placed in situations where they are exposed to conflicting information and opposing group pressures. Their political environment, unlike that of the upper classes, is definitely not homogeneous. The cross pressures to which workers are subjected may be one reason for their comparatively low voting turnout.

Miller and Riessman propose an alternative to Lipset's view. They argue that no class has a monopoly on authoritarianism. Both upper and lower classes have qualities which could be turned in the direction of authoritarianism under certain conditions. Workers do have a number of traits which incline them toward authoritarianism. These include preference for strong leadership and definite structure, anti-intellectualism, and a punitive attitude toward violation of law. But they also have attitudes, overlooked by Lipset, which incline them toward democracy. These include their anti-elitist stance, their preference for informality in personal relations, their sympathy for the underdog, and their acceptance of leadership with accompanying delegation of authority. Members of the middle class do have characteristics which encourage their support of democratic principles and their participation in democratic processes. These include their education, their participation in voluntary associations, their reading habits, their economic security, and their sense of political effectiveness. But they also have characteristic attitudes that Lipset fails to mention. Under certain conditions these can lead them in the direction of authoritarianism. Specifically, wealth, security, and knowledge can lead to smugness, elitism, intellectualism, and coldness.

Miller and Riessman's suggestions have yet to be thoroughly explored through empirical research. While the literature on authoritarianism is voluminous, no empirical studies have investigated the specific conditions under which members of different social classes are likely to exhibit politically relevant authoritarian tendencies. The particular characteristics of any linkages that may exist between social class, authoritarianism, and political behavior are not as yet understood.[81]

Research on authoritarianism has been plagued by a number of difficulties.[82] Nevertheless, those who have critically reviewed the literature tend to agree with Kirscht and Dillehay that "despite the many doubts . . . authoritarianism is a significant phenomenon worthy of further attention by social science investigators."[83] A number of contemporary political events suggest that the concept of authoritarianism may have some analytic utility. The vehemence of the reactions of some to civil rights activists and to community fluoridation issues in the early 1960s can serve as examples. So too can the attitudes and behavior of the more violence-prone student protesters on the one hand and "hard-hats" on the other later in that decade. Furthermore, the vastly increased centralization of power in American society has made the psychological dispositions of political leaders and those who surround them more important to understand. (However, this is not to suggest that in the foreseeable future there will be some "scientific" basis for understanding in social-psychological terms such acts as Richard Nixon's Watergate activities, Gerald Ford's pardon of Richard Nixon, or Jimmy Carter's permitting the Shah of Iran to enter the United States.) Finally, the apparent growth in the complexity of politically relevant social, economic, and moral issues which confront the public increases the probability that nonrational factors such as authoritarianism (which involves orientations toward power and authority) will influence people's political attitudes and patterns of routine participation. Many enthusiasts on both sides of the present issues of school busing to achieve racial integration, gay rights, women's rights, and nuclear power illustrate this.

Social Class and Religion

A number of features of the interplay of class and religious factors and their influence on routine participation have already been described. Here three general points bear repeating. First, different religious groups tend to be composed of different strata. The religions of different strata vary theologically and organizationally and these differences affect patterns of routine political participation. Second, despite differences in the class composition of their memberships, differences in the political behavior of members of different religious groups cannot be fully explained in socioeconomic terms: that is, there is a "religious factor" that has some significance as an independent variable. Third, while any given religious group tends to have a characteristic class membership, there are always numerous "deviant" cases—persons whose class membership does not correspond to what is modal for their religious group (e.g., working-class Jews).

In this subsection points two and three will be elaborated. Generally, class and religious factors tend to reinforce each other. However, in certain circumstances they do not. These circumstances are important to understand, for their analysis gives some clues as to the relative importance of class and religious factors as determinants of political behavior. Their analysis also gives some insight into the limitations of the generally accepted cross-pressure hypothesis discussed earlier in this chapter.[84]

The cross-pressure hypothesis leads to the expectation that persons who perceive that the politics of their religious group are at variance with the politics of the social class with which they identify are not likely to be strong partisans. Hence they are less likely to engage in routine participation than are those who perceive no such conflict. Assuming that this hypothesis has some validity, it does raise two empirical questions: (1) How great must the discrepancy be between the modal economic position of one's religious group and one's own economic position before persons generally feel cross-pressured and subsequently reduce feelings of partisanship and levels of participation? (For example, if the modal economic position of an individual's own religious group is lower middle class, will he generally feel cross-pressured if his income defines him as upper middle class—or, in general, must he be upper class before he experiences such feelings?) (2) In cases where persons do experience cross-pressures but do not totally withdraw from political action, will they generally tend to support the politics of their church or of their class?

These questions were raised by Hamilton in his study of class and politics in the United States.[85] His data on Catholic manual workers show that those having low and middle incomes are at least three-fourths Democratic. Of particular interest is the finding that this tendency increases in the higher of these categories. It is only in the highest income categories that increasing Republican support is seen. And even in these highest categories the level of Democratic support is nearly twice that of equivalent white Protestants. Hamilton therefore concludes:

> The findings provide eloquent testimony to the fact that, at best, level of income could have only a very restricted impact on the determination of outlooks. There is much more impressive support for the alternative

explanation—the notion of "social determinism"—the findings indicating much greater differentiation associated with the socio-religious factor.[86]

The preceding suggests that cross-pressures of religion and class which tend to reduce partisanship, and thereby reduce tendencies to participate in routine politics, are experienced primarily by those whose class membership (defined in economic terms) is vastly different from that which is modal for their religious group. Hamilton's analysis also indicates that purely economic factors are less potent determinants of routine political behavior than is widely assumed.[87]

Early Theories and Contemporary Micro-Research: Statification

Marx argues that factors which discourage the political participation of the working class—participation of the sort from which they would benefit—are manipulated by the bourgeoisie. There is some evidence to support this view. For example, Litt found that material presented in American working-class schools did not encourage a belief in the citizen's ability to influence government action through political participation. The material in the middle-class schools, on the other hand, stressed political participation as a means of influencing political processes and political decision making.[88]

Research reviewed in this chapter, though not conclusive, does suggest that workers have self-imposed, internal constraints on their political action. Purposive manipulation by others accounts for only some of the political inactivity of the working class in industrial societies. Other factors, such as socialization practices, reading habits, personal interests, and allocation of leisure time, all of which could encourage politicization, are such as to have a self-imposed, internal "enemy" of working class political interest as well as an objective, external "enemy." Even Marx's concept of "false consciousness" fails to take account of these relatively subtle internal limitations on the political involvement of members of the working class.

Marx's two-class model of Western industrial society eliminates from consideration a common group in this society—economically prosperous workers. These workers, who have no part of ownership of the social means of production, nevertheless have some interest in the perpetuation of the social-political order in which they are prospering. The concerns that motivate their political participation are often status concerns rather than economic concerns. When placed in a political situation in which they must choose between enhancing what they perceive to be their economic interests or enhancing their social status, it is not uncommon for them to opt for the latter. Data indicating the political importance of the religious factor and data on workers' reactions to cross-pressure situations in which they must choose between their material and ideal interests are not consistent with some basic components of Marx's position.

Weber clearly states that in political life people pursue status as well as economic objectives. Data indicating that in certain circumstances workers choose status goals over economic goals is anticipated in his discussions. His analysis of the importance of values in human conduct is consistent with findings indicating the independent contribution of the religious factor in structuring political behavior.

Weber's macroanalytic, historical-comparative perspective did not generate questions about the social-psychological attributes of workers in Western industrial societies. However, two of his discussions do have some bearing on these qualities. These are his analyses of status groups and rationalization. A status group refers to a set of persons who have in common life chances which are determined by the level of prestige granted them by others in their society. Members of any given status group share a specific style of life and tend to limit their social relations to those from whom this style of life can be expected. According to Weber, historically such groups have frequently engaged in collective political action.

Workers in contemporary industrial society may constitute a status group in Weber's sense of the term. When perceiving a threat to their material and/or ideal interest they are likely to respond through collective political action. It may be that the democratizing consequences of the continuing rationalization of Western industrial societies is perceived as a threat by members of the working class. Increasing rationalization means the increasing probability of being assessed for appointment or promotion to a work role in terms of universalistic criteria. It means the increasing probability of having to compete with members of status groups previously excluded from competitive consideration. Insofar as workers do manifest authoritarian tendencies, these may represent attitudinal reactions to threats to members of a group most likely to be adversely affected by increasing rationalization. Workers may believe that it is antithetical to their own interests to support the political rights and welfare of groups which in the future might displace them in power and prestige.

Durkheim argues that as a society's division of labor becomes more complex, the political significance of kinship, religion, and region diminish. He advocates the development of occupational associations which, in the context of modern society, could serve the political functions performed by these traditional groupings in less differentiated societies. Prior to the development and elaboration of such associations, societies undergoing rapid change lack the organization which provides people with clear rules of conduct. Such societies lack the ability to impose discipline upon their members. According to Durkheim's analysis, individuals lacking external controls will also lack self-control. Hence the most important political problem of rapidly industrializing societies is the threat of anarchy for, as Durkheim sees it, when anarchy prevails individual freedom is not possible.

Insofar as there is such a thing as a politically relevant authoritarian syndrome, it might be understood within the framework of this analysis. In rapidly changing societies individuals lacking self-restraint imposed by a stable normative order pursue, among other things, what they perceive to be their political self-interest. Supporting a set of principles, processes, and rules which appear to limit the ways and the extent to which they can pursue politically their own interests may seem personally self-defeating.

Authoritarianism may represent an expression of this judgment. Studies of right-wing extremism in the United States do indicate that political authoritarianism is most commonly expressed during periods of rapid social change.[89]

As previously noted, Durkheim underestimated the continuing significance of religion in the life of modern society. Findings such as those indicating that in conflict situations workers will sometimes favor the interest of their religious groups over their own economic interests is not anticipated by his analysis.

In industrial societies, particularly under conditions of rapid social change and instability, emerging political leadership is sometimes seen as possessing qualities which Durkheim claimed were the qualities characteristically attributed to centralized power in traditional societies. Had Durkheim not drawn so sharp a distinction between political life in traditional and modern societies, his analysis of the political consequences of anomie might have included discussions resembling Weber's analysis of charismatically led social movements.

SHARED BELIEF AND VALUE SYSTEMS

Introduction

In this chapter numerous beliefs and values which influence political participation have been identified. However, a major agent of political socialization—the school—has yet to be discussed. A second related topic, which also remains to be considered, concerns the effect on routine participation of widely shared feelings about political participation itself—feelings about the rights and obligations of citizenship.

In Western industrial democracies, a major responsibility of the school is the production of "good citizens." The school is expected to inform children how the political institutions of their society operate and motivate them so that, in the future, they will responsibly participate in them. Through formal instruction and informal interaction with teachers and peers, students are expected to adopt certain political norms—particularly the norm encouraging informed democratic participation. These expectations raise a number of questions: (1) How important is the school as an agent of political socialization? (2) Does the school actually perform its intended political functions? (3) How important is the norm encouraging political participation? These questions are explored below.

The School as an Agent of Political Socialization

Possibly the most important beliefs and values affecting political behavior are those concerning politics itself. All modern societies have some formal programs of political education aimed at transmitting a more or less well-defined set of beliefs and values. These programs are carried on, at least in part, within school systems which have compulsory attendance for youth of certain ages. No modern societies leave civic instruction entirely to traditional socialization agencies such as the family or the church. As Key states it, ". . . all national educational systems indoctrinate the oncoming generation with the basic outlooks and values of the political order."[90]

The agency primarily responsible for determining what shall be taught in the schools about politics varies greatly from nation to nation. In some nations political education is closely supervised by the central government and the ruling party. Elsewhere supervision may be less strict, may take place on the regional, state, or local level, and may be almost entirely independent of central control.

The presentation of explicit political subject matter is not the only way in which the school acts as an agent of political socialization. Teachers and administrators can serve as political role models. The perceptions of interested students of the political orientations of particular teachers or administrators can influence their own political beliefs, feelings, and values. In addition, in education systems in which officials determine career-linked courses of study for particular students, students may adopt political orientations favored by those officials in order to help insure their assignment to a course of study leading to a job or career they desire. Education systems differ greatly in the extent to which political considerations influence the assignment of personnel to (or removal of personnel from) teaching roles and the assignment of students to various career paths.

Although all modern societies rely on the school as an agent of political socialization, the relative importance of the school in this regard is far from clear. Early studies of political socialization focused almost exclusively on the correlations of the political attitudes of youth and those of their parents. However, it was soon recognized that "while positive, the *moderate* magnitude of the correlations . . . leads to the formulation that parents are only one of the many agents of such socialization and that their influence is not great."[91] It was also understood that "the *relative* influence of parental norms declines as peers and other agencies exert their influence on the growing individual."[92] These findings led to the question of how influential the family really is vis-à-vis other agencies of political socialization, particularly the school.

Hess and Torney present the strongest claim for the relative importance of the school as an agent of political socialization.[93] On the basis of a
study including more than 17,000 elementary school children from all
parts of the United States they conclude:

> The effectiveness of the family in transmitting attitudes has been overesti-
> mated in previous research. The family transmits preference for a political
> party, but in most other areas its most effective role is to support other
> institutions in teaching political information and orientations.... The
> school apparently plays the largest part in teaching attitudes, conceptions and
> beliefs about the operations of the political system. While it may be argued
> that the family contributes much to the socialization that goes into basic loy-
> alty to country, the school gives content, information and concepts which
> expand and elaborate these early feelings of attachment.[94]

Hess and Torney go on to note that in the United States the major
emphasis in civic education is on compliance to rules and authorities. The
only form of political participation receiving some attention is the political
action of the individual citizen—particularly voting. Little, if any, information is given concerning participation in organized political groups or about
the nature of political conflict. In short, the school encourages some limited
routine participation for the individual, but little more.

It thus seems that the family influences routine participation by
transmitting sentiments of system loyalty on the one hand and partisanship
on the other. The school channels this loyalty and partisanship by encouraging students to perform their duties as individuals—but in very limited ways, primarily by passive compliance and by voting.[95]

In addition to these orientations toward political community and regime and toward political participation itself, beliefs and feelings about oneself as a political actor are important factors influencing political participation. The extent to which one feels personally capable of manipulating
aspects of one's political environment, i.e., the extent to which one feels
politically effective, is another important orientation.

In his study of American and Jamaican students, Langton specifically
raised the question of the relative influence of family, school, and peer
group in developing the individual's sense of political efficacy.[96] He found
that each agency plays a somewhat different role. He also discovered that
the impact of each agency varies by social class. Specifically, the school
moves the student with a low sense of efficacy to a medium sense of efficacy
but has almost no influence in developing a high sense of efficacy. The
face-to-face peer group, on the other hand, can move students from
medium to high levels.

Langton's data indicated that, over all, the family is the most important agency in establishing a sense of political efficacy. It accounted for
almost four times more movement along the entire efficacy scale than

either peer group or school. However, the family appears to have less of an impact on upper-class students. Such students, Langton hypothesizes, "may be relatively more affected by class-bound cultural cues from outside the family—cues which are more readily transmitted through the informal school and peer environment."[97]

While every modern society assigns the school some responsibility for the political socialization of its young members, the research reviewed above shows that the school does not, in any real sense, politicize them. While the school may enhance the sense of political efficacy of some, it certainly does not encourage the development of political activists.

Sense of Civic Obligation

Whatever its source or sources in the socialization process, the belief that one ought to involve oneself in the political life of one's community, state, or nation encourages political participation. The more widespread such a belief in society, the higher the level of actual routine participation that can be expected in that society. Data confirming this expectation are presented by Almond and Verba in their five-nation study.[98]

Respondents were asked what role they thought individuals should play within their local community. Respondents were classified into those who believed that ordinary citizens should take some active part in the community (by doing things such as joining organizations involved in community affairs), those who believed that citizens ought to participate more passively in community life (by doing things such as keeping informed), those who felt that ordinary persons ought to participate only in church and religious activities, and those who did not think ordinary citizens had any responsibility to take part in community affairs. Data revealed large differences among the five nations with respect to the percentage of respondents who said they believed ordinary people should be active in their local community, even if the activity was minimal (United States 51%, United Kingdom 30%, Mexico 26%, Germany 22%, Italy 10%).

Actual opportunity for participation is a major factor accounting for such differences. For example, in the United States there are many opportunities to participate in the political life of one's community and a relatively large proportion of citizens stress the obligation to participate actively. "In Italy, on the other hand, the relative lack of opportunity to participate in an autonomous local community is accompanied by the absence of a set of norms favoring such participation."[99]

Almond and Verba found that in each of the five nations, those with some higher education were more likely than others to express adherence to the norms of participation. With prolonged exposure, it does seem that the school encourages routine participation. However, differences among the nations in the frequency of adherence to the norms of participation did not disappear when education was controlled. "In fact, a university educated person in Germany or Mexico is no more likely to express adherence to those norms than is a primary educated person in the United States or Britain, and the Italian university educated respondent is less likely to do so."[100] The ultimate influence of the school on patterns of routine political participation thus seems to be largely determined by prevailing societal belief and value systems.

Early Theories and Contemporary Micro-Research: Shared Belief and Value Systems

Studies reviewed above show that the school encourages routine participation which, by definition, is activity supporting an existing structure of power and authority. They also reveal that the school encourages political compliance and support of the status quo and excludes considerations of political dissension, conflict, and change-oriented collective action.[101] The fact that the obligation to participate is most strongly felt by those who have spent the greatest amount of time in the educational system is another indicator of the role played by the school as an agent of political socialization. All of this is consistent with the position of Marx that the dominant beliefs and values of any class society are the beliefs and values of its dominant class, and that agencies transmitting and attempting to inculcate these beliefs and values are tools of that class—tools used to perpetuate an existing structure of political-economic relations.[102]

The school performs legitimating functions which Weber claimed are important for the operation of all types of political systems. This legitimating function is performed by the school's exclusive emphasis on political consensus values and on the minimum obligations of citizenship.

By failing to inform students about and interest them in the wide range of forms of political involvement, the school does nothing to help offset the tendency in modern societies, observed by Weber, to relegate responsibility for making decisions on social policy to "experts." The school, which could operate as an agency increasing the democratic potential of rationalizing societies, does not do so. This represents grounds for Weber's pessimism about a more democratic future.

Durkheim emphasized the importance of restraining social norms in any political system in which some degree of individual freedom was to be possible. He felt that in modern societies it was primarily the occupational association which could instill norms. Contemporary work on political socialization also notes the necessity of individuals to limit their demands on the polity if it is to remain relatively responsive to citizen needs. However, as the research reviewed above shows, to a large extent it is the school which is responsible in modern society for performing this function. Furthermore, while imposing certain social norms does contribute to system maintenance, it is not clear that this contributes to the possibility of individual freedom—except in Durkheim's special sense of reducing the threat of anarchy under which individual freedom is seen as an impossibility.

Agencies of political socialization can enhance liberty by imposing some self-restraint. However, another important function they can perform in this regard involves informing individual citizens concerning the political action they can take to insure their rights. Socializing agents can encourage widespread and varied forms of political participation. In the United States, at least, the school does not appear to do this.

This chapter has reviewed some empirical research on the influence of kinship, religion, work, class, and certain shared beliefs and values on patterns of routine political participation. The research was primarily social-psychological and dealt with forms of political behavior which contribute to the maintenance of the political system in which they occur. The research was conducted almost entirely in Western industrial democracies. It is this type of research which has been most common in American political sociology.

We now turn to consider a less frequently initiated type of microresearch—that dealing with political behavior oriented toward changing features of a political system in ways which are not institutionalized.

NOTES

1. The conceptualization of political participation developed here includes the official acts of those occupying formal political offices. Hence, in modern political democracies, political participation includes not only the acts of ordinary citizens, such as voting, but also acts of political officials, such as service on congressional committees. Some of the acts of public officials are formally required—i.e., they are a part of the job. In this sense they differ from the participation of those who do not hold office.

2. Lester W. Milbrath, *Political Participation* (Chicago: Rand McNally, 1965), pp. 5–38. Milbrath also distinguishes between autonomous versus compliant participation. In this chapter compliant behavior is not considered a form of political participation.

3. Sidney Verba and Norman H. Nie, *Participation in America: Political Democracy and Social Equality* (New York: Harper & Row, 1972).

4. John F. Zipp and Joel Smith, "The Structure of Electoral Political Participation," *American Journal of Sociology*, 85, no. 1 (July 1979), pp. 167–177.

5. Abraham Maslow, "A Theory of Motivation," *Psychological Review*, 50, 1943, pp. 370–396.

6. James C. Davies, *Human Nature in Politics* (New York: John Wiley & Sons, 1963).

7. Actually, the proportion of the population of the United States that takes part in various political events is low in comparison to other countries in view of the education level of the American population. For example, 64% of those eligible voted in the national election in the United States in 1960 while 57% of those eligible voted in the national election in India in 1962. These relatively similar rates must be viewed in the light of India's low literacy rate (23.7%). See Reinhard Bendix, *Nation Building and Citizenship* (New York: Anchor Books, 1969), pp. 312–313.

8. See Nicholas L. Danigelis, "Black Political Participation in the United States," *American Sociological Review*, 43, no. 5 (October 1978), pp. 756–771.

9. For example, in the United States the proportion in a sample survey reporting nonvoting is almost invariably lower than the officially reported or estimated proportion of nonvoters in the total electorate. This is due, in part, to the fact that nonvoters have characteristics which make them less likely to be included in a sample survey. But it is also due to the fact that in the United States one is expected to vote if one is to be considered a good and responsible citizen.

10. Bruce M. Russett, Hayward R. Alker Jr., Karl W. Deutsch, and Harold D. Lasswell, *World Handbook of Political and Social Indicators* (New Haven, Conn.: Yale University Press, 1964).

11. A number of studies indicate that national levels of citizen participation in routine politics generally are related to urbanization, literacy and education, percentages of labor force in nonagricultural occupations, and communications development (measured by such factors as number of newspapers, radios, and telephones per capita).

12. Categories 4, 5, and 6 are derived from David Easton and Robert D. Hess, "The Child's Political World," *Midwest Journal of Political Science*, 6, no. 3 (August 1962), p. 233.

13. See James C. Davies, "The Family's Role in Political Socialization," *The Annals of the American Academy of Political and Social Sciences*, 361, (September 1965), pp. 10–19.

14. Seldom are all things equal. The groups are likely to differ with respect to internal political homogeneity, the importance they attribute to politics, and their punishments, if any, for political nonconformity. In making his choice, the individual may take into account such additional factors.

15. More often than not, children will find themselves in social settings in which the political orientations of their parents will be reinforced rather than contradicted. Children tend to associate with other children from similar socioeconomic, religious, and ethnic backgrounds whose parents have political views similar to those of their own parents.

16. See Angus Campbell, Gerald Gurin, and Warren E. Miller, *The Voter Decides* (New York: Harper & Row, 1954), p. 99.

17. This may not be true of persons who strongly identify with one parent but not with the other.

18. Richard G. Niemi, "Political Socialization," in *Handbook of Political Psychology*, Jeanne N. Knutson, ed. (San Francisco: Jossey-Bass, 1973), p. 128.

19. Herbert McClosky and Harold E. Dahlgren, "Primary Group Influence on Party Loyalty," *American Political Science Review*, 53, no. 3 (September 1959), pp. 757–776.

20. Eleanore Maccoby, Richard E. Mathews, and Anton S. Morton, "Youth and Political Change," *Public Opinion Quarterly*, 18, no. 1 (Spring 1954), pp. 23–38.

21. Dwain Marvick and Charles R. Nixon, "Recruitment Contrast in Rival Campaign Groups," in *Political Decision Makers*, Dwain Marvik, ed. (New York: The Free Press, 1961), p. 209.

22. Kenneth P. Langton, *Political Socialization* (New York: Oxford University Press, 1969), p. 144.

23. Robert Lane, *Political Life* (New York, The Free Press, 1959), p. 216.

24. Fred I. Greenstein, *Children and Politics* (New Haven, Conn.: Yale University Press, 1965), pp. 115–127.

25. For a critical review of the various explanations for differences in the political beliefs and behavior of men and women, see Anthony M. Orum, et al., "Sex, Socialization and Politics," *American Sociological Review*, 39, no. 2, (April 1974), pp. 197–209.

26. Niemi, "Political Socialization," p. 128.

27. L. Eugene Thomas, "Political Attitude Congruence Between Politically Active Parents and College-Age Children: An Inquiry Into Family Political Socialization," *Journal of Marriage and the Family*, 33, no. 2 (May 1971), pp. 375–386.

28. Philip Converse and Georges Dupeux, "Politicization of the Electorate in France and the United States," *Public Opinion Quarterly*, 26, no. 1 (Spring 1962), pp. 1–23.

29. Robert D. Hess and Judith V. Torney, *The Development of Political Attitudes in Children* (Chicago: Aldine, 1967), p. 105.

30. Langton, *Political Socialization,* Chapter 2.

31. Robert E. Lane, "Political Maturation in the United States and Germany," in his *Political Man* (New York: The Free Press, 1972), pp. 77–96.

32. Gabriel A. Almond and Sidney Verba, *The Civil Culture: Political Attitudes and Democracy in Five Nations* (Princeton, N.J.: Princeton University Press, 1963).

33. Richard Merelman, "The Development of Political Ideology: A Framework for the Analysis of Political Socialization," *American Political Science Review* 63, no. 3 (September 1969), pp. 750–767.

34. Merelman does not discuss participation but rather ideological thought. However, the conditions which facilitate the ability to think ideologically are also positively associated with political participation.

35. Merelman cites experimental evidence indicating that frustration, no matter what its source, has its own fixation properties. Frustrated individuals tend to settle on a few patterns of behavior as a response. These become almost purely ritualistic. Physical punishment leads the subject to focus primarily on his suffering rather than on the world around him.

36. Frank A. Pinner, "Parental Overprotection and Political Distrust," *The Annals of the American Academy of Political and Social Sciences,* 361, (September 1965), pp. 58–70.

37. Robert E. Lane, "Fathers and Sons: Foundations of Political Belief," *American Sociological Review,* 24, no. 4 (August 1959), pp. 502–511.

38. Richard E. Dawson and Kenneth Prewitt, *Political Socialization* (Boston: Little, Brown, 1969), p. 120.

39. Dean Jaros, *Socialization to Politics* (New York: Praeger, 1973), pp. 64–68. Also see Davies, "The Family's Role in Political Socialization," pp. 17–18.

40. Ronald Inglehart, "The Silent Revolution in Europe: Intergenerational Change in Post-Industrial Societies," *American Political Science Review,* 65, no. 4 (December 1971), pp. 991–1017.

41. Inglehart refers to a study by Richard Flacks showing that in the United States, in the late 1960s, students from relatively affluent homes who tended to emphasize intellectual, aesthetic, and humanitarian values were more likely to become political activists than students from less affluent homes who tended to emphasize material success, occupational achievement, conventional morality, and religiosity. The sources of nonroutine participation will be discussed in Chapter 5 of this book.

At present the American economy is in a sustained period of decline. This is also a period in which there is no highly conspicuous political participation on the part of American youth. Neither those who were politically active in the late 1960s and early 1970s nor a younger cohort now in their late teens to late twenties is significantly mobilized around a political issue or set of issues. This suggests that the impact of early political socialization on political behavior is significantly affected by immediate environmental factors, such as the state of the economy and the presence of issues highly salient to particular segments of society.

42. David Easton and Jack Dennis, *Children in the Political System: Origins of Political Legitimacy* (New York: McGraw-Hill, 1969), pp. 69–70.

43. Edward S. Greenberg, "Black Children and the Political System," *Public Opinion Quarterly* 34, no. 3 (Fall 1970) pp. 333–345. Also see Paul R. Abramson, "Political Efficacy and Political Trust Among Black Schoolchildren: Two Explanations," *Journal of Politics* 34, no. 4 (November 1972), pp. 1243–1275.

44. Alex Inkeles, "Social Change and Social Characters: The Role of Parental Mediation," *Journal of Social Issues,* 11, no. 2 (1955), pp. 12–23.

45. Easton and Hess, "The Child's Political World."

46. Dawson and Prewitt, *Political Socialization,* p. 92.

47. Under such conditions continuing political participation is likely to be carried on with little enthusiasm.

48. Gerhard Lenski, *The Religious Factor* (Garden City, N.Y.: Doubleday, 1961), p. 128.

49. Ibid., pp. 137–138.

50. See Andrew M. Greeley, "Political Participation among Ethnic Groups in the United States: A Preliminary Reconnaissance," *American Journal of Sociology,* 80, no. 1 (July 1974), pp. 170–204.

51. Jaros, *Socialization to Politics,* pp. 34–35.

52. Hess and Torney, *Development of Political Attitudes in Children,* p. 117.

53. Ibid.

54. Lenski, *The Religious Factor,* p. 181.

55. Milbrath, *Political Participation,* p. 137.

56. Ibid.

57. Lane, *Political Life,* p. 245.

58. Lenski, *The Religious Factor,* p. 328.

59. Ibid., p. 157.

60. "It has been said that Democratic bosses of certain Massachusetts cities on occasion have eagerly sought to have birth control referendum on the ballot in state elections because this enlisted the efforts of the church in getting out The Catholic—and Democratic vote." Lane, *Political Life,* p. 237.

61. Similar lists of job characteristics related to political participation are presented in Lane, *Political Life,* p. 334, and in Milbrath, *Political Participation,* p. 125.

62. There is some supporting evidence for this line of reasoning. Olsen conceptualized alienation as involving two dimensions: attitudes of incapability (powerlessness) and attitudes of discontent. His study of 154 residents of Ann Arbor, Michigan, showed both dimensions to have a generally negative association with various forms of routine participation.

The measure of incapability consisted of items such as: "I believe public officials don't care much what people like me think" and "People like me don't have any say about what the government does." Presumably, an individual's assessment of who constitutes "people like me" will be significantly influenced by his occupational identity. See Marvin Olsen, "Two Categories of Political Alienation," *Social Forces* 47, no. 3 (March 1969), pp. 288–299.

63. J. Milton Yinger, "Anomie, Alienation and Political Behavior," in *Handbook of Political Psychology,* Jeanne N. Knutson, ed., p. 189.

64. Ada W. Finifter, "Dimensions of Political Alienation," *American Political Science Review,* 64, no. 2 (June 1970), pp. 389–410.

65. This combination is hypothesized to be associated with separatist or revolutionary tendencies among persons who maintain a sense of *personal* efficiency.

66. Other research indicates the need to qualify the assertion that alienation is negatively associated with routine participation. Templeton found that alienated persons tend to withdraw from national but not from local politics. His explanation is that alienation does not reduce the tendency to participate when channels for the expression of discontent are readily available—as they are more likely to be on the local than on the national level. See F. Templeton, "Alienation and Political Participation: Some Research Findings," *Public Opinion Quarterly,* 30, no. 2 (Summer 1966), pp. 249–267.

For a case study of the participation of the alienated, see John Horton and Wayne E. Thompson, "Powerlessness and Political Negativism: A Study of Defeated Local Referendums," *American Journal of Sociology,* 67, no. 5 (March 1962), pp. 485–493. The authors conclude that those in the two Upstate New York communities studied who felt powerless and were power conscious voted against referendums as an expression of protest—a vote against the local "powers-that-be."

67. Melvin Seeman, "On the Personal Consequences of Alienation in Work," *American Sociological Review,* 32, no. 2 (April 1967), pp. 273–285.

68. The following analysis of the bearing of occupational isolation on routine political participation is based on discussions in Seymour M. Lipset, *Political Man: The Social Bases of Politics* (Garden City, N.Y.: Doubleday Anchor, 1963).

69. Ibid., p. 263.

70. Ibid., p. 76.

71. See Jeffrey M. Paige, *Agrarian Revolution* (New York: The Free Press, 1975), pp. 34–35.

72. Milbrath, *Political Participation,* p. 124, cites a dozen studies reporting this uniformity.

73. Seymour M. Lipset, Martin Trow, and James Coleman, *Union Democracy* (Garden City: Doubleday Anchor, 1962).

74. The authors note the importance of distinguishing between a set of voluntary associations which is deliberately organized and controlled by the central authority and a structure of voluntary associations independent of such control. The existence of either set of voluntary associations is associated with a high level of routine political participation. However, the deliberately organized system "will be negatively related with political democracy, while the (other) is one of the requisites for the institutionalization of democracy." Ibid., pp. 88–89.

75. Ibid., p. 86.

76. Ibid., p. 85–86.

77. See Harry M. Johnson, *Sociology: A Systematic Introduction* (New York: Harcourt, Brace, 1960), pp. 472–474.

78. Lipset, *Political Man,* Chapter 4.

79. S. M. Miller and Frank Riessman, "'Working Class Authoritarianism': A Critique of Lipset," *British Journal of Sociology,* XII, 1961, pp. 263–276.

80. Lipsitz reexamined Lipset's evidence for the claim that working-class men are more likely to give authoritarian responses than middle-class men. He concludes: "The greater authoritarianism of the working class as opposed to the middle class appears to be largely a product of lower education. With education controlled, middle class individuals who were surveyed in the early 1950's are not consistently less authortarian than working-class individuals. A comparison of those in both strata with high school education or less reveals that workers tend to be less authoritarian on questions more closely related to politics." Lewis Lipsitz, "Working Class Authoritarianism: A Re-Evaluation," *American Sociological Review,* 30, no. 1 (February 1965), p. 109.

81. Another empirical study also presents data which do not support the claim that manual and lower-middle-class workers are more authoritarian than upper-middle-class workers. The data concern tolerance of racial and ethnic minorities, attitudes toward civil liberties, preferences for "hard" versus "soft" options in the conduct of military policy, and the Wallace vote in the 1968 election. See Richard F. Hamilton, *Class and Politics in the United States* (New York: John Wiley & Sons, 1972), pp. 399–507.

82. For general reviews of the vast literature on authoritarianism, see Roger Brown, *Social Psychology* (New York: The Free Press, 1965), pp. 477–546; John P. Kirscht and Ronald C. Dillehay, *Dimensions of Authoritarianism: A Review of Research and Theory* (Lexington: University of Kentucky, 1967). For review essays on the bearing of authoritarianism on political life in particular, see Fred I. Greenstein, "Personality and Political Socialization: The Theories of the Authoritarian and Democratic Character," *The Annals of the American Academy of Political and Social Science,* 361, (September 1965), pp. 81–95; Nevitt Sanford, "Authoritarian Personality in Contemporary Perspective," in *Handbook of Political Psychology,* Jeanne N. Knutson, ed.

83. Kirscht and Dillehay, *Dimensions of Authoritarianism,* p. 130.

84. The cross-pressure hypothesis appears in most voting studies. These tend to show that where individuals or groups are exposed to pressures which operate in opposing directions they are likely to respond by losing interest and not voting. For a discussion of evidence for the hypothesis, see Lipset, *Political Man,* pp. 211–226. An extensive discussion and refinement of the hypothesis is presented in David R. Segal, "Status Inconsistency, Cross-Pressures and American Political Behavior," *American Sociological Review,* 34, no. 3 (June 1969), pp. 353–359.

85. Hamilton, *Class and Politics.*

86. Ibid., pp. 216–217.

87. A study of the voting behavior of Catholic Republicans in the 1960 presidential

election in which John Kennedy—a Catholic but a Democrat—ran for office also indicated the limitations of the cross-pressures hypothesis and the restricted influence of economic factors. See Ithiel de Sola Pool, R. P. Abelson, and S. L. Popkin, *Candidates, Issues, and Strategies* (Cambridge, Mass.: M.I.T. Press, 1965), p. 76.

88. Edgar Litt, "Civic Education, Community Norms and Political Indoctrination," *American Sociological Review* 28, no. 1 (February 1963), pp. 69–75. The data do not bear precisely on Marx's claim, for the concept "middle class" does not fit within his analytic scheme.

89. See, for example, Talcott Parsons, "Social Strains in America" in *The Radical Right,* Daniel Bell, ed. (Garden City, N.Y.: Doubleday, Anchor Books, 1964), pp. 209–238; Seymour M. Lipset and Earl Raab, *The Politics of Unreason* (New York: Harper & Row, 1970).

90. V. O. Key, Jr., *Public Opinion and American Democracy* (New York: Alfred A. Knopf, 1963), p. 316.

91. Herbert Hyman, *Political Socialization* (New York: The Free Press, 1959), p. 72.

92. Ibid., p. 105.

93. Hess and Torney, *Development of Political Attitudes in Children.*

94. Ibid., p. 217.

95. The emphasis in the schools on "good citizenship" in this sense is not unique to the United States. For example, Dawson and Prewitt report that in the East African countries of Kenya, Tanzania, and Uganda, nations vastly different from the United States, teaching students such orientations ranks first among a number of "purposes a school might have." See Dawson and Prewitt, *Political Socialization,* p. 162.

96. Langton argues that single-agency analyses of political socialization have ignored the questions of relative influence and therefore have not been able to investigate the possibility of the complementary and interactive effects agencies have on one another. See Langton, *Political Socialization.*

97. Ibid., p. 159.

98. Almond and Verba, *The Civic Culture.*

99. Ibid., p. 134.

100. Ibid.

101. See Easton and Dennis, *Children in the Political System,* pp. 47–70.

102. For an elaboration of a more extreme Marxist argument that schooling in Western industrial countries as well as in the Third World is part of a system of imperialist domination (i.e., schooling is organized to develop and maintain an inequitable organization of production and political power), see Martin Carnoy, *Education as Cultural Imperialism* (New York: Longman, 1974).

CHAPTER FIVE
PARTICIPATION IN NONROUTINE POLITICAL ACTIVITIES

THE CHARACTER OF NONROUTINE PARTICIPATION

In Chapter 4 political acts were defined as acts oriented toward the acquisition and use of power and authority within a specified social system. Those social systems which are of primary interest to political sociologists were described as being relatively large, including such systems as formal organizations, communities, and nations. Routine acts of political participation were defined as those political acts which are encouraged, as opposed to merely permitted, though not required, within a social system. Such participation was viewed as expressing a belief in the legitimacy of the structure of power and authority of the social system.

By way of contrast, acts of nonroutine participation are those political acts which are *not* encouraged, though some may be permitted, within a social system. Such participation expresses a belief that the existing structure of power and authority of the social system is less than fully legitimate. It expresses a belief that something is undesirable about existing political and socioeconomic conditions, and/or policies, and/or political officials and their activities. It is action aimed at change which also expresses the belief that routine varieties of political participation are less likely to bring about desired benefits in the form of political, socioeconomic change than alternative courses of political action.

Acts of nonroutine political participation are neither inherently less rational nor inherently more rational than are acts of routine participation.

Some political behavior, of both routine and nonroutine varieties, is primarily expressive in character. That is, it is primarily oriented toward meeting the actors' desire to demonstrate their loyalties or to give air to their grievances without the attendant goal of actually changing some aspect of the political-economic status quo. However, most political behavior can be seen as directed toward achieving some goal. This is as true of nonroutine participation as it is true of routine participation.

In pursuit of a goal actors will tend to select as means for its attainment the course of action they believe has the greatest likelihood of maximizing valued consequences. Hence, they will choose to engage in a routine form of political participation rather than a nonroutine form when they believe this course of action will have the best payoff. And they will choose to engage in a nonroutine variety of participation when they reach the opposite conclusion. No special set of psychological concepts is necessary to explain the choice of a nonroutine course of action. It is the result of the same kind of decision-making process which leads individuals to select the kind of response encouraged within the existing political system.

Horowitz and Liebowitz point out that those who engage in nonroutine politics are generally treated by political officials as deviants in need of punishment or therapy. They are not defined as legitimate combatants in social conflict but as a social problem—a problem for administrative policy to be handled by experts instead of being debated by the public. Horowitz and Liebowitz argue that the welfare state is an attempt to "cool out" relatively underprivileged strata, reducing the likelihood of their collective nonroutine political action and the potential danger to authorities such action would pose.[1]

Turner has argued that political sociologists must avoid assuming in the first place that there are objectifiable phenomena that must be classified as deviance, protest, or rebellion. Collective acts of nonroutine politics are sometimes viewed as expressions of social protest, and sometimes as crime or rebellion, leading to different community reactions. The protest interpretation, which is the only supportive view of nonroutine political action, is likely to occur only when the action is initiated by a group (1) whose grievances are already documented, (2) which is seen as deserving and powerless to correct its grievances, (3) which shows no signs of conspiracy or serious threat of violence or, if violence does break out, it is used in a constrained way, (4) which uses appeals for support and for change more conspicuously than threats, and when (5) an effort is being made by the community to avoid full-scale conflict.[2]

Gamson has noted that social scientists also have treated those who engage in collective nonroutine politics in a biased manner. He observes that they have maintained an unjustifiable distinction between "the politics of social movements" (nonroutine politics) and the politics of conventional groups and organizations. "The actors who engage in these two types of behavior are seen as different species. Conventional groups act to achieve goals (while non-conventional groups are viewed as) reacting to express distress."[3] Part of the appeal of this approach, according to Gamson, is its "serviceability as an intellectual weapon to discredit mass movements of which one is critical."[4]

The claim that political sociology has focused on the conditions that tend to maintain the basic institutional forms of Western industrial democracies was developed and illustrated in Chapters 2 and 3 of this book. There it was also argued that, for the reasons specified, American political sociology transformed some of the central analytic concepts of its Western European intellectual heritage into social-psychological concepts. The ways in which American political sociologists treat alienation and anomie clearly examplify this transformation. Those particular concepts, in their social-psychological form, appear frequently in the research literature dealing with nonroutine politics. This suggests the need for caution in interpreting the results of the studies in which they appear, some of which are reviewed below.

Most of those who believe that there is something illegitimate about the existing structure of power and authority in their society are neither alienated or anomic in the sense that they are clinically abnormal persons or in the sense that they are people who feel generally powerless or normless or that their lives are essentially meaningless. Nonroutine participation is not frequently motivated by individual psychopathology. Rather, it is most often initiated by a complex set of social and social-psychological factors discussed in this chapter.

The concept of alienation developed by Marx and the concept of anomie advanced by Durkheim referred to conditions of social structure which deprived persons of control of their own lives. They were frustrating structural conditions which people could change through their collective political action. In their analyses, such collective action would not be, in any sense, irrational. The intellectual tradition inherited from Marx, Weber, and Durkheim aids in the understanding of nonroutine politics. It has been the transformation of their contributions which has not helped the empirical understanding of such phenomena as demonstrations, riots, and revolutions—the phenomena which constitute the subject matter of this chapter.

Many of the empirical studies discussed below have in common with the writings of Marx, Weber, and Durkheim a historical-comparative orientation, a central concern with change, and a goal of developing generalizations which are applicable to a number of societies. They are all works which exemplify the likely course of political sociology's development which was discussed in Chapters 2 and 3. They are, however, microanalytic in the sense that they draw on research which makes inferences about collective manifestations of psychological variables. The use of the concept of *relative deprivation* and of the frustration-aggression hypothesis in the literature to be reviewed illustrates this approach. While the studies are microanalytic in this sense, none of those selected for discussion views a form of nonroutine politics as inherently irrational—as having its primary source in individual psychopathology. None takes the position that protestors, demonstrators, rioters, plotters, revolutionaries, or whatever defined social category is being studied, are deviants requiring control, therapy, or punishment. The goal of the studies is to understand the social forces which lead some to believe that the existing structure of power and authority of their society is less than fully legitimate and to feel that existing political and socioeconomic conditions ought to be changed, and to initiate political action aimed at change which takes forms not encouraged within their society.

VARIETIES OF NONROUTINE PARTICIPATION

There are undoubtedly some political sociologists who would argue that the concept "nonroutine political participation" is too broad to permit anything but vacuous generalizations about its sources. Those who write about what appear to be much more limited topics, revolution for example, are commonly attacked on the ground that *this* term covers too many diverse types of events (such as peasant jacqueries, urban insurrections, military coups d'état, conspiracies, domestically supported counterrevolutions, etc.) to permit useful comparisons and generalizations. And even if the topic of revolution is narrowed to include discussions of only the great revolutions of modern history (France, 1789; Russia, 1917; China, 1949) it is sometimes objected that these events occurred under socioeconomic, historical, and cultural conditions which were so diverse that understanding one will produce no insights into the others.

While there is merit in being cautious about the construction of typologies and the development of generalizations from what appear to be vastly different subjects, such efforts can never be rejected a priori. They can be judged only after the fact by checking them against established empirical evidence. Analytically useful typologies and empirically grounded theories of revolutions, internal wars, and other forms of nonroutine politics do exist within political sociology. While there is no such thing as *the* typology of nonroutine political acts or *the* theory of revolution, and so on, some insightful work has been produced. This chapter reviews some of this work.

As a starting point for an analysis of varieties of nonroutine participation, discussion will be limited to its "modern" forms. According to Tilly, in the history of Europe there have been three broad categories of nonroutine participation: "primitive," "reactionary," and "modern."[5] The primitive form, present until about 1600, involved social disruption on a small scale. Action had a local scope, was participated in by members of communal groups as such, and had neither explicit nor clearly political objectives. Examples include feuds, brawls among members of rival guilds, and mutual attacks of hostile religious groups. With the establishment of centralized states upon their victory over rival powers in towns, provinces, and estates, nonroutine political action took its second or "reactionary" form. Conflicts were on a small scale and pitted either communal groups or loosely organized members of the general population against representatives of those who held centralized power. This nonroutine participation was "reactionary" in the sense that it represented a reaction to changes seen as depriving of rights once enjoyed. Examples include revolts against tax collectors, attacks on machines, and forcible occupation of fields and forests by the landless. Such activity faded away by the nineteenth century. "Modern" nonroutine participation emerged with the proliferation and rise to prominence of special-purpose organizations like parties, firms, and unions. Disturbances involve specialized associations organized for political activity with relatively well-defined goals. Such disturbances can attain a large scale. Tilly terms this activity "modern" not only because it often involves complex organizations but also because participants tend to regard themselves as working for rights due them but not yet achieved; they are forward looking. Examples include demonstrations, violent strikes, and guerrilla warfare.

According to Tilly, the development of the city had a significant influence on the development of "modern" nonroutine politics. It did this by grouping people in larger homogeneous blocks than ever before (e.g., in the factory and in the working-class neighborhood), by facilitating the formation of special-interest associations which could inform, mobilize, and deploy large numbers of persons (e.g., the labor union and the party), and by massing the people posing the greatest threat to the authorities near the urban centers of power. Tilly argues that the "plausible presumption" that rapid urbanization produces social disruptions which in turn generate protest is not valid. Rather, there is, if anything, a negative correlation between the rapidity of urban growth and the frequency of collective nonroutine action. Such action is engaged in not by uprooted and anomic individuals, but by people integrated into urban political life who have organized and have developed a sense of collective political interest.

As it is viewed here, all forms of modern nonroutine political participation consist in some sort of involvement in a social movement in Gusfield's sense of "socially shared activities and beliefs directed toward the demand for change in some aspect of the social order."[6] To this will be added Turner's point that all major social movements depend upon and promote normative revision. They become possible when some social category rises in general power and standing and its members begin to demand as their right some social value of which they believe they have been deprived.[7]

The minimum level of participation in nonroutine politics consists in gathering information about, discussing, and expressing support for a social movement during its early phases. During its initial period, according to Blumer, social movements have relatively vague aims and no real organizational structure. Their media of interaction are primarily reading, conversations, talks, discussions, and perception of examples.[8] "Membership" in a movement at this point may involve nothing more than individual self-identification—people are "members" of the movement in the same sense in which most Americans are Republicans or Democrats.

Blumer observes that, over time, social movements tend to clarify their objectives and to develop a recognized and accepted leadership and a definite membership characterized by a "we-consciousness." They further develop a system of organizational rules, policies, tactics, and discipline as well as a body of traditions, a guiding set of values, and a general body of expectations.

The level of individual participation in a developed social movement ranges from nominal membership in an organization seeking limited change through the use of existing values and institutions to the total commitment of all of an individual's resources to an ideological group which seeks to reconstruct the entire social order, rejecting existing social values and institutions, and using strategies far outside legitimate modes of political conflict.[9]

Beyond nominal membership in a social movement the types of action with which this chapter deals occur when participants in a social movement plan, organize, encourage, or participate in an attack, physical or symbolic, on the political institutions, policies, or officials of their social system. Gurr terms such action participation in "civil strife" and identifies three varieties: *turmoil, conspiracy,* and *internal war*.[10] *Turmoil* is characterized by relatively spontaneous, unorganized activity with a low intensity of violence and substantial popular support. It includes political demonstrations, political strikes, riots, police clashes, and localized rebellions. *Conspiracy* is characterized by highly organized activity with limited participation. It aims at subverting a regime by striking at its key members. The category includes political assassinations, small-scale terrorism, small-scale guerrilla wars, most coups, mutinies, plots, and purges. *Internal war* consists of highly organized activity with widespread participation almost always accompanied by extensive violence. It includes large-scale terrorism and guerrilla wars, civil wars, and large-scale revolts.[11]

PRECONDITIONS FOR
NONROUTINE PARTICIPATION

All of the conditions for routine participation specified in the last chapter are also preconditions for nonroutine participation. In some cases this is obvious, but in other cases it is not.

It seems reasonable to assume that the legitimacy of a political system is most likely to be questioned and that collective action aimed at change through nonroutine political methods is most likely to be taken when social, economic, or political conditions reach some absolute level of deprivation. For example, it might be assumed that political instability is most likely to be found where there is widespread poverty and hunger, where a state frequently makes use of naked force and violence, or where there are vast social-economic inequalities. Such assumptions are incorrect. With respect to poverty and hunger, studies cited in Chapter 4 indicate that depoliticization follows physical deprivation—people become too absorbed in meeting their physical needs to take political action. Widespread poverty and hunger focus attention away from politics.

With respect to the use of coercion, a study by Feierabend and Feierabend drawing on data from eighty-four nations covering the period 1948–1962 shows that sufficiently coercive governments are capable of preventing acts of hostility against themselves.[12] The use of violence by the state is often an effective political strategy disorienting those at whom it is directed and thereby reducing the likelihood of their initiating political action. Violence is behavior which makes an environment undependable and unpredictable for its recipient.[13] It keeps an important precondition for political participation from being met.

With respect to the supposed relationship between extensive inequality and political instability, Russett's data on forty-seven countries show that extensive inequality in terms of distribution of agricultural lands leads to political instability *only* in those poor, predominantly agricultural societies where limitation to a small plot of land condemns one to poverty.[14]

A popular theme in political sociology during the 1950s and 1960s was that those who become involved in nonroutine politics are, to a greater or lesser extent, both psychologically and socially maladjusted; they are the alienated, the isolated. Eric Hoffer, for example, claimed that "faith in a holy cause is to a considerable extent a substitute for lost faith in ourselves"[15] and that "the unemployed are more likely to follow the peddlers of hope than the handers-out of relief."[16] As Hoffer saw it, social movements appeal as a cure for atomistic individualism, as activity which facilitates self-forgetting and affords the individual a chance for action and a new beginning.[17]

Kornhauser, expressing a similar theme, argued that nonroutine political activity (which he termed "crisis politics") is most likely to occur in societies in which there is an absence of independent groups between the state and the family. (According to this theory, the independent groups work to protect elites and nonelites from manipulation and mobilization by each other.) In such societies individuals lack psychologically and politically significant ties to one another. "In the absence of social autonomy at all levels of society, large numbers of people are pushed and pulled toward activist modes of intervention in vital centers of society; and mass-oriented leaders have the opportunity to mobilize this activism for the capture of power."[18]

This "mass society" approach did tend to discredit those involved in nonroutine action. It was a theory which took the view that political movements represented a "crisis" in relatively stable political systems. Modern Western democracies in particular seemed prone to attacks by personally alienated and isolated leftist and rightist extremists.

While there may be some truth to the notion that some of those attracted to social movements are isolated and anomic,[19] more recent work has not only revealed the ideological bias of this theoretical approach but has challenged its empirical accuracy as well. For example, on the theoretical level, Pinard argues that certain groups intermediate between the state and the family can and do act to *motivate* and *legitimate* individual as well as collective participation in a political movement. He points out that, at the very least, participants in various social groupings are more likely to learn about the leadership, goals, and successes of a social movement than are atomized people.[20] On the empirical level, Gary Marx's 1964 study showed that blacks supporting the outlook of conventional civil rights groups who had already or said they would take part in demonstrations tended to be among the socially privileged and not among the anomic and isolated. This was so clear that "on the basis of knowing that an individual is very low in social position (little education, low income, low occupational prestige) it is possible to predict that he will not be militant and be correct nine times out of ten."[21] Marx explains that only the relatively privileged have the energy, resources, morals, and self-confidence needed to challenge an oppressive and powerful system.

Findings such as those of Marx, together with America's Watergate experience, suggest that the greatest threat to modern Western industrial democracies is not to be found among alienated masses but in the psychosocial predispositions of its leaders and advisers.

In sum, high levels of physical deprivation, extensive government use of violence, the existence of vast economic inequalities, widespread alienation, and atomization are not the sources of collective nonroutine political action. On the contrary, each of these conditions tends to *reduce* the likelihood of its occurrence. As in the case of routine political action, participants in nonroutine politics tend to be relatively secure physically, socially, and psychologically.

Anomie and alienation do play an important role in nonroutine politics. However, they are not alienation and anomie of the sort considered in "mass society" approaches to nonroutine politics, that is, psychological states of individuals—particularly psychologically maladjusted, socially isolated, politically resourceless individuals.

The anomie involved in nonroutine politics is structural. It is anomie in Merton's sense of inconsistency in the extent of a society's emphasis on certain cultural goals and the extent to which the society provides access to institutionalized means for their achievement. Anomie is the gap between culturally universalized goals and structurally limited means.[22] Merton himself points out that "when the institutional system is regarded as the barrier to the satisfaction of legitimized goals, the stage is set for rebellion as an adaptive response."[23] The likelihood of nonroutine political participation vastly increases when members of a social unit are dissatisfied because of their sense of discrepancy between their aspirations and the institutionalized political means they have available to realize these ambitions. The alienation involved in nonroutine participation is also structural. It is a social condition by virtue of which certain social units have a highly limited, if any, capacity to achieve social, economic, or political objectives through routine political action. Alienation is a structural position of powerlessness.

Neither structural alienation nor anomie is a necessary precondition for the occurrence of nonroutine political participation. As noted earlier, what is essential is that a social unit makes the judgment that the use of nonroutine political patterns is more likely to bring desired results than following institutionalized political patterns. However, it does seem that such an assessment is most likely to be made when there is limited access to the use of institutionalized means and when the unit is in a relatively powerless position.

While objectively high levels of deprivation of various kinds are negatively associated with nonroutine participation, a number of studies suggest that *relative deprivation* of a social value or values is a precondition for such collective action. The strong belief that the group or groups with which one identifies are kept from obtaining what they perceive to be their deserved share of a valued social resource appears to be an important component of the set of beliefs which motivates nonroutine politics. The additional components of the set are the beliefs that (1) some aspect of the existing political system is a primary source of the frustration and that (2) nonroutine participation is more likely than the use of routine politics to open access to the desired resource.

In a number of situations social units will experience a sense of relative deprivation. Being in one of these situations appears to be a precondition for nonroutine participation. Gurr's study of "civil strife" occurring in 114 nations and colonies during the period 1961–1965 identified four different situations of relative deprivation.[24] The first, *aspirational depriva-tion,* occurs when a society's capabilities of providing values remain stable but the ambition of a segment or segments of its population increases. *Decremental deprivation* consists of a society's declining capabilities to provide values in the presence of stable expectations. Examples of this sort of rela-tive deprivation include groups being deprived of long-held civil liberties, groups on stable incomes suffering from increased taxes or inflation, and middle-class groups threatened with displacement by the upward mobility of those below them. *Progressive deprivation* involves a period in which a society has increased its capacity to provide values being followed by a period of substantial relative decline. In this situation expectations for in-creasing well-being are not met. This is the situation in which the so-called revolutions of rising expectations are likely to occur.[25] *Persisting deprivation* exists when some social units continue to expect and demand such condi-tions as greater educational opportunity, political autonomy, or freedom of religious expression that the society will not or cannot provide.

In another article Gurr specifies the psychological conditions which affect the strength of reactions to such deprivations:

1. Given the availability of alternative experiences and beliefs, the likelihood that the more aggressive of them will prevail tends to vary with the strength of anger.
2. The strength of anger itself:
   A. tends to vary directly with
      i   the intensity of commitment to the goal or condition with regard to which deprivation is suffered or anticipated
      ii the degree of effort previously invested in the attainment or main-tenance of the goal or condition
      iii the proportion of all available opportunities for value attainment with which interference is experienced or anticipated
   B. tends to vary inversely with the extent to which deprivation is held to be legitimate
   C. tends to vary as a power function of the perceived distance between the value position sought or enjoyed and the attainable or residual value position
   D. inhibition of aggressive responses by fear of external retribution tends in the short run to increase strength of anger, but in the long run to reduce it
3. The duration of increased anger under conditions of inhibition tends to vary with the intensity of commitment to the value with respect to which depriva-tion is suffered.[26]

Despite the intrinsic and theoretical appeal of such assertions, the role, if any, that relative deprivation plays in nonroutine political action, beyond serving as a precondition, remains unclear. The position taken here is only that some form of relative deprivation is a necessary but not a sufficient condition for the occurrence of nonroutine participation. Moore's investigation of historical situations of unrest (the German Revolution of 1848, the uprisings in the Ruhr around World War I, the reformist revolution between 1918 and 1920, the Russian Revolution, and the National Socialist movement) found no relationship between suffering—whether defined in objective or subjective terms—and rebellion.[27] Hibbs's analysis of internal war and collective protest, based on data from more than one hundred nations, concluded that relative deprivation has little value for explaining actual variation across nations in either of these dimensions of nonroutine political action.[28]

As an alternative to the relative-deprivation hypothesis, Snyder and Tilly suggest that two *political* variables—the extent of government repression and the degree of national political activity—can provide at least partial explanation for year-to-year fluctuations in levels of collective violence in a nation's history.[29] Specifically, they hypothesize a negative partial relationship between government repression (conceptualized as governmental activity which raises the cost of collective action by contenders for power) and the magnitude of collective violence. They also hypothesize that collective violence will tend to rise or fall, all things being equal, with the extent of nonviolent political activity. The theory underlying these expectations is that "collective violence results from changes in the relations between groups of men and the major concentrations of coercive power in their environments."[30] In short, collective violence (as well as nonviolent forms of collective nonroutine political participation) is viewed as a by-product of struggles for political power rather than as a reaction to relative deprivation.

Snyder and Tilly's data, involving time-series analyses of year-to-year fluctuations of collective violence in France from 1830 through 1960, suggest that their theoretical position has some merit and deserves further empirical exploration. They also indicate that expectation-achievement theories of nonroutine participation are not unambiguously established and do require further empirical investigation.[31] Despite the particulars of Snyder and Tilly's data, others have made as good, though not conclusive cases for the importance of relative deprivation in nonroutine politics. The need in political sociology for future macroanalytic, historical-comparative research which focuses on change and aims at the development of cross-societal generalizations is once again indicated.

Securing satisfaction of basic physical needs, meeting the needs for a relatively ordered, predictable, dependable environment, for association and for self-esteem and respect, a sense of relative deprivation (made likely by societal anomie and the alienation of one's group) plus sharing the belief that aspects of the existing political system are responsible for the deprivation, which is most likely to be removed by noninstitutional collective political action—these are the preconditions of nonroutine political participation. While the presence of all of these conditions does not make its occurrence necessary, the absence of any one of them makes such behavior unlikely.

The successful history of modern revolutions in which peasants played central roles (Mexico, 1910; Russia, 1905 and 1917; China from 1921; Vietnam from World War II; Algeria, 1954; Cuba, 1958) appears to call all of the preceding analysis into question. Commonly, peasants engage in little more than subsistence agriculture, where meeting even physical needs is often problematic. Because of their work, peasants are socially isolated; they tend to work on their own land rather than cooperatively. They are often competitors for available resources within their communities as well as for credit from without. Most peasants have been excluded from participation in decision making beyond the village level. The ceaseless routine of their labor keeps them from obtaining political knowledge and skills. In their societies peasants typically lack access to elites, who maintain a clear monopoly over the materials of coercive force as well as over the agencies of socialization. The cause of peasants in itself would seem to attract little support in their broader society. Finally, their lack of resources gives peasants no real ability to inflict great cost and violence on authorities or to protect themselves from the retribution of the authorities.

If this view of peasants were accurate, the facts of their apparently autonomous revolutionary action would invalidate virtually all of the propositions, set forth in this chapter, identifying factors which affect the occurrence of nonroutine politics. However, while this picture of peasants may be correct in very broad outline, a slightly more detailed consideration of their situation reaffirms the tenability of the propositions. Wolf's analysis of peasant revolutions makes the following points: (1) Those segments of the peasantry which engage in revolutionary activity are either a "middle-peasantry" with secure access to land of its own or a peasantry located in a peripheral area, outside the domain of landlord control, which sustains itself by subsidiary economic activity such as casual labor or livestock raising. For peasant revolutionaries, meeting physical needs is not problematic. (2) Peasant revolutions are centered in communities with considerable social solidarity, often derived from their ethnic and linguistic differences from the surrounding population.[32] For example, the peasants of Morelos (Mexico), Kabylia (Algeria), and Oriente Province (Cuba) showed the greatest tendency to rebel against central authority. Peasant revolutionaries are not socially isolated. (3) Rural peasant families commonly have members working in industrial towns. These members gather and transmit political information and ideas—ideas often expressing urban unrest. The peasantry also contains other middlemen who relay communications between urban and rural regions. They include, among others, economic brokers, teachers, and village notables. Peasant revolutionaries do not entirely lack political knowledge and skills. They have some access to elites. (4) Peasant revolutionaries are able to rely on external power to challenge central authority. For example, the Constitutional Army in Yucatan liberated the Mexican peons from debt bondage; the Russian Army collapsed in 1917 and a peasant soldiery emerged; the Chinese Red Army was an instrument designed to break up landlord power in the villages. Peasant revolutionaries do not lack outside support nor do they lack protection or the ability to inflict violence and costs.

Paige's study of agrarian revolution also supports the analysis presented above.[33] His data indicate that the greater the importance of land as a source of income for cultivators, the more likely they are to resist revolutionary political movements.[34] Paige cites a number of reasons for this. First, peasant agricultural production is precarious, and there are bleak alternatives which face the landless in most peasant societies. Second, personal profits and upward social mobility are possible through individual efforts in systems based on small landholdings. Incentives for economic competition weaken incentives for political organization. Third, peasants depending on land tend to be more structurally isolated and dependent on noncultivators. This too weakens the pressures for political solidarity. Hence, land-dependent peasants tend to be politically conservative. This political orientation represents a rational response to the economic conditions of peasant life. On the other hand, the greater the importance of wages in cash or land as a source of income for cultivators, the greater the acceptance of risk and the greater the receptivity to revolutionary appeals. When wages become more important than landholding, economic competition between cultivators is reduced. Agricultural wage laborers are usually brought together in work groups isolated from other classes. Both factors increase pressures for political solidarity, political organization, and collective opposition to a regime.

In sum, studies of peasant revolutions support and/or specify rather than disconfirm the propositions concerning participation in nonroutine politics that have been presented.

NATIONAL LEVELS OF NONROUTINE PARTICIPATION

There are no cross-national studies which present statistics on the frequency of nonroutine political action as it has been defined here. However, there are reports on the frequency of particular kinds of nonroutine political activities in a number of nations.[35] Each of these clearly indicates that nonroutine politics occurs in all societies with much greater frequency than the term suggests. "Nonroutine" is certainly not equivalent to "infrequent."[36] Figures provided in the studies noted below should be sufficient to establish the basic point that nonroutine politics is a major feature of the modern world's political life.

Neiberg reports that "the world (between 1945 and 1968) (saw) 12 limited wars, 48 coups d'état, 74 rebellions for independence, 162 social revolutions, and vast numbers of racial, religious and nationality riots."[37]

Feierabend and Feierabend found that eighty-four countries for which relevant data were available for the years 1948–1962 all had experienced some one or more of thirty types of internal political conflict. Data showed 704 occurrences of unrest including such events as large-scale demonstrations and general strikes, 333 occurrences of serious societal disturbances in the form of coups d'état, terrorism and sabotage, and guerrilla warfare, and 150 occurrences of events connoting violence, such as executions, severe riots, and civil wars. The authors note an inverse relationship between the frequency of occurrence of an event and the intensity of violence which it denotes.[38]

Gurr reports in his 114-nation study that, from 1961 through 1965, more than a thousand instances of civil-strife turmoil, conspiracies, and internal wars (counting waves of demonstrations, riots, or terrorism over related issues as single "events") were reported in general news sources.[39]

During the peak of the period of political activism in the United States, 216 incidents of protest were reported in the *New York Times* and in the *Washington Post* for the single-month period September 16 through October 15, 1968.[40] Contrary to what might be expected, examination of long periods of American history also shows considerable amounts of nonroutine participation. For example, at the elite level, Weisband and Frank found that between 1900 and 1970, 389 people from the rank of Assistant Secretary to Cabinet Officer resigned their high government offices because of their disagreement with prevailing administration policies.[41] For another example, Gamson's study of "challenge groups"—voluntary associations that challenged some aspect of the status quo in American society between 1800 and 1945—revealed between five and six hundred such groups. This is an impressive figure in the light of the extensive set of technical criteria required of a group to be defined as a "challenge group."[42]

SOME SOURCES OF
NONROUTINE PARTICIPATION

Once the preconditions for nonroutine political participation specified above are present in a society, additional variables affect the likelihood of its occurrence, when and where it does occur, its extent and duration.

Initially it must be pointed out that the existence of "social problems" per se does not guarantee that patterns of nonroutine political participation will develop within a society. Social problems do create demands that relevant political elites take actions which appear to insure substantially improved conditions in the future. However, as long as confidence is maintained that there will be future improvement because elites are both willing and competent to bring it about, such demands need not find expression through nonroutine participation. The literature on social movements suggests three classes of factors which are conducive to the development of collective nonroutine political action: *historical, motivational,* and *situational.* Each of these is considered below.

Historical Factors

Among historical factors, a past history of considerable nonroutine political action is particularly important in that such a history is likely to facilitate further such action in the future. "The assumption is that the greater the strife has been in a country's past, the more likely some of its citizens are to regard it as justifiable, and the more likely some would have found it partially successful in the past and hence regard it as potentially useful in the future."[43] For example, this is the case in India, where "protests are so common that they not only supplement formal procedures but supplant them and render them irrelevant. Protests are not used only when other avenues of accommodation have been exhausted, they have become a 'court of first resort.' "[44]

Motivational Factors

Motivational factors include those goals which individuals attempt to achieve through their participation in or through their identification with nonroutine politics. Their involvement may take the forms of continuing participation in nonroutine activities such as demonstrations, continuing membership in an organization related to a political movement, or continuing support through more passive means such as contributing money or displaying symbols.

Zygmunt has pointed out that a motivational explanation of individuals' participation in a social movement must rest on adequate theories of *alienation, attraction, conversion,* and *membership management.*[45] His discussion is applicable to involvement in nonroutine politics. First, Zygmunt notes that a motivational explanation must take into account the fact that identification with collective action which challenges the status quo can have negative repercussions for an individual's relations with others who do not have similar sympathies. Alienating consequences are most likely to occur when the individual is identified with nonroutine politics that are defined very negatively by society. Second, the explanation must account for why individuals get involved with one particular movement rather than another—for example, why they associate themselves with radical rather than with reform politics. Third, the explanation of motivation must recognize that preexisting motives are relevant mainly for understanding initial recruitment. Once one "joins" a political movement, it redirects one's prior motives and creates new motives to meet its own organizational requirements. Fourth, discussions of motives for continued association with a political movement must take into account the fact that the movement itself can play an active role in reducing the negative effects on an individual of facing adversity, disappointment, boredom, and the like.

Almond's 1954 study of persons who had joined and later left the Communist movement in four non-Communist countries—the United States, England, France, and Italy—provides some insights into the motives involved in nonroutine political participation and treats some of the topics described by Zygmunt.[46]

The study identifies two different types of appeal employed by the Communist party in an effort to attract members: exoteric and esoteric. *Exoteric* doctrines or appeals are relatively simple, pragmatic, concrete, and intended for mass consumption. The emphasis is on the actions of antagonistic parties such as the American government and capitalism; there is much less emphasis on the actions of the Communist movement. If the party is discussed directly, it is represented as peace-loving, freedom-seeking, and striving for democracy, humanitarianism, and national independence for their own sake. The arena of politics tends to be local and not worldwide. *Esoteric* party doctrines are contained in the classical writings of Marx, Engles, and Lenin. Such classics stress the actions of the Communist movement and place the actors in a worldwide arena. The movement is pictured as striving for the power of the party, the revolution, and the realization of socialism. Such works emphasize the need for militance, rationality, and organization in order to achieve such goals.

While the vast majority of recruits to the Communist movement in non-Communist nations are aware of the party's exoteric doctrines, their awareness of the esoteric party is primarily limited to knowledge of a few slogans or a brief exposure to some of the classic Communist writings. However, the majority does "register the fact that they are affiliating themselves with something that is esoteric, outlawed, iconoclastic, pitted against society."[47] This strongly suggests that it is not commitment to abstract ideological principles that primarily motivates nonroutine political participation.

Almond presents four categories of motives for joining the Communist party in non-Communist nations. First, there are *self-related interests:* personal objectives such as a career; a desire to participate in group activities with others from strata with which one does not usually associate because of one's racial, religious, or ethnic characteristics; a desire for understanding and having a position on social and political questions. Second, there are *group-related interests:* those objectives an individual might achieve by means of joining a political movement for a group or groups with which he is already identified; examples include helping to advance trade union objectives and facilitating the work of minority-group organizations. Third, there are *ideological interests:* commitments to the principles of the movement's exoteric doctrines resulting from personal knowledge and experience; the movement is seen as an advocate of aggrieved groups and as an opponent of immediate evils. Fourth, there are *neurotic needs:* feelings of rejection and resentment, unworthiness and inadequacy, confusion and uncertainty, which lead individuals to defy the modal patterns of their associates.[48]

Almond's data reveal significant differences among American, British, French, and Italian respondents as to the types of needs and interests which are most commonly related to joining the Communist party. Such differences are accounted for in terms of the differences in the likelihood in the various countries of exposure to esoteric and exoteric doctrines, the extent to which joining the party violated operative social and political norms, and the extent to which the Communist party operated as an effective proponent of the rights of those who suffered significant social, economic, and political disadvantages.

Such an analysis certainly suggests a general typology of motives related to recruitment to nonroutine politics. Future motivational research is needed which makes use of such a typology, which explores further the preconditions for nonroutine political participation, which attempts to answer the full range of questions posed by Zygmunt, and which gathers data on a number and variety of political movements in several societies.

Situational Factors

Situational factors refer to those aspects of a society's social structure and culture which affect the likelihood, extent, duration, and intensity of nonroutine political action within it. Included among these factors are *features of social structure,* particularly level of social-economic development and the character of existing social cleavages, *general social processes,* particularly the rapidity of social-economic change, and *features of political structure,* including the extent to which government authority patterns are congruent with other authority patterns of the society of which it is a part, the extent to which the mass public in general and skilled and educated strata in particular are denied political participation they desire, and the resources possessed by authorities and by those who challenge some aspect of the status quo through nonroutine political means.

The Feierabends' study of 84 nations for the 15-year period 1948–1962 investigated both the relationship between "modernity" and political instability and the bearing of rate of social change on political instability.

Their instability measure consisted primarily, though not exclusively, of the occurrences of nonroutine political events.[49] Specifically, it included resignations of cabinet officials, peaceful demonstrations, assassinations of significant political figures, mass arrests, coups d'état, and civil wars.

Eight indices (GNP, caloric intake, telephones, physicians, newspapers, radios, literacy, and urbanization) were used to construct both a social frustration index and a modernity index. Empirical thresholds were developed for each indicator to develop a composite picture of a stable country. According to the analysis, if all of these threshold values are attained by a society, there is an extremely high probability that the country will achieve relative political stability. Conversely, if measures are less than these threshold values—the more they fail to meet them—the greater the likelihood of political instability (i.e., the greater the likelihood of comparatively high levels of nonroutine political participation).

Data indicate that the stable society is one in which 90 percent or more are literate, with 65 or more radios and 120 or more newspapers per 1,000 population, with 2 percent or more of the population having telephones, with 2,525 or more calories per day per person, with no more than 1,900 persons per physician, with a GNP of $300 or more per person per year, with 45 percent or more of the population living in urban centers. All eight indicators did not predict degree of stability with equal efficiency. Level of literacy was the single best predictor. Comparatively, GNP was one of the weaker predictors, others of which were degree of urbanization, population per physician, and caloric intake per capita per day. Relatively unstable nations with high systemic frustration include Bolivia, Brazil, Bulgaria, Ceylon (now Sri Lanka), Chile, Colombia, Cuba, Cyprus, Dominican Republic, Ecuador, Egypt, El Salvador, Greece, Guatemala, Haiti, India, Indonesia, Iran, Iraq, Italy, Japan, Korea, Mexico, Nicaragua, Pakistan, Paraguay, Peru, Spain, Syria, Thailand, Turkey, Venezuela, and Yugoslavia. Relatively stable nations with low systemic frustration include Australia, Austria, Canada, Costa Rica, Czechoslovakia, Denmark, Finland, West Germany, Great Britain, Iceland, Ireland, Israel, Netherlands, New Zealand, Norway, Portugal, Sweden, Switzerland, United States, and Uruguay.

The Feierabends also found that, in general, the faster the rate of change in the modernization process within any given society, the higher the level of political instability within that society. While modernization does realize some social goals, it also creates new hopes and aspirations which certain strata may be impatient to satisfy. This "feedback effect" operates until a high enough level of satisfaction has been reached that a society will tend toward stability rather than instability.[50]

When rate of change is defined solely in terms of rate of increase in national income, an *inverse* relationship exists between rate of change and political instability. Rapid increase in national income occurs only after a society has become relatively modern and has achieved relatively high levels of literacy, education, and nutrition. The most modern nations that are the most stable show the greatest growth in national income.

Social cleavages which have organizational expression (e.g., political parties representing distinct strata) are particularly important for patterns of both routine and nonroutine politics. Gurr has found that strong, politically effective organizations beyond the family and community level, such as parties and trade unions, tend to minimize nonroutine politics in some groups of countries but not in others. Such organizations can limit the coercive potential of the government and can provide important resources for those dissatisfied with the status quo. In the most developed democratic nations, strong political parties and trade unions are associated with low levels of strife. However, commonly in Latin America, leaders of such associations oppose political authorities and their policies and direct their organizations into demonstrations and sometimes into violent oppositional activity.[51]

Eckstein found that the similarity or dissimilarity of government authority patterns and authority patterns existing elsewhere in a society affects the society's political stability.[52] Government will tend to be stable in a society in which a high degree of resemblance exists between authority patterns of government and authority patterns of associations closely related to government (such as parties and pressure groups); further, there will be found throughout the society, in the associations less closely related to government (such as schools and families), significant departures from functionally appropriate patterns of authority for the sake of imitating the governmental pattern, or, if not this, at least extensive imitation of the government pattern in ritual practices. On the other hand, government will tend toward instability if its authority pattern is substantially different from those of other social segments, or if very abrupt changes in authority patterns occur in organizations closely linked to government, or if several different authority patterns exist in social strata furnishing a large proportion of the society's active routine participants.

Eckstein theorizes that incongruity between authority patterns is a source of strain because individuals must repeatedly be resocialized for participation in different areas of social life. They try to deal with this strain by changing the government patterns under which they live, i.e., by collective nonroutine political action.

Gurr found that the general form nonroutine participation is likely to take in a society is related to the particular segments of the society which experience relative deprivation.[53] When society's more skilled, highly educated members are severely discontented, political action is likely to be highly organized and intense. Such strata possess the intellectual and organizational skills effectively to initiate and direct collective action. When the mass public experiences relative deprivation, but discontent is not felt by the skilled and educated strata, nonroutine participation is likely to be largely spontaneous and disorganized, to involve relatively large numbers of people but to be of low intensity. Whether organized and intense nonroutine participation is large-scale or small-scale is a joint function of the extent of mass deprivation and the strategic access of members of skilled and educated strata to existing political authorities.

The likelihood, extent, and duration of nonroutine political activity in a society, as well as the outcome of such activity, are influenced both by the types and amounts of resources possessed by those who would challenge existing authorities and the types and amounts of resources possessed by the authorities themselves. Any analysis of nonroutine political participation which considers only challenger resources or only incumbent resources is inherently inadequate.

Recognition of the importance of the distribution and use of various resources in accounting for patterns of nonroutine political activity indicates that theories of nonroutine politics which employ only social-psychological variables are unsatisfactory. McCarthy and Zald have pointed out that social-psychological theories which emphasize shared grievances and ideologies neglect many of the most important practical problems which confront regime challenging political groups.[54] For example, one such problem concerns how a disadvantaged group can get outside support. (If Southern civil rights leaders had been unable to enlist the support of Northern white Liberals, the history of the American civil rights movement would have been very different). Another such problem concerns choices of specific tactics which a political organization will employ. Heavy investment of money, facilities, and labor in pursuit of one political goal will leave few resources available for the pursuit of other objectives.

The two most commonly cited resources of authorities, i.e., ideal or material possessions which they can use for their benefit in political conflict (or to reduce the likelihood of conflict in the first place), are *legitimacy* and *effectiveness*. Lipset has defined *legitimacy* as involving "the capacity of the system to engender and maintain the belief that the existing political institutions are the most appropriate for the society,"[55] and *effectiveness* as "actual performance, the extent to which the system satisfies the basic functions of government as most of the population and such powerful groups within it as big business or the armed forces see them."[56] According to his analysis, political systems which are both effective and legitimate, such as those of the United States, Sweden, and Great Britain, tend to be stable. Ineffective and illegitimate regimes, like the regimes of Hungary and East Germany in the late 1950s, are by definition unstable and break down unless they are dictatorships maintained by force. From a short-range perspective, effective but illegitimate regimes, such as those of well-governed colonies, are more unstable than regimes which are relatively low in effectiveness and high in legitimacy, such as were the governments of various Western democracies in the 1930s. However, prolonged effectiveness over a number of generations may give legitimacy to a political system.

There is some question about the exact ways in which and the extent to which legitimacy and effectiveness are associated with nonroutine participation. For example, Lipset presents data indicating that the political stability of any given nation depends more on legitimacy than effectiveness in satisfying wants. On the other hand, Bwy presents data showing that, at least in Latin America, while there are high negative associations between measures of legitimacy and organized violence (guerrilla warfare, revolutions, government crises) no such negative associations exist among these measures and relatively spontaneous violence. That is, in Latin America, riots, strikes, and demonstrations break out just as frequently in highly legitimate political systems as in those with little legitimacy. Furthermore, in these nations, effectiveness (want satisfaction) has a strong negative association with both organized and relatively spontaneous violence (though the relationship is not as strong in the case of organized violence).[57] On the basis of data in his 114-nation study, Gurr argues that legitimacy has no important effect as a mediating variable on deprivation but acts much as a deprivation itself does: Low levels of legitimacy, or by inference feelings of illegitimacy, apparently motivate men to collective violence.[58]

It appears that, at times, legitimacy may not be independent of effectiveness and, in the long run, may be of secondary importance to want satisfaction in influencing patterns of regime opposition. This was illustrated by the 1979 revolution in Nicaragua. What always made the Somoza regime different from others in Latin America was the Somozas' personal control over the national economy. When President Somoza began operating the economy in ways that "violated the rules" which had given significant advantages to business, the Catholic church, and the National Guard, their support was withdrawn.[59] A series of staggering blows to Nicaragua's once robust economy accomplished what years of political struggle, guerrilla war, and unsubtle pressure from Washington failed to do.[60]

Whatever the precise character of the relationship, legitimacy and the ability to satisfy social wants are factors which, if possessed by existing political authorities, are likely to reduce overall levels of nonroutine politics in the society they govern.

The availability of institutional mechanisms that permit the expression of nonviolent hostility can reduce levels of nonroutine participation. Extremist voting and participation in millenarian religious movements serve as examples.[61] Closely related to this resource is the manipulative ability of authorities. This includes the ability to persuade the dissatisfied to employ routine political patterns in the pursuit of their goals or to accept limited adjustive concessions rather than pursue broader and more extensive goals, or to displace their aggression against minority groups or against other nations.[62] In all political systems ideology and propaganda are important methods of elite control. Finally, one of the most important resources of authorities is their "coercive potential"—the size of the coercive force available to them weighted for the degree of its loyalty to the regime. This resource can be applied only in certain ways to increase the likelihood of stability. In the case of societies with coercive political regimes, there is a greater likelihood of political stability if coerciveness is at a level high enough to act as a deterrent to aggression. Conversely, there is a greater likelihood of political instability—increased nonroutine participation—if coerciveness is at mid-level—not sufficient to act as a deterrent to aggression but sufficient to be a source of frustration.[63] Thus, to "coercive potential" as a resource must be added the provision of knowledge concerning how and when to use it.

The major resources which, if possessed by those who would change the status quo through nonroutine politics, increase the likelihood of their taking such action include a high level of motivation, widespread support, protection from the retribution of authorities, and the ability to inflict great costs and violence on authorities. Such factors are clearly related to one another.

Individuals are likely to be highly motivated if their sense of relative deprivation is strong, if they unambiguously blame some component of the political system—or the political system itself—for the deprivation, if they firmly believe collective nonroutine politics represents the best available strategy for the elimination of the deprivation, and if, in addition, they can satisfy through nonroutine political participation wants of the sort identified by Almond, which were described above. High levels of motivation are likely to be widespread when large numbers of individuals sharing such orientations are in frequent and continuous interaction with one another. They are also likely to be widespread when challengers have what they perceive to be an inspired leader or prophet. The 1979 revolution in Iran led by the Ayatollah Khomeini appears to illustrate each of these conditions.

While widespread, high levels of motivation may be an essential resource for initiating and continuing collective nonroutine action aimed at the radical restructuring of a political system, such motivation is not an essential (though it remains a useful) resource for the continuity and potential effectiveness of reform organizations. For example, Lewis has pointed out in the case of the American civil rights movement, "Neither the N.A.A.C.P. nor the Urban League has ever fired the loyalties of the rank and file. Court tests, behind the scenes negotiations and educational efforts are not the kinds of activities which evoke passionate commitments from those who live their lives largely outside the middle class context."[64]

Widespread support for nonroutine political action can serve as a resource in several ways. Large numbers not only increase the probability of success, but by doing so also increase motivation to participate. Widespread support means that individuals are more likely to receive social reinforcement for their political attitudes and participation in nonroutine politics. Widespread support also means that authorities may be less likely to attempt retribution for fear of provoking political conflict which they might lose. The conditions under which nonroutine political action is likely to receive broad support include the existence of persistent and continuous discontent with the existing social-political order and the presence of a well-organized political movement with a clear program for social reformation which has diversified appeal. According to Abel, it was precisely these conditions plus the added ingredient of a charismatic leader (confidence in leaders enhances expectations of success and hence increases motivation) that contributed to the Nazi success in Germany.[65]

A variety of factors determine the ability of authorities to inflict retribution on those who attempt to bring about significant changes in the existing political system or in one of its components.[66] First, there are general cultural factors—such as the society's toleration of coercion. Second, there are the orientations of the authorities themselves—some may be sympathetic to the demands of the discontented. Third, as noted above, there are the related factors of the size and loyalty of the authorities' forces on the one hand and the number and motivation of the challengers' forces on the other. Finally, there are geographical factors, such as the type of terrain the challengers occupy. Clearly, in situations where a society has little historical experience with coercion, where authorities are divided in their loyalties, where challengers are numerous and highly motivated, and where the terrain occupied by challengers makes them difficult to attack, the likelihood of retribution is small. In a similar manner, such factors affect the ability of challengers to inflict costs on authorities.

Every one of the situational factors just noted refers to an internal or "domestic" condition of a nation-state—for example, the level of its economic development or the character of social cleavages which exists within it. Here it must be added that the international and world historical contexts in which the nation-state is located cannot be ignored in accounting for patterns of nonroutine politics which occur within it. This point has been made most forcefully by Theda Skocpol in her historical-comparative study of the French Revolution (1787 through the early 1800's), the Russian Revolution (1917 through the 1930's), and the Chinese Revolution (1911 through the 1960's).[67] For example, she points out that modern social revolutions have happened only in countries situated in disadvantaged positions within international economic or military arenas or both. Such macroanalytic and historical factors will be considered more fully in Chapters 7 and 8.

EARLY THEORIES AND CONTEMPORARY MICRO-RESEARCH ON NONROUTINE POLITICS

In the first section of this book political sociology was conceptualized as the analytic concern with power and authority relations in relatively inclusive social systems, such as formal organizations, communities, and nations, as these influence and are influenced by the bonds of kinship, religion, and class, by interest groups based on other than purely ascriptive or economic ties, and by socially shared belief and value systems. The outline of Chapter 4 followed this definition. The chapter, dealing with microanalysis of routine politics, presented research on the role which family, religion, social class, school, work, and work-related association each plays in determining individuals' patterns of participation. The analyses of Marx, Weber, and Durkheim of the political roles of these social units was then considered in the light of these findings.

Thus far in this chapter, research bearing on the preconditions and the historical, motivational, and situational factors influencing the likelihood, scope, frequency, and intensity of nonroutine political participation within a given society has been considered. At this point the analyses of the modern founders of political sociology will be compared with this contemporary empirical work in order to suggest something of the changes and continuities in political sociology since its inception. Comparison cannot proceed as in Chapter 4 by considering, in order, what each theorist wrote about the role of the family, the religious organization, and so on. This is due to the fact that the role played by each of these units varies by historical instances of nonroutine political action. Systematic comparison can be carried out only by considering the analytic utility of the classic writings for a particular historical instance of nonroutine political action which has been selected as a case study. This will be done in the next section of this chapter. However, before presenting a case study, the general viewpoints of the classical authors will be considered in relation to the findings thus far described.

Marx's view that social conflict and change proceed from contradictions in social structure receives some empirical support from contemporary research literature. In many instances, those in positions of power and privilege do limit access to culturally legitimized means to achieve economic goals which, their ideology falsely asserts, are equally available to all. When such ideology fails to persuade—when a segment of society believes that the existing structure of power and authority of their society is less than fully legitimate—those in positions of power can and do attempt to maintain the status quo through the use of force. People whose structural location deprives them of control over their own lives, people who are alienated, can and do attempt structural change through collective political action, rejecting ideology and physically challenging the authorities. The goal of such collective political action frequently is to change the social rules under which people work and live and to change the ways in which these rules are established. Programs for the achievement of such objectives characteristically involve reference to introducing fundamental changes in the society's economic structure.

The research reviewed above shows that the deprivations experienced by those who challenge the status quo politically are neither absolute in any sense nor exclusively economic. Relative deprivation rather than absolute economic deprivation is a major precondition of collective nonroutine participation. Such action may be initiated to secure power, prestige, or other ideal or symbolic goals in addition to predominantly economic goals. Those who seek change through collective nonroutine political activity may or may not constitute a social class in Marx's sense. Finally, authorities do not invariably act essentially in the interest of economically dominant strata. Their use of diversionary mechanisms, strategic concessions, or coercion often represents nothing beyond efforts to keep *themselves* in positions of power.

Weber's contribution to understanding nonroutine participation includes his identification of some of its probable sources, the categories of antagonistic parties likely to be involved, and some of the factors which influence its form and outcome within a given society. According to Weber, all forms of domination—traditional, charismatic, and rational-legal—have inherent difficulties. They all have characteristics potentially productive of dissatisfaction and instability. In the case of modern rational-legal systems, at least within industrial democracies, widespread dissatisfaction can arise from the tendency, noted by Weber, for power to become concentrated in the hands of politically nonresponsible "experts." America's recent energy and economic crises suggest that such dissatisfaction is most likely to be felt when such "experts" apparently fail to find technical solutions to major socioeconomic problems confronting the society. Such failure can result in the decremental deprivation identified by Gurr as a major precondition of nonroutine political action and can lead to the development of support for nonroutine politics among those most directly affected by such failure. Weber's view that social change proceeds from conflict between groups pursuing incompatible ideal as well as material interests facilitates understanding something of the broad range of deprivations—including such values as social status, civil liberties, and political autonomy—which can prompt nonroutine political action. His position that beliefs and values can serve as determinants of behavior encourages examination of the ways in which a society's historical experiences and subsequent cultural emphases can facilitate or limit the use of various strategies by authorities and by challengers in political conflict.

The limitations of Weber's work for understanding nonroutine political participation lie in his possible overestimation of the importance of legitimacy and in the lack of a more extensive examination of the functions and dysfunctions of bureaucratic organization in diverse settings. It was pointed out above that present empirical research is inconclusive on the importance of legitimacy in nonroutine politics as compared with other factors, particularly regime effectiveness. With respect to bureaucracy, it was noted in Chapter 1 that following bureaucratic procedures does not have identical consequences in all types of organizations; an effective and efficient administrative structure for an army might not serve as an effective and efficient administrative structure for a factory or a hospital or a school. More specific to the analysis of nonroutine politics, government organization and operation according to strict bureaucratic procedures may have different social-political consequences in democratic and in nondemocratic political systems—in the politics of advanced industrial nations and in the politics of developing nations.

Durkheim tended to see disruptive social conflict as a problem to be avoided—as an indication that something was at fault in the social structure and moral order of a society. Serious political conflict could represent widespread anomie and could carry with it the threat of anarchy and loss of individual freedom. Such a view was useful in that it promoted the investigation of two central factors influencing nonroutine political participation: (1) poor integration of social values and social structure (where structure blocks the achievement of goals emphasized throughout the society so that supposed social values do not define and explain existing institutions) and (2) the associational structure of society. The view is limiting to the extent that it encourages analyzing political conflict within a society almost exclusively as a problem for authorities rather than additionally as an opportunity for challengers.[68] It is also limiting to the extent that it ignores the role which associations, including occupational associations, can and do play in developing support for political movements seeking radical change.

A CASE STUDY OF NONROUTINE POLITICAL PARTICIPATION: STUDENT ACTIVISM IN THE UNITED STATES IN THE 1960S

Student political activism that occurred in the United States during the period extending from 1964, when the "Free Speech Movement" emerged at the University of California at Berkeley, to the early 1970s, by which time such activism was comparatively rare on American campuses, can serve as a case study in terms of which the bearing of kinship, religion, economy, stratification, and shared belief and value systems on nonroutine political participation can be considered. The analytic utility of the views of Marx, Weber, and Durkheim on the parts played by these factors in the processes of political conflict and change can be explored by viewing their perspectives and their claims in the light of empirical studies of American student politics. Again it must be emphasized that it remains an empirical question as to whether any of the generalizations about the sources of student activism which occurred during this period are applicable to other historical instances of nonroutine political participation.

Student political activism was selected as the case study because a vast amount of empirical research on the topic is readily available[69] and because research can be located which treats the specific topics of the role played by the family, by the church, by the economy, by social class, and by cultural values and norms. However, there is one major precaution that must be taken in approaching this body of research literature. Perhaps because the political action was so "close to home" there was a stronger than usual tendency on the part of political sociologists to be judgmental in their analyses. To some, student protesters represented "young intelligentsia" in search of a better world[70] while to others they were youth manifesting the trauma of adolescence[71] or spoiled children in a society whose abundance lowered the value of effort and achievement in conventional occupational roles.[72]

Kinship and Stratification

In the analyses of student political activism, the influence of family is not separated from the influence of social class. Families are treated as the agencies through which class perspectives are transmitted and established.

The most frequently reported characteristic of the early student radicals (those active during the period of roughly 1964–1968, after which the social base of the student movement broadened considerably) was that they were drawn disproportionately from upper-middle-class households with politically liberal, socially democratic, humanistic, and egalitarian values, with a high degree of permissiveness with respect to self-regulation, and with an emphasis on values other than achievement—in particular an emphasis on the importance of living up to intellectual, political, or religious ideals.[73] Flacks argues that young people raised in such a family context have difficulty in submitting to adult authority, are unlikely to express unexamined allegiance to conventional values, and are likely to reject and oppose practices which conflict with their ideals. This, he maintains, is one major source of their inclination to nonroutine political action.[74]

Inglehart's 1970 study of student activists in the Netherlands, Belgium, Italy, France, Germany, and Great Britain produced findings similar to those on American students.[75] He, like Flacks, hypothesizes that youth who have been socialized under conditions of relatively high and stable affluence show preference for values such as free speech and political participation (which he terms "post-bourgeois" values) rather than for values such as economic security and domestic order (which he terms "acquisitive values"—values which are dominant in Western Europe at present). Post-bourgeois values, which do not conform to those of society as a whole, are hypothesized to be linked to a relatively change-oriented stand on current issues and preference for change-oriented political parties. Data support the hypothesis and also clearly show that those with post-bourgeois values in the five nations were considerably more favorable to student demonstrations than those with acquisitive values (71 percent versus 16 percent).

Studies of socialization to which student activists were exposed were not based on the assumption that socialization experiences within the family were the sole determinant of individuals' political involvement. It was the conjunction of such upbringing with certain subsequent experiences—particularly with the university and with the polity itself—experiences occurring within the context of a particular configuration of historical, social, political, and economic processes and events which prompted the activist response.[76] Nevertheless, research does suggest that the upper-middle-class family's role in promoting predispositions to left-wing activism was of considerable importance.

Findings on the class origins of student activists initially appear to contradict expectations based on Marx's theory. It was young members of the bourgeoisie rather than young members of the proletariat who led the left-wing rebellion. Furthermore, the values which motivated the behavior of the activists were not the values which Marx attributed to the bourgeoisie. Hence, as applied to American student activism of the late 1960s, Marx's analysis appears to be misleading.

There are two lines of reasoning which counter these criticisms of the Marxist perspective as applied to student activism. Both contend that, despite the upper-middle-class position of their parents, student activists could not be considered members of the bourgeoisie. First, data show that parents of student activists tended to be professionals, not corporate owners. It can be argued that with the increasing number of technical and professional personnel in the United States and with continuing concentration of corporate power, such strata are becoming increasingly alienated. More and more, the conditions of their labor and the character of the political system under which they live are being determined by those at the top of the "military-industrial complex." More and more, the objective interests of these strata correspond to those of the working class.

Second, the class location of students can be considered independently. For example, Pinner has argued that students constitute a "marginal elite" and, as such, can be expected to act in predictable ways.[77] He maintains that because of their segregation—their sense of identity and the ease with which communications can be established and maintained among groups living in relatively closed communities—marginal elites are easily mobilized for action. Together with the social position and the ideological predispositions of marginal elites, their high level of internal communication explains their sudden assumption of leadership roles at moments of political change.[78]

This second position denies the relevance of social status and class perspectives inherited from the family. Pinner maintains that, due to their structural position and cultural importance, marginal elites were particularly attracted to populist-type ideologies (including populist versions of Marxism-Maoism). Such marginal elites resemble the intellectuals whom Marx identified as playing an important role in developing working-class consciousness and furthering the proletarian revolution.

Weber did not present an extended analysis of the importance of the family in the political life of modern societies. Rather, he tended to argue that in rationalized society the political significance of kinships is considerably diminished. Nevertheless, his position that sets of beliefs and values serve as important components in systems of domination encourages a search for those points at which such orientations are established or fail to be established. In the case of student activism, such a search proved to be fruitful.

Durkheim, like Weber, believed that the family had a reduced political role in societies with a complex division of labor. Research on student activism indicates that Durkheim seriously misjudged the importance which traditional structures can have in modern society. The theoretically interesting point in this case is that a traditional structure, the family, was creating and transmitting nontraditional values which helped promote change-oriented political action. Research showed that activists' parents were "preparing their young to lead responsible, autonomous lives, but in accordance with inner-directed goals and values rather than externally defined roles."[79]

Religion

Little, if any, empirical research focused on the significance of specifically religious affiliations and orientations for student activism. Several studies reported that among activists there was a disproportionately high percentage of Jews and those expressing no religious orientation.[80] Beyond the statement of this uniformity, little has been offered by way of discussing possible links between religion and student politics.

Studies of black protest occurring at approximately the same time, however, did investigate the role of Christianity in militancy and do at least suggest some general hypotheses. For example, Gary Marx's 1964 study showed that religiosity (whether measured by the importance of religion to the respondent, the orthodoxy of the respondent's religious belief, or the frequency of attendance at worship service) tended to reduce militancy.[81] Nevertheless, Marx argued that although the net effect of religion is clearly to inhibit attitudes of protest, many religious people are militant. This is due to the fact that

> like most ideologies, both religious and secular, Christianity contains many themes, which if not in contradiction, are certainly in tension with one another. Here, no doubt, lies part of the explanation of religion's varied consequences for protest. One important strand of Christianity stresses acceptance of one's lot and glorifies the after-life. However, another is more concerned with the realization of the Judaeo-Christian values in the current life.... When one's religious involvement includes temporal concerns and acceptance of the belief that men as well as God have a role in the structuring of human affairs then, rather than serving to inhibit protest, religion can serve to inspire and sustain it.[82]

If this line of thought is correct, there is good reason to doubt Marx's dictum that religion is the opiate of the masses. Religion can provide a set of values with which to criticize the political status quo. Modern history provides a number of dramatic examples of this: In 1949 Hungarian Primate Joseph Mindszenty became a tragic embodiment of the opposition of church and political regime; ever since the South African government sanctioned apartheid in 1948 the South African Council of Churches has urged its followers to ignore apartheid laws; the Iranian revolution of 1979 was led by a Moslem fundamentalist sect. In addition, religion can provide an organizational structure in which political skills useful in nonroutine politics can be acquired, attitudes critical of the existing political system can be transmitted, and collective action aimed at change through nonroutine means can be directed.

Weber's theoretical contribution to understanding student activism lies, in part, in his emphasis on the importance of legitimation processes in systems of domination. His writings certainly suggest that in a modern society in which political structures and practices are not congruent with value systems maintained by socially significant religious groups, the likelihood of political stability would be diminished considerably. In a rationalized society, when religion does not support "the law" as it is expressed in political practices, the ability of a regime to govern effectively is hindered seriously.

Durkheim's major theoretical concern was with social instability and the threat of anarchy arising from anomie. His statements on this topic would lead one to predict that a society in which fundamental moral norms did not appear to many to guide political life would experience considerable turmoil. It is doubtful, however, that Durkheim would have attributed much importance to religion as a source of moral norms in contemporary society. Religion was seen by Durkheim, at the time of his writing, as performing integrative functions—reducing anomie and thereby reducing the likelihood of social-political instability.

Economy

Most theories of student activism refer to the fact that such nonroutine participation took place during an extended period of economic prosperity. Interpretations of the meaning of this fact for student activism varied considerably. In a study previously mentioned, Inglehart argued that values which he construed as motivating student activism represent "higher order" values in Maslow's sense—values which emerge as major motivators of behavior once basic needs, such as those for food, security, and a dependable environment, have been met. Similarly, Flacks hypothesized that students were part of a first generation in advanced industrial societies in which a substantial number of youth were both motivated to free themselves from conventional status concerns and could afford to do so. They represented a "liberated generation" in the sense that their affluence made it possible for them to ignore, at least temporarily, the occupational and status concerns which have long been important features of American middle-class social characteristics, in pursuit of values which were lacking in the occupational sphere.[83]

Aron, viewing the impact of prosperity differently, argued that young people born between 1945 and 1950 (most of the activists) simply lacked authentic experience with poverty, fascism, totalitarianism, and war. They represented a generation devoid of historical awareness in conflict with an older generation whose values and political views were shaped by the harsh political-economic realities of the 1930s and 1940s. According to Aron, they represented threats to democracy in the industrialized West for "there is a danger that everything will begin all over again because in their eyes everything begins with them."[84]

Whatever the interpretation of the fact of protest by the advantaged in the context of economic prosperity, any theory attempting to account for this fact would seem destined to contradict any explanations of student protest that could be developed from the theoretical framework provided by Marx. For example, in developing his thesis that student protest is to be understood as a form of generational conflict, Feuer makes an explicit point that the political interests of young workers and the political interests of students are and always have been vastly different. There has always been a psychological cleavage between workers and students of the same age. Young workers are motivated by class consciousness—a set of concerns about matters such as wages, working hours, working conditions, fear of unemployment, and fear of life always at the bottom. Students, on the other hand, are motivated by generational consciousness—a set of concerns about matters such as absolute ethical conceptions of justice and right.[85]

Despite observations such as those of Feuer, there is a viable Marxist interpretation of student protests. Flacks, for example, argued that several fundamental changes had occurred in advanced capitalist societies over the past several decades which created a "new working class" (elsewhere referred to by Flacks as the "intelligentsia" or "educated labor" and including students as the "young intelligentsia") capable of serving as the agency of revolutionary change.[86] The most important of these developments has been the introduction of a technology which has freed increasing numbers from direct dependence on material production for making a living and provides them with material security. However, the demands of capitalism for maintaining the imperatives of profit, economic growth, and individual consumption keep people from realizing the liberating promises of the new technology. In developing this position Flacks refers to an essay by Martin Nicolaus which suggests that Marx anticipated that within advanced capitalism the proletariat might be well fed and intellectually sophisticated and make the revolution in order to eliminate alienated labor and to achieve for all the promises embodied in the technological capacities of society.

Weber's contribution to understanding the bearing of the economy on student politics lies in his discussion of rationalization. The emphasis on principles of hierarchy, authority, and impersonality which Weber recognized as being essential to the survival of the modern economic organization were directly opposed to the values which upper-middle-class youth had had emphasized in their families. Rationalization embodied precisely those principles which student protesters rejected in their attack on the political-economic order.

Durkheim recognized that social instability could arise during periods of economic prosperity just as readily as it could arise during less prosperous times. The critical factor, in all cases, was the extent to which individuals were provided with a relatively well defined moral framework within which to conduct their lives. Durkheim further believed that in modern societies individuals' positions within the division of labor would have considerable moral significance for them. Even though Durkheim misjudged the significance of traditional structures such as the family in modern society, the occurrences of high levels of nonroutine participation during a period of prosperity when moral norms emphasized in the sphere of work directly contradicted moral norms emphasized in the family is consistent with his theoretical perspective.

Shared Belief and Value Systems

The beliefs and values of upper-middle-class families which contributed to the development of activist tendencies in their young have already been described. The beliefs and values discussed here are those which students acquire in the course of their academic training.

Research shows that student activists were disproportionately drawn from the ranks of those majoring in the humanities and the social sciences. There are numerous possible reasons to account for this uniformity. Activist tendencies of many liberal arts and social science students may have had something to do with the fact that, for the most part, training in these areas has little connection with occupational roles which students envision for themselves in the future, with the fact that faculty in these areas tend to be comparatively liberal and often support activities such as student demonstrations, with the possibility that those who choose to major in the humanities or in the social sciences tend to have liberal or radical activist orientations even before they enter academic programs, or with the possibility that beliefs and perceptions acquired as part of one's training in the humanities and social sciences somehow predispose one to liberal or radical activism. This fourth possibility will be considered here briefly.

Wasburn's 1967 study of approximately 750 students enrolled in social science courses at four colleges revealed that those with relatively high scores on a test of social science knowledge tended to be politically more liberal and to be more involved with politics than others (including participating in demonstrations protesting U.S. foreign policy).[87] The liberalizing influence of social science knowledge was predicated, in part, on the basis of the hypothesis that knowledge of some of the extent to which human beings' psychological constitution and the social world tend to limit their alternatives may lead to a general disposition to adopt perspectives such as these: "It's understandable why they do X or believe Z" or "If I were in their situation I'd probably do the same thing as they are doing." Such attitudes, it was reasoned, may be accompanied by a lessening of the tendency to impute responsibility and to assign blame. The result may then be a greater emphasis on "help" and "understanding" and, more important, upon changing social conditions rather than upon punishment, retribution, and "adjustment." The expectation that social science knowledge is positively associated with political participation, both routine and nonroutine, was based on two hypotheses: (1) Individuals who are knowledgeable in social science tend to be aware of a more extensive set of social consequences which can result from the adoption of social policies and therefore are more likely to view policy decisions as important. (2) In cases where social science knowledge leads to increasing liberalization of politically relevant attitudes it will lead to increasing partisanship—which is an expression of policy preference. Viewing politics as important and partisanship are both positively associated with political participation.[88]

In Marx's theoretical scheme ideal factors do not serve as independent determinants of social behavior. Dominant social ideas were primarily tools used by the privileged to help maintain their position. In Chapter 2 several sociological accounts of the history and present character of sociology were described which argued, in a Marxist manner, that the basic features of this idea system in particular was developed to meet the needs of industrial welfare democracies. In this view of American sociology, students were being trained to be deployables for private corporations and for government. They were being trained as technicians with usable skills rather than as intellectuals with critical and innovative orientations. If this is so, it is surprising that the students who had the greatest contact with idea systems supporting the status quo were the very ones who were most critical of it and were most likely to participate in nonroutine politics.

Weber's major contribution to understanding nonroutine politics in general lies in his recognition of the importance of legitimating belief and value systems for maintaining systems of domination and in his analysis of the relationship between these belief and value systems and the different organizational forms associated with different systems of domination. It is consistent with his analysis that major criticism of and attack upon existing authorities should come from those directly tied to the society's central belief- and value-shaping institutions; in the case of advanced, industrial societies, these institutions are colleges and universities. The conflict between democratic values and bureaucratic norms was cited by Weber as a source of tension in modern society. Student protests against the impersonality and nonresponsiveness of the authorities of the state and the authorities of the university can be seen as a response to that tension.

Durkheim's work directs attention to three related features of society: the division of labor, moral integration, and organizational structure. Students have an unusual position in modern society with respect to each of these. They have no economically productive role in the division of labor; the moral norms emphasized in their homes (at least the homes of upper-middle-class students) and expressed, however implicitly in their classrooms (at least in those of humanities and social science students), were often at variance with those apparently operative in the world of work; they lacked psychologically meaningful and politically effective organizations to mediate their relations to their universities and to their state. Persons in such a position are very poorly integrated into their society and, reasoning from Durkheim's writings, would seem to be among those likely to challenge established institutions.

The case study of student activism indicates that many of the approaches, concepts, and hypotheses presented by Marx, Weber, and Durkheim have considerable analytic utility today. At some points particular lines of thought did appear to be misleading. At many other points they proved to be insightful. Some overall assessment of the advantages and disadvantages acquired through empirical application of their work should provide a sense of political sociology's changes and continuities. Progress in political sociology will not be achieved through a priori rejection of the works of its theoretical forebears but by a systematic building upon what has been found to be of value in their ground-breaking efforts.

NOTES

1. Irving Louis Horowitz and Martin Liebowitz, "Social Deviance and Political Marginality: Toward a Redefinition of the Relation between Sociology and Politics." *Social Problems,* 15, no. 3 (Winter 1968), pp. 280–296.

2. Ralph H. Turner, "The Public Perception of Protest," *American Sociological Review,* 34, no. 6 (December 1969), pp. 815–831.

3. William A. Gamson, *The Strategy of Social Protest* (Homewood, Ill.: Dorsey, 1975), p. 132.

4. *Ibid.,* p. 133. For example, Gamson notes that *The Authoritarian Personality* discredited the fascist movements of the 1920s and 1930s by depicting the followers of Hitler and Mussolini as irrational victims of a sick society.

5. Charles Tilly, "Collective Violence in European Perspective," in *The History of Violence in America: Historical and Comparative Perspectives,* Hugh Davis Graham and Ted Robert Gurr, eds. (New York: Praeger, 1969). Tilly's categories of collective violence have been extended here to include nonroutine political activity which is not necessarily violent. Tilly himself includes political demonstrations, which can be nonviolent, in his discussion. For his more recent general theory of collective political action, see Charles Tilly, *From Mobilization to Revolution* (Reading, Mass.: Addison-Wesley, 1978).

6. Joseph Gusfield, ed., *Protest, Reform and Revolt* (New York: John Wiley & Sons, 1970), p. 2.

7. Ralph H. Turner, "The Theme of Contemporary Social Movements," *British Journal of Sociology,* xx, no. 4, 1969.

8. Herbert Blumer, "Social Movements," in his *Principles of Sociology* 3rd ed. (New York: Barnes and Nobel, 1969).

9. For a discussion of ideological groups and a description of the individual commitment involved in belonging to them, see Vladimir Nahirny, "Some Observations on Ideological Groups," *American Journal of Sociology,* 67, no. 4 (January 1962), 397–405.

10. Ted Robert Gurr, "A Comparative Study of Civil Strife," in *History of Violence in America,* Graham and Gurr, eds., pp. 572–626.

11. The term "internal war" was originally proposed by Harry Eckstein. He used it to denote any resort to violence within a political system to change its constitution, rulers, or policies. It is conducted practically without mutually observed normative rules and involves serious disruptions of settled institutional patterns. All species of internal wars have in common the use of force to achieve purposes which can also be achieved without violence. All indicate a breakdown in the legitimate political order and the existence of collective frustration and aggression in the population. All presuppose certain capabilities for violence by those who make the internal war and a certain incapacity for preventing violence among those on whom it is made; all tend to scar societies deeply and to prevent the formation of consensus indefinitely. See Harry Eckstein, ed., *Internal War, Problems and Approaches* (New York: The Free Press, 1966).

12. Ivo K. Feierabend and Rosalind L. Feierabend, "Systemic Conditions of Political Aggression: An Application of Frustration-Aggression Theory," in *Anger, Violence and Politics,* I. K. Feierabend, R. L. Feierabend, and T. R. Gurr, eds., (Englewood Cliffs, N.J.: Prentice-Hall, 1972), pp. 136–183.

13. "Violence is either behavior which is impossible for others to orient themselves to or behavior which is deliberately intended to prevent orientation and the development of stable expectation with regard to it." Chalmers Johnson, *Revolutionary Change* (Boston: Little, Brown, 1966), p. 8.

14. Bruce M. Russett, "Inequality and Instability: The Relation of Land Tenure to Politics," *World Politics,* 21, no. 3 (April 1964), 442–454.

15. Eric Hoffer, *The True Believer* (New York: Mentor Books, 1958), p. 22.

16. *Ibid.,* p. 24.

17. *Ibid.,* pp. 27–28.

18. William Kornhauser, *The Politics of Mass Society* (New York: The Free Press 1959), p. 41.

19. Despite its pejorative aspect, the theory may be applicable to utopian or to retreatist movements, which are unlikely to recruit mass memberships in Western industrial societies.

20. Maurice Pinard, "Mass Society and Political Movements: A New Formulation," *American Journal of Sociology*, 73, no. 6 (May 1968), p. 682-690.

21. Gary T. Marx, *Protest and Prejudice* (New York: Harper & Row, 1967), p. 64.

22. Robert K. Merton, *Social Theory and Social Structure*, enlarged ed. (New York: The Free Press, 1968), pp. 185-248.

23. *Ibid.,* p. 210.

24. Gurr, "A Comparative Study." Civil strife is defined as all collective non-governmental attacks, physical and symbolic, on persons or property that occur within a political system, excluding individual crimes.

25. See James C. Davies, "Toward a Theory of Revolution," *American Sociological Review*, 27, no. 1 (February 1962), 5-19. Davies explains Dorr's Rebellion of 1842, the Russian Revolution of 1917, and the Egyptian Revolution of 1952, as well as other civil disturbances, in these terms.

26. Ted Robert Gurr, "Psychological Factors in Civil Violence," *World Politics*, 20, (January 1968), 245-278.

27. Barrington Moore, Jr., *Injustice: The Social Bases of Obedience and Revolt* (White Plains, N.Y.: M. E. Sharpe, 1978).

28. Douglas A. Hibbs, Jr., *Mass Political Violence* (New York: Wiley-Interscience, 1973).

29. David Snyder and Charles Tilly, "Hardship and Collective Violence in France, 1830 to 1960," *American Sociological Review*, 37, no. 5 (October 1972) 520-532. Data do not directly challenge the position taken here—that some form of relative deprivation is a *precondition* for nonroutine participation. Rather, data are presented which call into question assertions connecting levels of relative deprivation to levels of collective violence. Research containing such assertions is described in this chapter.

30. *Ibid.,* p. 520.

31. For criticisms of Snyder and Tilly's research and for their replies, see Charles N. Halaby, "'Hardship and Collective Violence in France': A Comment," *American Sociological Review*, 38, no. 4 (August 1973) 495-501, and Snyder and Tilly, "How to Get From Here to There," Ibid., pp. 501-504; James C. Davies, "The J-Curve and Power-Struggle Theories of Collective Violence," *American Sociological Review*, 39, no. 4 (August 1974) 607-610, and Snyder and Tilly, "On Debating and Falsifying Theories of Collective Violence," Ibid., pp. 610-613.

32. Eric R. Wolf, "Peasant Rebellion and Revolution," in *National Liberation: Revolution in the Third World*, Norman Hiller and Roderick Aya, eds. (New York: The Free Press, 1971), pp. 48-67.

33. Jeffery M. Paige, *Agrarian Revolution* (New York: The Free Press, 1975).

34. *Ibid.,* p. 36.

35. See, for example, the table compiled by Rudolph J. Rummel and Raymond Tanter from data for 84 nations covering the period 1955-1960. Data concern assassinations, general strikes, guerrilla wars, major government demonstrations, revolutions, and numbers killed in domestic violence. Table 13 in *Anger, Violence and Politics*, I. K. Feierabend, R. L. Feierabend, and T. R. Gurr, eds., pp. 400-405.

36. Experimental studies show that "a substantial proportion of people do what they are told to do, irrespective of the content of the act and without limitations of conscience so long as they perceive that the command comes from a legitimate authority." Stanley S. Milgram, "Some Conditions of Obedience and Disobedience to Authority," *Human Relations*, 18, no. 1 (February 1965), 57-76. However, nonroutine political participation is, by definition, behavior which expresses the belief that an existing structure of authority is less than fully legitimate.

37. H. L. Nieburg, "Politics of Confrontation," in *The Sociology of Dissent*, R. Serge Denisoff, ed. (New York: Harcourt Brace Jovanovich, 1974), p. 347.

38. Ivo K. Feierabend and Rosalind L. Feierabend, "Aggressive Behaviors within

Polities 1948–1962, A Cross National Study," *Journal of Conflict Resolution,* 10 no. 3 (September 1966), 249–271.

39. Gurr, "A Comparative Study." p. 574.

40. National Commission on the Causes and Prevention of Violence, *The Politics of Protest* (New York: Simon and Schuster, Clarion Books, 1969), p. 3.

41. Edward Weisbrod and Thomas M. Frank, *Resignation in Protest* (New York: Grossman-Viking, 1975).

42. Gamson, *The Politics of Protest.* Definitional criteria are presented on pp. 16–18.

43. Gurr, "A Comparative Study." p. 605.

44. David H. Bayley, "Public Protest and the Political Process in India," in *Protest, Reform and Revolt,* ed. J. Gusfield, p. 304.

45. Joseph F. Zygmunt, "Movements and Motives: Some Unresolved Issues in the Psychology of Social Movements," *Human Relations,* 25, no. 5 (November 1972), pp. 449–467. In this context *alienation* merely refers to antagonistic, hostile, or unfriendly social relationships.

46. Gabriel A. Almond, *The Appeals of Communism* (Princeton, N.J.: Princeton University Press, 1954). The study deals with two types of Communist movements—the small deviational movements of the United States and Great Britain, and the mass, working-class parties of France and Italy. Data consist in analyses of Communist doctrines and propaganda and in extensive interviews with 221 former party members. Most respondents had had a long tenure in the party and had held formal positions in the party hierarchy. The validity of findings based on the sample of ex-Communist respondents was checked by reference to available biographical data on then current members of the Central Committees of the Communist Parties of France, Italy, and the United States.

The study is not without major methodological problems. First, the validity of data depends on the ability of subjects to accurately recall their behavior, opinions, motives, and perceptions in emotionally charged contexts in the somewhat distant past. Second, the usual criticisms of the use and validity of various psychological tests and the interpretations of test results are applicable.

47. Ibid., pp. 231–232.

48. Nonroutine participation is not usually motivated by some form of psychological maladjustment. Earlier in this chapter it was argued that, in their psychological interpretations, *alienation* and *anomie* are negatively associated with nonroutine participation. However, under certain circumstances such factors do promote activity. As Almond's own data indicate, this is most likely to occur in situations where such participation is likely to have little, if any, instrumental significance.

49. Feierabend and Feierabend, "Aggressive Behaviors."

50. A study of political instability in Latin America notes that during the initial phases of economic development, the majority of the population sees its more obvious manifestations such as new factories, roads, and municipal institutions. Yet they frequently do not directly benefit from this development. Hence such manifestations of growth may serve to aggravate an already existing sense of deprivation. See Manus Midlarsky and Raymond Tanter, "Toward a Theory of Political Stability in Latin America," *Journal of Peace Research,* no. 3 (1967), pp. 209–227.

51. Ted Robert Gurr, "A Causal Model of Civil Strife: A Comparative Analysis Using New Indices," *American Political Science Review,* 62, no. 4 (December 1968), 1104–1124.

52. Harry Eckstein, "A Theory of Stable Democracy," *Research Monograph* No. 10, Center of International Studies, Princeton University, 1961.

53. Gurr, "Psychological Factors."

54. John D. McCarthy and Mayer N. Zald, "Resource Mobilization and Social Movements: A Partial Theory," *American Journal of Sociology,* 82, no. 6 (May 1977), 1212–1241.

55. Seymour Martin Lipset, *Political Man* (Garden City, N.Y.: Doubleday, Anchor Doubleday edition, 1963), p. 64.

56. *Ibid.*

57. Douglas P. Bwy, "Political Instability in Latin America: The Cross-Cultural Test of a Causal Model," *Latin American Research Review,* 3, no. 2 (Spring 1968), 17–66.

58. Gurr, "A Causal Model." p. 1121.

59. Stephen Kinzer, "Nicaragua: Universal Revolt," *Atlantic Monthly,* 243, no. 2 (February 1979), 4–20.

60. "An Ostracized Regime Runs Out of Money," *Business Week,* no. 2571 (February 5, 1979), 38.

61. Gurr, "Psychological Factors," p. 269.

62. For an illustration of the ways in which authorities attempt to persuade the dissatisfied to use institutional procedures and to use them in ways which actually help to maintain the status quo, see Harvey Molotch, "Oil in Santa Barbara and Power in America," *Sociological Inquiry* 40, Winter 1970. With respect to the strategy of authorities making adjustive concessions for their own benefit, Horowitz and Liebowitz observe that the welfare state is an attempt to "cool out" the marginal lower classes and minimize the potential political danger they pose. See Horowitz and Liebowitz, "Social Deviance," p. 294.

63. See Gurr, "A Causal Model," p. 1121.

64. Michael Lewis, "The Negro Protest in Urban America," in *Protest, Reform and Revolt,* Joseph R. Gusfield, ed. (New York: John Wiley & Sons, 1970), p. 156.

65. According to Abel, the Nazis provided a political program appealing to (a) those who were in power before World War I and were deposed, (b) nationalists deeply dissatisfied with the Versailles Treaty, (c) those discontent with government ineptitude in a parliamentary system that lacked democratic traditions, (d) those in both business and labor suffering from economic disturbances both before and after 1929. See Theodore Abel, *Why Hitler Came to Power* (Englewood Cliffs, N.J.: Prentice-Hall, 1938).

66. For a detailed discussion of these factors, see Eckstein, *Internal War.*

67. Theda Skocpol, *States and Social Revolution* (Cambridge: Cambridge University Press, 1979).

68. For an extensive discussion of these two perspectives, see William A. Gamson, *Power and Discontent.* (Homewood, Ill.: Dorsey, 1968).

69. See Riley E. Dunlap and Dennis L. Peck, "Student Activism: A Bibliography of Empirical Research" (Monticello, Ill.: Council of Planning Librarians, Exchange Bibliography 709, December 1974).

70. Richard Flacks, "Young Intelligentsia in Revolt," *Trans-action,* 7, no. 8 (June 1970) 49–55.

71. Lewis Feuer, *The Conflict of Generations* (New York: Basic Books, 1969), esp. pp. 10–35.

72. Raymond Aron, "Student Rebellion: Vision of the Future or Echo from the Past?" *Political Science Quarterly,* 84, no. 2 (June 1969), pp. 289–310.

73. See Richard Flacks, "The Liberated Generation: An Exploration of the Roots of Social Protest," *Journal of Social Issues,* 23, no. 2 (July 1967) 52–63, and David L. Westby and Richard G. Braungart, "Class and Politics in the Family Backgrounds of Student Activists," *American Sociological Review* 31, no. 5 (October 1966) 690–692.

74. Flacks, "The Liberated Generation."

75. Ronald Ingelhart, "The Silent Revolution in Europe: Intergenerational Changes in Post-Industrial Societies," *American Political Science Review,* 65, no. 4 (December 1971), 991–1017.

76. Frequently noted among these conditions were the presence of the military draft, the continuation of the Vietnam War, prolonged economic prosperity and a "good job market" for students, and the emergence of the "multiversity."

77. Frank A. Pinner, "Students—A Marginal Elite in Politics," *Annals of the American Academy of Political and Social Science,* (May 1971), 127–138. Pinner characterizes marginal elites as differing from other population groups in the following ways:

1. They are producers of collective goods the need for which is most keenly felt by political and religious leaders. (Students produce "social intelligence," in the widest meaning of the term.)
2. As producers of collective goods they do not engage in exchange of goods and services with specific members of the community. To some extent they always "live off the community."
3. They attain elite status by recruitment or by formal admission.
4. Members of marginal elites are often physically separated from the rest of the community.
5. They are given special privileges and immunities—the most important of which is the subjection to a separate system of law and to the jurisdiction of a separate court system.
6. They simultaneously have both populist and elitist attitudes. They protect their own privilege while at the same time maintain concern for the common man and the community or polity as a whole.

78. Ibid.

79. Jeanne H. Block, Norma Haan, and M. Brewster Smith, "Socialization Correlates of Student Activism," *Journal of Social Issues,* 25, no. 4 (Autumn 1969) 143–177.

80. See Seymour Martin Lipset, *Rebellion in the University* (Boston: Little, Brown, 1972), pp. 84–87. For an explanation of the overrepresentation of Jews among student activists see Arthur Liebman, *Jews and the Left* (New York: John Wiley & Son, 1977).

81. Gary T. Marx, *Protest and Prejudice* (New York: Harper & Row, 1967).

82. Ibid., pp. 104–105.

83. Flacks, "The Liberated Generation."

84. Aron, "Student Rebellion," p. 294.

85. Feuer, *The Conflict of Generations,* pp. 10–35.

86. Richard Flacks, "On the New Working Class and Strategies for Social Change," *Social Policy,* 1, no. 6 (March–April 1971) 7–15.

87. Philo C. Wasburn, "Some Political Implications of Student's Acquisition of Social Science Information," *Social Forces,* 48, no. 3 (March 1970) 373–383.

88. Similar linkages might be expected between serious concern with the humanities on the one hand and leftist activism on the other. Interest in philosophy, music, literature, and art would seem to be prima facie evidence of a broad cultural and intellectual interest which is associated with social participation in general and political participation in particular. The social, political, and psychological characteristics of those recruited to the humanities as well as the lack of relationship between humanities training and occupational goals may contribute to the tendency of those found to be knowledgeable in the humanities to criticize the existing social order and to the development of leftist leanings. See Philo C. Wasburn, "Literature, Music, Art and Political Involvement," *Proceedings of the Indiana Academy of Social Sciences,* Third Series, Vol. 2, 1967, pp. 171–180.

CHAPTER SIX
POLITICAL IDEOLOGY IN THE UNITED STATES

THE CONCEPT OF POLITICAL IDEOLOGY

Ideology is possibly the most confounding term in the literature of political sociology. It is one member of a set of terms including *authoritarian, bureaucratic,* and *totalitarian* that presents two major difficulties. First, for each term there exist a number of alternative and sometimes incompatible conceptualizations—and many of these tend to be vague and ambiguous.[1] Second, the terms are almost always used pejoratively—to be authoritarian or bureaucratic or totalitarian or ideological is somehow bad—at least in the context of contemporary American society.

There is a third, unique, and more difficult problem which ideology presents: It is sometimes difficult to differentiate *ideology* from *social science.* The problem stems from several facts: (1) ideology and social science arose during the same period of Western European history; (2) both, at least in part, represent efforts to explain major social and intellectual transformations; (3) both call into question prevailing modes of thought and existing institutional arrangements—particularly political arrangements; (4) both express, if sometimes only implicitly, a vision of a better society.

In this first section an effort will be made to develop a conceptualization of *ideology* which sufficiently eliminates the ambiguities of the term to permit empirically grounded discussions of the role of ideology in political life at the microanalytic level.

Reinhard Bendix argues that ideology, in most of the senses in which the term is used today, emerged in the seventeenth or eighteenth century with the decline of the traditional view of the world according to which people uncritically accepted beliefs because they were long held and sought to discover uniformities in nature only to glorify God through an understanding of His wisdom.[2] Human beings traditionally questioned neither the existence of moral law nor the divine ordering of the universe. According to Bendix, "Historically, the Age of Ideology came into its own when critical questions were raised concerning man's ability to reason and the degree to which he is capable of defining and realizing the ends of his actions."[3] Francis Bacon in particular is credited with advancing the view that people should not accept uncritically received opinion and that they should investigate nature with the end in view of benefiting humankind.[4]

The term *ideology* itself was coined about 1796 by Destutt de Tracy to refer to a "science of ideas" that was closely tied to zoology. De Tracy believed that such an empirically based science would produce certain knowledge of the ways in which ideas are formed and would help to determine the kinds of social norms and institutions best suited to human beings. Like Bacon, he saw significant political implications in the empirical study of man's psychological and social nature. Napoleon Bonaparte soon found the views of De Tracy and his associates incompatible with his political interests. They were dismissed from their academic positions in 1803 on grounds of being impractical, wrong-minded visionaries. (This appears to be the historical origin of ideology's negative connotations.)

This very brief sketch of the origins of ideology is sufficient to indicate several enduring components of subsequent conceptualizations of it. At a base the term refers to these characteristics:

1. A more or less integrated set of explicit beliefs about the nature of man and society which are held to be empirically true by members of some social unit (e.g., class, status group, political association, nation).
2. The set of beliefs is associated with an explicit program for social action for the unit, i.e., defending or challenging the existing distribution of rights and advantages and the existing uses of power and authority to create, maintain, or change them. (Ideologies are intended to be linked with politically relevant collective behavior.)
3. The program for social action proceeds explicitly or implicitly from a set of values in terms of which the existing institutional orders (particularly existing political, economic, and stratification systems) are defended or found in need of change.
4. Those who do not support the proposals for social action which are part of the ideology tend to deny the empirical validity of the ideology's assertions about the nature of man and society. They also tend not to believe that the proposals for social action will be effectively carried out.

Most discussions of ideology generally include two other related characteristics:

5. The sets of beliefs and values are relatively closed to change. Neither the presence of new information nor the development of new social circumstances is likely to bring about alterations.
6. The beliefs and values are associated with strong feelings; they are maintained to some extent on the basis of emotional commitment. While it is not an identifying characteristic of all ideologies, many have an authoritative body of sacred doctrine such as manifestos and declarations and a set of heroes such as originators or great interpreters. These tend to help maintain emotional commitment.

Ideologies can differ from one another with respect to any of these characteristics. Hence they can differ with respect to:

1. Their cognitive components
   a. the specific topics addressed by the belief system[5]
   b. what specifically is believed about each topic
   c. the degree of integration of beliefs within and between topics
   d. the extent to which the most central beliefs in the system are open to change in the light of new arguments and/or empirical information[6]
2. The social units which are their carriers
3. Their programs for collective social action
   a. the explicitness with which they are stated
   b. whether they are aimed at defending or changing existing systems of rights, advantages, power, and authority
   c. the courses of action which are advocated[7]
4. Their value orientation
   a. the specific value or values which are supposed to motivate belief and action
   b. the extent to which this value or values are made explicit
   c. in cases where more than one value is involved, the degree of value integration
   d. the degree of value-action integration, i.e., the extent to which the specific actions advocated are consistent with the specific values that are supposed to motivate belief and action. (The lack of such integration is a major problem for groups advocating violence for the achievement of humanitarian goals.)
5. The social units which oppose the carriers of the ideology. An ideology is identified by its enemies as well as by its supporters.

There are a number of social and psychological functions which ideologies can serve. For individual actors an ideology can provide a "cognitive and moral map of the universe," particularly needed during times of social crisis when the previously prevailing outlook has become unacceptable.[8] During such times ideology can also link individuals' actions with a "wider set of meanings and, by doing so, lend a more honorable and dignified complexion to social conduct."[9] Hence it can enhance individuals' feelings of self-worth and further provide social support for this enhanced sense of self by uniting them with others who share their perspective.

The social functions of ideology include its roles in motivating, guiding, and coordinating collective behavior. As Bell puts it: ". . . ideologies are, in effect, attempts to unite ideas, behavior and character; they demand a hardening of commitment. The communist (or fascist, or the kibbutznik, or the 100 per cent American) is not only supposed to believe certain things; he is supposed to act, to be something and, in acting to fix his character. If one is 'serious' one 'lives' one's ideology."[10] Parsons emphasizes that ideologies unite individuals in belief and in action by defining an ideology in part, as "a system of ideas which is oriented to the evaluative integration of the collectivity."[11] Similarly, Johnson observes that "by simplifying complex situations (ideologies) help many diverse people to cooperate toward the same goal. They define the situation and justify a particular course of action."[12]

Finally, an ideology can serve the social unit which carries it to relate more successfully to other social units which are actually or potentially hostile. Miner observes that "ideologies relate a social unit to its context by interpreting it for relevant audiences and making it understandable and acceptable according to external standards."[13] Lane also notes that ideologies "constitute an argument; that is, they are intended to counter opposing views."[14]

The components and functions of social science can now be compared with those of ideology. Like ideology, social science presents a set of beliefs about the nature of man and society which are held to be empirically true. However, in contrast to ideology, the belief system of social science is normatively committed to change in the light of new empirical information which indicates the inadequacies of existing theoretical formulations. Ideologies tend to resist change by ignoring new information which cannot be assimilated, by denying its validity or relevance, or by selectively viewing new empirical data in such a way that they do not call into question the tenability of existing doctrine. This does *not* mean that ideologies are inherently and totally false. Whether or not a particular belief component of an ideology is true or false (assuming that it is the sort of belief which is empirically verifiable or falsifiable) is always a matter for scientific inquiry—not a matter which can be determined a priori. It is the members of social units which oppose the social carriers of an ideology who view its belief components as inherently false. They render this judgment not on the basis of empirical evidence but on the basis of political interests. The notion that ideologies are inherently false interferes with their study by social scientists. As Geertz puts it:

> If the critical power of the social sciences stems from their disinterestedness, is not this power compromised when the analysis of political thought is governed by such a concept, much as the analysis of religious thought would be (and, on occasion has been) compromised when cast in terms of the study of "superstition."[15]

Social science is "disinterested" in the sense discussed above, i.e., it is normatively committed to change its truth claims to correspond to the demands of new empirical data. It is this openness to change which represents its primary distinguishing characteristic from ideology. In addition, several secondary differentiating qualities can be noted. First, while ideologies involve explicit statements of value orientations, social science theories generally do not contain such statements. Social science theory and research are commonly said to "express" or "reflect" the values of those who produce them; they very seldom contain explicit statements of such values. Second, social science is primarily and explicitly concerned with enhancing empirical understanding of social structures and processes. Ideology, by way of contrast, is at least as equally concerned with motivating and directing social behavior as with maximizing intellectual clarity. Hence, the belief components of ideologies are characteristically presented in ways intended to evoke feeling as well as to convey analyses of social situations.

Third, while ideologies characteristically advocate explicit programs for political action, theories of social science generally do not. (This does not mean, however, that the theoretical and research activities of social scientists are not influenced by their own views of what constitutes the good society and what are the best ways to bring about its realization.) While the products of social science are often "relevant" to policy formation, historically its role has been that of supplier of information rather than that of advocate of particular action. However, this distinction is rapidly becoming blurred in practice. Apter observes that:

> Ready or not, social scientists are being asked to do research leading to policy formation. What happened first in natural and physical sciences is now beginning in the social sciences—that is the modification of change through the application of planning and control. Some years ago Bertrand Russell made a comment about the role of science that is increasingly applicable to social science as well. "Science used to be valued as a means of getting to *know* the world; now, owing to the triumphs of technique, it is conceived as showing how to *change* the world."[16]

The view of ideology developed here contrasts sharply with the commonly encountered position according to which ideologies inherently involve distorted perceptions of social reality, value commitments, and programs for political-social change while social scientific theories involve none of these (with the possible exception of cognitive errors which, when discovered, are eliminated as rapidly as possible). The major difference between social science and ideology is to be found in the norm of social science that the structure of its truth claims correspond to empirically observed social structures and processes and that they must be revised when such correspondence is not found. It is this commitment to cognitive openness and change which is social science's qualitative difference. Like ideologies, theories of social science express value commitments and visions of a more desirable social world. However, in social science, unlike ideology, expressions of such orientations remain largely implicit.

Some belief components of ideologies may be empirically valid—this is a question for research. Some of the presently maintained belief components (propositions) of social science may turn out to be demonstrably false when more reliable and valid data become available—this is, in part, the question of replication and is also a question for research. Sometimes the pet theories of social scientists, like the belief components of ideologies, die hard. The differences between ideology and social science are greater than ideologists like to think but are certainly less than social scientists often like to persuade themselves. Ideologies posing as social science have been produced by "objective" academics as well as by impassioned revolutionaries and threatened beneficiaries of the status quo.

COMPARISON WITH CLASSICAL VIEWS

The conceptualization of ideology developed here differs in several respects from the views of Marx, Weber, and Durkheim as well as from the positions of some contemporary writers. For Marx, ideologies inherently were distorted sets of ideas about the economic and political order. Ideologies were the belief systems of the dominant economic class, serving as its intellectual weapons and reflecting existing, though transitory, sets of economic relationships. For example, Marx argued that under industrial capitalism bourgeois ideology asserted that private ownership of the means of production was both natural and permanent and that workers' wages represented all that in the market they could be paid. As conceived above, any real social unit (e.g., class, status group, occupational association), not only a society's dominant economic class, can be the bearer of an ideology. While ideologies do function as intellectual weapons, they are not viewed here as necessarily reflecting existing economic relationships. The character of any linkages that may exist between a set of ideas and the social situation of the social unit which accepts them is always a question for research. As conceived above, the empirical truth or falsity of a given belief component of an ideology also is always a question for research. The examples of truth claims of "bourgeois ideology" cited above do indeed appear to be empirically false. However, this is not a matter to be assumed a priori, or on theoretical grounds, or denied by means of definitions.

Weber, like Marx, saw ideologies as belief systems which justified and motivated the activities of social units with material interests. (Unlike Marx he did not require that the units be social classes.) For example, Weber argued that the religious beliefs associated with the Crusades were promoted by feudal lords with imperialist aspirations who were interested in securing fiefs for their descendants. For Weber, however, such beliefs were not inherently false. Rather, they represented sets of ideas selected for their affinity with the interests of certain social units. Ideas which did not have such an affinity were eventually abandoned by the unit. This leaves open the question of whether the individual ideas which are retained are empirically true or false—a position congruent with the view developed here. Weber went on to assert that ideas, to some extent, follow developments of their own; they are not merely reflections of the interests of the social units which maintain them. According to Weber, particularly during the initial stages of the development of an ideology, there can be considerable tension between the social unit's beliefs and the effective pursuit of its material interests. Weber attributed considerable importance to people's ideas and ideals in the process of social and political change.

For Durkheim, shared belief systems, such as sets of religious beliefs, represented the symbolic expression of a social unit's shared experiences—particularly its members' experience with their own social structure. Such symbolic formulations were regarded neither as the conscious creations of individuals nor as merely long-enduring, though factually groundless, myths. Durkheim argued that:

> a collective representation presents guarantees of objectivity by the fact that it is collective: for if it is not without sufficient reason that it has been able to generalize and maintain itself with persistence. If it were out of accord with the nature of things, it would never have been able to acquire an extended and prolonged empire over intellects. At bottom, the confidence inspired by scientific concepts is due to the fact that they can be methodically controlled. But a collective representation is necessarily submitted to a control that is repeated indefinitely; the men who accept it verify it by their own experience. Therefore it cannot be wholly inadequate for its subject. . . .[17]

Durkheim went on to argue that the occasional "strange appearance" of collective belief systems could be accounted for, in part, by the imperfections of the symbols that are used to express experiences. This, he noted, is also a problem of science, whose symbols are themselves never more than approximative. Another factor accounting for the character of accepted belief systems is their congruence with other held beliefs. In this respect as well, Durkheim maintained, science and other collective belief systems are no different.

> It is not enough that (concepts) be true to be believed. If they are not in harmony with other beliefs and opinions . . . they will be denied; minds will be closed to them. . . . Today it is generally sufficient that they bear the stamp of science to receive a sort of privileged credit, because we have faith in science. But this faith does not differ essentially from religious faith. In the last resort,

the value which we attribute to science depends on the idea which we collectively form of its nature and role in life; that is as much to say that it expresses a state of public opinion. . . .[18]

The position taken here is compatible with Durkheim's view of the influence of symbols in theoretical formulations and with his analysis of the importance of belief congruence. However, the fact that a collectively held belief has long endured is no guarantee of its empirical validity. Socially useful fictions can long endure. Durkheim's error stems from his failure to distinguish between pragmatic "truths" and empirical truths.

Before turning to empirical studies of ideology, a modern theoretical discussion of the topic deserves consideration. The approach, that of Lewis Feuer, is both extensive and provocative.[19] Feuer argues that ideology involves a dramatic interpretation of history, a specification of an oppressed, exploited, or deprived group (class, stratum, nation, etc.) which is to play a major role in developing historical processes, a designation of an elite (invariably marginal young intellectuals) whose mission it is to lead the chosen group, and a vision of historical culmination. For example, in the 1930s young student Fascists claimed their mission was to rescue the Italian people from the exploitation of European capitalism, which treated them as mere laborers. Through their leadership, the Italian people, who had guided Europe into civilization, would have their proper dignity restored and Italy would be resurgent. Other "heroic" people and groups which have been chosen similarly to be led by young intellectuals include the proletariat, the peasants, the blacks, the American Indians, the hoboes, Latin American guerrillas, and the North Vietnamese. The social unit which ideologists conceive of as "their" chosen people is one which embodies the values they most prize and which does not appear to possess those defects they most despise. Ideologists also tend to believe that the thought processes of their chosen people yield higher-order truths than those produced by the application of scientific method.

Ideologies, according to Feuer, contain purported demonstrations of the truth of their claims about social-political history. Such demonstrations consist in showing that the claims are based on fundamental metaphysical and epistemological tenets (e.g., materialism, idealism, relativism, pragmatism, existentialism, etc.) which are the current fashion. For example, advocates of competitive capitalism in nineteenth-century England saw a direct link between their position and the Utilitarianism of Jeremy Bentham—arguing that the greatest happiness of their countrymen would be achieved by dismantling the system of aristocratic privileges and expanding competitive enterprise. However, Feuer points out, there is no necessary connection between any philosophic doctrine and a concrete set of political proposals. Utilitarianism, like all such philosophies, was available for ideological use by left, right, and center. Hence, John Stuart Mill, quite possibly the most influential of all of the Utilitarians, later moved toward a socialist position. It seemed to him that the system of private property had not led to the greatest happiness of the greatest number.

According to Feuer, the ideological use of philosophical ideas follows a definite pattern. The same idea in the course of its history moves through the political and social spectrum from left to right or right to left. Ultimately, in its time it will be associated with contrary political positions. The time span of this process begins when a new generational group adopts the set of perspectives. These eventually are accepted by more conventional sections of their own generation and finally by their slightly older opponents and their relative elders. By the time this occurs the philosophical perspective has become lifeless and the time has come for a new insurgent generation to define its own independent character by articulating a new set of philosophical tenets. The philosophical orientations the new generation chooses will express the emotions which were most repressed by the previous philosophical scheme. For example, determinism repressed the drive for spontaneity; voluntarism is at odds with the desire for orderly explanation, and empiricism represses the impulses to fantasy.

Finally, Feuer argues that ideologies attempt self-validation by "demonstrating" not only that a political program is based on widely accepted philosophical tenets but also that its principles are structurally similar to the basic principles of the physical world. For example, Marx wrote that Darwin's work served him with a basis in natural science for the class struggle in history; social struggles could be seen as an extension of the struggle for existence among all living things.

Feuer's work deals with several questions central to the understanding of ideology: Who initiates ideologies? When and why do they do so? What are the most basic features of ideologies? What types of efforts are made to intellectually justify ideologies? In what ways do ideologies change over time? Some of the answers he provides are extremely interesting and suggest further research, while others are doubtful.

Some ideologies, such as those espoused by student activists in the late 1960s, can be viewed as the creation of a generational group—or at least a particular segment of a generational group. (Young industrial workers who were the age peers of the activists could hardly be classified as supporters.) However, the idea that ideologies are entirely the product of marginal young intellectuals overlooks the creation of ideologies by various elite groups to enhance their social and political positions. Such uses were understood clearly by Marx and Weber. While ideologies can serve emotional needs, as Feuer correctly points out, they also serve social and economic interests. Hence they arise not only under the conditions Feuer notes, but also when various kinds of social groups find uses for them. For example, as we shall see in a later section of this chapter, historical data indicate that extreme right-wing ideological movements in the United States appear during periods of rapid social and economic change during which certain status groups are socially dislocated.

All ideologies, as defined earlier in this chapter, do not have all of the specific components listed by Feuer—e.g., the designation of an elite. Hence, his characterization may be too narrow for certain analytic purposes. However, the notions that ideologies are constructed to derive support from basic metaphysical and epistemological positions and that they meet or express emotional needs suppressed by institutionalized modes of thought deserve further historical investigation. They also suggest further empirical research into the psychological functions of political doctrines and their various forms of symbolic expression.

Feuer is no doubt correct in his observation that a single philosophy can be used to support a number of ideological positions, including those which are contraries. In order to secure widespread support an ideology requires some demonstration that the beliefs, values, sentiments, and programs set forth are consistent with widely held epistemological notions and with socially shared feelings about social justice and morality.

Finally, Feuer is also correct in noting that ideas which originate with one social group are often picked up by other groups with divergent political interests. In the course of this successive adoption the ideas become vapid. However, what is not certain, and what remains a subject for empirical inquiry, is the extent to which divergent ideological groups represent different generational groups. Here Feuer's thesis concerning the dynamics of ideological change is in some doubt. Weber's theory that ideas are created, adopted, maintained, and discarded according to their affinity with the interests of the social unit which promotes them is at least as equally plausible as that of Feuer.

FORMAL AND INFORMAL IDEOLOGIES

Discussing the conceptual components of ideology sheds little light on the role which ideology actually plays in ongoing political life. To initiate consideration of this topic it is necessary to introduce a distinction between *formal* and *informal* ideologies (although the distinction is intended to be suggestive rather than rigorous).[20] Formal ideologies, which have all of the characteristics of ideology described above, represent the articulated well-developed political belief systems of informed partisans such as conscious Marxists or Liberal Democrats or Fascists. Informal ideologies, by way of contrast, address a comparatively limited set of topics, display less integration of beliefs within and between topics, and often lack explicit programs for collective social action. They often lack value orientations that are made explicit and reveal less value integration and value-action integration than do formal ideologies. Informal ideologies represent the loosely structured unreflective beliefs of the "ordinary person." The research literature reviewed in the following sections of this chapter focuses on informal ideologies.

The distinction between formal and informal ideologies can be illustrated by reference to Gabriel Almond's distinction between the "esoteric" and the "exoteric" appeals of Communism which were described in Chapter 5.[21] His analysis indicated that esoteric doctrine (formal ideology) played little role in attracting people to the Communist movement in four non-Communist countries. This certainly suggests that since formal ideology has little bearing on this particular form of nonroutine participation, it is unlikely to be important in explaining many other forms of political behavior. On the other hand, it also suggests that informal ideologies may have some association with political action. While most people have little contact with, concern about, or even interest in sophisticated political belief systems, many do maintain sets of political beliefs and values, however loosely structured and poorly articulated, which influence the extent and course of their political involvement. Such beliefs and values are likely to reflect, rather directly, their own social and economic experiences. For example, Almond found that the majority of his respondents joined the Communist party because they perceived it as an advocate of specific aggrieved groups with which they identified and a militant opponent of immediate social evils which they knew first hand.[22]

Robert Lane's study of the political belief system of the American "common man" also illustrates the formal-informal ideology distinction.[23] In this work Lane sketches the basic features of an informal ideology which is likely to be widely shared among members of America's working class. The belief system Lane describes concerns the central ideas of American political culture: freedom, equality, and democracy.

Interviews indicated that the common people focus their attention upon the importance of economic functions in defining *freedom*. Lane observes that the lives of most Americans are much more concerned with the business of buying and selling, earning and disposing of things, than they are with more abstract political discussions or concepts. One could caricature the "common man's" view of freedom by the expression "I don't care what I am allowed to say, so long as I can buy what I want, work where I want, and go where I want."

The American "common man's" understanding of *equality* is also quite concrete and grounded in economic experiences. He knows that he receives less income, less deference, and less preferment in public places than members of the middle class. Yet, he does not respond with hostility coupled with a desire to change the system. He does not view the distribution of social rewards as being highly unjust. He is not so blind as to think he has equal opportunity with everyone else; but he "knows" that he has more opportunity than he is using.

Democracy in the minds of Lane's respondents referred "neither to majority rule nor minority rights but something of a hybrid—majority rights."[24] They typically thought of democracy in terms of the right of the majority to do what is conventionally approved. Democracy as a popular concept centers in the freedom of the nondeviant individual to do what the majority thinks is right. Nevertheless, there is also a general willingness to tolerate conflicting political opinion.[25] The American "common man" does express a preference for hearing more than one side of a political issue.

One final study, Huber and Form's analysis of "the American political formula" can be cited to illustrate the concept of informal ideology.[26] The study is based on data gathered in 1967 from 354 residents of Muskegon, Michigan. Respondents were selected to represent the full range of income categories in the community.

The conceptualization of ideology used throughout the work is congruent with the view developed above and with discussions of "politics" developed in the first section of this book. *Ideology* is used to "describe the explanations and justifications which people use to legitimize a stratification system."[27] Huber and Form add that:

> as a whole, an ideology cannot be true or false because it is an inextricable mixture of normative and empirical propositions about society. Ordinarily, the norms, myths and facts in the ideology are not critically examined except during crises: they are usually taken as social givens.[28]

The first reference assigned to the term is consistent with the position that socially shared, politically relevant belief and value systems are those which focus on relations of power and authority and which serve to help create, maintain, or change the social distribution of rights and privileges. The second statement is at variance with the position developed here only insofar as it is maintained here that the normative and empirical components of ideologies are, at least in principle, separable.[29]

The authors' major hypothesis, which is supported by their data, contends that those who are in privileged positions maintain an ideology quite different from that believed in by the poor. The ideology of the privileged stresses equal economic opportunity. Such a view prevails over all of the industrialized world because it is an efficient way to motivate people to participate in work with mainly instrumental rather than intrinsic rewards. The belief is just as useful in the Soviet Union as in the United States. In the case of the United States, the ideology maintains that elementary and secondary schools are free, scholarships to colleges and universities are available to those with academic ability who cannot pay, and that hard work and talent will always be rewarded. Unequal rewards are seen as necessary in society because they motivate people to work harder. And, in the long run, hard work helps everyone. Furthermore, the informal ideology of the privileged asserts that

> because educational opportunity is equal, and because everything depends on how hard a person works, the system is fair to everyone. Should the rewards become unfairly distributed, the system could be adjusted and improved because every man has a vote in a political system devoted to protecting individual achievement. Therefore, individuals get the rewards they earn and people get the government they deserve.[30]

In the United States the poor have less faith in the normative components of this ideology and tend to deny some of its empirical claims. For example, they do not tend to believe that individual hard work is always rewarded; they tend to see social structural factors rather than individual factors as primarily responsible for the distribution of wealth and income.[31] The poor do not tend to believe that one's vote gives one a share of control over the system. Nor do they believe that there is any guarantee that, in the long run, individual interests are represented when policies are decided. They do not think the political system works as it should because it does not redistribute resources and equalize political and social opportunities.

The existence of such divergent informal ideologies in the United States is not accompanied by overt social-political conflict. Lane has suggested several reasons for this (see note 25). An additional reason is to be found in the fact that these ideological differences are often submerged beneath apparent agreement with general American values. For example, while most Americans espouse belief in "equality," some would find unacceptable a black family moving into their neighborhood. Such an absence of value-action integration is characteristic of informal ideologies. Because informal ideologies also lack specific programs for collective social action, they are less likely than formal ideologies to motivate conflict.

THE EXTENT OF "IDEOLOGICAL THINKING"

Studies thus far cited have sketched informal ideologies in America which center around broad concepts such as freedom, equality, and democracy. Characteristically, such belief systems do not include programs for collective social-political action. However, one might expect that they have at least some sort of systematic connection with the policy preferences and with the political party affiliations of individuals. For example, adoption of the ideology of the poor described by Huber and Form would seem to encourage preference for political-economic policies quite different from those promoted by the ideology of the rich. Hence, the poor might be

expected to support the expansion of social security and sharply progressive income taxation while the rich generally might be expected to oppose
such policies. An extension of this line of reasoning leads to the commonly
encountered proposition that the rich tend to support the political right or
relatively conservative political policies and programs while less affluent
strata tend to support the political left or relatively liberal or radical programs and their carriers.

The proposition that different strata tend to support different parties
does not mean that the rich tend to support certain parties because they are
conservative or that the poor tend to support certain parties because they
are liberal or radical. The ways and the extent to which formal or informal
ideology influences party support are questions for empirical research.

Several studies show that, at least in the United States, the policy
preferences of individuals are not systematically linked; they do not represent a set of preferences which reflect a more or less consistent set of beliefs
and values. For example, Axelrod, using national survey data, found that:

> American public opinion on policy issues has no single clear pattern, and
> there is hardly a trace of an over-all left-right dimension. This is true for the
> informed and the concerned, for the well-educated and the uneducated, for
> the rich and the poor, for the participant and the nonvoter.
> ... Apparently people tend to view each issue independently of the others,
> perhaps, for example, thinking of sick people when asked about government-
> insured medical care and about local school facilities when asked about aid to
> education.[32]

Possibly the most widely cited empirical investigation of the role of
ideology in influencing Americans' party affiliation and policy preferences
is that of Converse.[33] In the study *ideology* is defined as a belief system
which has a wide range, which allows some centrality to political objects,
and which has some relevance to political behavior. Each of the components of this definition requires brief explanation.

As Converse uses the term, a *belief system* is a configuration of beliefs
and attitudes in which the elements are bound together by some sort of
constraint or functional interdependence. The *range* of a belief system refers to the number and diversity of objects that are referents for the beliefs
and attitudes in the system. For example, Marxism as a formal ideology
links control of the means of production with the social functions of religion and a doctrine of aesthetics "all in one more-or-less neat package" and
hence is a belief system which has an extremely broad range. The *centrality*
of a belief system element refers to its resistance to change—the more
central the element, the more resistant it is.

Converse develops important hypotheses with respect to each of these
defining features of ideologies. First, he identifies three types of constraint:
logical, psychological, and social. Logical constraints refer to the objective,

logical consistencies that exist between the idea elements of a belief system. Converse finds that the existence of logical inconsistencies between elements of a belief system does not ensure that the constraint will be subjectively felt by the actor. For example, he notes that many Americans believe that government expenditures should be increased, that government revenues should be decreased, and that a favorable balance of the budget should be achieved all at the same time.

Psychological constraint refers to the quasi-logical consistencies that characterize the relationship between idea elements of a cogent argument. For example, arguments are sometimes based on premises about the nature of social justice or "natural law." The existence of this sort of consistency in a belief system may serve as a substitute for objective consistency.

Social constraint refers to an individual's subjective feeling that certain ideas are interrelated because he or she has been provided with social cues—i.e., an elite source of information, such as an officeholder or party official, has said, "If you believe this, then you will also believe that, for it follows in such and such ways." In this situation, people "know" that several ideas go together, but do not know *why*. For example, many Americans know that "Communists are atheists," but this perceived correlation cannot be explained by them. Converse argues that any set of individuals who support a position tends to show more consensus on specific implications of the position as a result of the social diffusion of "what goes with what" than it would if each member were required to work out the implications individually, without help. Information concerning "what goes with what" is socially diffused much more than information about *why* certain idea elements go together because such information is less complex. According to Converse, different ideas that are in the political interest of individuals or groups that have the ability to communicate to the broad public are put together and "sold as packages." The public subsequently comes to see them as natural wholes. It is this packaging and selling process which is the chief source of most people's sense of what politically relevant ideas and values "go together."

Converse finds that as one moves from elite sources of a belief system downward on an information scale several changes occur. Constraint declines—increasingly one finds not only individuals whose political belief systems contain logical inconsistencies but also many whose belief systems lack even quasi-logical integration, and still others who even lack information about the identity of the objects of political beliefs and attitudes. Among the less educated, the range of political belief systems becomes narrower and narrower. The character of the objects that are central in their belief systems also changes. Abstract principles are replaced by increasingly simple and concrete objects such as particular social groupings or charismatic leaders and finally "close-to-home" objects such as family and job.

Only 2.5 percent of Converse's sample made active use of an abstract conceptual dimension such as liberal-conservative in understanding and evaluating political parties, political programs, and public figures. Another 9 percent mentioned such a dimension but did not appear to have full understanding of its meaning or to really use it in understanding and judging the objects of their political world. The majority of the sample, 42 percent, made no use of an abstract conceptual dimension. Rather, they understood and evaluated parties, policies, and candidates in terms of their expected favorable or unfavorable treatment of various social groupings in the environment such as blacks, farmers, workers, and so on. Another quarter of the sample used only minimal policy considerations in their understanding and evaluation. Parties and candidates were thought of and appraised primarily in terms of their temporal association in the past with broad societal states of war or peace, prosperity or depression (e.g., supporting the Democratic party because of its original association with the social security program). Finally 22 percent of the sample reacted politically in ways totally unrelated to policy considerations. For example, during political campaigns such respondents directed their attention to personal qualities of candidates or felt loyal to one party or the other but could say nothing about the differences between the parties.

Converse's study concludes with three important assertions. First, the ability to think ideologically—i.e., to use abstract concepts to organize systematically politically relevant information and systematically render relatively consistent judgments on the basis of such information—is positively associated with both partisanship and political activism. As many voting studies have shown, the political "independent" tends to be relatively uninformed and uninvolved.

Second, party strategies differ in response to recognized differences between sophisticated and nonsophisticated audiences. Political sophistication is strongly associated with education and social class. Hence as one moves from the conservative parties of the relatively prosperous and well educated to the liberal-radical parties of the relatively less prosperous and less educated, in most political systems there is an increasingly overt stress on group loyalty and cohesion per se. Converse notes that:

> for Left parties, the transmission of gross, simple group-oriented cues is a functional imperative. For Rightist parties there is much to lose and nothing to gain in such publicity, for the basic clientele can be counted for fair support without blatant cues and the tactical needs are to avoid the alienation of potentially large-scale "haphazard" support from the lower-status clientele.[34]

Finally, Converse observes that serious ideological conflict between various elite groups in a society may go on unperceived by large segments of the mass public. Despite the facts of a high literacy rate and a mass media system that makes politically relevant information available to everyone, the mass public is sometimes largely unaware of what elites perceive to be the principal ideological struggles of some historical periods.

Converse's study suggests that the proportion of the American mass public which "thinks ideologically" is relatively constant. Field and Anderson investigated this hypothesis through the analyses of national sample survey data dealing with public perceptions of parties and candidates during the presidential election years 1956, 1960, and 1964.[35] The 1964 data were particularly interesting because during the election the Republican presidential candidate, Barry Goldwater, explicitly defined the election as an ideological plebiscite. The data reveal significant differences in the proportions of respondents making explicit ideological references in their discussions of parties and candidates. In 1964, 16 percent of the sample made explicit references to ideology in discussing political parties as compared to 8 percent in 1956 and 13 percent for 1960. This indicates that characteristics of the political environment as well as attributes of individuals influence the extent of ideological thinking in a society at a given point in time.[36]

Continuing research on the political attitudes of Americans indicates substantial changes in the direction of increasing levels of conceptual sophistication since 1964. For example, Nie, Verba, and Petrocik present data indicating that by 1972 about one-third of the American population both made references to issues and employed ideological terms in their evaluations of candidates and/or parties, and about half made at least some use of ideological terminology in their political evaluations.[37] However, they also point out that the percentage of Americans who make use of an abstract conceptual dimension in understanding and in evaluating political objects increased from Converse's figure of 2.5 percent to about 6 percent. While this is a major change, the percentage remains very small. This latter figure corresponds very closely to a finding by Klingemann in his study of ideological conceptualization in five nations.[38] He reports that those who think in terms of an abstract ideological dimension in their political evaluations range from 4 percent in Britain and Austria up to 9 percent in the Netherlands, with Germany and the United States both at 7 percent.

Data on the 1972 and 1976 elections, gathered by the Institute for Social Research at the University of Michigan, indicate that traditional party identification can change, at least temporarily, as a result of the perceived extent of liberalism or conservatism of the presidential candidates of each party. In 1972 about 40 percent of the Democrats defected and voted for Richard Nixon. This defection was related to comparisons they made between their own views and the views of the candidates on a liberal-conservative continuum. In 1976 there was a return to partisan politics after it reached a twenty-year low in 1972. According to the I.S.R., a major part of Jimmy Carter's success was his ability to obfuscate issues. If Carter had emphasized clear-cut liberal Democratic policies, the outcome could have paralleled 1972 because of the set of conservative Democrats willing to defect on the basis of issues.[39]

The fact that comparatively few people "think ideologically" under most circumstances does not mean that ideology plays an inconsequential role in political life. The bearing of ideology on the political behavior of individual citizens will be considered in the last section of this chapter. Here, the significance of ideology on the community and national levels will be noted.

Individuals with the capacity and inclination to think ideologically tend to have characteristics associated with assuming social leadership positions. The social impact of the views of a few leaders of socially influential groups or organizations can be considerably greater than the views of a large number of individual citizens. For example, Samuel Stouffer found that all categories of community leaders tend on the average to be more respectful of the civil rights of those of whom they disapprove than the average person in the general population, either of the same cities from which the leaders came or of the nation as a whole.[40] He observes that the maintenance of civil liberties depends more upon the orientations of such leaders than upon support of the mass public.

Since Stouffer's 1954 study there has been a substantial increase in public support for democratic principles. Differences between the political values of civic leaders and the mass public are not so great as they once were. Nevertheless, many antidemocratic attitudes are widely held (e.g., willingness to deny freedom of speech to admitted Communists), and leaders continue to play an important role in protecting civil liberties.[41]

The ideological orientations of organizational elites thus have considerable social importance. The influence of such leaders derives from their ability to make binding decisions for the organizations they head or to influence disproportionately the making of such decisions. It also derives from their ability to influence the political perceptions of others. Leaders of community organizations and those who influence the schools and the mass media have ready audiences for the consumption of their interpretations of the political world.

While ideologically inclined elites influence political policies and perceptions, their own behavior is limited, to some extent, by the prevailing broad ideological commitments of the mass public. The ordinary American's ideas of freedom, equality, and democracy circumscribe the behavior of political leaders in much the same way as do the beliefs which serve as the bases of legitimacy for the various forms of domination described by Weber. To maintain effectiveness, political leaders must do more than just obey the law. They must be sensitive to prevailing ideological notions of the mass public as well as to their associated ideas and feelings about what is right and what is wrong, what is fair and what is unfair. Whether or not any American president can ever be "above the law," it is clear that he can never be "above" the general notions of justice and ethical conduct held by most citizens. Another type of constraint on political leaders is imposed by the necessity of the day-to-day agreements and compromises they must make with others in the process of governing. Ideological purity and fervor at times inevitably must give way to practical considerations. If they do not, tenure in office is likely to be brief.[42]

THE "END OF IDEOLOGY" DEBATE

Sometime in the early to mid-1950s several influential political analysts began writing about the "end of ideology." The discussions such writings prompted continued for more than a decade. Vestiges are seen even today. One reason for such prolonged consideration was lack of agreement of exactly what *ideology* meant in this context; much discussion was at cross-purposes. Another reason was that, whatever *ideology* meant, some writers hailed its supposed demise while others argued that if ideology had indeed ended, the social and political consequences were both serious and undesirable.

While the end-of-ideology debate involved considerable ambiguity, there was agreement on at least a few points. First, the ideologies under discussion were those found in Western industrialized nations. No one appeared to argue that ideologies had "ended" in the nations of Asia, Africa, and Latin America. It was clear that Third World ideologies had different emphases from those found in the industrialized West. There, emphasis was on political integration, economic development, and national power. On the other hand, Third World ideologies were (and are) more oriented toward increasing economic productivity than promoting economic equality and expanding popular political participation.[43] In the Third World also, in contrast to the industrialized West, ideologies were the creation of acting political leadership rather than of other strata. Second, those who had ceased being ideological in the West were "intellectuals," i.e., the stratum directly involved in the creation, maintenance, dissemination, and analysis of political ideas and values. The debate was not focused on the beliefs of the mass public. Third, the ideologies in question were *formal* ideologies in the sense described above. Classical socialism in particular was said to have lost its importance as a politically relevant idea system.

Two "facts" were also agreed upon; to some these were synonymous with "the end of ideology" while to others they were not. In the 1950s many Western intellectuals appeared to display little, if any, interest in forcefully arguing for long-range political and social goals which expressed some vision of a social order substantially different from the one in which they lived. In the 1950s there also appeared to be a remarkable lack of political issues which divided the various strata of industrial societies. Associated with this was an absence of severe conflict between strata—particularly between social classes (understood in economic terms). Political conflict appeared to have given way to social and economic compromise and adjustment. And the working classes of the Western industrial societies no longer seemed susceptible to the appeals of Communism. If it is assumed for the time being that these statements about the politics of the 1950s are true, then the explanations offered to account for them can be presented.

One of the most widely cited positions, that of Lipset, argued that ideology had ended because some of the basic problems produced by the industrial revolution finally had been solved. (As noted earlier in this chapter, and in Chapter 1, ideology and social science arose, in part, as intellectual attempts to deal with questions raised by the French and industrial revolutions). Specifically, Lipset argued that:

> ... the workers have achieved industrial and political citizenship; the conservatives have accepted the Welfare State; the democratic Left has recognized that an increase in over-all state power carries with it more dangers to freedom than solutions for economic problems. This very triumph of the democratic social revolution in the West ends domestic politics for those intellectuals who must have ideologies or utopias to motivate them to political action.[44]

According to Lipset, political conflict between left and right had become a relatively inconsequential debate over a little more or a little less government ownership and economic planning. It no longer made any real difference which political party controlled the domestic policies of individual nations.

Bell presented a similar thesis when he claimed that:

> in the Western world ... there is today a rough consensus among intellectuals on political issues: the acceptance of the Welfare State; the desirability of decentralized power; a system of mixed economy and of political pluralism.[45]

Bell interpreted this consensus as the similar reactions of intellectuals to major events of the political and economic history of the 1930s and 1940s. Political events included the Moscow Trials, the Nazi-Soviet Pact, the Nazi concentration camps, and the more recent Soviet suppression of Hungarian workers. Economic changes included major modifications of capitalism such as the increasing role of government in the economy (both as consumer and regulator) and the rise of the welfare state.

Another set of explanations of the supposed "end of ideology" can be roughly organized around Weber's concept of rationalization. It was argued that all large-scale industrial societies, capitalist and socialist, the United States and the Soviet Union alike, were faced with similar complex problems of political and economic administration. In these societies, science had become increasingly specialized and increasingly committed to probabilistic models. Increasing specialization was associated with a decrease in holistic thinking. Political and economic problems were seen as too complex for "simplistic" solutions presented in sweeping utopian schemes. They could be dealt with efficiently and effectively one by one in a piecemeal and pragmatic fashion by bureaucratically appropriate managers and technically appropriate experts.

Thus far, the explanations given for the supposed end of ideology were presented by those who viewed ideology's demise as a benefit to human society. As they saw it, the end of ideology represented the end of unrealistic expectations of miraculous changes either from revolutions or from ambitious social and economic plans. It represented recognition of the dangers of totalitarianism inherent in ideologically inspired mass movements of the political left or right. Above all it represented "an end to apocalyptic beliefs that refuse to specify the costs and consequences of the changes they envision."[46]

Others were considerably less enthusiastic about the assumed end of ideology. Mills, for example, characterized the themes of Lipset, Bell, and others as "an intellectual celebration of apathy,"[47] and Haber termed it "a status-quo intellectual formulation designed to rationalize the incorporation of intellectuals into the American way of life."[48] Such perspectives prompted different explanations of the end of ideology. As Haber suggested, one reason was the incorporation of intellectuals into mainstream positions and activities. They were no longer segregated in university communities but played important roles in corporations, foundations, churches, and government itself. They now received money for research that was rationalized in terms of the national interest. Intellectuals, no longer an independent class, now profited rather directly from the maintenance of the status quo. In addition, large-scale organizations such as unions and universities, which formerly were creators and carriers of divergent idealogies, were also viewed as having been coopted.

The concentration of vast resources in the hands of the state also contributed to the end of ideology. The state has the power to provide a variety of material and nonmaterial rewards to dissident groups and thereby to diffuse, at least partially, emotional commitment to idea systems promoting radical change. Furthermore, the modern industrial state's monopoly over the vast and terrifying array of modern military hardware makes ideological thought, at least revolutionary thought, somewhat less than fully rational. Finally, the modern state has considerable ability to symbolically manipulate public opinion in ways which undercut ideological appeals while at the same time perpetuating the social conditions which promote protest. For example, Edelman has pointed out that in the United States regulative agencies such as the National Labor Relations Board, the

Interstate Commerce Commission, the Federal Communications Commission, and the Office of Price Administration create and sustain an impression that the economic interests of the public are safeguarded from corporate tactics that might be expected to produce resentment, protest, and resistance. However, such agencies, he notes, operate only symbolically in this fashion. Analysis of their actual operation shows that they should be understood as economic and political instruments of the parties they supposedly regulate.[49] Lack of ideological activity may reflect neither that wants have been satisfied nor that there is at that point in time an "attachment to moderation in action and orderliness and stability in change."[50] Rather, if Edelman is correct, it means that public political quiescence has been achieved through symbolic reassurances by government.

Not all political sociologists agreed that ideology "ended" in the 1950s. Evidence that ideology was alive and well in the industrialized West was seen in the large mass base of the Communist party in Italy and France, the influence of the left wing of the Social Democratic parties in Germany and England, and the widespread support of the civil rights and peace movements in the United States. Furthermore, as Harrington pointed out, ". . . perhaps some of the proclaimers of the finished and un-ideological society will have mistaken a passing historical moment for an entire future."[51] In his view, continuing mechanization, automation, and cybernation have considerable potential for producing future social problems, class alignments, and ideological and political responses. Harrington's view repeats Marx's insight that as people alter the tools with which they transform the physical world to meet their needs they also necessarily change their relationships to one another.

The so-called end-of-ideology debate should not obscure two important points. Whether or not "intellectuals" have lost interest in formal ideologies (in the sense of explicit statements of long-range political goals for a new and substantially different social order from the present one—statements intended to arouse mass sentiment) the American mass public still maintains belief systems of the sort described by Lane and Huber and by Form. Their ideas about democracy, freedom, equality, and distributive justice, though perhaps vaguely formulated and poorly articulated, influence their perceptions and evaluations of political personalities, structures, and processes and, to this extent, their political behavior. The second point is that whether or not ideology temporarily or even permanently lost its interest for Western intellectuals, ideology (in the sense of general expressions of abstract societal values and goals which demand affective attachment) never loses its interest for government. As Weber pointed out, all forms of domination rest, in part, on systems of belief which require periodic reinforcement. The enactment of all political policies bestows benefits on some while it extracts costs from others. Those required to pay the costs require some reassurance that the demands on them are justified. In

Western industrial nations this is partially accomplished by political socialization and by government presentation of extensively documented
claims, dramatically stated, and transmitted by an elaborate system of mass
communication that reaches virtually all social strata. Government claims
emphasize that sacrifices are essential in order to achieve collective goals;
values are sacrificed in the "national interest."

More basically, however, Western industrialized nations rely upon the
principle that if individuals believe they have participated in a decision-
making process, they are more likely to accept the outcome of that process.[52] Routine political participation, in the sense in which it was discussed
in Chapter 4, performs this legitimating function. This is the point of
Edelman's characterization of voting:

> This is participation in a ritual act . . . only in a minor degree is it participation
> in policy formation. Like all ritual, whether in primitive or modern societies,
> elections draw attention to common social ties and to the importance and
> apparent reasonableness of accepting the public policies that are adopted.
> Without some such device no polity can survive and retain the support or
> acquiescence of its members.[53]

In the industrialized West, government emphasis on the necessity of citizen
sacrifice for "the national interest" and on citizen participation in routine
politics "for the maintenance of freedom and democracy" certainly did not
end in the 1950s.

What occurred in the 1950s, at least among American intellectuals, is
best viewed not as the "end of ideology" but as the ascendance of a particular approach to the analysis of political life. For the reasons discussed in
Chapter 2, American political analysis has tended to be microanalytic, ahistorical, and noncomparative and to focus on social and political stability.
These characteristics, which were most strongly emphasized during the
early to mid-1950s, were the antitheses of the major qualities of previous
ideologies. Political ideologies such as communism, socialism, and fascism
dealt with social classes, institutions, peoples, and societies; they were macroanalytic. Such idea systems were concerned with historical development
and change—more often than not change brought about through conflict
between social strata with opposing interests. They placed actors in historical perspective to explain the course and outcome of political movements.
Such ideologies were explicit about the values they sought to realize
through collective political action. Social science, the professional identification of many of the "end-of-ideology intellectuals," at the time was ahistorical and nonabstractive and focused on factors promoting the stability of
Western political institutions as they were presently constituted. It was
widely held that social science itself did not support any particular set of

political values—except, perhaps, political values which were compatible with the uninhibited conduct of social science research.

IDEOLOGY AND THE EXPLANATION OF POLITICAL BEHAVIOR

Research reviewed earlier in this chapter indicated that formal or esoteric ideologies have little influence on routine political action such as voting and little effect on nonroutine action such as joining the Communist party in non-Communist nations. It was also shown that informal ideologies have some bearing on routine participation such as voting—an influence, the magnitude of which, though never great, varies with historical circumstances. Informal ideologies appear to have some influence on the desires of individuals to participate in nonroutine politics. Existing research thus indicates that, at least in the recent history of the industrialized West, ideologies originating from elite sources have less effect on overall patterns of national political behavior than do ideologies which emerge from people's everyday social, economic, and political experiences. However, it is difficult to assess the extent to which interpretations of such experiences are influenced by exposure to elite-dominated agencies of political socialization such as the schools and the mass media.

Recognition of the relative importance of personal experiences in the structuring of political behavior has reinforced the tendency of American political sociologists to emphasize personality characteristics in their explanatory schemes. However, the specific qualities hypothesized to account for particular modes of behavior commonly reflected the investigator's attitude toward that activity. Because, as noted in earlier chapters, academic sociologists in the United States have tended to support the general features of the social-political status quo, positive qualities were attributed to those engaged in routine politics. One revealing review of the research literature on political participation concluded in this way: "People with well-adjusted personalities are likely to be active politically (*in non-extremist politics, that is*)."[54]

In a similar manner, studies reviewed in Chapter 4 indicated that people who did not participate in routine or conventional politics were seen as personally deficient. For example, nonvoters were shown to be relatively unconcerned, uniformed, lacking a sense of personal and political efficacy, and lacking a sense of civic obligation. Participants in political movements aimed at influencing policies in directions which social scientists found undesirable were often analyzed in ways suggesting that there was something faulty, blameworthy, or lacking in their personality structure and social perspectives. In the past few decades, supporters of Joseph McCarthy, opponents of fluoridation, opponents of school-bond issues, Black Panthers, those supporting "Hawkish" policies during the Vietnam War, Weathermen, members of the John Birch Society, supporters of George Wallace, anti-pornography crusaders, working-class opponents of school busing, and supporters of the Moral Majority have all been viewed as alienated, or anomic, or authoritarian, or anxious, or uprooted, or socially displaced, or status threatened. Work reporting such findings appears to have been motivated as much by the desire to deny the empirical validity of ideologies which are disliked and by the need to discredit the ideologies' carriers as by the interest to explain why certain types of individuals respond positively to certain types of ideological appeals.

Studies of ideologies and their carriers, such as those mentioned above, are all, at best, partial analyses. Characteristically they have ignored the historical, cultural, structural, and explicitly political settings in which the behaviors occurred. It was this feature, and not the motivation for the studies per se, which produced the results just noted.

It may be true, for example, that there is some correlation between status anxiety and supporting the ideological positions of the so-called radical right.[55] However, the establishment of such an association represents only the beginning of an explanation. It tells us little if anything more than does the "explanation" that a particular group discriminates against blacks because its members are racist. The correlation raises questions rather than provides answers. For example, what other general social attitudes are associated with favoring "far right" ideas and ideals? With what group affiliations and identifications is the position associated? What individual or group experiences, reflecting historical circumstances, might account for a person's status anxiety or more directly for his "ultra" conservatism? Does the individual's stated position reflect primarily personal commitment or conformity to group or cultural norms? These questions touch on the possible roles of kinship, religion, class, stratification, and shared beliefs and values in political life. They deal with people's perceptions of their ability to collectively change the political structure of their society. They concern the importance of ideas and ideals in the process of social and political change. The questions concern the development and maintenance of the political orientation; they are microanalytic. Nevertheless, their thrust is closer to the thrust of the major questions raised by the founders of the sociological tradition. Analyses of ideologies and their carriers which are guided by such a set of questions are unlikely to produce truncated studies which suggest ideological bias.

The set of questions noted above suggests, in broad outline, a model of political behavior in which the role of ideology is clearly specified. It promotes a model indicating the ways in which attitudes and ideology are shaped by personal and group experiences and by the historical, cultural, structural, and political settings in which they occur. It encourages the development of a model which links all of these factors, in some determinate way, to political action.

TOWARD A MODEL OF THE ROLE OF IDEOLOGY IN POLITICAL ACTION

The model of political action developed below embodies the perspective that the political behavior of the individual represents the outcome of the interaction of a number of factors over time. It does not reject the possibility that earlier studies of ideologies and the social units which maintain and promote them do contain some insights—despite their often truncated approaches. It takes into account the criticisms of politically relevant personality and attitude research—particularly those criticisms presented in empirical studies focusing on alternative sources of political action.[56] It considers the possible sources of ideological orientations as well as their hypothesized consequences.

The model is based on a number of general assumptions about the various types of factors which interact with one another and, in turn, influence political behavior. These factors, most of which are associated in some way or another with family, religion, economy, stratification, and shared beliefs and values, are arranged in a hypothetical temporal sequence and organized into five general categories. For purposes of this chapter, the major feature of the model is the location of political ideology in the hypothesized causal sequence of interrelated factors which together structure the political behavior of the individual. The model is also designed to apply to all forms of political participation. Hence, the findings reviewed in Chapters 4 and 5 should be compatible with the model.

First, it is hypothesized that, temporally, *ascriptive characteristics* (age, sex, race, ethnicity, and religion) are the initial factors which structure political behavior. While their influence is viewed as indirect, the role played by each of these variables does not make it possible to subsume them under the headings of status groups or social classes. While members of a particular age, sex, race, ethnic, or religious category may be assigned rather clear class and status positions in a society, it is always empirically possible that they will respond to political situations in ways opposing others sharing their locations in these social hierarchies. In fact, this often happens. The view of the impact of ascriptive characteristics developed here is more differentiated than that of Marx (which would assign class identities to ascriptive categories on the basis of the role their members characteristically play in the relations of production in their society) and that of Weber (which would assign status-group identities to ascriptive categories on the basis of their life chances, which are determined by the specific positive or negative social estimation of their honor).

A cluster of three factors is seen as next in the temporal sequence of variables. Each of these is viewed as directly linked to ascriptive characteristics. The cluster includes *associational ties, social experiences,* and *political or quasi-political group affiliations.*

Associational ties refers to the attributes of the associations to which individuals "belong" which serve as major sources of their self-concept and social identity. The associations themselves need not be interaction systems. For example, occupational categories bestow on their members socially and psychologically significant qualities. At present, even in the most "rationalized" societies, consideration of ascriptive characteristics plays some part in the assignment of socially important roles. Occupational hiring and promotion practices which discriminate against blacks, women, and older workers in our society serve as obvious examples. Hence, a direct link is predicted between ascriptive characteristics and associational ties. The hypothesis reflects currently institutionalized practices.

Social experiences refers to the qualities of interaction individuals commonly initiate and receive in the course of their social life—whether generally rewarding or punishing, dominant or subordinate, conforming or innovative, and so on. Social experiences, so defined, are predicted to be directly linked both to ascriptive characteristics and to associational ties. Most societies differentially evaluate their members according to age and sex. Such differential evaluation generally finds expression in differential treatment. For example, in the United States and most other societies, women tend to be in subordinate positions to men in most of their interactions. Societies also tend to differentially evaluate and differentially treat their members according to qualities they possess by virtue of their associational ties. For example, the high prestige bestowed by one's occupation is recognized by others outside the occupational context.

Political or quasi-political group affiliations refers to individuals' membership in groups and organizations which at least occasionally articulate positions and sponsor programs of action to maintain or change the policies and activities of civil government and/or the government of the various organizations to which individuals belong. Membership in such groups is hypothesized to be directly tied to ascriptive characteristics and to associational ties. Ascriptive characteristics can affect organizational membership in three ways. First, organizations simply can include or exclude from membership persons with a certain ascriptive quality or set of qualities. Second, individuals may join political or quasi-political organizations which they perceive to benefit the ascriptive category with which they identify. Third, individuals may join a political or quasi-political organization for traditional reasons—people with their ascriptive qualities "have always" supported it. Similarly, there are three ways in which associational ties influence membership in political or quasi-political organizations. Such organizations can represent the political organization of a social category such as an occupation—labor unions and professional associations which carry on political activities serve as examples. Apart from such linkage, political organizations may be joined because of their perceived benefit to members of the category or because of some traditional link between members of the category and the political organization.

Most generally, the hypotheses thus far presented maintain that ascriptive characteristics structure politically relevant social action by influencing associational ties, organizational memberships, and social experiences. It is now hypothesized that attitudes are next in the sequence of factors which together channel political behavior. A cluster of three broad classes of attitudes constitutes the third temporal segment of the model. This cluster includes *general social attitudes, political ideology,* and *specific political attitudes.*

General social attitudes refers to individuals' beliefs about, evaluations of, and feelings about the social world, its components, and their relationship to them. Most commonly, general social attitudes are measured by attitude scales and involve concepts variously labeled "values," "attitudes," or "personality factors." Examples include subcultural values, alienation, authoritarianism, faith in human nature, status anxiety, sense of personal efficacy, and so on. All have cognitive, evaluative, and affective components which, research indicates, predispose individuals to certain modes of political behavior. Here it is hypothesized that general social attitudes are directly or indirectly linked to every one of the ascriptive and associational factors noted above. General social attitudes are seen as a function of all of individuals' experiences—those resulting from the way in which their society treats persons with their ascriptive qualities at a particular point in time, those reflecting the ways they are treated as a result of their associational ties, recurring features of the interaction they have by virtue of the social positions into which they have been channeled, and their experiences in organizations which present them with sets of shared social and political perspectives. The relative weight of each of these factors in the determination of some particular values, attitudes, or personality factors in specific populations can be determined only by empirical research.

Political ideology as conceptualized in this chapter refers to individuals' relatively stable, more or less integrated set of beliefs, values, feelings, and attitudes about the nature of human beings and society and their associated orientations toward the existing distribution of social rewards and the uses of power and authority to create, maintain, or change them. Research reviewed above shows that most American citizens do not have an ideology in any formal sense. However, studies did indicate that most members of the public have some notions about the central ideas of their political culture, such as freedom, equality, and democracy, and about the ways in which the rewards in their society get distributed. Like general social attitudes, political ideology is viewed as a function of all of an individual's social roles and experiences. It is also hypothesized that ideologies represent, at least in part, the political expression of general social attitudes. On the other hand, ideologies acquired within associations and political or quasi-political groups (which issue their own interpretations of political events, policies, parties, personalities, and presentations of the mass media), or emerging as a response to social experiences, can generalize subsequently to other areas of social life in the form of general social attitudes.

Specific political attitudes refers to individuals' orientations toward particular political objects such as a political party, a politically relevant group or organization, a public official, a public policy, and so on. It is hypothesized that individuals acquire such attitudes within the political and quasi-political organizations to which they belong and from interaction with others who share their associational ties. This relationship can also run the other way because political attitudes can motivate political and quasi-political group membership. A direct link is also predicted between specific political attitudes and political ideology. While the political belief systems of individuals often exhibit little consistency, within limits and for at least comparatively well educated segments of the population, it is still possible to predict attitudes toward specific political objects from indicators of ideological perspective.

Finally, we come to the *political behavior* of individuals. This refers to acts which are oriented to the acquisition and use of power and authority to maintain or change the distribution of rewards in any social unit (organization, community, or nation) in which individuals are involved. While political behavior is seen as the outcome of the interaction among all of the variables of the model, it is hypothesized to be linked directly only to specific political attitudes which immediately precede it in the model and to organization membership. Specific political attitudes are seen as mediating experiences, more general attitudes, and behavior—as shaping the character of political responses to personal experiences. The direct link between organization membership and political behavior expresses the fact that some political behavior reflects nothing more than the attempt to receive the rewards or avoid the punishment of some political or quasi-political group to which one belongs.

Figure 6-1 expresses the relationships just considered. It is particularly intended to clarify the view developed in this chapter of political ideology's location in the network of interacting factors which together structure political behavior.

This model emphasizes the view that political action, whether routine or nonroutine, is not usefully understood as a function of an isolated trait, syndrome, or organizational identification. Traits and syndromes have

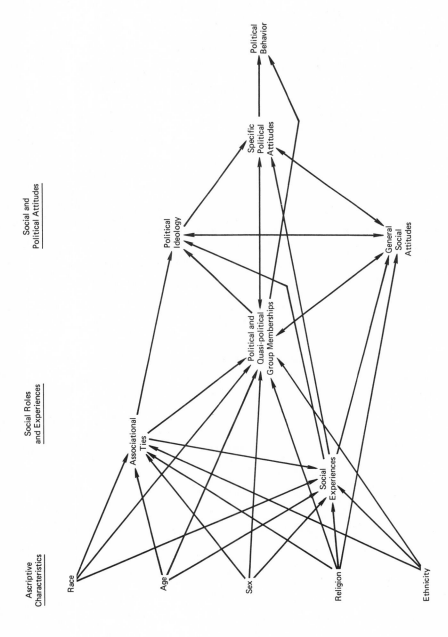

Ascriptive
Characteristics

Social Roles
and Experiences

Social and
Political Attitudes

263

their social origins, and organization memberships reveal features of a society's history and social structure. Such basic ideas are easily forgotten when one attempts to explain the politics of those one does not like.

It may seem inappropriate to employ a highly abstract model to emphasize that political action—particularly the political action of groups which carry ideologies to which one is opposed—is a response of people whose full range of experiences, beliefs, attitudes, and values acquired within their families, religious groups, work contexts, and class associations are reasonably consistent with taking the action. However, it may be that starting analysis at relatively high levels of abstraction makes it easier to avoid substituting pejorative characterizations for social science explanations.

The model developed here is intended to be applicable to all forms of political action—those which are system maintaining and those which are system challenging—those which are widely supported and those which are "controversial." Future research which applies the model to a variety of political actions and which employs numerous alternative operational definitions of its components such as *social experiences, social values,* and *political ideology* will indicate its analytic utility. The model is intended to stimulate research and is open to modification and change in the light of empirical evidence. Such research should produce, on the microanalytic level, some insights into the role which kinship, religion, work, and social class play in structuring political behavior. It should also reveal something about how much importance is to be attributed to people's ideas and ideals in the process of social and political change.

NOTES

1. For a discussion of several major conceptual-theoretical ambiguities in the literature on ideology, see Willard A. Mullins, "On the Concept of Ideology in Political Science," *American Political Science Review,* 66, no. 2 (June 1972), 498–510.

2. Reinhard Bendix, "The Age of Ideology: Persistent and Changing" in *Ideology and Discontent,* David E. Apter, ed. (New York: The Free Press, 1964), pp. 294–327.

3. Ibid., p. 297.

4. A critical orientation toward what is accepted as traditional wisdom and the belief that a better world can be created through the application of what is felt to be superior understanding of observable structures and processes in nature are both major components of *ideology.* They are also major components of the theories of the major founders of the sociological tradition—Marx, Weber, and Durkheim—and find explicit expression in the writings of the founding fathers of American sociology such as Ward and Giddings.

5. Johnson contends that ideologies focus on points that are crucial to the operation of the social system. They identify present sources of strain and the extent of that strain, courses of action for the reduction of strain, other social systems with which the system of reference is compared (revolutionary movements often focus on an imaginary society of the future while conservative movements tend to romanticize the past in which people realized truths and values now allegedly lost or being lost), and the nature of the dominant value system and its implications (radical ideologies tend to emphasize the failures of the social system to realize

dominant values). See Harry M. Johnson, "Ideology and the Social System" in *International Encyclopedia of the Social Sciences, V. 7,* David L. Sills, ed. (New York: Macmillan and The Free Press, 1968), pp. 77–84.

Parsons notes that an ideology involves interpretations of the empirical character of the social unit which carries it and the situation in which this unit is placed. It also involves interpretations of the processes by which the unit developed to its given state, the goals to which its members are oriented, and their relation to the future course of events. See Talcott Parsons, *The Social System* (New York: The Free Press, 1951), p. 349.

According to Lane, the belief components of ideologies imply an empirical theory of cause and effect in the world and a theory of the nature of man. Such beliefs are inevitably torn from their context in a broader belief system and share the structural and stylistic properties of that system. See Robert E. Lane, *Political Ideology* (New York: The Free Press, 1962), p. 15.

Mullins defines an ideology as ". . . a logically coherent system of symbols which, within a more or less sophisticated conception of history, links the cognitive and evaluative perception of one's social evolution—especially its prospects for the future—to a program of collective action for the maintenance, alteration, or transformation of society." See Mullins, "On the Concept of Ideology," p. 510.

6. Converse describes ideologies as differing with respect to what is believed, what beliefs are most central (resistant to change), their level of constraint or interdependence (the probability that a change in the perceived truth or desirability of one idea element would psychologically require, from the point of view of the actors, some compensating change(s) in the status of elements elsewhere in the configuration), and range (the extent to which the belief system links apparently diverse social phenomena). See Philip E. Converse, "The Nature of Belief Systems in Mass Publics," in Apter, *Ideology and Discontent,* pp. 206–261. For a further elaboration of this approach, see Giovanni Sartori, "Politics, Ideology and Belief Systems," *American Political Science Review,* 63, no. 2 (June 1969), 398–411.

7. Of particular importance is whether the social unit chooses to pursue a single issue or to make multiple demands upon those in positions of power and authority, whether or not it attacks the legitimacy of the existing distribution of wealth and power, and whether it chooses to attempt to influence or the replace those holding power and authority. See Roberta Ash, *Social Movements in America* (Chicago: Markham, 1972), p. 230.

8. Edward Shils, "The Concept and Function of Ideology" in Sills, *International Encyclopedia,* v. 7, p. 69. One particular way to do this is to provide people with symbolic enemies. This can reduce inner tensions resulting from rapid and/or unwanted social changes by explaining such changes in conspiratorial terms. Ambiguity, doubt, and a vague sense of guilt thereby can be converted into a more manageable sense of anger. Such anger is then available for political mobilization. In addition, reduced levels of personal tension make it easier for individuals to perform their routine social roles.

9. David Apter, "Ideology and Discontent" in Apter, *Ideology and Discontent,* p. 16.

10. Daniel Bell, *The End of Ideology* (New York: The Free Press, 1960), p. 316.

11. Parsons, *The Social System,* p. 349.

12. Johnson, "Ideology and the Social System," p. 77.

13. David W. Minar, "Ideology and Political Behavior," *Midwest Journal of Political Science,* 5, no. 4, November 1961, 317–331.

14. Lane, *Political Ideology,* p. 14.

15. Clifford Geertz, "Ideology as a Cultural System," in Apter, *Ideology and Discontent,* p. 51.

16. Apter, *Ideology and Discontent,* p. 18. When social scientists advocate social policy which is unpopular with their colleagues, those colleagues tend to react in the way in which members of ideological groups respond to their opponents. For example, in April 1975, University of Chicago sociologist James S. Coleman reported that school desegregation in large cities was contributing substantially to white flights from these cities and questioned the wisdom of existing desegregation orders. For Coleman's account of reactions to his research (which included efforts to discredit research results and to explore the possibility of taking legal action against him), see his letter in *A.S.A. Footnotes,* November 1976, p. 4.

17. Emile Durkheim, *The Elementary Forms of Religious Life* (Glencoe, Ill.: The Free Press, 1948), p. 437.

18. Ibid.

19. Lewis S. Feuer, *Ideology and the Ideologists* (New York: Harper & Row, 1975).

20. This distinction is based on Robert Lane's differentiation of "forensic" and "latent" ideologies. See Lane, *Political Ideology*, p. 15.

21. Gabriel Almond, *The Appeals of Communism* (Princeton, N.J.: Princeton University Press, 1954).

22. Ibid., p. 242.

23. Lane, *Political Ideology*.

24. Ibid., p. 83.

25. Lane discusses a number of factors which contribute to the "common man's" willingness to tolerate differences in political beliefs and attitudes. First, he notes, Americans find that "what matters most has been settled for them beforehand." While there are many ideological cleavages in America, the common man feels no problem of choice among competing and organized formal ideologies such as communism, monarchism, fascism, and so on. Second, in the United States, ideological conflicts are not associated with other sorts of conflicts. Third, in America, political conflicts are less intense since they do not coincide with strong group loyalties such as ties to church, union, or ethnic group. Fourth, Lane contends that his respondents were willing to tolerate conflicting political opinion in part because such conflict has low salience. Their sense of disengagement from government gives them the capacity to bear and internalize political conflicts without excessive discomfort.

26. Joan Huber and William H. Form, *Income and Ideology* (New York: The Free Press, 1973).

27. Ibid., p. 2. It should be noted ideologies explain and justify *a* stratification system, not necessarily *the* stratification system operating in a society at the time the ideology finds support. Hence the poor and the powerless may have an "ideology." However, the system of stratification they see as valid is likely to be quite different from that which is presently institutionalized.

28. Ibid., p. 15–16.

29. Huber and Form themselves accept the principle of the separability of the components of ideologies, noting that: "Clearly, any attempt to study ideology should separate normative and empirical statements" (page 5). Furthermore, they note that many of the claims of the ideology of the rich are empirically false—i.e., do not correspond to data collected by social scientists. One of the most important of these questionable claims is the belief that in American society there is equal opportunity for all. Clearly this claim is not true for such collectivities as blacks, Chicanos, American Indians, and women.

30. Ibid., p. 4.

31. Huber and Form note that, due to their experience with structural barriers to economic oportunity, middle-income blacks disbelieve the dominant ideology more than poor whites. The "poor whites" interviewed by Huber and Form did not express views much different from the "common man" interviewed by Lane.

32. Robert Axelrod, "The Structure of Public Opinion on Policy Issues," *Public Opinion Quarterly*, 31, no. 1 (Spring 1967), 51–60.

33. Philip E. Converse, "The Nature of Belief Systems."

34. Ibid., p. 249.

35. John Field and Ronald Anderson, "Ideology in the Public's Conceptualization of the 1964 Election," *Public Opinion Quarterly*, 33, no. 3 (Fall 1969), 380–390.

36. The findings do support Converse's generalization that the proportion of ideologues in the population is extremely small, even under conditions which would seem to encourage viewing and judging the political world in ideological terms.

37. See Norman H. Nie, Sidney Verba, and John R. Petrocik, *The Changing American Voter*, enlarged ed. (Cambridge, Mass.: Harvard University Press, 1979), pp. 110–122.

38. See Hans D. Klingemann, "Measuring Ideological Conceptualizations" in Samuel

H. Barnes, Max Kaase et al., *Political Action: Mass Participation in Five Western Democracies* (Beverley Hills, Calif.: Sage, 1979), pp. 215-254.

39. See *I.S.R. Newsletter,* Winter 1977, pp. 4-5.

40. Samuel A. Stouffer, *Communism, Conformity and Civil Liberties* (Garden City, N.Y.: Doubleday and Company, 1955).

41. See Clyde Z. Nunn, Harry J. Crockett, Jr., and J. Allen Williams, Jr., *Tolerance for Nonconformity* (San Francisco, Calif.: Jossey-Bass, 1978), pp. 142-160.

42. "The ideologue in office has to be a politician since he has to compromise with powerful and intrenched interest and to meet problems of an everyday nature which do not concern the ideologue out of office. In short, the ideologue in office is almost a contradiction in terms: he is, as Lenin put it, 'not a revolutionary but a chatter-box.'" Robert E. Dowse and John A. Hughes, *Political Sociology* (London: John Wiley & Sons, 1972), p. 255.

43. See Samuel P. Huntington and Joan M. Nelson, *No Easy Choice: Political Participation in Developing Countries* (Cambridge, Mass.: Harvard University Press, 1976).

44. Seymour M. Lipset, *Political Man* (Garden City, N.Y.: Doubleday Anchor Books, 1963), pp. 442-443.

45. Daniel Bell, *The End of Ideology,* p. 373.

46. Daniel Bell and Henry David Aiken, "Ideology—A Debate," in *The End of Ideology Debate,* Chaim I. Waxman, ed. (New York: Simon and Schuster, 1969), p. 261.

47. C. Wright Mills, "Letter to the New Left," in Waxman, *The End of Ideology Debate,* p. 126.

48. Robert A. Haber, "The End of Ideology as Ideology," in Waxman, *The End of Ideology Debate,* p. 205.

49. Murray Edelman, *The Symbolic Uses of Politics* (Urbana, Ill., University of Illinois Press, 1964), Chapter 3.

50. See Edward Shils, "The End of Ideology," in Waxman, *The End of Ideology Debate,* pp. 49-63.

51. Michael Harrington, "The Anti-Ideology Ideologies," in Waxman, *The End of Ideology Debate,* p. 348.

52. For a review of experimental findings supporting this proposition, see Sidney Verba, *Small Groups and Political Behavior* (Princeton, N.J.: Princeton University Press, 1961).

53. Edelman, *The Symbolic Uses of Politics,* p. 3.

54. Bernard Berelson and Gary A. Steiner, *Human Behavior: An Inventory of Scientific Findings* (New York: Harcourt, Brace and World, 1964), p. 425. (Italics added.)

55. See Daniel Bell, ed., *The Radical Right* (Garden City, N.Y.: Doubleday Anchor Books, 1964) and Seymour M. Lipset and Earl Raab, *The Politics of Unreason* (New York: Harper & Row, 1970).

56. For example, Wolfinger et al. found that poor education and low income and traits associated with these did not account for membership in the Christian Anti-Communist Crusade. Rather, party identification (Republican) was an important explanatory variable. See Raymond Wolfinger, et al., "America's Radical Right: Politics and Ideology" in Apter, *Ideology and Discontent,* pp. 262-293.

PART THREE
MACROANALYTIC STUDIES

CHAPTER SEVEN
SOME HISTORICAL, STRUCTURAL, AND CULTURAL FEATURES OF WESTERN DEMOCRATIC POLITIES

THE CHARACTER OF WESTERN DEMOCRATIC POLITIES

Democracy is another confounding term in the literature of political sociology. Even without the analytic problems presented by the term's emotional connotations, there exist many disagreements about the concept's most central defining characteristics. For example, while some argue that democracy refers to a general type of political structure,[1] others argue that democracy refers to a type of process, which can be carried on within a variety of structures, by which political decisions are formulated. Many attempts to define democracy involve questions of political-moral philosophy where concern centers around the problem of what constitutes the best set of political relations under which people can and therefore should live. The discussion of democracy which follows is intended to be a conceptualization useful for organizing some major findings of macroanalytic empirical studies of the political systems of several Western industrial nations— political systems that are commonly referred to as democracies. The discussion involves both the defining characteristics of democracy and the major conditions which contribute to its development and sustain its existence. Historical, cultural, social structural, and explicitly political factors will be considered.

Shils has usefully identified three defining qualities of political democracy.[2] It is a regime of civilian rule, with representative institutions and public liberties. Each of these conditions requires brief discussion.

Democracy involves civilian rule in at least two senses. The first is that in a democratic system accessibility to office and to routine political participation in general is not the exclusive privilege of an aristocratic elite or of a professional class of civil servants. All adults, regardless of class, are citizens and elegible participants. In a democracy popular participation is emphasized and there is, in principle, equal right of access to government. Democracy also involves civilian rule in the sense that political decisions have to be justified publicly. Hence, those outside the formal authority structure have some influence over the formulation and enactment of policy.

Democracy involves representative institutions in the sense that the authority to govern is derived from election by citizens. In complex societies democracy is expressed in the competitive struggle between political elites who must seek, find, and maintain support from those they govern by at least appearing to represent their interests. Hence, the decisions they make must take into account citizen preferences.

Democracy involves the maintenance of public liberties in the sense that citizens have certain rights, such as the rights of free communication and free assembly, which the state must respect. The state has limited authority based on uncoerced agreements. Hence, violence, intimidation, and fraud are barred in principle and the rights of minorities are guaranteed in principle.

With some noteworthy exceptions, political sociologists have tended to pay relatively little attention to the *historical conditions* which are conducive to the emergence of political democracy. This has occurred despite the historical interests of figures such as Marx, Weber, and Durkheim and despite the fact that many of the most influential political sociologists have argued that the study of the social conditions of democracy is the defining concern of the field. *Cultural factors* associated with democracy have been interpreted as orientations, such as sense of personal political competence, trust of public officials, and some sense of civic obligation, which allow representative government to act fairly freely yet without abusing its freedom to act. Such orientations, which are properties of individuals and which were discussed in Chapters 4, 5, and 6, have been a primary interest of political sociology. However, other interpretations of cultural factors, which do not focus so much on individual orientations as on shared definitions of political phenomena, such as shared understandings of political symbols, have received relatively little attention. There has been considerable research on *social structural factors* associated with the operation of the polities of the so-called Western industrial democracies. Many of these studies are in the general tradition of research, broadly suggested by Marx, which investigates the impact of class structure on macropolitics. Other studies, following leads provided by Weber, seek to understand the antidemocratic consequences of bureaucratic organization. A third body of research, related to the concerns of Durkheim, has studied the political role of voluntary organizations and, in particular, the importance of occupational associations. Most of the work on democracy and social structure either tends to emphasize the concentration and hierarchial organization of power within industrial societies or tends to focus on the ways in which power is dispersed through such societies. These approaches lead to very different conclusions about the existence and viability of democracy in industrial societies. Finally, the bearing of explicitly political factors, such as party structures, on the existence and maintenance of democracy characteristically has been ignored by sociologists who study politics, although it has been a paramount concern of many political scientists. The apparent division of labor in which sociologists study the political impact of factors such as social attitudes or class structure and political scientists limit their investigation to explicitly political variables has no justification. Quite possibly, the distinction originated in the legitimacy battles fought by each field. Sociology, seeking to establish itself in American colleges, came to emphasize the relationship between self and society, the ways in which individuals come to internalize shared prescriptions for behavior in commonly encountered social situations, and the bearing of the social distribution of attitudes on institutional forms. In contrast, political scientists came to emphasize such topics as the history of political thought, the provisions of constitutions, the structures of governments and party systems. In this chapter such a division of labor is rejected.

SIMILARITIES AND DIFFERENCES IN HISTORY

Introduction: Moore's Thesis

For more than a decade, Barrington Moore's *Social Origins of Dictatorship and Democracy* has been one of the most influential studies of the historical events which gave rise to modern Western democracies—or, more specifically, to the type of political democracy which developed in England, France, and the United States.[3] Because of its prominence, because it takes an explicitly macroanalytic, historical-comparative approach to political institutions, and because it focuses on conflict and change, the work will be considered in some detail. The study will also serve as a background for discussing additional historical factors which have shaped some more specific features of several contemporary political systems.

According to Moore, scholars concerned with building general theories of the historical development of dictatorship and democracy have failed to appreciate the importance of two central factors which are related to one another: the role played by those living in the countryside and the contribution of open and violent social conflict. Moore hypothesizes that the occurrence and outcome of a civil war or a revolution is the key event in the transformation of a preindustrial society into a modern society. While trading and manufacturing classes in cities and gradual structural and cultural changes undoubtedly played important parts in modernization, the political institutions which finally emerged in the modern world were shaped largely by the results of patterns of conflict and cooperation between landed upper classes and peasants as they reacted to the challenges of commercialized agriculture.

Moore argues that there have been three major courses of development from the preindustrial to the modern world. The first involved the successful revolution by a group in society with an independent economic base, which destroyed previously existing obstacles to a democratic version of capitalism. Groups opposing this historical thrust, sometimes a landed aristocracy and in other cases a peasantry, were virtually destroyed. The histories of England, France, and the United States exhibit such a pattern. Each of these cases is described below.

The two other paths of development, outlined by Moore, will be described in Chapter 8. However, they should be mentioned here in order to give some comparative perspective. The second route to the modern world was also capitalist, but it took a reactionary form—in the twentieth century it led to Fascism. For example, in the cases of Germany and Japan, bourgeois revolutions, if they took place at all, were unsuccessful, and a coalition between agrarian and industrial elites triumphed. The third route was Communism and is exemplified by the cases of Russia and China. In these countries, agrarian bureaucracies inhibited commercial and industrial development. Urban classes were weak and a huge peasant stratum remained. The peasantry, subject to strains toward modernization, was the main revolutionary force which overthrew the old order and helped establish Communist rule. However, in turn, the peasants proved to be the primary victims of Communism. The following pages will describe Moore's account of the cases of England, France, and the United States, nations which followed "the first course of development to the modern world." In Chapter 8, Moore's treatment of Germany and Russia will be considered.

The development of democracy in England begins in the fifteenth century with the dismantling of feudalism. Two major factors contributed to its decline. The first was the War of the Roses (1455–1485), which destroyed the aristocracy, enabled some consolidation of royal power, and subsequently led to the establishment of peace in the countryside. The second was the further growth of the considerable wool trade aided by the peace, which promoted a "commercial outlook" in both the countryside and the towns.

Among the most important components of the new commercial outlook was a transformation of the medieval conception of land. Whereas land was formerly the basis of political functions and obligations, it became an income-yielding instrument and agricultural production now was for profit rather than for consumption. Members of the landed upper class, once preoccupied with their power relative to other members of their class and with maintaining political independence from the crown, and frequently engaging in private warfare, now had far greater concern with efficiency and financial profit. They came to view their estates almost exclusively in terms of their profit-yielding abilities.

Money rather than birth ultimately became the basis of the new order. A primary goal of men of property was to free themselves from any restrictions on the ways they might use their land for personal profit. In support of this goal they maintained that the unlimited ability to use private property produced, through the mechanism of the market, increasing prosperity for the society as a whole. Such values and beliefs serve as a foundation of capitalism.

The English Civil War (1642–1649) removed the two obstacles to fully and efficiently exploiting the material resources of the state for individual profit: the king and the peasants. Since the power of the king diminished with substantial increases in the independent wealth of an already prosperous landowner class that was engaged in commercial agriculture, it was in his interest to impose limits on expanding production. He therefore was a protector of the peasants and upheld their rights to cultivate open fields, to use the common for pastureland and for the collection of wood, and so on.

Technological improvements in the seventeenth century, such as increasing use of fertilizer, new crops, and programs of crop rotation, made large farms considerably more profitable. Profits from the wool trade also made increasing production attractive. The Civil War eliminated the king as the last protector of the peasants. The landed upper class, which had exerted pressure on the peasants before the war—pressure often in the form of violence and coercion—now successfully engaged in a number of legal and semilegal acts which deprived the peasants once and for all of their land rights. The results, the enclosure acts, ultimately destroyed the medieval peasant community.

English history, in which violence and the commercialization of agriculture played key roles, produced conditions conducive to the emergence of capitalist, parliamentary democracy. The Civil War eliminated a strong, divine-right monarchy.[4] The destruction of the peasantry removed a social stratum which, at certain points in the histories of other nations, such as Germany, Japan, and India, had conservative and reactionary responses to modernization or, as in the cases of Russia and China, served as the social base of Communist revolution. The success of the commercially minded elements of the landed upper class meant that they would not strongly oppose democracy. Rather, the class's most influential members "prepared England for rule by a 'committee of landlords,' a reasonably accurate, if unflattering designation of Parliament in the eighteenth century."[5] And, in doing so they "acted as a political advance guard for commercial and industrial capitalism."[6]

The origins of democracy in France, which Moore considers next, were vastly different from those in England. Nevertheless, here too, violence and the commercialization of agriculture were of paramount importance. The categories of social actors that were central in initiating the development of democracy in France were the same as those in England: the crown, the landed aristocracy, the bourgeoisie, and the peasantry. However, the circumstances of each stratum were different.

In seventeenth-century France the crown was strong. The landed aristocracy lacked an independent economic base and lacked, as well, inclination to engage in commercialized agriculture. The bourgeoisie was not pushing for the expansion of production and trade but rather was oriented toward the production of arms and luxuries for a restricted clientele. The peasantry was sharply divided between a peasant "aristocracy" with strong interest in expanding private property and a destitute peasant majority.

The relationships each of these categories formed with the others were also vastly different from the relationships seen in English history. Royal absolutism was able to control the landed aristocracy. The nobles for the most part lacked any equivalent of the English wool trade to give them financial independence. The thrust toward economic modernization was initiated by the crown. When pressures for revenue were exerted on the aristocrats they responded not by increasing agricultural production for market profit, but by increasing the rents they collected from their peasants. Rather than initiating an extensive enclosure movement and expanding production, the large proprietors were interested in preserving peasant tenants because they served as their economic base. In striking contrast to the situation of peasants in England, many French peasants were in a position approaching de facto ownership of the land they worked. The relationship of aristocracy to bourgeoisie was also considerably different from the English situation. In England, the shared commerical interests of these strata often united them in their opposition to the monarchy. However, in France during the seventeenth and eighteenth centuries, the crown sold offices in the bureaucracy to the bourgeoisie, who treated the purchased offices as private property which, among other things, could be inherited. By converting members of the bourgeoisie into aristocrats in this manner, the crown turned them into staunch supporters and defenders of the status quo. This sale of offices was the base of the king's independence of the aristocracy and of any effective control by a parliament.

The French Revolution (1789–1799) violently destroyed the entire system of monarchy and aristocratic privilege. According to Moore, the revolution occurred as the monarchy was weakened by the fusion of nobility and bourgeoisie which it itself had created. This strong conservative alliance limited the crown's ability to act, to adapt to the intrusion of capitalism into the countryside, and to decide what sectors of French society were to bear the burdens of modernization. The revolution itself initially was carried out by the Parisian poor, upon whom the burdens were placed, supported by the majority of the impoverished peasants. These strata sought to establish a regime insuring a "fair" distribution of necessities to the poor. To this end they rose to abolish royal absolutism, the system of feudal obligations, and the sale of offices in the government bureaucracy. They established equality before the law, the rights of small-property ownership, and the access of all to public services.

At the height of the revolution, radicalism in the countryside reinforced and supported radicalism in the cities. The urban poor were also joined by segments of the bourgeoisie that had no ties to the old order. Finally, however, the need to get food to the urban poor and to the revolutionary armies ran against the interests of the "peasant aristocracy." Their increasing resistance deprived the Parisian poor of food and ultimately halted the radical revolution. (More basically, for some time prosperous peasants had been at odds with poor peasants by opposing the division of property as part of their drive toward more modern—i.e., commercial—use of private property in the form of land.) Hence, Moore concludes that while the urban poor made the revolution, the peasants determined just how far it could go.

In broad historical perspective, the most significant political consequence of the French Revolution was the destruction of a landed aristrocracy and its union with the upper ranks of the bourgeoisie which the monarchy had created. In Moore's view, without the revolution this combined stratum might have continued and led France on a conservative course of modernization similar in many respects to the course followed by Germany and Japan. The revolution destroyed the social bases of potential right-wing authoritarian regimes that, under the pressures of industrialization, have tended to result in Fascism in other nations. By destroying the seigneurial system the revolution also served as a historical alternative to the development of commercial agriculture free of preindustrial characteristics. In many major countries where such development did not occur, Communist movements found a social base in the peasantry and established themselves through violent revolutions.

Moore locates the origins of American political democracy in the Civil War rather than in the War of Independence. He argues that the War of Independence was not a revolution in any real sense because it did not produce any fundamental changes in the structure of American society. It was unlike twentieth-century anticolonial revolutions, which characteristically aim at disposing of foreign domination in order to establish a new form of society with substantial socialist elements. Rather, its main effort was to promote political unification of the colonies and the separation of this unit from England.

Unlike England and France, America was a new nation which had no monarchy, established church, or aristrocracy to overthrow by political revolution. Commercialized agriculture was important from the beginning—as in the Virginia tobacco plantations. There was no previous feudal order to destroy in order to make commercial expansion possible. Capitalism predominated in both North and South, although in the South it was not bourgeois, i.e., it was not based on an urban population.

In the South, those expanding commercial agriculture and capitalism, contrary to their European counterparts, defended the concept of hereditary status and privilege. Bourgeois notions of freedom and equality, which were focal points in the English, French, and American revolutionary wars, were subversive doctrines to the South. Southerners emphasized qualities found in their society such as courtesy, grace, and cultivation, which they contrasted with the crude money-grubbing which they felt predominated in the North. Such a set of political and cultural values was used by the plantation aristocracy in support of the system of slavery, which produced the commercial profits that were the base of the aristocrats' social and political position.

In the North and South, then, different economies had produced different social structures with contrasting ideals. The Civil War was a consequence of both economic and moral conflicts. Its conclusion marked the dividing line between the agrarian and industrial periods of American history. According to Moore, its critical feature for the development of democracy in America was that the conflict was not compromised. The coalition of Northern industry and Western family farmers ruled out a reactionary solution to the problems of growing industrialism. Such a solution would have involved an alignment of Northern industrialists and Southern planters against slaves, small farmers, and industrial workers. Such a situation would have paralleled the "marriage of iron and rye"—the German combination of industry and Junkers—with possibly parallel political consequences.

Before turning from Moore's historical analysis, two critical points should be made. First, despite its title, his book contains few *general* hypotheses useful for understanding the social origins of dictatorship and democracy. Propositions are tied to the specific histories of England, France, the United States, and so on. (Perhaps too much more is not possible. Many of the criticisms aimed at Marx, Weber, and Durkheim also stem from their handling of the extremely difficult problem of generalizing about structural process from historical case studies.) Second, Moore's book gives the impression that the development of the political structures of a nation is almost entirely determined by factors internal to that nation. The Soviet Union's use of armed force in Hungary in 1956, in Czechoslovakia in

1968, and in Afghanistan in 1979 quickly reminds us that this is not always so.

Revolutionary and Nonrevolutionary Origins

Moore's thesis that the American Revolutionary War was not a crucial factor in the formation of American democracy is debatable. For example, Lipset claims that the Revolutionary War was a key determinate of the particularly egalitarian character of American political democracy.[7] This can be seen, he argues, by contrasting political life in the United States with that of Canada.

Canada never had a revolution of its own. Colonial Tories were successful in erecting a relatively conservative and rigidly stratified society. They were joined by many who emigrated from America following the Revolutionary War while radical segments of Canadian politics emigrated south. The result was the development of a political culture in which liberty and democracy were identified more often with legal traditions and procedures than with populism, the rights of the people to rule, or with freedom of business and enterprise. The diffuse elitism in Canadian politics is also expressed in Canadians' generally greater respect for public authority and stronger collectivity sentiments.[8] Stronger commitments to the "rules of the game" and to elected officials has meant that Canadians are not as likely as U.S. citizens to support slogans such as "the best government is the one that governs least." This has several important consequences. First, civil liberties for unpopular groups find stronger support in Canada than in the United States. Second, Canadian elites are more able to control populist movements which express intolerance, such as McCarthyism. Third, in Canada proposals for policies such as medicare, grants for large families, government intervention in the economy, and public ownership of major industries encounter much less opposition than they do in the United States.

The American Revolution, then, is certainly not without significant political consequences beyond nation and state building. What does seem clear is that the persistence of social groups and institutions which act to rigidify political and social structures, by demanding deference and by limiting access to positions of power and privilege, influences the extent to which democracy in a nation will take on populist characteristics. The very existence of any form of democracy depends upon extensive dismantling of impenetrable social structures that thwart commercial growth in agriculture and industry and that preserve a caste or castelike social order. In societies with feudal histories, such dismantling has required social revolution.

The historical occurrence of a revolution, even one that successfully overthrows a traditional elite, redistributes wealth, reduces exploitation, and increases economic opportunities, does not rule out the subsequent reemergence of conservative social and political groups and institutions, i.e. those which work to maintain or increase substantial existing social and political inequalities.

Kelly and Klein's study of stratification in postrevolutionary societies notes that many nations which have experienced revolutions which initially reduced inequalities experienced over time increasing inequality and status inheritance.[9] Their analysis deals with the predominantly rural, pre-modern, peasant-dominated societies in which most revolutions have oc-curred. Specifically, they hypothesize that in the *short run* a radical revolu-tion (1) produces a more equal distribution of material resources and re-duces status inheritance, (2) shifts the stratification system from an ascrip-tion to an achievement basis, and (3) benefits those who possess certain achieved qualities (knowledge, technical and linguistic skills, etc.) or who have been able to retain material resources. In the *long run* a radical revolu-tion (4) makes peasants better off materially than they were initially, (5) generates social forces which produce steadily increasing economic in-equality among peasants, (6) produces increasing educational inequality among peasants, (7) produces social forces which tend to create more status inheritance among peasants through both economic advantages and educa-tion, and (8) will result in low levels of inequality and status inheritance among peasants if nonpeasants remain well off and there is no economic development in the countryside, but will result in rising levels of material and status inequality in poor societies in which there is substantial economic development.

If these hypotheses are correct, then while revolutionary overthrow of an economically and politically restrictive social order may be a precondi-tion for the emergence of some form of political democracy from a non-democratic history, subsequent factors are required to sustain it. Such forces include the development of certain types of formal political systems and the enfranchisement of all sectors of the work force. These are dis-cussed immediately below. Additional factors that sustain political democ-racy, such as features of economic and stratification systems and cultural variables associated with these, will be discussed in later sections of this chapter.

Formal Political Structures

There are two important social developments which must take place if political democracy is to emerge and be maintained. Once the historical scene is cleared of traditional elites and traditional structures which se-riously inhibit commercial growth and markedly restrict social mobility, it is important that such changes be institutionalized in the form of a constitution and by the presence of a system of competitive political parties. While the existence of an effective constitution and a genuinely competitive party system does not necessitate that a society will have a political democracy, in the absence of either political democracy is most unlikely.

Democratic government requires the introduction of a constitution in the sense that there must be an effective set of fundamental rules which authoritatively define the rights and obligations of citizens and of those who govern them. Constitutional government is opposed to rule by elites with undefined or vaguely defined powers. Constitutional government subjects rulers to the control of the ruled. It imposes what Weber termed a system of rational-legal domination.

In such a system a sharp distinction is made between office and incumbent. The constitution itself specifies procedures for replacing incumbents. This can take the form of providing for periodic elections by universal (adult or male) suffrage. (The role of political parties in this process is discussed below.) It also specifies procedures for changing the structure of political offices. Such change involves modifying the constitution itself. However, political democracy requires that there be limits on the ways in which a constitution can be changed. Specifically, it requires that civil liberties cannot be abridged. This involves guaranteeing the existence of an independent judiciary to protect rights of citizens against the government, maintaining acceptance of responsible opposition as a necessary part of the political system, continuing commitment to the principles of free expression and association, and maintaining the principles of equal access to government and government responsiveness to citizen demands. Hence democracy cannot be equated with majority rule because it is possible that a majority could eliminate any or all of these constitutional guarantees through routine political participation.

Constitutional provisions and their enactment are not in fact as clear-cut as the preceding suggests. They can be subject to differing and sometimes incompatible interpretations. Political elites can sometimes devise strategies to circumvent them or can conceal their violation. To the extent that constitutional provisions limiting political authority or guaranteeing civil rights are ignored or violated in one way or another, the maintenance of democracy is threatened.

There is a considerable body of research in political sociology which indicates the undemocratic and oligarchic tendencies of political parties. Nevertheless, political democracy itself requires the development of a system of competitive political parties. What constitutes a genuinely competitive party system and what forms such a system can take are matters of some debate. Here the approach provided by Giovanni Sartori will be followed because it represents a general theory of party-based politics which rests on an elaborate base of empirical evidence accumulated over the last twenty years.[10]

According to Sartori's analysis, modern political parties arose after the industrial revolution. Their acceptance as legitimate organizations was contingent upon the widespread realization that diversity and dissent are not necessarily incompatible with or disruptive of political order. That is, parties had to be seen not as organized factions standing in opposition to the existing political order but as necessary parts of orderly political systems in which rights to political dissent and to restrained conflict over policies were both important and desirable. Parties themselves probably arose in the competition between members of parliament and governing elites as both sides attempted to have their voices gain more weight by demonstrating that they truly represented their constituents. "Responsible" government, government by elites presuming to serve the best interests of a segment of the citizenry and to rule competently, was organized around a peer- (i.e., elite-) oriented parliamentary party. Later competition between elites encouraged them to appeal to their constituents, producing the first extension of the suffrage (which initially was very restricted) and the development of the vote-seeking party. At some point such parties tend to "solidify" in the sense that they come to be held together not only by political principles but also by the electoral advantages of being stable.

The development of stable parties was the beginning of "responsive" government, i.e., government attentive to and influenced by citizen preferences and demands. It was also the beginning of party government because the party obviously could not meet the demands with which it competed for votes unless it could govern.

With the presence of constitutional and responsive government, widespread (though not necessarily universal) enfranchisement and elections, a party system comes into being. For political democracy to be present as well, the party system must be *competitive*. Sartori identifies several varieties of the competitive party system, all of which involve more than one political party. There are scholars who argue that a single party can freely develop factions and therefore that democratic political competition can exist within the framework of a single-party state. Sartori notes that when there is competition between more than one party, a party governs insofar as it is responsive to the governed. But when a single party governs permanently, any competition is limited to concern with who will govern the party itself—a question whose resolution is unlikely to result in change of the state's outlook. In short, intraparty rivalry cannot be a substitute for interparty competition. The typology of competitive party systems includes the following:

1. *Polarized pluralism:* A polity in which there are at least two anti-system parties, i.e., those which undermine the legitimacy of the regime they oppose. Such parties are mutually antagonistic and mutually exclusive—often being of the Communist or Fascist varieties. In such a polity, along the left-to-right dimen-

sion the center of the system is occupied. Under these conditions cleavages are likely to be very deep, consensus is low, and the legitimacy of the system is widely questioned. Examples include the German Weimar Republic in the 1920s, the French Fourth Republic, Chile until 1973, and present-day Italy.

2. *Moderate pluralism:* A system of three to five relevant parties—parties which over time are occasionally needed or put to use for a feasible coalition majority or which affect the tactics of party competition. Moderate pluralism lacks relevant and/or sizable antisystem parties; there is relatively small ideological distance among its relevant parties. Examples include the German Federal Republic, Belgium, Ireland, Sweden, Iceland, Luxembourg, Denmark, Switzerland, the Netherlands, and Norway.

3. *Two-party systems:* While this is the most widely discussed category of competitive system, it has few members, at most five or six: England, the United States, New Zealand, Australia, Canada, and possibly Austria since 1966. In this system two parties are in a position to compete for the absolute majority of seats; one of the two parties actually succeeds in winning a sufficient parliamentary majority. The winning party is willing to govern alone. Change of the party in power always remains a genuine possibility. In this system both parties must accommodate as many groups, interests, and demands as possible in order to maintain their competitiveness. This tends to minimize ideological conflict within the society.

4. *Predominant-party systems:* A more-than-one-party system in which changes in the party in power have not occurred historically. Over time, the same party consistently manages to win an absolute majority of seats in parliament. Examples include the Solid South in the United States, India, Chile until 1973, Japan, Israel, Turkey, Italy, and Uruguay until 1973. While minor parties in this system are not successful in gaining power, they do represent legal and legitimate competitors of the predominant party. The possibility always exists that the predominant party can be replaced. This represents an equality of opportunity which simply has no equivalent for minor parties in hegemonic systems such as those of East Germany or Poland.

All of the party systems described above are *competitive*—all permit contested elections. Political competition is a structure, or rule of a political game. It ceases to exist whenever contestants and opponents are deprived of equal rights. Competitive systems vary with respect to the amount of actual competition going on within them at any point in time. For example, a given election might involve a number of candidates for public office going unopposed. At the other extreme, an election might involve a bitterly fought contest in which one political party wins by a very thin margin. However, whatever the actual state of competitiveness at some particular point in time, there is always the potential for competitiveness in each of the party systems outlined above.

A political party is any political group that presents at elections, and is capable of placing through elections, candidates for public office. Parties serve as instruments for democratic government when they can effectively convey to authorities the demands of the public as a whole. This can occur within the context of a competitive party system in which parties manage to balance, to a greater or lesser extent, loyalty to themselves and to the state, party interest and general interest, and, when in power, partisanship and impartial governing.

A competitive system of responsible parties leads to *democratization* in the sense specified by Weber:

1. Prevention of the development of a closed status group of officials in the interest of universal accessibility of office.
2. Minimization of authority of officialdom in the interest of expanding the sphere of influence of public opinion as far as practicable.[11]

The development of parties and competitive party systems in the nineteenth century represented a second step in the history of democracy's development in the West. Its necessary predecessor occurred a century earlier with the establishment of civil rights (of habeas corpus, freedom of the press, freedom to choose one's work). A possible future consequence of its development is the institutionalization of an expanding set of social rights (e.g., to a minimum wage and to a certain level of economic security).[12] This has already occurred in varying forms in Western industrial democracies.

Aspects of the complex relationship between political democracy and social equality are considered below. As a prelude to this topic it is important to consider the historical role of the working class in Western democracies. This role is related to the emergence of modern political parties in the industrialized West, to their various ideological stances, and ultimately to possible future developments of the welfare state.

The Incorporation of the Working Class into the Polity

The emergence of the working class as a recognized force in the politics of Western nations is remarkably recent. The process, described by Moore, which removed feudal and feudal-like structures standing in the way of commercial expansion, reduced the rigidity of stratification systems, and made possible nonreactionary solutions to the problems posed by rapid industrialization, took centuries in some cases such as England. The development of competitive party systems, outlined by Sartori, did not occur until the nineteenth century. In many nations, such as Germany, Austria-Hungary, Sweden, and Belgium, universal suffrage was not granted until shortly before or during World War I.[13]

The consequences of the working class gaining rights of political participation have varied considerably from nation to nation. The historical setting in which the working class was incorporated into a polity not only helped determine the particular political issues with which it had to deal at that time, it also set the political agenda for that working class for the indefinite future. Even today, many international differences in working-class political orientations reflect differences in the contexts of their original incorporation.

Major features differentiating these contexts include rigidity of the stratification system, the pattern of industrial-urban development, and the extent to which existing political cleavage cut across or corresponded to class cleavages. For example, England and Germany, which have always been more sharply status divided societies than the United States, also have been societies in which political parties always have been more clearly class linked. Members of the working class in England and Germany have long exhibited greater deference to public authority, political rights, and the legal traditions that guarantee public liberties than have their American counterparts.

American workers never did battle with an established aristocracy or an established church. They did not have to fight their way into the polity. Universal adult male suffrage existed in the United States before the development of any urban-industrial working class. Hence, American workers did not confront established social, religious, and political orders as members of a self-conscious class which was deferential to certain aspects of constituted authority on the one hand while demanding social and political rights on the other. Their orientation to the polity was neither deference nor hostility. They never developed a class-conscious party.

The concerns of American workers centered almost exclusively on the immediate and concrete problems of their everyday existence in the rapidly growing American cities of the mid to late nineteenth century. These problems, well analyzed by early American sociologists such as Lester Frank Ward and later by various members of the Chicago school, in large part stemmed from the incapacity of previous kinship, religious, and economic ties to serve as an effective political infrastructure under the prevailing conditions of expanding, laissez-faire capitalism.

The American working class followed no ideology which guided them in a holy war as did many European working-class socialists. Their concern was for streets, street lighting, bridges, interurban transportation systems, satisfactory sanitary conditions, building inspection, control of crime and delinquency, fire-fighting equipment, hospitals, and above all else, jobs. These needs, in addition to the perpetuation of outmoded city governmental structures and the desires of business to avoid government regulation while simultaneously selling government the material and services necessary for urban expansion, promoted the first formal political organization in the United States—the city machines.[14]

With mass suffrage, mobilization of the urban working-class vote required disciplined, bureacratically structured, professionally administered organizations. In exchange for the vote, effective organizations, such as Tammany Hall, provided jobs, helped immigrants adjust to life in urban industrial America, and provided numerous welfare state functions. They also frequently aided local business by encouraging lax enforcement of city codes, loose auditing of municipal funds, and purchasing supplies and letting contracts in exchange for political support. Knowledge of such political activity reinforced the tendency of American citizens to view authority as always subject to the exercise of some form of influence.[15] Feelings of deference were partially replaced by feelings that the polity, including officeholders and legal traditions, can be manipulated. Incorporation of the working class into Western industrial political life was democratizing in the sense that it vastly increased the numbers of persons outside the formal authority structure of their nation who had legally based influence over the formation and enactment of policy. However, in all nations it did not in itself vastly increase the numbers of persons unreservedly committed to the support of democratic principles such as rule by law and the maintenance of public liberties.

In the West, the working classes have successfully promoted public spending on elaborate and sustained national programs for universal schooling, medical care, the elderly, the unemployed, and guaranteeing satisfactory working conditions. However, particularly in the past two decades or so, working classes appear less and less willing to bear the burdens of taxes, government regulations, and unanticipated social consequences which inevitably accompany these programs.[16] Significant increase in dissatisfaction with government might represent a critical point in the political life of the working class and might prompt the development of new political structures to meet working-class demands. In the United States, in addition to problems of taxation and regulation, the working class has seen the civil rights movement, student activism, the women's movement, and environmental action groups produce changes in the family, religion, the economy, and class, ethnic, and race relations about which it feels, at best, ambivalent. Hence the likelihood of new political directions for the working class appears particularly strong.

Early Theories and Contemporary Macroanalysis: Historical Variables

Political democracy developed hand in hand with capitalism in England, France, and the United States following the destruction of social and political obstacles to commercial and industrial expansion. In this broad sense in which political life is determined by prevailing economic relations, Marx was essentially correct. There is considerable utility in attempting to understand the development of democracy in a nation in terms of certain specific changes in its economic structure. It is also instructive to view these fundamental economic changes as resulting from structurally generated conflict between social classes. Furthermore, once stable, centralized political authority is established in a nation, a condition necessary for conducting modern commercial and industrial activity, internal political struggles center around the distribution of the gross national product. Social classes are the chief parties in these struggles. In general, only during prolonged periods of economic prosperity do other political issues emerge and other social bases for political conflict arise.

In historical perspective, the major social groups whose conflicts shaped basic features of modern Western industrial democracies can be termed "social classes" in the sense of social groups in similar objective circumstances that organize to promote their collective material interests. However, such "social classes" did not always correspond to Marx's *bourgeoisie* and *proletariat*. In the next chapter it will be seen that none of the major groups involved in the development of Fascism in Germany and the establishment of Communism in Russia correspond to the classes Marx specified.

Marx's analysis of the historical development of Western industrial democracy failed to attribute sufficient importance to the political enfranchisement of the working class. The right to form unions and parties in the context of universal male suffrage and competitive party systems made it necessary for governing elites to attend to working-class demands. Despite the not infrequent cooptation of union and party leaders by those in positions of power and privilege, the working class has systematically extended the domain of what it can claim as its political and social rights through institutionalized political means—particularly through the vote. At least in the United States, it is difficult to imagine any candidate for national office seriously seeking electoral victory on the basis of a campaign pledge to *reduce* welfare state provisions.

The very success of the working class in promoting the welfare state may pose a threat to the future of responsive and responsible government. The administration of already existing programs has spawned an enormous bureaucracy. Its members constitute a large political stratum not directly responsible to the electorate. Because this stratum either makes public policy (in practice if not always in principle) or provides technical advisers to those formally responsible for making public policy, its influence is considerable. Recognition of the inevitability of this development led Weber to discuss the antidemocratic potential of all bureaucratically administered organizations, particularly the state.

Weber's contribution to historical understanding of modern Western polities begins with his discussion of democratization and its link to rational-legal domination. Rule according to abstract, rational-legal principles frees people from the arbitrary demands of the powerful, reduces social and economic differences between rulers and the ruled, and presents opportunities for members of all strata to hold authority by making technical competence rather than kinship, religious, or class associations the basis for appointment.[17] In principle, Weber is correct in all of this.

Weber himself constantly emphasized that he was engaging in "ideal type" analysis. Observed structures can be described in terms of the ways in which and the extent to which they diverge from ideal patterns. However, when empirical patterns consistently differ from ideal types in significant ways, questions must be raised about the analytic utility of the concepts. Specifically, the continuing importance of social class in determining political opportunities in all modern polities suggests that Weber underestimated the extent to which and the numerous ways in which power and authority are used to maintain privilege.

Most discussions of the development of political democracy in the West, including the most recent analyses, emphasize the importance of competitive party systems. Weber must be credited with the early recognition of the limits on the role which parties play in promoting democracy. First, he realized that parties tend to respond to citizen interests only when they feel that such attention is necessary. Second, he noted that the stated goals of modern parties involve references to improvements in material standards of living. Characteristically they do not include reference to increasing democracy and equality.

Weber recognized that expanding political bureaucracy would lead to the proliferation of public policy which the public played little role in making. Impersonal rule could become nonresponsive rule. In the United States the mass public has come to the same realization. This recognition can be seen in voters responding with increasing favor to "antibureaucracy" or "anti-Washington" campaign rhetoric despite their favoring the increase of federal government services.

Durkheim pointed out that under conditions of modern social organization, political leadership is no longer accorded extraordinary qualities. Once the religious aura of political authority is gone, it becomes less absolute and more susceptible to demands placed on it by society's members and subgroups. In this sense the polity becomes more democratic. This line of reasoning helps explain the historical importance of efforts to limit the powers of an established church in the process of commercial and industrial expansion and the extension of rights of political participation. The church granted religious legitimation to rulers in exchange for political protection and vast property rights. This pact ran counter to the interests of all newly emerging strata.

Like Weber, Durkheim understood that industrialization would be accompanied by political centralization. Government would take increasing responsibility for protection, public health, education, transportation, and so on. Also like Weber, he was concerned with the antidemocratic consequence of this centralization. Durkheim felt that unless countervailing forces in the form of a network of occupational groups developed, the political, economic, and social rights of individuals could readily be destroyed by the state.

Durkheim was correct in arguing that effective politically independent voluntary associations play an important role in maintaining political democracy. However, he failed to consider the historic contribution of the franchise and the democratizing influences of competitive party systems. Even more than the threat of the overpowering state, Durkheim feared the possibility of political anarchy presented by extensive and rapid social change. While such a potential does exist, such periods of change can also lead to a clarification of moral norms and to the development of more democratic political systems. Historically this has been the goal of many social movements and the result of much nonroutine political participation. The civil rights movement and the women's movement in the United States can serve as examples.

DEMOCRACY AND SOCIAL STRUCTURE

Introduction

The historical events and social changes which made possible the emergence of modern democratic political systems were discussed above. Concern here is with the social consequences of democratic political systems once they are more or less established.

The social revolutions from which democracy emerged in Western Europe destroyed the power and authority of monarchy, aristocracy, and church which each used to maintain its privileges. In the United States as well as Western Europe, destruction of feudal or feudal-like structures facilitated commercial and industrial expansion. This, in turn, vastly increased the wealth of the societies. Since the new industrial working classes all eventually organized and won or were granted the franchise, they had some control over the distribution of this social wealth. Like all strata, they used the power they had gained to secure some material advantages. With increasing size and with better organization the working classes could use their political rights to establish social rights. Hence it would seem that political democracy inevitably promotes substantial improvement in the material conditions of working-class life. Material improvement, however, is not material equality. An important question for political sociology involves the extent to which (or even if) political democracy has promoted economic equality.

In a similar manner it would seem that political democracy promotes improvement of mobility opportunities for the working class. Political power can be used to remove obstacles to working-class entry into mobility channels, particularly through education but also through politics itself. Improved mobility opportunities, however, are not social equality. Another important question for political sociology involves the extent to which (or even if) political democracy has promoted equality of social opportunities. This question is distinct from the question of whether political democracy has promoted economic equality, for substantial material inequality can exist in social systems where there is equality of opportunity. This fact underlies the ideology of meritocracy. Differences in emphasis on *equality* as opposed to emphasis on *achievement* are at the heart of present political controversies in the United States over "affirmative action programs" and practices of "reverse discrimination."

It would also seem that political democracy promotes greater equality in the distribution of political power. It is true by definition that in a political democracy authority is derived from the governed. In complex societies this is expressed in the competitive struggle between political elites who must get support from those whom they govern. However, it is clear that some groups can provide greater support than others because of their greater resources. It is equally clear that such groups will have greater ability to have their preference realized in the process of public policy formation. The formal political equality of individuals does not guarantee the equality of power and influence of the social units they form. While the franchise is of considerable importance, so too is the distribution of politically relevant resources. Hence, a third important question for political sociology involves the distribution of power in putatively democratic systems.

Whether or not democratic political systems promote material, social, or political equality are empirical questions. These are considered in the following three subsections. Such topics rapidly give rise to normative questions: *Should* democratic political systems work toward the achievement of material equality? *Should* they lead to social equality for all citizens? *Should* power be in the hands of all the social groups that make up a complex, heterogeneous society? Some answers proposed for these questions at the border of normative and empirical theory are considered below. In the concluding subsection, contemporary empirical research and normative theory are compared to the positions of Marx, Weber, and Durkheim.

Democracy and Material Equality

In his historical-comparative study of social stratification, Lenski finds a basic trend of increasing inequality of power and privilege from hunting and gathering to horticultural to agrarian societies.[18] However, he notes that inequalities of power and privilege are less pronounced in mature industrial than in agrarian societies. The appearance of mature industrial societies thus marks the first significant reversal in the evolutionary trend toward ever increasing inequality.

Lenski observes that in agrarian societies government is almost entirely an instrument of the few and privileged. Those few who control government are able to determine the rules governing the competition for material rewards available in the society and by virtue of this power are able to influence significantly the outcome of this competition. While in modern industrial societies upper strata still benefit disproportionately from the activities of government, the mass public also benefits to an extent vastly exceeding the share it typically received in agrarian societies. This is surprising since, given the increased productivity of industrial societies and the increased power of the centralized state, one might predict even greater inequality than in agrarian societies.

Lenski explains the decline of inequality in terms of a number of factors.[19] One of the most important of these is the changed role of government in modern industrial societies. While industrialization does not make democracy inevitable, it does create conditions favorable to the growth of political democracy. Such conditions include the spread of literacy and the extension of education, a standard of living giving workers more time, energy, and money to devote to political activity, the development of modern patterns of warfare which involve the entire population (inequality tends to be greater in societies where the military constitutes a distinct stratum), and the spread of the new democratic ideology which asserts that the state belongs to the mass public and that powers of government may no longer be used for the benefit of the few at the expense of the many. All this has meant that in the majority of the more advanced industrial societies (all the Scandinavian countries, Great Britain, all the English-speaking overseas members of the British Commonwealth, the Netherlands, Belgium, Luxembourg, Switzerland, West Germany, Austria, France, Italy, the United States, and Japan) three conditions have prevailed:

1. There is universal, or virtually universal, adult suffrage.
2. The right of organized political opposition is protected by both law and custom.
3. Disadvantaged strata are permitted to organize and engage in collective action in their own behalf.

According to Lenski, the extension of the suffrage to more disadvantaged groups and the growth of competitive elections has resulted in increased material equality over and above the effects of economic development itself. The rise of democracy, then, is a major factor accounting for the decline in the degree of material inequality in modern industrial societies relative to agrarian societies.

Lenski's thesis runs counter to the position taken by both functionalists and conflict analysts.[20] Both positions maintain that political democracy has little or no effect on reducing material inequality. However, the reasons given by the contrasting theoretical approaches differ. Functionalists argue that the needs of industrial economic systems determine the character of their stratification systems. For example, Kerr and others contend that changes in the distribution of material rewards in industrial societies are the result of technological and economic changes which impact on the division of labor and through this alter the pattern of rewards.[21] Increasing technological sophistication increases the number of higher-level positions in the occupational structure. These positions require considerable education and receive substantial prestige and economic rewards. Advanced technology not only creates vastly enlarged middle strata, it also vastly increases productivity. The first effect tends to reduce the number of cases of extreme wealth. The second effect tends to reduce the number of cases of extreme poverty by making some surplus available to those at the bottom of the stratification order. Hence, industrial development leads to a reduction of the range of material inequality. Such effects are produced in all advanced industrial economies leading to convergent patterns of development. Political structure plays little if any role in this.

Conflict analysts also argue that the democratic political systems of Western industrial nations have little or no impact on reducing material inequality. For example, Parkin contends that only in cases where lower classes have used the franchise to elect socialist governments has there been any chance for greater equality.[22] He asserts that nonsocialist governments simply are not concerned with the redistribution of material rewards or with social equality. Parkin compares Western nations which have had extensive periods of socialist government (the Scandinavian countries and Great Britain) and other Western European nations in terms of the extent to which their governments reduced material inequality by providing social services and by reducing income inequality. Using the proportion of gross national product devoted to social service expenditures as a measure of government redistribution programs and the ratios of the average earnings of different occupational groups as a measure of income inequality, Parkin finds that there are no differences in either the provision of social services or in income differentials among occupational groups between the two groups of countries.[23] Hence even socialist democracies do not seem to foster material equality.

Also contrary to Lenski, Jackman finds that political democracy exerts no significant effects on material equality.[24] His data indicate that when democratic performance (measured in terms of degree of electoral participation, amount of political competition, freedom of access to information, and degree of electoral regularity) is specified as an intervening variable it does not interpret or add to the basic relationship between economic development and economic equality. Jackman notes that this finding cannot be interpreted to mean that political structures, policies, and actions have nothing to do with the distribution of material rewards. Rather, there are important political factors that do play a role, but they are factors that have little to do with how democratic a nation is. There are two possible reasons for this: Either (1) political rights were extended to less advantaged groups but then the groups did not engage in effective collective political action in their own behalf or (2) the rights to such collective action were not adequately extended in the first place.

Jackman's study indicates that political programs in the area of social welfare have, in fact, contributed to reduce material inequality. Nations with greater "social insurance program experience" (i.e., programs covering work injury, sickness or maternity, old age, invalidism and death, family allowance and unemployment) are nations with less income inequality. Jackman thus replaces the hypothesis that political democracy promotes material equality with the hypothesis that economic development leads to greater policy effort in the area of social welfare, which, in turn, leads to a greater degree of material equality.

A subsequent study by Hewitt argues that much previous work on the effect of political democracy on material equality (particularly the work of Parkin and Jackman) has had both theoretical and methodological shortcomings.[25] With respect to theory, Hewitt argues that it is not a nation's present political situation as regards democracy or socialism that must be considered but rather the nation's historical experience over the last few decades. With respect to methodology, he proposes several different measures. One dimension of material equality is government distribution. This Hewitt defines as that proportion of social service expenditures which is raised from direct taxes. A second measure of material equality is income equality. Hewitt measures this in terms of individual or household distribution data.[26] As a measure of a nation's historical experience with democracy Hewitt proposes the number of years the nation has had full democracy (universal male adult suffrage, secret ballot, responsible government). His measure of socialist party strength is the annual average proportion of seats held by socialist parties in the national legislature over the first twenty postwar years. Using these measures Hewitt finds:

1. The more democracy or socialism a country has experienced, the lower the share of national income that is taken by the highest income categories.
2. The more the democratic experience, the narrower the range of earnings between high- and low-paid workers.
3. Strong socialist movements are associated with a greater proportion of the national income being redistributed.[27]

The contradictory findings on the relationship of political democracy and material equality make it impossible, at present, to formulate a hypothesis which is likely to go uncontested. Nevertheless, some general conclusions seem warranted. In all societies, material inequalities are the results of and are maintained by the use of power and authority. In political democracies lower strata can use the power of the franchise, within a framework of competitive party systems and responsible government, to reduce material inequalities by electing parties promoting extensive programs of social welfare. Political democracy in itself seems to have done nothing to promote material equality. Much of the reduction in the amount of material inequality from agrarian to industrial societies is the result of technological and economic development. It seems reasonable to conclude tentatively that industrialization promotes the development of the welfare state and that both produce some reduction in material inequality.

Democracy and Social Equality

If political democracy promotes social equality in modern industrial nations, then more democratic nations (however this is defined) should have higher rates of social mobility and greater access to higher education by young from lower social strata. Current rates of occupational mobility say something about the present openness of a stratification system; relatively high mobility rates, both upward and downward, suggest that power and authority are being used less extensively to maintain social inequalities. Present proportions of lower-strata youth enrolled in institutions of higher education might say something about the future openness of a stratification system. In industrial societies education is the chief channel of social mobility. Relatively high enrollment of lower-strata youth might suggest that, at present, power and authority are being used less extensively to insure future inequalities.

With respect to social mobility in Western industrial societies, Lipset and Bendix found relatively little difference in the rates of social mobility—as measured by the shift across the manual-nonmanual line—in Germany, Finland, Sweden, Norway, and the United States.[28] The similarity of rates is attributed to several processes inherent in all modern social structures: (1) changes in the number of available vacancies, (2) different rates of fertility, (3) changes in the rank accorded occupations, (4) changes in the number of inheritable status positions, and (5) changes in legal restrictions pertaining to potential opportunities. In short, mobility patterns in Western industrial societies are determined by the occupational structure. Political democracy plays no part in this process. Extending this line of analysis, Rubinson and Quinlan argue that there is much stronger empirical support for the hypothesis that occupational structure and the social forces which shape it affect democratization than there is for the hypothesis that democratization negatively affects social inequality.[29]

With respect to educational opportunities in Western industrial societies, data do show increasing enrollments of lower-strata youth in institutions of higher education. However, by themselves, these data are insufficient to suggest anything about social equality. They must be supplemented with data on the types of institutions of higher education which are attended. It is quite possible that lower-strata youth are overrepresented in lower-status schools and in programs leading to middle and lower-middle positions in the occupational structure while the opposite is true of upper-strata youth. Increasing enrollments do not necessarily represent increased social opportunities. They might simply represent an increase in the technical requirements of middle to lower-middle occupational roles. Power and authority might be used to open access to certain types of schools and/or programs while simultaneously restricting access to other types of schools and/or programs—those linked to highly rewarded positions. As yet there is no empirical evidence unambiguously supporting the contention that political democracy fosters equality of educational opportunities.

The tentative conclusion about the bearing of political democracy on social equality parallels the tentative conclusion about the relationship of political democracy to material equality. Further macroanalytic and historical-comparative research is needed in these areas. If data from such studies force the conclusion that political democracy itself promotes neither material nor social equality, then very basic questions must be raised about the ways in which political power and authority *can* influence the distribution of material and social rewards in advanced industrial societies.

Democracy and Political Equality: The Pluralist-Elitist Debate

The pluralist-elitist debate concerns opposing theories of the way in which power is distributed in communities and in nations. There are a number of points of similarity between the debate and the "end-of-ideology" debate discussed in Chapter 6. In part, both of them stem from a lack of consensus on how the subject matter (ideology or power) is to be defined. In turn, different definitions lead to different measurement procedures. These methodological disagreements finally produce different sets of data often supporting conflicting hypotheses.

Underlying differences in concepts and hypotheses are divergent approaches. In the case of the end-of-ideology debate, there were those who saw the "good society" as close to realization in the industrialized democratic West. These analysts viewed the demise of ideology as a desired and desirable sign. They were confronted by others who saw substantial inequalities and injustice at present and in the foreseeable future of Western nations. Insofar as they believed there was any decline in the production and spread of ideological thought, they were not pleased. As they saw it, ideology motivated individuals to collective action in order to realize a vision of the good society. Any end of ideology was an end of social vision and of the hope for a better tomorrow through collective political action.

In the case of the pluralist-elitist debate, there are those who see the distribution of power in Western industrial democracies, or at least in the United States, as being as fair or as democratic as is possible in the context of modern highly differentiated societies. While they certainly do not see all individuals and groups as having equal power, they maintain that most have some power to achieve their ends in issue areas that are of particular interest to them. Such theorists or "pluralists" are confronted by others, who see the distribution of power, whether local, or national, as being anything but fair or democratic. In their view, the ability to decide the full range of important political issues is concentrated in the hands of a very few persons—an elite—who are not formally responsible to the mass public or to any sector of it whose interests are affected by their decisions.

The elitist and pluralist positions are sketched below. This will be followed by an appraisal of both approaches and by a description of some research which overcomes some of their characteristic problems.

Elitists generally view *power* as participation in making social policy. For example, Mills writes that "power has to do with whatever decisions men make about the arrangements under which they live . . . in so far as decisions are made, the problem of who is involved in making them is the basic problem of power."[30] Those who are reputed to participate in such decision making are those who control major social organizations and institutions. In the case of individual communities this generally involves business leaders. In the case of the nation it involves only those who command major institutions, such as high-ranking leaders of the government and the military, and the owners and executives of the largest corporations.

Hunter's study of Atlanta is the classic illustration of the elitist position with regard to the distribution of power in communities.[31] Hunter found power concentrated in the hands of a group of leaders of the business community who interacted socially and who determined social policy informally and without publicity. The group consisted of forty industrial, commercial, and financial owners and top executives of large enterprises. There were no formal ties between this group and the city government. However, the presence of its members on policy-determining committees and their links with other powerful institutions and organizations of the community made government subservient to their interests—interests which were generally promoted by maintenance of the political-economic status quo.

Mills's *Power Elite* is undoubtedly the most widely cited elitist study of the distribution of power in the United States.[32] His thesis is that continuous and important social power resides with those who hold the highest decision-making positions in the nation's political, economic, and military institutions. The *power elite* itself consists of "those political, economic and military circles which, as an intricate set of overlapping cliques, share decisions having at least national consequences. In so far as national events are decided, the power elite are those who decide them."[33]

The unity of the power elite lies in the similarity of its members social origins, education, and style of life; the criteria of admission, honor, and promotion that prevails among them; the structural coincidences of interest which connect their institutional areas (e.g., industry and the military), and, at times, some explicit coordination.

Such sources of unity make it possible for members of the power elite to take on another's point of view and to interchange top roles in the different institutional orders. The admiral who was a banker and a lawyer and who headed a major federal commission, and the corporation executive whose company was a leading war materials producer who became Secretary of Defense serve as two of Mills's examples. Such persons "define one another as among those who count and who, accordingly, must be taken into account."[34]

According to the elitist image, at least as it is expressed by Mills, the mass public is politically passive, disorganized, and unable to play a part in the formulation of public policy. It would seem that citizens would have some power through their involvement in interest groups and associations. However, according to Mills and others, such organizations have ceased being both psychologically meaningful and politically effective for their members.[35] This is the result of the enormous gap between members and leaders now found in mass associations. As soon as a man becomes a leader of a mass association with significant resources he is coopted by the elite and comes to see himself as one of its members. He thereby ceases to be a delegate of the association whose interests he supposedly represents. The interests he now takes into account are the interests of other elites. He discusses, debates, and resolves issues with them and "sells" the results to the membership of his mass association. He is no longer a delegate of the association but a spokesman for the elite. This analysis is intended to apply to political parties as well as to other mass associations. Hence, elections are viewed as contests between leaders who are not truly representative of their groups. Party leaders sell a political program to their supporters rather than work for their interests as these have been communicated. Consequently, in the United States "there is little live political struggle. Instead, there is administration from above, and a political vacuum from below."[36]

There are a number of versions of the elitist image in addition to that of Mills. At least two of these merit independent discussion. One, developed by William Domhoff, claims that the United States has a distinctive upper class which controls or dominates its political life on the national level.[37] His studies of the backgrounds of people in key decision-making positions in the federal government (such as cabinet members, presidential advisers, and members of the Supreme Court) and in large corporations revealed that they disproportionately tended to come from a privileged class. The class is united by its members having attended exclusive schools and elite universities, where they belonged to the "right" fraternities. Now they belong to exclusive clubs, visit the "right" resorts, support similar charitable and cultural organizations, and so on. According to Domhoff, the upper class exerts its influence to preserve the prevailing order of power and privilege in America not only by occupying key positions but also by making political campaign contributions, lobbying, and joining national policy-planning organizations such as the National Planning Association, the Committee for Economic Development, the Advisory Council, the Twentieth Century Fund, the Brookings Institution, and the Council on Foreign Relations.

Domhoff's thesis is an extension of Mills's analysis of the social sources of cohesiveness of the power elite. Like Mills's work it expresses a profound sense of dissatisfaction—a sense that democracy is betrayed—by the political structures and processes it describes. A very different orientation is offered by Charles Lindblom.[38] Lindblom agrees that, in particular, executives of large corporations constitute the core of a newly constructed upper class of wealth and overpowering political resources. As he puts it:

> The executive of the large corporation is, on many counts, the contemporary of the landed gentry of an earlier era, his voice amplified by the technology of mass communication.[39]

However, rather than expressing distress at the vastly disproportionate power of big business in America, Lindblom sees it as a power structure which inevitably accompanies private-enterprise, market-oriented economies. He is explicitly critical of theorists such as Mills and Domhoff in arguing that:

> to understand the peculiar character of politics in market-oriented systems requires . . . no conspiracy theory of politics, no theory of common social origins uniting government and business officials, no crude allegations of a power elite established by clandestine forces. Business simply needs inducements, hence a privileged position in government and politics, if it is to do its job.[40]

In Lindblom's view, in Western democracies government is held largely responsible for levels of employment, economic growth, prices, and the balance of payments. If there is widespread dissatisfaction with government performance in these areas, as during periods of depression or inflation, a government can be brought down. Therefore, government must see to it that businessmen perform their tasks. Hence government helps business in a number of ways: (1) through subsidies (e.g., to water, rail, highway, and air transport), (2) in fair trade regulation, (3) in overseas trade promotion through foreign ministries, (4) in subsidized research and development (e.g., to aerospace industries), and (5) by bailing out failing industries with loans (e.g., $1.6 billion to Chrysler Corporation in 1980). Hence:

> In the eyes of government officials . . . businessmen do not appear simply as the representatives of a special interest, as representatives of interest groups do. They appear as functionaries performing functions that government officials regard as indispensable.[41]

In short, in Lindblom's elitist image, a politically dominant business elite is necessary to the operation of industrial democracy—democracy and political inequality go hand in hand.

The United States is a political democracy in the senses of having universal adult suffrage, regular elections, the legal right to organized political opposition, freedom of access to information, the freedom of disadvantaged strata to organize and engage in collective action, and so on. If Mills, Domhoff, Lindblom, and several others are correct, all of this has failed to produce anything approximating a system of political equality. As Mills, at least, sees it, America is a nation run by "the huge corporation, the inaccessible government (and) the grim military establishment."[42]

Pluralists generally view power as the ability or potential of individuals or groups to realize their own will in political conflict. Individuals or groups who possess the resources which make it possible for them to impose their will on others in a given situation are regarded as those who possess power in that situation.

Pluralists argue that there are many power-relevant resources. For example, Dahl points out that these include, among other things, money and credit; control over jobs; control over the information of others; social standing; knowledge and experience; popularity, esteem, and charisma; legality, constitutionality; ethnic solidarity, and the right to vote.[43] Obviously, such resources are not equally distributed. To the extent that they are dispersed rather than concentrated in the hands of a few, power is also dispersed.

In addition, to the extent that particular resources have different political values in different contexts or issues, power is also dispersed. For example, ethnic solidarity and the right to vote may be crucial in determining the outcome of a particular election but may have little bearing on the formation of economic policy. The opposite might be true for control over jobs. Pluralists, whether studying the distribution of power in an individual community or in the nation, tend to find that power-relevant resources are dispersed and that given resources have different values in different areas of political conflict. This might not be a sufficient basis for claiming that American communities in general and the nation as a whole can be characterized as having a "fair" or genuinely democratic distribution of power, or that an approximation of the good society has been found. Nevertheless, pluralist studies do give the impression that their authors hold such a view.

Pluralists also argue that there are a number of additional factors which reduce the possibility of concentrated power being used effectively by a small elite stratum to further its material and ideal interests. These include:

1. Competitive elections require elected officials to make some effort to support policies desired by the electorate.
2. Disadvantaged groups can combine resources to produce aggregate strength and possibly can use their available, though limited, resources with greater efficiency.
3. There are often major social forces which shape issues in ways beyond the control of any one group, no matter how powerful it is.
4. Social norms set limits on political objectives which can be pursued and on the methods by which they are pursued. Rational manipulation can take place within this framework but not in spite of it.
5. There are constitutional and other forms of legal constraints on power. Many of these have the additional support of public opinion. While, at times, the powerful can get around laws, many times they cannot.
6. There are often counter-elites pursuing their individual or group interests. The powerful have to contend with each other when their interests do not coincide and at times with organized opposition in such forms as civil rights groups, environmental groups, youth groups, trade associations, and other voluntary associations.

In their studies of the distribution of power, pluralists tend to focus on particular issues of significant political controversy. Those who have power are those who were active or instrumental in their resolution. The data characteristically reveal a pattern in which power is widely shared among individuals or social units that are specialized with regard to issue areas. That is, those active and instrumental in the resolution of issues in one area of social organization generally are not the same as those powerful in other issue areas. In terms of community power, for example, Dahl's study of New Haven, Connecticut, revealed a system of noncumulative or dispersed inequalities in political resources marked by six characteristics:

1. Many different kinds of resources for influencing officials are available to different citizens.
2. With few exceptions, these resources are unequally distributed.
3. Individuals best off in their access to one kind of resource are often badly off with respect to many other resources.

4. No one influence resource dominates all the others in all or even in most key decisions.

5. With some exceptions, an influence resource is effective in some issue areas and in some specific decisions, but not in all.

6. Virtually no one and certainly no group of more than a few individuals is entirely lacking in some influence resources.[44]

This set of characteristics does not indicate that in the pluralist view political democracy and equality of power are inseparably linked. There are always inequalities in the distribution of political resources. In given issue areas there are always power differentials. However, the pattern of dispersed inequality is interpreted as representing a kind of political system which, if not exactly a fair and equal one, constitutes a reasonable approximation.

Pluralist studies of power in the nation present a similar view. For example, Rose's study of power in the United States concludes that American society is composed of many small elite groups each exercising its power in different areas of political life.[45] Some have their power through economic controls, others through political controls, and still others have power through military, associational, religious, and other controls. Rose acknowledges that in American society there are masses of individuals who have no social ties which give them some amount of political influence. Nevertheless, he maintains that the majority of the population consists of groupings of individuals who have some political information, interest, and concern, who have varying degrees of power, and who communicate their opinions to political elites. As a result, Rose maintains that the majority is not readily susceptible to manipulation or control by a political elite. For Rose, Dahl, and other political pluralists, political inequality is dispersed in America.

Both pluralists and elitists present considerable amounts of empirical data which support their diverse positions. Since each uses a somewhat different set of concepts and methodological approaches, it might be that their divergent findings are little more than reflections of these divergent points of analytic departure. If this is so, then what is needed to shed some light on the central issues of the pluralist-elitist debate are entirely new studies of the distribution of power. Such studies should critically evaluate what, if anything, can be learned from the vast amount of research already conducted and then, on the basis of this assessment, generate new, additional hypotheses to be tested through the use of new and, insofar as possible, unbiased methods.

Progress along such lines has already been made in the analysis of community power. Walton's review of thirty-three studies dealing with fifty-five communities indicated that results of community power studies to date were related to the methodology used.[46] Specifically he found that:

1. The reputational method (in which informants are asked to identify the most influential people in their community when it comes to getting things done) tends to locate power structures which are monolithic, monopolistic, or a single concentrated leadership group.

2. The decision-making approach (in which the focus is on specific community issues, and leaders are those persons active or instrumental in their resolution) tends to identify power structures in which there are at least two durable factions or in which there are fluid coalitions of interest usually varying with issues.

3. Studies focusing on governmental issues tend to find factional and coalitional structures, while a focus on nongovernmental issues more frequently results in an elitist description.

The review of the community studies also revealed some support for these hypotheses:

1. Socially integrated, heterogeneous populations have less concentrated power structures.

2. There are regional differences in the distribution of power.

3. The more industrial the community, the less concentrated its power structure.

4. Communities with a high proportion of absentee ownership tend to have less concentrated power structures.

A major methodological and theoretical advance was introduced by Perrucci and Pilisuk in their study of Lafayette, Indiana.[47] The explicit purpose of the study was "to measure power as an *institutional* variable and to put the question of pluralism versus elite control to a methodologically different test from what (had) yet appeared in the literature."[48]

The authors argue that both the reputational approach and the decision-making approach are incomplete since they only attempt to identify powerful individuals. The power any person has stems from occupying a high decision-making position within an organization whose operations affect the larger community. The greater the effect of the organization's activities on the community, the greater the individual's power. Further, when a person is in a position to influence the decisions of additional organizations in the community by overlapping membership, he has still more power. And when a person is part of a chain that connects organizations in the community, this constitutes a network of organization resources he can draw upon to influence community decision making. Hence, to use Perrucci and Pilisuk's example, the community banker who also sits on the executive board of three other community organizations will occupy a more powerful situation than the banker who does not hold other executive positions.

On the basis of these considerations the authors set forth their major position that it is not the potency of any individual or set of individuals but the shape of the network of organizational ties in the community which depicts the structure of enduring community power. Four hypotheses are offered:

1. There exists in communities a relatively small and clearly identifiable group of interorganizational leaders (IOLS), or persons who hold policy-making positions in "many" organizations.
2. Organization leaders (OLS), or persons who hold equally high positions in "few" organizations, will be less often identified as having influenced the outcome of an actual community issue than will their counterpart IOLS. The groups will also differ with respect to the frequency with which they are identified as being likely to exert influence on the outcome of a hypothetical community issue, but less so than on real issues.
3. IOLS will show greater similarity of values and primary or social ties among themselves than will OLS.
4. Those IOLS who are part of the same resource network will be judged more powerful by their peers and will show greater value similarity on matters of local and national political-economic policies and more frequent social ties.[49] (Using the operational definition of the study, a resource network is said to exist when: (a) three or more IOLS share executive positions on the same organization, and (b) they are also linked to each other by one or more other organizational ties, and (c) in such a fashion that the network is "closed" in the sense that all persons are directly linked to each other by first or second order connections.)

The results of testing this set of hypotheses in a particular community will not be methodological artifacts. A full range of outcomes is possible. A small and identifiable group of IOLS might not be found. In this case, it can be concluded that there is the greatest possibility that power in the given community is shifting and amorphous. The nature of value similarity and structural ties among the identified leaders can then be examined to determine whether any other pattern of power exists. If IOLS are identified with interconnections which form a resource network but are not identified as actual influentials or potential influentials on hypothetical issues, then it can be concluded that power is likely distributed according to the pluralistic model. If IOLS are identified and the same interorganizational resource networks are found to consist of men who are both reputational and actual leaders, and if they also reveal value similarity and primary or social ties among themselves, then a ruling elite has been found.

The authors found an elite structure existing in Lafayette. The details of their methodology and findings are too extensive to report here. What is important is that the researchers developed an approach to the distribution of community power which does not bias results. What is equally important is that power is treated as an institutional variable rather than as an attribute of individual persons. The study treats power structures rather than the social psychology of powerful persons. The approach invites comparative studies and suggests a view of changes in the distribution of power which involves considerably more than changes in personnel.

Additional progress in developing the concept of power structure has been provided by the work of Laumann and others.[50] The authors begin with the standard sociological understanding of social structure as a recurrent pattern of social relationships among social positions. Using this definition, they treat the structure of a community elite, whether a single concentrated leadership group or sets of leaders dispersed in different issue areas, as a regularized pattern of communication and information exchange among its members on community matters.

Two factors are of particular importance in determining patterns of elite communication: the extent to which there is agreement among members of the elite on outcome preferences on various community issues (*issue consistency*) and the nature of the ties among community elites—whether based on factors such as membership of shared business and professional organizations and legally required associations in formal governmental structure (*instrumental ties*) or based on factors such as similarity of value orientations and religious affiliation (*solidary ties*). These and several additional variables noted below influence the development of one or the other of two patterns of elite communication or "models for issue resolution." In the *bargaining model,* highly involved persons on each side of a community controversy negotiate the outcome by compromise and trading of concessions on the points at issue. Active participants in the controversy carry on considerable communication both with those who support them in order to mobilize as much support as possible, and with active opponents to explore possible bases for compromising their differences. The *oppositional model* describes a polarized community in which there are sharp differences of opinion and often considerable mutual antagonism. Direct discussion among active persons with opposed preferences is avoided. Reduction of controversy in such situations is likely to be carried out, if at all, via mediation by less highly committed persons rather than by direct negotiation among active partisans. This model implies intensified communication within groups of persons sharing the same strongly held views.

The authors' data were drawn from two American and one West German community of moderate size. They suggested the following set of propositions:

1. The greater the economic and social differentiation of a community,
   a. the greater the range of decisions faced by an elite
   b. the greater the likelihood that various bases of interest similarity crosscut one another, and
   c. the greater the importance of organizations versus persons as significant community actors.
2. The greater the range of decisions and the greater the extent of crosscutting solidarities, the lower the issue consistency of elite actors.
3. a. The lower the issue consistency, the greater the importance of organiza-

tions as actors; and the greater the extent of crosscutting cleavages, the more likely the use of instrumental ties in constructing the influence structure.

b. the higher the issue consistency, the lower the importance of organizations as actors; and the greater the extent of overlap among bases of interest similarity, the more likely the use of solidary ties in constructing the influence structure.

4. a. The lower the issue consistency and the greater the use of instrumental ties in constructing the influence structure, the more likely the appearance of a bargaining model for issue resolution; and

b. the higher the issue consistency and the greater the use of solidary ties in constructing the influence structure, the more likely the appearance of an oppositional model for issue resolution. . . .

5. The greater the use of instrumentally based linkages in constructing the influence structure and the more issues for which a bargaining model for issue resolution appears, the more frequently decisive outcomes are reached.

6. The greater the use of solidary linkages in constructing the influence structure and the more issues on which an oppositional model for issue resolving appears, the higher the level of open controversy involving mobilization of nonelite members of the community.

7. The larger and more differentiated a community, the more institutionalized the elite contact pattern. . . .

8. The institutionalization of elite contact patterns bears a curvilinear relation to output levels. More specifically, moderately institutionalized systems will have higher rates of issue consideration and resolution.[51]

Progress in understanding how power is distributed and exercised parallels the progress which has been made in understanding the determinants of voting behavior described in Chapter 2. In both substantive areas, sociological research using increasingly sophisticated conceptual and methodological tools has advanced from analysis of the analytically isolated individual to genuinely structural concerns. Many statements which were previously seen as expressing invariant features of individual social behavior have come to be understood as applying only in particular historical circumstances. Comparative studies have revealed the inadequacies of previous work and have raised new questions for research.

The emerging image of the structure of power which comes from the findings of studies like those of Walton, Perrucci and Pilisuk, Laumann and his colleagues, and others, is neither an elitist nor a pluralist image. What is indicated is that under specifiable sets of empirical conditions the terms "elitist" and "pluralist" can serve more or less adequately as summary terms for describing the distribution of power in a particular social system at a particular point in time. The terms cannot be taken to suggest anything about the distribution of power at some future point in time. The dynamics of structural change have yet to be adequately studied.

Early Theories and Contemporary Macroanalysis: Democracy and Social Structure

In Marx's view greater material, social, and political quality would result from the establishment of political democracy. However, democracy was not to be identified with "bourgeois" political structures but with a postrevolutionary stateless society in which class distinctions no longer had validity and social life was no longer determined by the relations of production. In a bourgois democracy, material, social, and political inequality are inevitable. It is a political system which best promotes industrial capitalism.

Much empirical research on community power, including research utilizing methodologies permitting a full range of findings, has produced a picture which, though not Marxist in detail, does reveal the concentration of power in the hands of the economically privileged. Some research has also indicated that such power is used to maintain and enhance the material interests of such a stratum. Studies of national power indicating, among other things, the influence of corporate interests, have been consistent with the notion that political life is largely determined by prevailing economic relations. There is need for further macroanalytic research and historical-comparative research on national power. Marx's approach of *historical materialism* and his concepts of *class* and *state* might have considerable value in such analytic undertakings.

Weber argues that bureaucratic administration tends to reduce social and economic differences between administrators and the governed by presenting opportunities for members of all strata to hold administrative office, by prohibiting officials from using office for personal gain, and by recruiting on the basis of technical qualifications. However, he also notes that in the political realm, as rationalization proceeds and bureaucracy expands, power comes to be increasingly concentrated in the hands of political leaders and more and more decisions come to be made by "experts." An extensively bureaucratized political system, even with civilian rule, representative institutions, and public liberties, still tends to be one in which there is considerable inequality of power. This is true all the more as political decisions appropriate for public debate come to be treated as technical decisions appropriate for the judgment of experts. Such analysis has been useful in understanding the question of power structures in communities dealing with such matters as fluoridation, public school needs, and environmental protection.

Weber's discussions of several of his central concepts have considerable potential for illuminating the relationships of democracy to material, social, and political equality. His analysis of status groups suggests hypotheses about the recruitment process of political elites, the interaction patterns they are likely to have, and the types of material and ideal interests they are likely to pursue. His discussion of bureaucracy leads the way toward a structural understanding of power and to the ways in which such administrative structure both promotes and inhibits equality. It also suggests that power can reside in positions of authority within well-defined social structures and leaves as an empirical question the matter of whether or not, in given situations, it is relations of production in the more narrow economic sense which are important in determining structures of material, social, and political inequality. Even with its flaws, it is valuable to keep in mind Weber's notion of ideal type analysis when discussing the nature, origins, and consequences of elite and pluralistic distributions of power. Only approximations of these patterns exist in reality. Notions of material equality, social equality, and political equality similarly refer to analytic constructs. In all societies there are material, social, and political inequalities which result from and are maintained by the users of power and authority.

It was Durkheim who called attention to the central role which occupational associations were to play in the political life of modern industrial society. Understanding the character of that role is the key to understanding the linkages of democracy and equality.

Clearly, occupational associations have both increased and reduced material inequality. For example, organized labor has been effective in reducing material inequalities through its lobbying efforts. On the other hand, some unions, as well as business and professional associations, have helped perpetuate and increase material and social inequalities by excluding minority groups from membership. In an industrial democracy, occupational associations, even those with internal democratic structures and processes, often develop a leadership stratum with material interests and political perspectives which make them less likely to direct the organizations in ways promoting material and social equality. The question of the extent to which such organizations are or can be effective advocates of their mass membership's interests is at the heart of the pluralist-elitist debate.

In modern industrial societies organizations not directly linked to the division of labor have had considerable significance in reducing inequalities. Civil rights, ethnic, religious, student, feminist, and environmental groups serve as examples. While Durkheim never claimed that *only* occupational associations were likely to be important in modern societies, he did not attend sufficiently to the political importance of organizations with other such bases of association.

The presence of a vast network of occupational associations in Western industrial democracies has served to direct popular political action into institutionalized channels. Collective political action which has occurred has produced neither enduring chaos nor anarchy. Material, social, and political equality as well as political democracy itself are not possible when social chaos and anarchy prevail. This is a fundamental and important proposition of political sociology which Durkheim emphasized.

CULTURAL DIFFERENCES AND SIMILARITIES

Introduction

Thus far, *culture* has been treated as the system of beliefs and values shared by members of a group which provides the basis for its members' mutual orientation. In Chapters 4 and 5 research on the political importance of culture in this sense of the term was described. There studies of culture involved the use of sample surveys and investigated the beliefs and values of individuals—what they thought about and how they evaluated political participation, themselves as political actors, the political behavior of others, government, the regime under which they lived, their political community, and other political systems. They were microanalytic studies. In addition, only aspects of political culture were discussed, that is, certain beliefs and values concerning manifestly political objects, including the self as a political actor.

In this section, the concept culture is to be understood more broadly in several senses. First, aspects of general culture which shape the political culture of a group are considered.[52] Second, macroanalytic studies are discussed. Concern will not be with the beliefs and values of individuals per se but with certain abstract patterns of beliefs and values present in a given social system. Third, in addition to beliefs and values other components of culture will be considered. These include ideas which do not purport to be empirically grounded (e.g., belief in God or in the intrinsic goodness of man), sentiments, motives, and symbols.

In this section the political importance of kinship and religion will be discussed again. Here, however, they will be considered neither as agents of political socialization nor as the institutional loci of interest groups such as churches and families. The discussion of kinship deals with the cultural emphasis on family ties as appropriate determinants of political-economic behavior. The discussion of religion deals with the interplay of religious and political orientations which shape the political life of a nation. Finally, the section concerns abstract patterns of beliefs about and expectations of political institutions.

The Importance of Kinship

The lack of emphasis on family-owned business and on precapitalist patterns of maintaining family fortune, power, and status from generation to generation have facilitated the development of both industrialization and political democracy in Western nations. As Lipset notes, this relationship can be seen by contrasting the political-economic role of kinship in Latin American nations with its role in Western nations with large-scale bureaucratized industries.[53]

Where private family property is seen as the foundation of the social-economic order, kinship relations structure power and authority relations. Particularistic loyalties are expected from workers. Stable definitions of rights and obligations, clearly defined and impersonal sets of authority relations, and publicity of decisions tend to be absent. Under these conditions rights to collective bargaining generally are denied. Any attempts to limit the rights of the ownership class or to introduce changes in the political, economic, or educational systems are vehemently opposed. Legitimate and effective trade unions and workers parties are difficult to establish and maintain. The absence of such organizations means that existing levels of material, social, and political inequalities are unlikely to be changed. This encourages the development of highly antagonistic ownership and working classes which are bearers of antithetical ideologies.

Where family-based businesses have been replaced by large-scale bureaucratic industries, there has been a greater willingness on the part of ownership and managerial classes to accept trade unions and workers parties as legitimate. Where this has occurred, management-labor relations tend to be less hostile and the appeal of radical ideologies to the working class is considerably reduced. In bureaucratized industries elites tend to support economic growth and expanded economic, social, and political opportunities. Such modernizing elites promote cultural values opposed to those characteristic of traditional elites. The latter emphasized rights associated with family property, which led them to oppose such changes not merely because they ran against their own political and economic interests but because they were seen as destructive of the very moral foundation of their society.

The Religious Dimension

In the previous chapters discussion of religion as a factor influencing political life dealt with religious organizations as agents of political socialization, as transmitters of specific beliefs legitimating or challenging particular types of political structures, and as political interest groups. In the present analytic context in which it is considered as a cultural-level variable, discussion will deal with religion as a society's basic self-conception which finds expression in a set of beliefs, symbols, and rituals.

It was Durkheim who first called attention to the fact that all groups have this kind of religious dimension in their collective life. Its features are revealed in public ceremonies, by the symbols society's leaders use in attempts to win support and achieve solidarity, in a society's aesthetic productions, and in its dominant value system. The diffuse nature of a society's religious dimension makes it difficult to establish clear empirical links between it and specific features or events of national political life. Valid and reliable indicators of this cultural variable need to be developed.

Historical-comparative studies utilizing such indicators could then be undertaken to investigate associations between varying religious traditions and varying political structures, processes, and events.

In the absence of such empirical studies there is still some conceptual work suggesting relationships between the religious dimension and politics. Undoubtedly the most widely discussed study of this type is Bellah's analysis of what he terms America's "civil religion."[54] The study is described here briefly to illustrate the way in which religion, considered as a macroanalytic cultural variable, can be conceptualized as impacting on the political life of a Western democracy.

Bellah argues that in the United States, despite the importance of the separation of church and state, politics has a religious dimension. There are, he claims, certain common elements of religious orientation, which are neither sectarian nor in any sense Christian, that the majority of Americans share. These have played an important role in the development of the American polity. This public religious dimension, which is expressed in a set of beliefs (e.g., America as the chosen people), symbols (e.g., the Statue of Liberty), and solemn rituals (e.g., presidential inauguration) and which has its own prophets (e.g., Washington, Jefferson), martyrs (e.g., Lincoln, Kennedy), sacred events (e.g., Memorial Day), sacred places (e.g., Arlington National Cemetery), and sacred scriptures (e.g., the Declaration of Independence, the Constitution), he terms the American "civil religion." It has served, among other things:

1. to reaffirm the religious legitimation of the highest political authority
2. to provide a basis for national religious self-understanding
3. to provide symbols of national solidarity
4. to mobilize deep levels of personal motivation for the attainment of national goals

It seems clear that the American polity does have such a religious dimension. However, what remains unclear as yet are the specific ways in which the American civil religion has influenced particular political structures and events in the past or can influence them in the future. Bellah does argue that events such as the antislavery movement in the nineteenth century and American rejection of socialism ever since the 1850s cannot be fully understood without reference to religious motives. He also contends that the present threat of political control by unresponsive bureaucracies is, in part, to be accounted for in terms of the displacement of a national religious self-understanding by calculating reason. Such reason treats political issues as exclusively technical problems to be dealt with by experts rather than as indicators that national priorities and ultimate goals need public consideration. At present, such contentions, whatever their merit, are difficult to treat empirically. How analytically useful the particular concept "civil religion" is in attempting to understand various political phenomena has yet to be demonstrated in empirical, historical-comparative research.

Views and Expectations of the Polity

What members of a society generally expect from their political system has some influence on its operation. National differences in shared expectations concerning what the political system should provide, how it should perform, and what, in turn, the political system is owed accounts in part for national differences in amounts and types of political participation and the development and maintenance of both formal and informal structures and processes, and also finds expression in national ideological differences.

No Western industrial democracy has a population all of whose members have the same expectations of their political system. Class, ethnic, regional, religious, and other differences are found in all of them. Nevertheless, such within-nation differences often are not nearly as large or as important in their political impact as are between-nation differences in citizen expectations of the polity. In many ways, the political orientations of American workers are more like the political orientations of American middle-class citizens than they are like the political orientations of English, French, Italian, German, or even Canadian workers.

There are a number of kinds of expectations which citizens can have concerning their political *rights*.[55] These include expectations concerning:

1. goods and services to be supplied by the polity (welfare benefits, housing, educational facilities)
2. regulations to be maintained by the polity (job safety rules, rules pertaining to health and sanitation, price controls)
3. information to be supplied by the polity (concerning the ongoing conduct of government, policies, policy intent)
4. symbolic activity to be provided by the polity (public affirmation of national values by political elites, displays of national symbols, conducting national ceremonies)
5. political rights to be maintained by the polity (to vote, to hold office, to organize political associations)

There is a corresponding set of expectations concerning *obligations* of citizens to the polity. These include expectations concerning:

6. goods and services required by the polity (payment of taxes, military service)
7. obedience to laws and regulations required by the polity
8. information to be supplied to the polity (concerning income, residence, occupation)

9. symbolic activity required by the polity (taking oaths, paying deference or respect to public authority, symbols, and ceremonials)
10. providing support through routine political participation (by voting, attending to governmental communications)

Almond and Verba's study of the political cultures of five Western democracies revealed major differences in the patterns of such expectations held by citizens of the various nations.[56] Expectations differed with respect to:

1. how *fairly* the political system would disperse goods and services, enforce regulations, uphold political rights, and so on
2. how *predictably* or *reliably* the political system would operate in enforcing regulations, in providing accurate information about its operation, and so on
3. how *responsive* the political system would be to citizen demands

The researchers found that Italians tended to look upon government and politics as frequently unfair, as unpredictable and sometimes even threatening, and as not responsive to their demands. Such a pattern does not support a stable and effective democratic system.

The Mexican pattern showed inconsistencies. On the one hand, Mexicans tended to attribute comparatively little significance to government and had the lowest citizen expectations of fair treatment in the hands of political bureaucracy and police. The system was not seen as generally reliable. On the other hand, a large proportion of Mexican respondents indicated that they believed their political system was responsive because they felt they could do something about an unjust law. They frequently maintained they could be effective, even though such expectations were not associated with being politically informed, with membership in voluntary associations, or with political activity. Almond and Verba suggest that this pattern of expectations indicates that Mexican citizens have democratic aspirations which may begin to consolidate as the Mexican political system increasingly offers opportunities for political experience.

The authors found that patterns of citizen expectations in West Germany reflected that nation's advanced technology, highly developed and widespread educational and communications systems, and its traumatic political history. Germans tended to view their political system as fair, predictable, and responsive. There was relatively widespread satisfaction with the performance of the polity. They had a high level of confidence in the administrative branch of government and a strong sense of competence in dealing with it. However, such expectations were not associated with a strong diffuse attachment to the polity. Germans tended to be detached, practical, and almost cynical about politics. This suggests that there is no perfect association between particular patterns of citizen views and expectations and patterns of attachment to the polity at the symbolic level.

Almond and Verba found that American citizens tended to feel that their political system was highly responsive to citizen demands. They also tended to be satisfied with the predictability and reliability of the polity and to express diffuse satisfaction with the political system as a whole. However, they had reservations about the fairness of the political system. Expectations of consideration by bureaucratic and police authority ranked below those held by the Germans and the British. These cultural patterns are attributed to America's revolutionary origins and to the American tendency to subject all governmental institutions, including the judiciary and bureaucracy, to direct popular control.

Like American citizens, the British tended to expect their political system to be responsive to citizen demands. They tended to be satisfied with the predictability and the reliability of their polity and to express diffuse satisfaction with the system. However, the British exhibited considerable deference to the independent authority of government. They more often expected fair treatment from government which is expressed in such deference.

It seems reasonable to hypothesize a circular relationship between views and expectations of the polity which form part of a nation's culture and other political variables such as that nation's patterns of political participation, its political structure and processes, and its dominant ideology. Shared views and expectations arise, in part, from shared experiences. Experiences themselves are evaluated and reacted to, in part, as the result of existing expectations and are expressed symbolically in ideologies. Structures are not only maintained on the basis of expectations (e.g., that particular goods and services will be provided with a certain degree of efficiency and effectiveness, that rights will be upheld, etc.), they are also changed because they fail to meet long-existing or newly emerging expectations (see the studies of nonroutine participation reviewed in Chapter 5).

It should be noted again that the views and expectations of the polity discussed in this section are those which are widely shared by members of a society. They are the views and expectations which, for the most part, transcend differences between race, age, sex, religious, ethnic, and other categories of the population. Within a nation, members of such different categories may tend to have different associational ties, social experiences, political and quasi-political group memberships, political ideologies, social and political attitudes which eventuate in different patterns of political behavior. The model of circular causation suggested in this section describes the operation of macroanalytic variables. Such variables provide the overarching context within which operates the linear causal model of microanalytic variables which was sketched in Chapter 6. The ideas and ideals which are shared most generally within a society and the political structures which operate within it channel the roles which kinship, religion, economics, stratification, and more specific beliefs and value systems play in the political life of a society.

Early Theories and Contemporary Macroanalysis: Shared Belief and Value Systems

Marx's postulate of historical materialism contends that shared belief and value systems by themselves have no political impact. Rather, it is economic relations which shape cultural factors. That does not mean that such factors have no real social importance. On the contrary, Marx argues that a society's dominant ideas serve the interests of its dominant economic class. In the case of capitalist societies, emphasis on the sanctity of private family property works in this way. Cultural supports for property inheritance can help perpetuate economic and political inequalities. Such a line of thought is consistent with present analysis and is particularly useful in understanding politics during early periods of capitalist development.

The importance of private family property may seem insignificant in the context of Western industrial nations whose economic life is dominated by giant corporations run by a professional managerial class. However, Marxist sociologists, among others, point out that in the case of the United States, one percent of the population holds almost four-fifths of the corporate stock. Furthermore, major stockholders are frequently not only directors but managers as well. The majority of these stockholders acquired their fortunes through family inheritance.

Marx's discussion of religion focuses on the ways in which it contributes to the maintenance of political-economic inequalities by legitimating existing property and political relationships and by obscuring the objective opposition of social classes. While religion can work in this way it also performs legitimating functions in ways more clearly identified by Durkheim than by Marx. Collective social experience by itself generates fundamental religious beliefs which find symbolic expression. Such symbols, which can have considerable power, can be manipulated in ways supporting the material interests of a particular segment of society over and against the interests of other segments. However, religion and religious symbolism can be used to evaluate and to criticize existing systems of rights, advantages, power, and authority as well as to maintain them. For example, religious leaders and organizations were frequently at the forefront of the American civil rights movement and antiwar protests in the late 1960s. Religion can have radical ideological functions as well as conservative ones.

Similar arguments can be set forth with respect to views and expectations of the polity. Marxist analysis suggests that what the majority of a nation expects from the polity by way of rights and obligations is precisely what those in positions of power and privilege want them and have led them to expect through their control of the agencies of communication and socialization. When working-class expectations do, on occasion, run contrary to the material interests of the dominant class, they can be managed symbolically. For example, regulatory agencies can be established which appear to exercise some control over corporations but which actually serve corporate interests. However, while it seems clear that such processes do occur, data on nonroutine participation do show that under certain circumstances, the failure of the polity to meet citizen expectations can produce complete disruption of the political order.

Weber's hypothesis that distinctive belief systems legitimate different systems of domination constitutes the most fundamental contribution to understanding the impact of culture on politics. His analysis contains explanations of the channeling effects of culture on the types of political structures, political processes, and inherent political conflicts in various types of societies.

Weber's discussion of rationalization indicates that the political role of kinship in Western industrial nations would be significantly less than it was in societies with traditional or with charismatic systems of domination. However, he does not rule out the possibility that kinship might have appreciable political influence, even in highly rationalized societies. In his description of bureaucracy he carefully notes that the supreme chief of an organization with such an authority structure occupies his position by virtue of appropriation by election or by having been designated for succession rather than by virtue of technical qualification. Kinship constitutes a major basis for allocation to supreme position. In this connection, kinship is politically important in rationalized societies to the extent that (a) family ownership and control is an important factor in the corporate economy, and (b) the operation of the corporate economy strongly influences the operation of the political system.[57] The extent to which these conditions are found in any Western industrial democracy at any point in time is always an empirical question. Answers to such a question would indicate the operation of one important set of nonrational factors within rationalized societies.

Weber's discussion of rationalization also indicates that, overall, the political role of religion in modern society would be less significant than in traditional society. In modern industrial nations, religion itself undergoes rationalization. Theological and other worldly emphases tend to give way to concern with the social role of religious organizations. When this occurs, religion helps to support the political-economic status quo, not by providing supernatural support for existing social norms and institutions, but by providing welfare and thereby reducing discontent. On the other hand, Weber also recognizes that, even in the most rationalized societies, religion can serve as the basis for status groups which actively pursue ideal interests. On occasion these may run counter to existing political and economic policies and practices.

Weber's discussion of rationalization provides insights into the cultural sources of several basic political "issues" in the contemporary United

States. As participants in a highly rationalized society, Americans generally expect some degree of predictability, reliability, and effectiveness from their institutions—including the polity. When a government is widely thought to be failing to meet whatever standards do exist, resentment is expressed in public opinion polls in which dissatisfaction with "big government," "bureaucratic waste," "the helpless giant," and so on is indicated.

In recent years the federal government has established and pursued a number of policies, the intent and/or implementation of which were far from clear. "Affirmative action" programs, various desegregation rulings, and welfare programs of all sorts serve as examples. The government has also exhibited a lack of technical competence in areas ranging from controlling accidents at nuclear power plants to controlling inflation. The more rationalized a culture, the less likely are such failures to be tolerated. Accompanying rationalization, particularly in light of such failures, efficiency and effectiveness will replace ideology and intent as primary criteria for assessing political parties, programs, and candidates.

One of Durkheim's major contributions to understanding the bearing of culture on political institutions involves his recognition of the religious-moral qualities of rule. He may have overemphasized these qualities in his study of premodern societies and underemphasized their importance in modern systems of rule. Nevertheless, his very identification of this dimension provides political sociology with a valuable discussion useful for explaining shared views and expectations of the polity—particularly as expressed in the strong emotional and moralistic reactions of American citizens to a variety of public events. These range all the way from the assassination of President John Kennedy (where an extended period of remarkably intense national mourning had all the qualities of a solemn religious observance) to Watergate (where revelations that high public officials had violated laws produced angry public demands that they be removed from office and prosecuted) to published tales about the professional behavior of members of the Supreme Court (when little was revealed beyond facts that Justices are sometimes petty in their relations with one another and sometimes use nonrational criteria in decision making but which seriously damaged the venerability of the Court).[58] Durkheim's discussion also helps explain the cultural origins of the "civil religion" described by Bellah.

A number of historical, social structural, and cultural factors were responsible for the development of political democracy in Western nations and remain responsible for its preservation. Some of these factors were reviewed in this chapter. Those which were selected for discussion reflect the view of political sociology developed in this book: the analytic concern with relations of power and authority as these influence and are influenced by kinship, religion, class, interest groups of various kinds, and by shared beliefs and values. In particular, attention was paid to the ways in which kinship, religious, class, and other associational units use what power and authority is available to them to maintain or extend rights and privileges. Given unequal resources, such political activity has meant that political democracy has produced neither material equality nor social equality nor political equality. Some approaches, concepts, and hypotheses provided by the founders of the sociological tradition were shown to be helpful in understanding these topics.

While political democracy has not led to equality among people, it is hardly necessary to point out that nondemocratic political systems have not produced material, social, or political equality either—despite any ideological rhetoric to the contrary. In no human society have all individuals or groups been treated equally. Chapter 8 concerns some historical, structural, and cultural features of several political systems which appear as far removed from democratic systems as modern history has recorded.

NOTES

1. This discussion is concerned with *political* as distinguished from *social* democracy. Analyses of the relationship between democratic social structures and democratic political structures and processes constitute a central focus of this chapter.

2. Edward Shils, *Political Development in the New States* (The Hague: Mouton, 1968), pp. 51–60.

3. Barrington Moore, Jr., *Social Origins of Dictatorship and Democracy* (Boston: Beacon Press, 1966).

4. Repudiation of the theory of the divine right of kings was a highly significant cultural change which also furthered the advance of capitalism and democracy. The concept had originally served the interests of capitalism by fostering the conditions for a dependable environment in which economic activity might flourish. However, from the seventeenth until the end of the nineteenth century, commerce and industry on the whole were hampered by government regulation and hence by belief systems which legitimated them. "Capitalism which began by supporting the new absolutism ended by demanding *laissez-faire*."
See A. D. Lindsay, "The Modern Democratic State," in *Political Sociology*, S. N. Eisenstadt, ed. (New York: Basic Books, 1971), pp. 352–356.

5. Moore, *Social Origins*, p. 9.

6. Ibid., p. 30.

7. See Seymour M. Lipset, *The First New Nation* (Garden City, N.Y.: Doubleday Anchor Books, 1967), pp. 98–102; Seymour M. Lipset, *Revolution and Counterrevolution* (New York: Basic Books, 1968), pp. 31–63. For another comparative analysis of the role which revolutionary, nonrevolutionary, and counterrevolutionary origin have played in the histories of Australia ("Born of Revolutionaries but without a revolution"), Canada ("Born out of forces opposed to Revolution"), Great Britain ("Evolved under the guidance of an aristocracy"), and the United States, see Robert R. Alford, *Party and Society* (Chicago: Rand McNally, 1963), pp. 1–31.

8. What, if any, effect the increasingly separatist policies of Quebec will have upon the orientations remains to be seen.

9. Jonathan Kelley and Herbert S. Klein, "Revolution and the Rebirth of Inequality: A Theory of Stratification in Postrevolutionary Society," *American Journal of Sociology*, 83, no. 1 (July 1977) 78–99.

10. Giovanni Sartori, *Parties and Party Systems* (Cambridge: Cambridge University Press, 1976).

11. Hans Gerth and C. Wright Mills, eds., *From Max Weber: Essays in Sociology* (New York: Oxford University Press, 1958), p. 226.

12. See T. H. Marshall, *Citizenship and Social Class* (New York: Cambridge University Press, 1950).

13. Maurice Duveger, *Political Parties* (London: Methuen, 1954), p. 46.

14. See Fred I. Greenstein, *The American Party System and the American People* (Englewood Cliffs, N.J.:, Prentice-Hall, 1963), pp. 37-53.

15. For data indicating the pervasiveness of this orientation in the United States as compared with Great Britain, Germany, Italy, and Mexico, see Gabriel Almond and Sidney Verba, *The Civic Culture* (Boston: Little, Brown, 1965), Chapters 5-8.

16. Much of the tax burden and many federal regulations are not associated with welfare state programs but rather with military programs and with policies which have the effect of subsidizing big business.

17. The relationship between political equality and social equality will be discussed in a later section. More specifically, questions about the relationship between democracy and socioeconomic equality are among the most central in the field of political sociology.

18. Gerhard E. Lenski, *Power and Privilege* (New York: McGraw-Hill, 1966).

19. (1) Increased complexity of control requires elites to delegate authority to subordinates in order to preserve efficiency and productivity. (2) In an expanding economy ruling elites can make economic concessions in relative terms without suffering any loss in absolute terms. This reduces worker hostility and accompanying losses from strikes, disorders, etc. (3) Slowed population growth makes possible real and substantial gains in per capita income, thereby reducing the intensity of competitive pressures. Thus the lower classes are able to bargain for wages in markets no longer glutted with labor. (4) Increased levels of skill and technical knowledge increase rigidity in the labor market that favors the sellers of labor.

20. Sociological functionalism, conflict analysis, and Lenski's interest in theoretical integration of the two were discussed in Chapter 2.

21. Clark Kerr, John T. Dunlap, Frederic H. Harbison, and Charles A. Myers, *Industrialism and Industrial Man* (New York: Oxford University Press, 1964).

22. Frank Parkin, *Class Inequality and Political Order* (New York: Praeger, 1971).

23. Parkin does find that social mobility and educational opportunities are greater in the social democratic countries. This finding will be discussed in the following section dealing with social (as opposed to material) equality.

24. Robert W. Jackman, "Political Democracy and Social Equality: A Comparative Analysis," *American Sociological Review*, 39, no. 1 (February 1977), 29-45.

25. Christopher Hewitt, "The Effect of Political Democracy and Social Democracy in Industrial Societies: A Cross-National Comparison," *American Sociological Review*, 42, no. 3 (June 1977) 450-463.

26. Parkin and others use the proportion of gross national product devoted to social service expenditures as a measure of government redistribution effort. Jackman and others measure income inequality in terms of the disproportion of income and population between occupational sectors.

27. In direct contradiction of Parkin, Hewitt finds no association between democracy and access to higher education by non-middle-class youth. His data show that socialist societies are more equal materially but are less open than less socialist societies. Social equality will be discussed in the following section.

28. Seymour Martin Lipset and Reinhard Bendix, *Social Mobility in Industrial Society* (Berkeley: University of California Press, 1959).

29. Richard Rubinson and Dan Quinlan, "Democracy and Social Equality: A Reanalysis," *American Sociological Review*, 42, no. 4 (August 1977) 611-622.

30. C. Wright Mills, *Power, Politics and People*, ed. I. L. Horowitz (New York: Oxford University Press, 1963), p. 23.

31. Floyd Hunter, *Community Power Structure* (Chapel Hill: University of North Carolina Press, 1953).

32. C. Wright Mills, *The Power Elite* (New York: Oxford University Press, 1956).

33. Ibid., p. 18.

34. Ibid., p. 283.

35. For an elaborated statement of this position, see William Kornhauser, *The Politics of Mass Society* (New York: The Free Press, 1959).

36. Mills, *The Power Elite,* p. 308.

37. See G. William Domhoff, *Who Rules America?* (Englewood Cliffs, N.J.: Prentice-Hall, 1967); G. William Domhoff, *The Higher Circles: The Governing Class in America* (New York, Vintage Books, 1971).

38. See Charles Lindblom, *Politics and Markets* (New York: Basic Books, 1977).

39. Ibid., p. 356.

40. Ibid., p. 174.

41. Ibid., p. 175.

42. Mills, *The Power Elite,* p. 308.

43. Robert A. Dahl, *Who Governs?* (New Haven, Conn.: Yale University Press, 1961).

44. Ibid., p. 228.

45. Arnold M. Rose, *The Power Structure* (New York: Oxford University Press, 1967).

46. John Walton, "Substance and Artifact: The Current Status of Research on Community Power Structure," *American Journal of Sociology,* 71, no. 4 (January 1966), 430–438.

47. Robert Perrucci and Marc Pilisuk, "Leaders and Community Elites: The Interorganizational Bases of Community Power," *American Sociological Review,* 35, no. 6 (December 1970) 1040–1057.

48. Ibid., p. 1041.

49. Ibid., p. 1044.

50. See Edward Laumann and Franz U. Pappi, "New Directions in the Study of Community Elites," *American Sociological Review,* 38, no. 2 (April 1973), 212–230; Edward Laumann, Peter Marsden, and Joseph Galaskiewicz, "Community Elite Influence Structures: Extension of a Network Approach," *American Journal of Sociology,* 83, no. 3 (November 1977), 594–631; Joseph Galaskiewicz, *Exchange Networks and Community Politics.* (Beverley Hills, CA: Sage Publications, 1979).

51. Laumann, Marsden, and Galaskiewicz, pp. 625–627.

52. Lehmann presents this example of such "shaping": ". . . the overarching culture of Medieval Europe encouraged feudal values within the political culture. In the modern world, a general culture glorifying equality and achievement makes a democratic political culture more likely. Conversely, it makes a political culture resting on the doctrine of divine right of Kings improbable." Edward W. Lehman, *Political Society: A Macrosociology of Politics* (New York: Columbia University Press, 1977), p. 24.

53. See Seymour M. Lipset, *Revolution and Counterrevolution* (New York: Basic Books, 1968), Chapter 3.

54. Robert N. Bellah, "Civil Religion in America," *Daedalus,* Winter 1967. Robert N. Bellah, *The Broken Covenant: American Civil Religion in Time of Trial* (New York: Seabury Press, 1975).

55. The particular list presented here was suggested by David Easton, *A Systems Analysis of Political Life* (New York: John Wiley & Sons, 1965) and by Gabriel Almond and G. Bingham Powell, *Comparative Politics: A Developmental Approach* (Boston: Little, Brown, 1966).

56. Almond and Verba, *The Civic Culture,* Chapter 12.

57. See Charles H. Anderson, *The Political Economy of Social Class* (Englewood Cliffs, N.J.: Prentice-Hall, 1974), especially Chapters 4, 5, 6, and 8.

58. The book which evoked this reaction was Bob Woodward and Scott Armstrong, *The Brethren* (New York: Simon and Schuster, 1979).

CHAPTER EIGHT
SOME HISTORICAL, STRUCTURAL, AND CULTURAL FEATURES OF MODERN NONDEMOCRATIC POLITIES

INTRODUCTION: FROM TOTALITARIAN STATES TO TRANSNATIONAL CORPORATIONS AND CARTELS

The literature of contemporary, empirically grounded political analysis abounds with typologies of political systems. These vary according to the analytic purposes they are intended to serve and according to the theoretical (and often rather manifestly ideological) perspectives they express. This chapter, in conjunction with Chapter 7, rests on a very basic distinction between two kinds of political systems—democratic and nondemocratic. Obviously, these are ideal types. Actual polities can be considered to be only more or less democratic according to some clearly defined set of criteria.

Chapter 7 suggested that political systems are democratic to the extent that they have civilian rule, representative institutions, and public liberties. These properties, in turn, tend to be associated with the presence of a constitution guaranteeing universal adult suffrage and the right of all social strata to organized political action—including political opposition. They also tend to be associated with the presence of a system of competitive political parties. Given this characterization, it follows that a modern political system cannot be considered democratic if it lacks an operative constitution. Even if a polity is constitutional, then it is nondemocratic to the extent that the right to routine political participation is limited, nonroutine participation is not permitted, and party competition is absent.

The first part of this chapter focuses on nondemocratic polities. Discussion will begin with a consideration of regimes which represent two of the most unambiguous examples of modern nondemocratic systems— Fascist Germany and Russia under Stalin. These particular historical regimes were selected for several reasons. First, their analysis can be expected to reveal some of the historical, social structural, and cultural conditions within individual nations which are most inhospitable to political democracy. Second, studies of these regimes are available that suggest something of the ways in which family, church, economy, stratification, and shared beliefs and values have operated within nondemocratic political contexts. Third, such studies also reveal something of the uses of essentially unrestrained national political power to determine the distribution of social and economic rights and privileges. Fourth, these particular historical regimes can serve as clear case studies for examining the utility of certain approaches, concepts, and hypotheses provided by Marx, Weber, and Durkheim for understanding nondemocratic polities. Finally, a consideration of Fascist Germany and Stalinist Russia necessarily involves a review of the defining qualities of two of the most important political movements in modern history—Communism and Fascism.

For these reasons, then, a review of the characteristics of extreme nondemocratic polities has considerable value. They define one end of the democratic-nondemocratic dimension along which nations might be located and along which they might historically move. Today, it is perfectly clear that most of the world's people are ruled neither by polities with long-standing democratic traditions nor by regimes as totally lacking democratic characteristics as were Fascist Germany and Stalinist Russia.

Polities are not only more or less democratic, they also undergo constant change. Throughout the 1960s and 1970s, political sociology was particularly concerned with the study of those nations whose political destinies along the democratic-nondemocratic dimension appeared to be most uncertain. For the most part, these were the world's low-income countries.[1] The second section of this chapter critically reviews these studies of "political development." Newer lines of theory and research are sketched which suggest that, for the foreseeable future, the political lives of low-income countries will be lived closer to the nondemocratic end of the spectrum of modern political systems than earlier theories would lead us to believe.

A consideration of modern nondemocratic polities necessarily involves more than a discussion of extreme cases of individual nations such as Fascist Germany and Stalinist Russia and a look at the lack of democratic potential in the future of present-day economically poor nations. It must also involve some analysis of the potential for Western industrial democracies to develop nondemocratic features. The third part of this chapter reviews some recent studies which suggest that, often, the political and economic policies of modern democratic nations represent reactions to international pressures rather than responses to citizen inputs. The studies identify the existence of transnational forces that can override the political significance of whether or not a nation has civilian rule, representative institutions, and public liberties. It may be that, in the future, the political lives of modern democratic countries will be moved closer to the nondemocratic end of the political spectrum than many would like to believe.

The studies in parts two and three of this chapter which deal first with the antidemocratic potential of economically poor nations and then with the antidemocratic potential of the world's rich nations are macroanalytic and historical-comparative. They have increased considerably our understanding of the historical conflicts and resulting changes that have helped shape the present political world. Such theoretical approaches represent a departure from the standard orientations of empirical sociological research in the United States. They represent a return to the types of concerns expressed in the writings of Marx, Weber, and Durkheim. The linking of sociology's past, present, and potential future will be discussed in the final section of this chapter.

Earlier in this book it was argued that sociology's future would involve a major concern with a number of specific topics. Three of these are (1) illegitimate uses of power and authority, (2) patterns of noninstitutionalized political conflict, and (3) widespread political dissatisfaction and political distrust. Understanding the ways in which international factors impact on domestic politics in ways inimical to the operation of democratic processes should contribute to our understanding of each of these.

Some of the most dramatic and historically important illegitimate uses of power and authority have been made by aggressive and expansionist nondemocratic states such as Fascist Germany and Russia under Stalin. More recent and somewhat less obvious examples of illegitimate uses of power and authority involve the activities of multinational corporations. Examples range from widespread bribing of public officials to efforts at destabilizing democratically elected regimes. New studies which express an increased awareness of the international determinants of political life are likely to increase our understanding of the social conditions under which such nondemocratic processes are likely to occur as well as factors affecting their probable outcomes.

New macroanalytic comparative studies of the major revolutions of the modern world which understand these events in their world-historical contexts represent significant contributions to our knowledge of noninstitutionalized political conflict. Such studies are described in this chapter.

Much political dissatisfaction in the United States, and undoubtedly elsewhere in the world today, stems from the apparent inability of national leaders to deal effectively with political problems which have transnational sources. For example, during his administration, Jimmy Carter took considerable blame for the failure of the United States to develop a coherent energy policy. The need for such a policy was necessitated largely by economic pressures exerted by the Organization of Petroleum Exporting Countries. In May, 1981, France elected a Socialist president who promised that he would push for the widespread nationalization of banks and industry, sharp increases in the minimum wage, and tax reforms that would substantially redistribute the nation's wealth. The choice of such policies by the French after 23 years of center-right control of the presidency was due largely to the failure of the government to control France's rapidly rising inflation rate and soaring unemployment. However, some of the major sources of these conditions which prompted the French to seek fundamental political, economic, and social changes were located outside of France's boundaries and outside of the direct control of her government.

Some political distrust undoubtedly stems from the failure or inability of government to influence the policies of transnational corporations. For example, Western European governments have frequently been unable to keep major transnational corporations from moving their manufacturing and production to other nations with lower labor costs. For each nation such moves have resulted in increased unemployment, an increased impact of foreign goods, a decline in the value of the national currency relative to other currencies, and increased inflation. Government failure to deal effectively with such consequences has not promoted the political trust of Western European workers. A related source of political distrust involves the complicity of a host nation in a transnational corporation's efforts at influencing the internal political affairs of other nations. A concrete example of public distrust generated by perceived links of government to a transnational corporation occurred in the United States in the early 1970s. At that time it was widely believed that the International Telephone and Telegraph Corporation in collusion with some officials of the United States government attempted to overthrow the democratically elected government of Marxist Salvador Allende in Chile. New macroanalytic studies which attend to the social and political conditions which permit such occurrences will provide needed insight into social sources of the personal reactions of political discontent and political distrust.

If any general theoretical approach does achieve some degree of dominance in the future of American political sociology, it is likely to be the one which best helps us to understand the uses of power and authority to create, administer, and transform social policy. New studies which are taking a macroanalytic, historical-comparative approach are beginning to produce such understanding. In particular, such studies are helping us to see the limits which are placed on the exercise of democratic rule in contemporary nations, both poor and rich.

THE CHARACTER OF EXTREME NONDEMOCRATIC POLITICAL SYSTEMS: THE CASES OF FASCIST GERMANY AND RUSSIA UNDER STALIN

Introduction

In modern history a number of political systems have been more than "nondemocratic" in the sense that they limited routine political participation, outlawed nonroutine participation, and lacked competitive party systems. These are regimes which have been actively repressive above and beyond being nonresponsive. From the late 1930s through the 1960s such regimes were the topic of considerable discussion and were frequently referred to as *totalitarian.* More recently the term has fallen into disfavor, primarily because of the history of the ideological rather than the analytic uses to which it was put. However, the term will be revived here, at least in a limited context—a consideration of Fascist Germany and the Soviet Union under Stalin. In the discussion of these particular historical regimes the concept has considerable analytic utility. These regimes are clearly among the most nondemocratic, by any standard, in modern history.

Friedrich and Brzezinski developed the most widely cited analysis of totalitarian regimes.[2] According to these authors, a totalitarian political system is composed of a cluster of six traits.

1. The political system has an elaborate ideology which supposedly governs all areas of social life.
2. There is a single mass party. Membership is limited to a small proportion of the population. The party has an oligarchic structure which either dominates or is completely intertwined with the governmental bureaucracy.
3. A system of terror, administered through the party and secret police, is used as a mechanism of control.
4. The media of mass communications are controlled by the party and the government.
5. Weapons in the society are monopolized by the party and the government.
6. Government and party control the entire economy.

The authors note that there may be additional traits which often accompany these six. Among the most important of these are administrative control of justice and the courts and political expansionism. However, they argue that these are not to be regarded as defining characteristics of totalitarian rule. In addition, they point out that each of the six characteristics is not necessarily of equal importance in all totalitarian regimes. For example, the ideology of Russia under Stalin was more specifically committed to certain principles than was the ideology of German Fascism—where ideology was formulated by the leader of the party himself.

Each of the two brief case studies will begin with a discussion of the historical conditions associated with the development of the extreme nondemocratic political system. Here particular attention will be paid to Moore's historical thesis concerning the social origins of dictatorship.[3] Conditions of social structure which existed under each regime will then be discussed. This will involve descriptions of the concrete ways in which kinship, religion, education, and economy operated under two totalitarian regimes. Attention will then shift from social structure to culture, with some account of the basic themes of the prevailing ideologies of the two regimes. (It is in this context that the defining characteristics of Fascism and Communism will be reviewed.) Finally, there will be a discussion of the ways in which power and authority were exercised in the totalitarian regimes to create inequalities in social rights and advantages.

Fascist Germany (1933–1945)

The establishment of capitalism in both agriculture and industry in Germany turned it into an industrial country. However, this economic transformation occurred without a popular revolution. A powerful landed aristocracy remained. New industrial and commercial classes emerged which were accumulating resources but which lacked real political power. Seeking wealth rather than political power per se, the upper segments of the new classes formed a coalition with the elite of the agricultural stratum. According to this analysis of Barrington Moore, these conditions formed the historical foundation of German Fascism.[4] In his view, it was the "coalition between those sectors of the upper strata in business and agriculture that was the main feature of the political system."[5] Fascism represented a "revolution from above." Germany attempted to set itself on a course of economic modernization without significantly altering its class structure. It sought to develop profitable commercial agriculture and industrialization without sharing the benefits of the new economic system with peasants and industrial workers.

On top of these historical and structural conditions, a set of social and economic crises occurred in Germany after World War I which were favorable to the advance of Fascism and the rise of the Fascist regime.[6] Defeat in the war and the provisions of the Treaty of Versailles generated widespread and intense nationalism in Germany. However, the Weimar Republic was weak and proved ineffective in its efforts to deal with the vast inflation of the German currency, with the growing power of monopolies, and with the economic slump of the early 1930s. While Germany had undergone considerable economic modernization, it had a relatively low standard of living. Apparently the government was so unpopular that many voters supported opposition groups and parties, irrespective of their particular political stances.

A large number of former commissioned and noncommissioned officers returned from the war to find no jobs waiting. A large number of diverse social groups, representing a considerable proportion of the German population, were threatened by social and economic changes occurring in Germany. (Among the most important of these were segments of the lower middle class—artisans, independent tradesmen, small farmers, lower-grade government employees, and white-collar workers.) A large number of middle-class and lower-middle-class youths at schools and universities faced an unattractive social and economic future for which the postwar governments were held largely responsible. In short, after World War I, a vast, socially heterogeneous segment of German society experienced deep-felt social and economic dissatisfaction and located the source of many of their difficulties in the political system. Such a mass of citizens was unlikely to resist mobilization by a well-organized political party which promised to take direct and immediate action to remedy existing social and economic ills and to provide a strong, proud, and well-integrated nation.

According to Linz, Fascist movements, such as the one which developed in Germany, are characteristically hypernationalistic and define themselves by the things against which they stand.[7] Hypernationalism was expressed in the German case in the form of hostility to philosophies, movements, groups, and organizations that possibly could be viewed as harmful to or diverting attention and energy from the ultimate goal of national social integration and greatness. It was expressed in its exaltation of the authority of the state and its supremacy over all other social groups. German Fascists saw their cause as being above narrow class and party interests.

Fascism was opposed to Marxism and Communism on grounds of their ideological internationalism. Opposition to Marxism and Communism was also based on the support Marxists and Communists gave to the trade union movements and to the political parties which supported them. Fascists saw trade unionism as furthering the separate and divisive interests of only one segment of German society—the working class. Not only was Fascism anti-proletarian in this special sense, it was also antibourgeois for the same reason. Fascism substituted for the conflict between the proletariat and the bourgeoisie within a nation a conflict between nations rich and poor.

Most important for the analytic purposes of this chapter is the fact that German Fascism was violently opposed to democracy—or, more accurately, it opposed common core features of political structures and processes of Western industrial nations. There were several reasons for this. Germany had little historical experience with democratic structures. Democratic political forms were seen as imposed on Germany as a result of defeat in the war. As Linz points out, this does not mean that all German Fascists viewed themselves as antidemocratic. On the contrary, some Fascists argued that political systems in which the public participates only occasionally by voting and using the secret ballot permitted a very low level of citizen involvement in national decision making. In their view, Fascism offered a more genuine democracy by directly involving citizens through extensive personal participation in a political movement that represented the feelings and sentiments of the whole people.

Many of the interpretations of the rise and success of Fascism in Germany have been essentially psychological and have long received considerable popular attention. The most extreme psychological positions, represented by the works of Harold Lasswell and Theodore Adorno and his colleagues, focused on the characteristics of individuals which supposedly make them susceptible to antidemocratic appeals. Such traits included obedience, subordination, love of an authority figure, and ego-defensive needs which are met by hostility and aggression against various outgroups.[8] More recent critical views of such psychological investigations have noted the ideological biases inherent in them.[9] The assumption of such works was that supporters of antidemocratic politics suffer from some form of psychopathology. Such an assumption is aimed more at discrediting those whose politics one finds particularly distasteful than at understanding the conditions which give rise to and sustain nondemocratic polities.

A more social-psychological approach to the appeal of Fascism in Germany is represented by the works of Eric Fromm and Karl Mannheim.[10] The position taken in their studies reflects some of the insights of Durkheim concerning the plight of individuals during the early stages of industrial capitalism. With the breakdown of the traditional social order in Western Europe at the end of the nineteenth century, individuals were freed from many previous sources of social, economic, ideological, and political oppression. However, many of those same traditional bonds had provided a firm sense of individual identity and a clear vision of place in a reasonably intelligible social world. Vastly increased freedom made it possible for individuals to be socially critical and politically active. But such freedom also made them feel more isolated, insecure, and powerless.

These negative feelings associated with social change were particularly intense in Germany after World War I, which saw the breakdown of the class structure and the system of political parties based upon it. Before the war, the political response of the mass of the German population to the impact of industrialization was apathy and resignation. However, defeat suffered in the war and the utter failure of governments and parties to achieve widely hoped for social, economic, and political goals finally transformed mass apathy into violent mass opposition. According to Fromm, masses of Germans sought escape from feelings of frustration, powerlessness, and meaninglessness by identifying with and participating in a new political movement. In this movement isolated individuals were offered a new refuge and security. In the movement one was "taught to project all his human powers into the figure of his leader, the state, the 'fatherland' to whom he has to submit and whom he has to worship. He escapes from freedom into a new idolatry."[11] Mannheim took a somewhat similar position. He argued that those who led and those who supported the Fascist movement were among the least integrated into the social structure associated with inchoate industrial capitalism. In his view, marginal intellectuals diverted masses who lacked a sense of understanding the changing social world. Such masses desperately desired social action which, in their eyes, would restore Germany to its greatness and, above all else, create for them strong ties of community.

Such analyses have a certain intrinsic appeal. Yet, they are not accompanied by compelling data. Furthermore, like the primarily psychological interpretations of Fascism, they raise the question of ideological bias.

A rather different approach to the rise of Fascism understands it in predominantly economic terms—although psychological factors are incorporated in the explanatory framework. For example, Organski argues that Fascism in Germany arose as massive inflation of the economy in the early 1920s and the depression of the early 1930s undermined the German welfare state.[12] Mass democracy failed to protect workers from unemployment and extreme social and economic hardships. An elite, consisting primarily of a rising but not yet fully established stratum of industrialists and a strong, though declining agricultural class, united to exclude the masses from democratic political participation—just as they had been excluded in the period before the Weimar Republic. The new elite produced a stage of economic development in which the principal function of government was to make possible the accumulation of capital which could be reinvested in the means of production. The new system also attempted to meet some of the rational welfare needs of the masses. Vast social services were instituted. The nation was put back to work. Now, however, work was carried on in the context of a highly centralized economy controlled by giant corporations and geared toward rearmament and the preparation for war. According to Organski, the Fascists also brought to the surface previously suppressed irrational drives of the German people. Hate and extreme aggressiveness were mobilized to achieve loyalty to the regime, acceptance of its extreme demands, and unquestioning opposition to the enemies which it identified.

It is important to understand correlations between patterns of economic development and the structures of political institutions. However, such correlations are always far from perfect. Fascism might prosper alongside a number of diverse economic systems. Furthermore, many of what appear to be characteristic economic activities of the Fascist regime, such as the concentrating of capital and elaborately planning economic expansion, represent little more than activities of any modern regime promoting industrial capitalism.

A fourth theoretical approach to the rise of Fascism in Germany argues that what was critical in determining the specific way in which prevailing beliefs, attitudes, and feelings were expressed politically and the concrete ways in which the severe economic conditions were to be dealt with politically were the mobilizing activities of the Nazis. For example, Lepsius contends that the success of the Fascists in Germany was to be located in their ability to penetrate and control a complex network of interest groups whose members had some predisposition to their cause.[13] Such a position contradicts the view that Nazi success was due to their attraction of socially and psychologically isolated individuals. Lepsius notes that countries lacking a rich network of politically relevant social groups, or those with such a network which contained groups resistant to infiltration, did not embrace Fascism—even when they were undergoing severe social and economic crises. Belgium, the Netherlands, Switzerland, Denmark, Norway, Sweden, and Great Britain all had Fascist parties which were unable to retain their initial momentum. Clearly, the mobilizing capacities of movement-related organizations must be taken into account in any adequate explanation of the success or failure of any collective efforts to change regimes.

Studies reviewed above identified interrelated historical, social-psychological, and organizational factors which facilitated the rise of German Fascism. After its initial establishment, the relationships which most clearly mark the Fascist regime as totalitarian—as most extremely nondemocratic—are those which it worked to establish with the other institutions of German society—kinship, religion, economy, and stratification, as well as the belief and value system which it attempted to impose on the society. It is to these that we now turn.

Friedrich and Brzezinski coined the phrase "islands of separateness" to refer to institutional spheres which might serve as centers of resistance to at least some of the all-embracing demands of totalitarian government.[14] Family, church, occupation, and class each represented a potential object of loyalty, dedication, and involvement which could replace or oppose the state. Hence, the Fascist state could not ignore them. Two courses of action were available. On the one hand, the state could make efforts to reduce the functional importance of these institutions by taking over the roles that they played. The alternative was for the state to penetrate these institutions and then use them in ways which appeared to support regime interests.

In the case of the German family, the Fascists pursued both courses of action.[15] They sought to strengthen families so that families would be fruitful and multiply. The regime wanted a large future generation of young

Germans who would advance their political cause. To this end, they made available loans to young couples seeking to get married, prizes for mothers with many children, and aid during pregnancy, especially for women who were working. While the procreative function of the family was encouraged in these ways, all other family-related policies and programs aimed at undermining family cohesion. Women were encouraged to work in industry. Youths were involved in extensive state-sponsored organizational activities outside the home. Men and women were similarly involved in continuous political meetings and government-supported collective activities. Even leisure activities were organized by the state. In these ways the Fascists worked to replace involvement in and devotion to family with commitment to the hypernationalistic regime.

The relations of the German Fascist regime to the church shifted over time. Initially, Fascists had the approval of many churches because of the movement's opposition to Marxism. In addition, the Fascists seized whatever religious support they could get and found some among the Lutheran clergy, particularly in the northern regions. Fascists promoted views combining religion and nationalism. Such ideas proved to be popular and provided the Fascists with some respectability. Eventually many citizens joined the "German Christians' Faith Movement," which strongly and explicitly approved Fascist doctrine and which later received government support.[16]

From the very first, however, Fascist influence was least in mainly Catholic districts in the south and west of Germany and in predominantly liberal Protestant cities such as Württemberg. The Catholic church attracted and held the commitment of many traditional segments of the German population, particularly those segments which had been displaced by social and economic modernization in Germany. These were the very groups from which the Fascists sought support. Hence, the Catholic church was a direct competitor for loyalty. The Catholic church was also directly opposed to the secularization and the anticlerical position which the Fascists often expressed. Among the Protestants, the Confessional Church arose as an ardent antagonist of the Fascists. Other liberal churches continued to espouse humanistic core values which were the antitheses of those promoted by the Fascists. This represented serious ideological opposition to the regime.

The cost of this Catholic and Protestant opposition was extreme. Countless thousands of priests, nuns, and lay religious leaders were arrested, imprisoned, and murdered. Most church-affiliated Germans passively accepted the new Fascist regime and its intervention in church affairs. While some German churches continued to struggle desperately as centers of political opposition, most churches, realistically fearing ruthless government intervention, ceased operating as "islands of separateness" and were turned into functioning components of one of the most extreme forms of nondemocratic state.

As Durkheim most clearly pointed out, in industrial societies, occupational groups are potentially the most important associations for effective resistance to unpopular regime demands. The Fascists in Germany could not and would not tolerate any political opposition. This was particularly true in the sphere of work. The entire economy, from the war machine to the social welfare system, was subject to the most detailed and centralized control by the government and party.

The economy was to serve the goals of the regime. Work associations were headed by functionaries of the state bureaucracy. Trade unions were, in fact, eliminated. They were replaced by the German Labor Front. The function of this organization was neither collective bargaining nor working-class action but pursuing industrial peace and promoting schemes of social welfare.[17] Industrial workers produced goods required by the military. Teachers, who were compelled to join the National Socialist Teacher's League, transmitted beliefs and values promoting loyalty to the regime and worked to develop narrow technical skills particularly useful to the state. Scientists and technicians provided the knowledge and hardware necessary to conduct sophisticated warfare abroad and to operate a system of propaganda, terror, and central planning ensuring total political control at home. And so on.

This description of the relation of the Fascist regime to the German work force illustrates its expressed goal of *Gleichschaltung*—complete subordination of all groups to its control. In some spheres of work, however, the regime eventually recognized that total subordination could be counterproductive. Such was the case with regard to the conduct of scientific work.[18] When ideological acceptability and loyalty to the regime took the places of empirical confirmation and technical competence as the basis for assessing and rewarding scientific production, results were less likely to serve well as the source of tools and programs needed by the regime. Hence, at least one category of occupation—scientists—was somewhat immune from regime pressures. Such an occupational category, then, had the potential to serve as a context for the development of opposition politics.[19]

The Fascists' penetration of family, church, and work was a structural feature and the hallmark of its totalitarian character. This kind of penetration is particularly disquieting to all those who view these spheres of life as "private"—as contexts within which individuals can attempt to realize life's most basic values. The obliteration of the distinction between private and public is thoroughly unacceptable to those socialized in democratic polities. Consequently, this aspect of the regime prompted many of its analysts to condemn this form of political organization rather than to attempt to fully understand its historical origins, structural and cultural features, and the everyday patterns of its operation. However, the features of German Fascism which finally compelled many social scientists to view this extreme form of nondemocratic polity as thoroughly pathological was not its effects on social structure so much as its political culture.

Under Fascist rule, members of the mass public were to love "the

German race" and "the Fatherland"—a combination of undiluted racism and extreme chauvinism. They were to hate many others—particularly Communists and Jews—who were identified as the ultimate sources of Germany's critical social and economic problems. They were to dedicate themselves without question to their nation, for the community was all important and the individual totally insignificant apart from the nation. They were to give their unquestioning total loyalty and obedience to their Führer, Adolf Hitler, who was to be considered the infallible representative of the true will of the German people. They were to attend marches, huge mass rallies, and to sing songs which reinforced these prescribed loves and hates. They were to deal with the enemies identified by the regime in a ruthless and often violent manner (humanitarian ideals were thoroughly repudiated and notions of rule by law often put aside).

The inhumanity that was promoted by this political culture has seen few equals in world history. Between 1941 and 1945 the German Fascists systematically killed millions of men, women, and children because they were Jews, Gypsies, or Slavs and were defined by the dominant ideology as threatening to Germany. The events of this time and place have come to be known as the *Holocaust.* It is far beyond the ability of any text to provide any reasonable understanding of what occurred in terms of human suffering. A vast literature on the Holocaust does exist.[20] It should be consulted by anyone interested in the exercise of absolutely unrestrained political power.

It is little wonder that many could understand Fascist Germany only in terms of its expressing mass pathology. However, to the extent that this tendency displaced other empirically grounded macroanalytic, historical, and comparative efforts to understand German Fascism, it impeded the development of theory which might have value in predicting any rise of future Fascist movements.

Russia under Stalin (1927–1953)

The usual historical starting point for a consideration of any modern Russian regime is the Bolshevik revolution of 1917. Prior to that cataclysmic event, the Russian czars, beginning with Peter the Great, had established an extensive empire. The strength of this political system varied, reaching its peak about 1815 and suffering a severe setback after the Crimean War (1848). Several aspects of Russia's imperial experiences influenced the course of the revolution and subsequent patterns of political development. First, Russia became an even more multi-ethnic political system comprised of many peoples either indifferent or overtly opposed to the central regime. Their numbers were added to the peasants, who made up the vast majority of Russia's population and who were already hostile to their exploiting landlords and czars. Second, the geographically vast polity was bordered by nations posing both economic and military threats. This combination of internal and external enemies promoted increasingly autocratic rule. Third, the empire made Russia a major part of the European political system. As such, many of her political officials, military officers, traders, and intellectuals had considerably increased contacts with European societies. Such contacts made these functionally important segments of the population acutely aware of, and critical of, Russia's political, social, and economic backwardness.

Military defeats and high casualties in World War I finally led to the forced abdication of Czar Nicholas in March, 1917. A liberal provisional government was established but failed to end the war. Subsequently, through shrewd political maneuvering, the small and well organized Bolshevik Party led by V. I. Lenin violently overthrew the provisional government and successfully established claim to state power.

Lenin was joined by revolutionary intellectuals, many of whom were Marxists.[21] Earlier, Lenin had studied the works of Marx and Engels and had accepted their values and vision of social change. However, ever since the 1890s, when the writings were first widely read, there had been continuous, extensive, and sometimes rancorous disagreements among supporters as to how Marxism, which specified the course of revolutionary change in advanced, industrial, capitalist societies, was to be applied to Russia with its overwhelmingly peasant population and low level of industrialization. At one extreme were the orthodox Marxists, who argued that socialism in Russia could be realized only in the far-distant future. The present responsibility of Russian Marxists, as they saw it, was to help promote industralization and a subsequent bourgeois-democratic revolution. They would then encourage the development of a mature proletariat within the capitalist order. This mass proletariat would constitute the final political force that would forever smash autocracy and build the socialist society in Russia.

Lenin, on the contrary, did not believe in the necessity of the long wait for a bourgeois-democratic revolution, industrial development, and a mature proletariat. In his view, the liberal bourgeoisie in Russia was too weak and unreliable to play a significant historical role in destroying czarist absolutism and establishing an industrially based bourgeois state. Rather, the revolution was to be carried forward in the present by the proletariat and the peasantry. However, neither of these two strata was entirely politically dependable. The proletariat was weak and did not merit the assumption that it would, by itself, become a "class for itself," i.e., become politically self-conscious and revolutionary. It seemed to Lenin more likely that the working class, rather than turning to revolution, would opt instead for trade-union bargaining. The peasants had little interest in revolutionary action once the resources of landlords and rich farmers had been redistributed. Their chief concern was to maintain autonomy from any centralized regime so that they might pursue, unimpeded, their own agricultural activities and mode of life. What was required for Russian socialism, then, in Lenin's view, was the creation of a select, well-organized, highly disciplined party. Such a party was to be directed by an elite who understood the laws of political history. This party was to organize, mobilize, and direct the Russian proletariat and peasantry on the course toward the final realization of socialism in Russia.

In 1918, before the Bolsheviks had fully consolidated their power, a civil war broke out in Russia. It was the continuation of social, economic, and military crises exacerbated by further struggles with counterrevolutionary forces (the White armies), the intervention of Western expeditionary forces (from the United States, France, Japan, and Great Britain), and a war with Poland. Faced with such serious challenges, the Bolsheviks responded with severely repressive emergency measures. They attempted to establish total state control over the economy. They organized the Cheka (political police), who maintained social order through the extermination of enemies of the regime and through the widespread use of terror. Opposing political parties were abolished and virtually all mass organizations were turned into "transmission belts" for carrying out the policies of the regime. This was the period of the "Red Terror" or "War Communism" (1918–1921) in which Russia became a highly centralized one-party state.

After the civil war had been won, the Bolsheviks soon lost considerable support because of the remarkable harshness of their rule. They therefore found it necessary to dismantle many of their extreme measures. They adopted a New Economic Policy (NEP) that permitted the reestablishment of some trade-union power and reintroduced private enterprise in peasant agriculture, in medium and small industry, and in domestic trade. (Heavy industry and foreign trade remained under the control of the party and government.) These policies facilitated general economic recovery and were of particular benefit to well-to-do peasants and small businessmen. However, the vast majority of the peasants were disadvantaged by the NEP. Furthermore, many within the leadership of the party argued that the NEP was politically undesirable because it significantly enhanced the political power of the petty bourgeoisie and economically undesirable because it did little to lead Russia out of economic backwardness.

Lenin's death in 1924 and the steadily increasing alienation of the peasantry from the central regime and from the national economy meant that Russia must have a new government with new policies. After considerable struggle within the party, in 1927 the party's general secretary, Josef Stalin, established his full control of its machinery. Stalin had four clearly defined political goals: (1) eliminating his rivals for political power, (2) integrating the peasantry, the vast majority of the Russian population, into national political and economic life, (3) dramatically improving Russia's economy, and (4) strengthening Russia's military defenses. The end in view of Stalin and his supporters may have been the establishment of socialism in Russia and the realization of Marx's humanitarian and democratic ideals, but the actual outcome of the pursuit of Stalin's four goals was precisely the opposite. The consequences of the Bolshevik revolution, as carried forward by Stalin, were the creation of a political system in which routine political participation was entirely manipulated by the regime, in which any serious competition for leadership which occurred within the one existing political party was eliminated, and in which political dissent was suppressed. The revolution against czarist absolutism led to Communist totalitarianism. One nondemocratic polity replaced another.

Stalin saw his goals as related to one another. In his view, rivalry for leadership would weaken the party and the government at a time when authority needed to be clearly established, unambiguous policies needed to be formulated, and directives needed to be followed without question.[22] Initially, he had defeated elite competitors through the skillful, though often heavy-handed, use of his position as general secretary. He had seen to it that those who ran the various party organizations at all levels were loyal and obedient. In later years (1935–1938) he initiated the "Great Purge" in which almost all dissenters (real, suspected, or imagined) in the party, in the schools, in the military, and in the professions were sent to labor camps or executed.

Russia's peasants had little incentive to involve themselves with the national economy or with the regime. Traditionally they engaged in subsistence agriculture. The lands they had won during the revolution were secured primarily through their own efforts. There were few important consumer goods available to them which could be purchased with the profits they might make by marketing surplus grain. There were no values to be gained in becoming soldiers in the Red Army or workers in the industrializing urban centers.

Stalin realized that the peasantry could no longer remain essentially autonomous. Russian cities needed grain, factories and the army needed manpower, and economic growth needed investment capital. To achieve these ends, Stalin forced the collectivization of agriculture. Under state control, agricultural production increased. Peasants were paid low fixed prices for the products of their work on collective farms and grain was sold in urban areas and exported at substantial profits for the state. Peasant exploitation became a major basis for acquiring the capital needed for industrial development. Dislocated peasants whose labor was not needed on the state farms were channeled into the army or into the expanding industrial proletariat.

Stalin decided that the quickest and most effective solution to the problems of the Russian economy was to engage in a crash program to develop heavy industry. For workers, this meant long hours of hard labor at low pay with few rewards available in the form of purchasable consumer goods. State-controlled work in the industrial areas, like state-controlled work in the countryside, involved making considerable sacrifices—supposedly for the Russian nation and its future. Such sacrifices were not freely chosen by peasants and industrial workers but were imposed by Stalin's government.

To ensure that peasants and industrial workers contributed according to his plan, Stalin increased the managerial and coercive capabilities of his government. Many of the features of social structure which were present during the period of War Communism were reintroduced. Two other features of political life under Stalin were added: the institutionalization of a system of grossly unequal social and economic rewards, and the dissemination of an official ideology to justify state controls, the use of coercion by the state, and the state's use of power to determine the distribution of social privileges.

Managerial capabilities of Stalin's regime were radically improved through vast increases in the size of state administrative organizations and through extreme centralization and bureaucratization. Stalin first introduced such structuring in the party. His personal secretariat became the effective center of political decision making. As in Fascist Germany, all political, economic, military, and even neighborhood organizations were made part of one hierarchical structure, much like a giant corporation with the party head on top.[23] Coercive capabilities were expanded in a similar manner. There were significant increases in the size of the police and the military. Both were put under the direction of newly created party organizations such as the Party Control Commission, the State Security Committee, the Political Commissariat in the Armed Forces, and so on.

Kinship, religion, and class were also affected by policies of Stalin's regime in ways intended to increase its control over Russian society. Possibly one of the best illustrations of regime attitudes toward the family is seen in the story of Pavlik Morozov.

> Although the name is unfamiliar to most Westerners, it is a household word in the U.S.S.R. A Young Pioneer (Communist youth group member) during the period of collectivization, Pavlik denounced his own father as a collaborator with the Kulaks (peasant landowners) and testified against him in court. Pavlik was killed by people of the village for revenge, and is now regarded as a martyr in the cause of communism. A statue of him in Moscow is constantly visited by children, who keep it bedecked with fresh flowers, and many collective farms, Pioneer palaces and libraries bear his name.[24]

From the very beginning the Bolshevik regime was intensely hostile toward religion. Severe persecution of clergy and church members was carried out from the 1920s until the end of the Great Purge in the late 1930s. In addition, major antireligious campaigns were conducted in the schools and a "League of Militant Atheists" was established. The Russian

Orthodox Church (which itself was the creation of the czars after the fall of the Byzantine empire, and which traditionally had served the state) offered little resistance to the new regime after the early period of coercion. Patriarchs and clergy were utilized by the government for various propaganda purposes. However, other religious groups, such as Roman Catholics and Moslems, continued to struggle despite arrests and executions of clergy. As an outcome, they were permitted to continue operating, though on a severely limited basis, and were kept from involving themselves with secular issues. Stalin, despite the repressive measures he approved, appears not to have fully grasped the ways and the extent to which the church can serve as an institutional basis of opposition to party supremacy. He is reported to have dismissed the pope with the cynical quip "How many divisions has he got?"[25]

Not all of Stalin's measures aimed at consolidating power and rapidly modernizing the economy took the form of extreme coercion. There was an elaborate system of rewards as well as negative sanctions. The new regime used its power to create a structure of extensive social inequality.[26] This distributive system was justified in terms of its motto: "To each according to his work." Its stated practical purpose was to provide work incentives and reward those who contributed most to the common good. Its consequence was the institutionalization of a sharply graded system of unequal social rewards which had little relation to its rationalizing motto.[27] Certain occupational categories, particularly political workers, military and paramilitary personnel, and those engaged in scientific activities who were cooperative with the government, often enjoyed higher salaries (several times the average wage), direct tax advantages, access to more and higher-quality food, housing privileges, access to institutions of higher education, internal and foreign travel prerogatives, prizes, and ranks and insignia of office. The extent to which reward differentials were emphasized even at the symbolic level is suggested by Skocpol's observation that "by the 1940's both the Soviet civilian administration and the officer corps of the Red Army had institutionalized official titles, ranks and uniforms that were just as elaborate and ostentatious—and in fact exactly parallel to—those established under the Old Regime by Peter the Great."[28]

The Bolshevik revolution was fought in the name of democracy and equality. Russia under Stalin had a totalitarian political system governing a society characterized by gross social, economic, and political inequalities. Marxism, the guiding ideology of Russia's revolutionary intellectuals, and later the official creed of the Russian nation was built on a core of humanitarian values and implored people everywhere to put an end to exploitation and alienation. Stalin's Russia was the setting for political assassinations, expropriation of personal property, forced labor, the widespread use of terror as a means of political control, and mass executions.

Several steps were taken by the regime in an attempt to reconcile its extreme actions with Marxist social thought and present itself as the legitimate heir of the revolution. A number of these steps were also extreme in themselves. First, prominent Russians who were fully aware of and espoused Marxist doctrine, and used it to criticize the regime, were eliminated. Many of the intellectuals who had played key roles in the revolution of 1917 were killed off in the Great Purge. Later Marxist critics of the regime met the same fate. Second, under Stalin, Marx's works were available in Russia only in expurgated editions. Much of Marx's writing was suppressed—particularly the earlier works, which explicitly expressed his humanitarian values and used alienation as a focal point of discussion. Works that were most widely available emphasized two themes in particular: (1) the intentional manipulation of economic structures for the realization of all social and political goals, and (2) the threat of bourgeois imperialism. Because the writings of Marx are open to many interpretations, a third step taken by the regime was to establish the party as the sole source of the true accounting of his views. The official party pronouncements on Marx's thoughts presented them as justifications for the crash programs of industrialization and political integration the regime was pursuing.[29] Rapidly expanding production was presented as consistent with Marx's views of the way out of any unjustifiable inequality at home and out of insecurity in the face of antagonistic capitalist nations. Marx's ideas were transformed from radical critiques of oppressive social institutions into an ideology justifying Stalin's totalitarianism.

The brief case studies of Fascist Germany and Stalin's Russia do suggest, in broad outline, some of the interrelated social conditions which were favorable to the development of extreme nondemocratic political systems. These include:

A. *Historical conditions*
   1. A long tradition of autocratic rule.
   2. Long-standing antagonisms and conflicts with other states.
   3. Persistence of severe and worsening economic conditions resulting from a low level of economic development and resource depletion created by nonproductive investment of wealth (e.g., as in wars or maintaining elite privileges).
   4. If and when relatively democratic political institutions were installed, they failed to win popular support or to deal effectively with existing social and economic problems.
   5. The presence of a highly centralized, well-organized political movement with a leadership committed, overtly or covertly, to extensive and rapid industrialization and to significantly increasing national political and economic integration.

B. *Structural conditions*
   1. Low levels of national political and economic integration.
   2. The institutions of kinship, religion, and education are either weak or lack experience in promoting orientations opposed by any regime.

   3.   Power and authority have long been used to maintain a sharply graded
        structure of social and economic inequality.
C.   *Cultural conditions*
   1.   A traditional value system emphasizing social order and the recognition
        of hierarchical relationships.
   2.   A new and widespread sense of nationalism born out of military defeat
        and subsequent national humiliation.

The relative importance of each of these conditions, and the combination of conditions most likely to promote the development of extreme
nondemocratic political systems are matters which can be determined by
future historical-comparative research based on many additional case
studies. Results of such research should be of more than academic interest.
Many of today's economically poor nations exhibit a number of the historical, structural, and cultural conditions listed above. They therefore appear
to have considerable potential for developing along extreme nondemocratic lines.

LACK OF DEMOCRACY IN
CONTEMPORARY LOW-INCOME
COUNTRIES

Until fairly recently, any interest American political sociologists showed in
low-income countries was generally expressed within the context of
elaborating theories of "political development." The theories tended to be
assessments of the ways in which political change in the world's poor nations might move in increasingly democratic directions. The analyses shed
little, if any, light on the nondemocratic potential of such nations. Below it
will be argued that this possible line of political change is much more likely
than is the probability of increasing democracy.
    The studies of "political development" had two additional shortcom-
ings. First, they focused on internal variables such as the character of political cleavages and the context of shared, politically relevant beliefs and
values. They tended to ignore the historical and international context in
which the "developing" nation was located. This approach revealed nothing about the ways in which, and the extent to which, the internal variables
were themselves consequences of transnational forces. In particular, they
did not recognize the extent to which the economy of a poor nation must be
understood as a part of a world economic system. Second, the studies
appear to have been based on the implicit assumption that economic development and political development (defined as increasing democratization) will tend to be compatible. This assumption is, at best, questionable on
both theoretical and empirical grounds. Economic modernization can be

impeded by the inclusion of the mass public in processes of political-economic decision making. This can occur in cases where there are extensive citizen demands for more consumer goods and more social services. Meeting such demands makes it virtually impossible to accumulate capital for investment in industry. Two of the most dramatic examples of rapid and effective economic development occurred under the extreme non-democratic polities of Fascist Germany and Stalin's Russia.

In their study of political participation in economically poor countries, Huntington and Nelson observed that the major goals of most such nations include rapid economic growth, increased socioeconomic equality, and increased political participation.[30] However, such goals can conflict with one another. In the early phases of modernization, a conflict exists between the goals of socioeconomic equality and political participation. In the countryside, as industrialization begins, many peasants are displaced from the land. Peasants become absorbed in personal problems and further lack political organization. In the cities, an urban middle class develops and joins the traditional rural elite as participants in the political process. The new urban class develops political organizations and skills which it uses to improve its economic position. This produces a widening gap between rural and urban standards of living; social and economic inequality are increased. (Huntington and Nelson's data show that significant land reform, the program most likely to reduce peasant inequality, is more likely to be introduced by nondemocratic governments.) In later stages of economic development, there is a conflict between economic growth and political participation. As noted above, as industrial production begins to create new resources, there are increasing demands on the polity for goods (e.g., schools, hospitals, roads) and services (e.g., public health programs, social welfare provisions). Meeting such demands interferes with reinvestment of capital necessary for industrial expansion and economic growth. Furthermore, whether some efforts are made to meet such demands or not, as long as the state exercises considerable control of the economy, the level of political democracy is likely to remain low.[31]

According to Huntington and Nelson, it is the dominant political elites of economically poor nations who choose the relative priorities given to the national goals of equality, participation, and economic development. It is they who also determine the means to achieve them. The authors argue that, at least in the short run, the values of political elites and the policies which governments pursue are more decisive than any other factors in determining the political life of "developing" nations. The choices of elites have what they term a "cascading effect." Such choices create the contexts for choices made by those at lower levels of political organization.

The prominence of the role played by political elites in economically poor nations might diminish over time. Eventually the mass public could be encouraged to play a large part in political decision making. Notions of civilian rule, representative institutions, and public liberties could come to have greater meaning for the citizens of poor nations. However, a number of factors tend to work against movement in the direction of increasingly democratic rule. First, those in positions of power and authority are unlikely to promote expansion of political participation because increases might lead to challenges to their positions. (Only if an elite believes it lacks a sufficient power base and is vulnerable to overthrow by military action or replacement by an opposing political elite will it be likely to attempt to expand participation.) Second, in economically poor nations, political participation generally is not highly valued in and of itself. The vast majority of the population, peasants and the urban poor, "usually take little part in politics because participation seems irrelevant to their primary concerns, futile, or both. The most pressing problems for many of the poor are jobs, food and medical aid—for today, tomorrow, or next week."[32]

It is not only reluctant elites and disorganized masses that keep the political lives of economically poor nations toward the nondemocratic end of the political spectrum. Important international factors also contribute to this consequence. Included among such factors are:

1. the military actions of the powerful nations of the world—overt, or covert, actual or threatened
2. the activities of multinational corporations
3. the position of economically poor nations in the world economy

Brief reference to some contemporary history can serve to illustrate the ways in which each of these factors can operate so as to make extremely difficult political, economic, and social self-determination by the inhabitants of economically poor nations.

The southwest African nation of Angola gained independence from Portugal in 1975 after a guerrilla war that had lasted thirteen years. However, after supposedly achieving independence, the people of Angola were not alone to determine how power was to be acquired, authority exercised, and rewards distributed to their new nation. These outcomes were determined by military conflict among political groups supported by foreign nations: the National Front, based in Zaire; the Popular Movement, backed by the Soviet Union; and the National Union, supported by the United States and South Africa. The battles killed thousands of blacks, drove most whites to emigrate, and destroyed the weak economy. Finally, some 15,000 Soviet-sponsored Cuban troops and massive Soviet aid helped the Popular Movement win control over most of the country. The established regime then operated in ways responsive to the Soviet Union, which maintained its influence through the presence in Angola of an estimated 25,000 Cuban, East German, and Portuguese Communists. A similar military action destroying political self-determination was initiated by the Soviet Union in

Afghanistan in 1979. Troops invaded Afghanistan to put down increasingly effective Islamic resistance to the regime and to replace a government which was not as positively responsive to demands from Moscow as its predecessors had been.

The operations of multinational corporations can also work to override the importance of expressed citizen preferences concerning the exercise of rule in economically poor nations. The modern multinational corporation originated with the great trading companies of the seventeenth and eighteenth centuries, such as the East India Company, the Hudson Bay Company, La Compagnie des Indes, the Company of Adventurers of London Trading into Africa, and other such organizations in Spain, Russia, Italy, and Germany. Many of these companies undertook to govern as well as to trade.[33] Nevertheless, such companies were basically national companies with secondary foreign operations. Since World War II, the number, size, wealth, and influence of such companies has expanded considerably. The organizations now not only have a large amount of their resources invested in international business and gain a significant amount of their income from abroad, they also engage in production and manufacturing in a number of countries and use a worldwide perspective in management and decision making. However, "what (really) distinguishes the global corporation of today from its prewar predecessor is its heightened structural mobility, i.e., its increased capacity to change when and what it produces and an accelerating change in its managerial techniques for controlling that production."[34] The major consequence of this structural mobility is that multinational corporations are little constrained in their institutional jurisdiction to their home nation. The importance of this lack of constraint on multinational corporations is quickly grasped when one looks at the statistics which indicate that multinational corporations have accumulated more power-relevant resources than most nation-states. For example:

- —51 of the world's largest 100 political and economic entities are multinational corporations, not nation-states
- —General Motors has a larger annual product than Switzerland or Pakistan
- —Standard Oil (New Jersey) has a larger annual product than Norway or Denmark
- —Ford Motors has a larger annual product than Austria or Yugoslavia
- —If the 300 largest multinational corporations would join together, their combined resources would be exceeded only by those of the United States and the Soviet Union.[35]
- —The United States Chamber of Commerce estimates that by the year 2000, 54 percent of the world's projected wealth—some \$4 trillion in assets—will be controlled by a few hundred multinational firms.[36]

These statistics have led many political sociologists to agree with Braungart that "multinational corporations constitute the third most powerful force on the earth."[37] As such they pose potential problems for all nations, particularly for those that are poor.

The major problems presented by the multinational corporations center around conflicting interests. Such corporations are, in effect, autonomous states with their own interests and foreign policies, which they place above any national allegiance.[38] The primary interest of any multinational is maximization of economic profits. On occasion such a goal has been achieved by pursuing policies which were politically and economically detrimental to a country in which a company did business. However, since corporations can account for a substantial proportion of the gross national product of a nation and the taxes paid by multinational corporations finance a large part of all government expenditures, it is difficult for the government of a poor nation to pursue policies contrary to corporate interests. Some analysts believe that as a result of situations such as this, the overall effect of multinational corporations on the economies has been extremely negative. They believe that this has happened despite the fact that multinationals do spread goods, capital, and technology and employ hundreds of thousands of workers around the world—often paying more than the prevailing wage. For example, Barnet and Müller argue that multinational corporations have contributed to

> . . . the deterioration of living standards, employment rates and economic justice around the world (and this) has occurred despite the fact that many corporate officials would like it to be otherwise and believe that it can be. The unfortunate role of the global corporation in maintaining and increasing poverty around the world is due primarily to the dismal reality that global corporations and poor countries have different, indeed conflicting, interests, priorities and needs. This is a reality that many officials of underdeveloped countries, lacking alternative development strategies, prefer not to face.[39]

While Barnet and Müller may overstate the case, the fact remains that the actions of multinational corporations impact on the political and economic life of poor countries in ways that cannot be controlled by the political leaders or by the mass publics of these countries. The importance of civilian rule, representative institutions, and public liberties is significantly diminished when national policies and the outcomes of national programs are largely decided in foreign corporate board rooms rather than in domestic voting booths or in parliaments.

Multinational corporations do more than inadvertently influence the economies of economically poor nations. At times they have made deliberate efforts to determine directly nations' internal political affairs. The example of I.T.T.'s involvement with the removal of the Allende government in Chile has already been mentioned. Other examples include the direct political involvement of the United Fruit Company in Guatemala in the 1950s and the political involvement of several American-based corporations in Katanga in the 1960s. Less dramatic and probably more effective forms of direct intervention include bribery of host country politicians, large contributions to political parties and to candidates, lobbying of legislators, and use of the mass media for propaganda purposes.[40]

The position of poor nations in the world economy also reduces the ability of their leaders and ordinary citizens to choose for themselves, through whatever political mechanisms might be available, the social and economic structures under which they are to live.

As Immanuel Wallerstein pointed out,

> (N)ational states are not societies that have separate, parallel histories, but parts of a whole reflecting that whole. . . . (T)o understand the internal class contradictions and political struggles of a particular state, we must first situate it in the world economy.[41]

Wallerstein first fully explicated his concept of world economy in a highly influential work published in 1974.[42] In brief, he argues that a world mode of production came into being in the sixteenth century. Northwestern Europe diversified its economic production, engaged in increasing long-distance trade, and developed strong state mechanisms. It became the core area of a worldwide system of economic production, distribution, and exchange. England, France, and Spain in particular colonized much of the non-European world. Eastern Europe and the Western hemisphere became peripheral areas of the world economy, exchanging primary products and raw materials (basically wood, grain, cotton, sugar, and gold) for relatively expensive goods (e.g., textiles, worked iron, luxury manufactured goods) from the core of the world system. There rapidly developed a world division of labor in which the core regulated the exchange processes and established domination over the periphery. The result was the institutionalization of a system of unequal exchange in which the core controlled economic surplus. The core became increasingly diversified economically as well as increasingly industrialized, rich, and militarily powerful. Peripheral societies became increasingly overspecialized economically, providing raw materials and inexpensive labor for the core. Peripheral societies tended to be relatively weak and subject to political and economic exploitation by the core. They tended to become increasingly less egalitarian socially and economically.

They also tended to become increasingly more unstable and less democratic politically. In the world economy there are also semi-peripheral societies—occupying an intermediate position between core and periphery. Such societies are weaker than the core but are undergoing industrialization and economic diversification. They represent a potential challenge to the future of the core.

There are objections to the world-economy thesis as presented by Wallerstein. For example, Skocpol argues that the position amounts to economic reductionism—nation-states are seen only as instruments used by economically dominant groups pursuing the expansion of economic production and profit on a world scale.[43] In her view, nation-states can be better understood as organizations oriented to maintaining power and authority in their home territory and to the possibility or actuality of military competition with other nation-states. The international system of states is seen as a structure of military competition. The structure was not created by capitalism. Its operation is related to the dynamics of world capitalism, but not reducible to it. Other factors such as administrative efficiency, political capacities for mass mobilization, and international geographical position also influence the international structure of military relations.

Clearly both interdependent variables (position in the world economy and position in the world military structure) have considerable impact on the character of social, economic, and political relationships in poor countries. Economic underdevelopment and lack of political democracy (themselves related factors) are as much, if not more, products of relations with other states (particularly those which are economically developed and militarily powerful) and with multinational corporations as they are the results of "internal" variables. This fundamental point became obvious to political sociologists only fairly recently as more analysts began macroanalytic, historical-comparative studies investigating political, economic, and social change.

THE NONDEMOCRATIC POTENTIAL OF WESTERN INDUSTRIAL NATIONS

Domestic Factors

Chapter 7 presented the position of the "elitists"—those theorists of political power who argue that, at least in the United States, despite the presence of formal democratic institutions, the ability to decide many issues of national and international importance does not ultimately reside with the mass public but with a very few persons who are not formally responsible to the public. Among the factors political analysts cite to account for the nondemocratic pattern which they identify are included:

1. Concentration of political influence resulting from the concentration of economic resources (i.e., the development of monopolies, near-monopolies, interlocking directorates, and conglomerates).
2. The presence of a large, influential, and permanent military establishment. (In the view of some, the conjunction of (1) and (2) produces the so-called military-industrial complex.)
3. The vast expansion of government size, organizational complexity, and in-

fluence in most spheres of social life. (This growth supposedly has made government simultaneously more important and less accessible to the public.)

4. Cooptation of leaders of large secondary associations (particularly labor unions) which might otherwise serve as sources of countervailing influence to the corporations, the military, and the government.

To the extent that the elitists are generally correct and big business, big military, big government, and the coopted leaders of big secondary associations largely determine, through whatever mechanisms, political policy in Western industrial nations, the operation of genuine political democracy in these nations is seriously compromised. Civilian rule, representative institutions, and public liberties that are present in these nations will, in fact, have little political meaning. If the elitists are, in general, correct, then the continued growth of corporations, the military, government, and certain secondary associations in Western nations increases their nondemocratic potential.

Changes in other institutions of Western industrial nations also contribute to their nondemocratic potential. Because the political consequences of these changes have not been the subjects of extensive empirical investigation, the changes will be added only tentatively to the list. They include

5. Family instability
6. Increasing secularization of religion
7. Increasing vocationalism in education

The failure to investigate the bearing of these changes in kinship, religion, and education on political democracy is surprising in light of the fact that most political sociologists consider the impact of society on the polity to be the defining concern of the field. The following discussion of these factors is intended to suggest plausible hypotheses for future research. Each might be explored profitably through the use of macro-analytic historical-comparative perspectives.

Rates of divorce, separation, and abandonment have increased in all of the Western industrial democracies over the past decades, and two reasons are commonly given to account for this instability. One reason is the family's loss of important social functions it once performed. A second reason accounting for the instability is the extreme importance of the family's specialized affective function. (In increasingly mobile and competitive societies, the family becomes the exclusive context in which love, security, and the general concern of others for one's welfare can be depended on. Should a family prove at all undependable in meeting basic and important affective needs, it is likely to be dissolved.)

To the extent that the family has become weakened, its roles as an effective agent of political socialization and as a locus of primary involvement and loyalty are diminished. Its operation as the major "island of separateness" is reduced. Political socialization functions are taken up by social units closer to government and state—such as the schools—which are more amenable to manipulation by those in established positions of power and privilege. Some loyalty is also transferred from the family to social units close to government and state—such as recreational groups—which can also be used as "transmission belts" for belief and value systems supporting the political-economic status quo.

The secularization of religion in Western industrial nations potentially has both democratic and antidemocratic consequences. On the one hand, secularization encourages the active participation of the church in social affairs. It can involve the church in political socialization and in collective political action consistent with religious ideals. Secularization might be a means of keeping the church "relevant" for certain sectors of the population and therefore keeping the church viable as a center of loyalty as well as critical thought and political action. On the other hand, there are at least two ways in which secularization might have antidemocratic consequences. First, one dimension of secularization involves taking stands on the controversial political and social issues of the society. To the extent that the church takes stands and claims exclusive validity for its positions, it is operating in a way which discourages the functioning of democratic processes such as recognizing the validity of political opposition, exercising the right of dissent, and engaging in open public debate. For example, the "religious right," which developed in the United States in the late 1970s, claimed that its positions on such diverse matters as abortion, school busing to achieve racial integration, voluntary prayers in the schools, homosexuals, and the Equal Rights Amendment were both morally correct and were supported by the majority of American citizens. Opposing views and groups which maintained them were characterized as clearly "wrong," in the moral sense and vaguely "un-American." Second, secularization of religion moves the church further in the direction of the "civil religion." Regime and government become beneficiaries of attitudes which previously found expression limited to purely religious contexts. Some churches inadvertently can promote views of the nation and its leaders which are reminiscent of Durkheim's description of the deferential political views of people living in less structurally and culturally differentiated societies. While all stable political systems require some degree of deference to political authority, there is some point at which deference can begin to inhibit criticism and opposition and therefore the operation of political democracy. When it operates primarily as a purveyor of the "civil religion," the church also ceases to be one of the "islands of separateness" necessary to maintain democratic rule.

Increasing vocationalism in the schools, at all levels, can be associated with the development of nondemocratic polities in three ways. First, programs of vocational and technical education can replace various programs in the arts, humanities, and social sciences. Study in these areas is intended, among other things, to give students a more reflective and critical view of the world around them as well as better analytic and communication skills. At least in theory, it is citizens who are reflective, analytic, and critical and who communicate their politically relevant perceptions to others who are the foundation of political democracy. When people with such capacities become rare in a population, democracy is threatened. Second, vocational and technical programs are often funded by government, private corporations, and foundations. Funding tends to give such agencies more extensive control over educational content and over the uses to which acquired knowledge and skills are to be put. It further concentrates power. Third, vocational and technical education can increase respect for and dependence on "expert" opinion. It can promote attitudes favoring technical—as opposed to political—solutions to social problems. Such orientations support technocracy rather than democracy.

It must be emphasized again that the discussion presented here of the ways in which family instability, secularization of religion, and increasing vocationalism in education might increase the nondemocratic potential of Western industrial nations is entirely theoretical. Considerable empirical research would be required to determine its actual merits. Furthermore, this list of changes is intended by no means to be exhaustive. Clearly, additional changes, such as serious fluctuations in national economies, might well produce other, more serious, pressures toward the development of nondemocratic rule. The appearance of factors such as this, however, cannot be predicted with any degree of certainty. By way of contrast, family instability, secularization of religion, and vocationalism in education are long-established tendencies of Western industrial nations which we are unlikely to change substantially in opposite directions in the foreseeable future.

Transnational Factors

In addition to domestic or internal factors, forces that transcend national boundaries also influence the nondemocratic potential of Western industrial nations. Some of these are the same forces which have antidemocratic consequences for the world's poor nations—world military conditions, activities of multinational corporations, and position in the world economy. In this context these forces are now being viewed from the other side.

The position of a Western industrial nation in the world military structure (its relative standing in the hierarchy of world military power and the character of its alliances with other nations) will influence at least three related features of its political system: (1) the role of the military in the formation of the nation's foreign policy, (2) defense spending, and (3) operative political definitions of what constitutes the "national interest."

It seems reasonable to assume that when a nation's position in the world military structure is defined, by its political leaders, influential groups, and/or by a significant proportion of its mass public, as being threatened, the political influence of the military in the nation will increase, national defense spending will increase, and political definitions of what is, and what is not, in the national interest will have more serious social consequences. Each of these results can diminish the importance of democratic structures and processes in a nation. An increase in the political influence of the military means some decrease in the actuality of civilian rule and in the representativeness of public institutions. An increase in military spending can represent a weakening of democratic rule if public support for such an allocation of scarce resources has not been expressed. This is most likely to happen when resources for such an allocation for the military must be diverted from long-established welfare state provisions. There probably are not very many occasions on which the public will opt for guns over butter.

Possibly the greatest threat to the maintenance of political democracy or, more specifically, to the maintenance of public liberties, occurs when officials of government attempt to suppress political dissent in the name of "national interest." This is most likely to happen before, during, or shortly after a period of war. For example, serious threats to civil liberties were present in the United States during the "McCarthy period" of the early 1950s (associated with the Korean War) and during the "Watergate era" of the mid-1970s (associated with the Vietnam War).

In a speech delivered in early 1950, Senator Joseph R. McCarthy of Wisconsin claimed that the Department of State was full of Communists and that the Secretary of State knew their names. This began a four-year period in which intimations, allegations, and undocumented accusations of disloyalty and even treason were directed against literally thousands of government employees (including those in the military), writers, journalists, educators, entertainers, and many others having contact with the public. Reputations were ruined and careers were disrupted or destroyed. Most of this occurred in clear and direct violation of the civil rights of the accused by such agencies as investigative divisions of the State Department, the FBI, the Civil Service Commission, and Army Intelligence. It was justified on grounds of ridding the United States of an internal threat of Communist subversion. This was, in turn, somehow thought to be linked to an international conspiracy aimed at Communist world domination.

Much the same thing occurred in the mid-1970s. As Nunn, Crockett, and Williams observed:

> Although the tactics of the Nixon era were more subtle than those employed by McCarthy, the Nixon administration abuses of civil liberties perhaps surpassed those of McCarthy. Not only was the White House violating civil liberties, the FBI, CIA, Army Intelligence, IRS and other agencies had files on

more than a million citizens, illegally opened nearly a quarter million pieces of mail, monitored millions of telegrams and telephone calls and used a variety of techniques to harass and defame private citizens. George Orwell's world of 1984 seemed dangerously at hand.[44]

Such historical events raise questions about future responses of democratic governments to situations which they define as threatening to national security. These questions are particularly salient in light of the apparent increase in acts of international terrorism. In recent years bombing, assassination, airplane hijacking, kidnapping, and hostage taking, carried out by terrorist organizations, has deeply affected the political lives of many nations, including political democracies such as the United States, France, Israel, Italy, West Germany, Great Britain, Ireland, and the Netherlands, among others. The responses of heads of state to these events suggest that attempts to deal effectively with terrorism can move a nation in a less democratic direction.[45] For example, in response to the bombing of a Paris synagogue in 1980, French President Valéry Giscard d'Estaing said that his government would ban neo-Nazi meetings and dissolve "racist organizations." In response to the 1979 takeover of the United States Embassy in Iran by militants, President Jimmy Carter called on the Congress in his State of the Union message to remove "unwarranted restraints" on U.S. intelligence-gathering capabilities. Such examples clearly indicate that terrorism now operates as a transnational stimulus to the development of nondemocratic practices in Western industrial nations.

Transnational *economic* factors also contribute to the nondemocratic potential of Western industrial nations. Many of these factors center around the activities of multinational corporations and the resulting location of the nations involved in the world economy. Multinational corporations take control of many features of a nation's political-economic life away from its government. The generalization applies to Western industrial nations as well as to economically poor nations. Viewed from the perspective of economically poor nations, multinational corporations appear as extensions of the power of their home country. Since most of the world's multinationals originate and have their headquarters in the United States, such corporations frequently are seen as agencies of United States foreign policy. As noted above, this view is not without some basis. However, the point here is that multinational corporations are largely independent forces which can, to some extent, influence the policies of any nation. Such influence is exerted to achieve corporate rather than national goals. Such goals need not coincide and, in fact, can conflict. For example, multinational corporations based in the United States have sold strategic goods to both Russia and China, despite federal regulations which prohibit such sales. American-based multinationals have also induced the United States government to intervene in the affairs of other nations in order to protect corporate interests. (The case of I.T.T. in Chile, noted earlier, is the most widely cited example of this process.) The future possibility that multinational corporations based in democratic nations will be neither effectively controlled nor effectively resisted by the governments of these nations suggests that the meaning of political democracy at the nation-state level is somewhat in doubt. Democratic rule is not enhanced when, in some politically important situation, law has little force and policies are formulated in response to the demands of giant corporations rather than in response to the wishes of the citizenry expressed through their democratic institutions.

Short of an unpredictable national calamity, war, or an unprecedented military coup that might promote limitations of civilian rule, representative institutions and political liberties, it seems rather unlikely that any Western industrial democracy will develop into a totalitarian state—despite the presence in each of these nations of vast organizational and technological capabilities that could make totalitarian rule exceedingly effective. A more likely threat to democracy in Western industrial nations lies in the possible recurrence of "McCarthy eras" or "Watergates" justified in the name of national security. Shifting world political alliances, political and economic instability in all parts of the globe, and the growth of international terrorism all increase this nondemocratic potentiality. However, the most serious threat to the continuation of viable democratic government comes from transnational corporations and cartels. The sovereignty of democratic nations is increasingly called into question. The threat of a nondemocratic future is not that a political democracy will give way to a totalitarian state. We are not now living in the dramatic future envisioned by George Orwell in his *1984*. Rather, we are living in a time in which the complex activities of transnational corporations and cartels, which impact directly and indirectly on the lives of millions of people, continue to be largely unaffected by the rules of nations and the desires of their citizens. Excluding war, the future threat to democracy is not so much the great power of any national government as it is the *irrelevance* of all national governments.

EARLY THEORIES AND CONTEMPORARY MACROANALYSIS: NONDEMOCRATIC RULE

Marx, Weber, and Durkheim each explored past systems of nondemocratic rule. Each was concerned about the nondemocratic potential of the rapidly developing industrial societies of the Western world. Each provided valuable theoretical insights into these topics. As political sociology further pursues its analysis of nondemocratic rule, through the initiation of new macroanalytic, historical-comparative studies, their works should be read with renewed interest.

Marx's concern for democracy was a concern with the social conditions under which exploitation and alienation would be forever removed from the human social scene. He was not interested in the maintenance of civilian rule, representative institutions, and public liberties as these were found in the Western industrial nations of his time. In fact, in his view, these were components of *bourgeois* democracies—political systems that *promoted* exploitation and alienation. In such systems the notion of democracy was a sham. Under bourgeois democracy civilian rule means rule by the owners of the means of production; political institutions represent the interests of the dominant economic class; public liberties represent legal provisions which meet the needs of industrial capitalism.

From the perspective of attempting to understand nondemocratic rule, Marx's approach has noteworthy strengths and weaknesses. The contemporary analytic utility of his view is located in his linking political alienation to property relations on an international scale. As argued above, in the modern world system, the concentration of ownership of the means of production in the hands of a relatively few transnational corporate entities has removed a considerable amount of political power from the hands of nation-states, their leaders, and ultimately their citizens. Democratic rule is diminished to the extent that citizens lose control, through whatever means, of their national political and economic life. Marx provides a theoretical foundation for understanding this major threat to present-day democracies. While the will of those representing vast amounts of concentrated economic power can be resisted and possibly even manipulated by those with purely political resources, recent history suggests that in the long run, economic interests tend to prevail.

The major shortcoming in Marxist analysis of nondemocratic polities lies in its lack of utility for understanding totalitarian rule—such as that exemplified by the cases of Fascist Germany and Russia under Stalin. Totalitarianism can exist in conjunction with a wide variety of economic systems—as the Fascist and Communist examples indicate. Totalitarianism is a form of political organization which cannot be adequately described or explained primarily in terms of economic factors. Marxist analysis also offers little insight into the role of social institutions under totalitarian rule. Marx's general position is that in all class societies, family and church operate so as to perpetuate political and economic inequalities. However, under totalitarian rule, family and church are more usefully seen as potential refuges from alienation and as potential loci of resistance rather than as automatic contributors to the maintenance of the existing distributive system.

Three concepts explicated by Weber are particularly helpful for understanding modern nondemocratic rule: rationalization, political party, and charismatic rule. In his discussion of rationalization, Weber points out that a number of principles which increase efficiency and effectiveness in organizations operate at the cost of giving consideration to the wishes of all organization members or to their representatives. Rationalization in the political realm, embodied in large, centralized, bureaucratically structured states, has led to the concentration of vast power and to processes of government decision making often based more on "expert opinion" than on the expressed desires of citizens. Rationalization in the economic realm, embodied in large, centralized, bureaucratically structured corporations, has produced the concentration of vast resources that can be applied to achieve corporate goals which can conflict with the desires and interests of democratic governments and of those whom they rule.

Weber's understanding of political party clarifies important structural features of totalitarian rule. First, he correctly emphasizes that a party need not be class based. Second, he notes that parties tend to be dominated by a small central group of individuals and tend to have primarily passive mass memberships. Weber also makes the useful point that the primary goals of a political party are the acquisition and use of power. This approach to parties makes considerably more intelligible the process by which successful revolutionary parties later develop despotic tendencies.

At this point, Weber's concept of charismatic rule can become relevant. The party leader who is widely believed to possess extraordinary qualities can, by virtue of this shared perception, transform the structure of one-party rule into a system of charismatic domination—such as happened, to a considerable extent, in the cases of Hitler and Stalin. Weber's discussion clarifies important cultural features of some extreme nondemocratic regimes and the system of rule which supports them.

The major failing in Weber's analysis of nondemocratic rule is his lack of sufficient attention to the important role that propaganda and coercion can play in systems of domination. Hitler's Germany and Stalin's Russia indicate that this role can be central. Several students of the totalitarian variety of nondemocratic rule argue that it represents a uniquely modern form of despotism. Its uniqueness lies in the fact that the government employs science to keep itself in power and to achieve its fundamental goals despite serious opposition (physical science, engineering, and technology to provide means of transportation, communications, and weapons systems, and psychology to provide techniques of persuasion and intimidation). Weber, who was particularly interested in the social conditions under which people will employ reason to subjugate nature, did not fully explore the social conditions under which some people will employ the products of reason to subjugate other people.

Durkheim identified two major threats to democracy in industrial society. The first was anarchy, which could arise in a society when the normative order was poorly defined, i.e., when social guides for conduct were unclear. The second was the development of a strong, centralized state with unrestrained power which could infringe on individual rights. Durkheim advocated the development of independent occupational groups which would serve as contexts within which moral norms appropriate to societies with advanced divisions of labor could be created and transmitted and which also would serve as countervailing forces limiting the state's exercise of power.

Durkheim's work suggests future empirical study of the relationship between levels of normative consensus and the maintenance of civilian rule, representative institutions, and public liberties. His analysis suggests that under some historical, cultural, and social conditions, very high levels of normative consensus actually might promote totalitarian dictatorship. Durkheim found that traditional societies with high levels of moral integration often had leaders who exercised largely unrestrained political power and had systems of repressive laws. His discussion suggests why, historically, rampant nationalism often has been associated with the emergence of dictatorship and political repression. On the other hand, under some historical, cultural, and social conditions, very low levels of normative consensus might promote anarchy, a political condition under which, according to Durkheim, freedom and equality cannot be realized. Future macroanalytic, historical-comparative studies which follow these leads would have considerable potential for increasing our understanding of the ways in which the character of leadership in any society reflects the basic features of that society's social structure and culture. At present, understanding of this topic in cases of modern nondemocratic polities is quite limited.

One major weakness of Durkheim's sociology of nondemocratic rule is his failure to foresee the importance of force, violence, and coercion in modern political life. Another is his failure to consider the possibility that the moral norms of a society, factors of central importance in his conceptual scheme, could be imposed on an entire society by a small, privileged, and powerful segment to serve its narrow interests. However, it is only fairly recently that modern empirically based political analysis itself has attended to these fundamental points.

NOTES

1. For an identification of these countries and a specification of their social and economic characteristics, see The World Bank, *World Development Report 1980* (New York: Oxford University Press, 1980).

2. Carl J. Friedrich and Zbigniew K. Brzezinski, *Totalitarian Dictatorship and Autocracy* 2nd ed. (New York: Frederick A. Praeger, 1965), pp. 15–27.

3. Barrington Moore, Jr., *Social Origins of Dictatorship and Democracy* (Boston: Beacon Press, 1966).

4. Ibid., pp. 433–452.

5. Ibid., p. 440.

6. Except when otherwise noted, the following discussion of the establishment of Fascism in Germany is based on Francis L. Carsten, *The Rise of Fascism* (Berkeley: University of California Press, 1969).

7. Juan J. Linz, "Some Notes toward a Comparative Study of Fascism in Sociological Historical Perspective," in *Fascism: A Reader's Guide*, Walter Laqueur, ed. (Berkeley: University of California Press, 1976), pp. 3–121.

8. Harold Lasswell, *Psychopathology and Politics* (New York: Viking Press, 1930); Theodore W. Adorno, Else Frenkel-Brunswick, Donald J. Levinson, and R. N. Sanford, *The Authoritarian Personality* (New York: Harper, 1950).

9. See, for example, Nevitt Sanford, "Authoritarian Personality in Contemporary Perspective," in *Handbook of Political Psychology*, Jeanne N. Knutson, ed. (San Francisco: Jossey-Bass, 1973), pp. 139–170.

10. Eric Fromm, *Escape from Freedom* (New York: Holt, 1941); Eric Fromm, *The Sane Society* (New York: Holt, 1955); Karl Mannheim, *Ideology and Utopia* (New York: Harcourt Brace and Co., Harvest Book edition, 1959), see pp. 136–146. (Originally published in German in 1929; Expanded English version first published in 1936.)

11. Eric Fromm, *The Sane Society*, p. 237.

12. See A. F. K. Organski, *The Stages of Political Development* (New York: Alfred A. Knopf, 1965), especially pp. 170–177.

13. Ranier Lepsius, "The Collapse of an Intermediary Power Structure: Germany 1933–1934," *International Journal of Comparative Sociology*, 9, nos. 3–4 (September-December 1968) 289–301.

14. Friedrich and Brzezinski, *Totalitarian Dictatorship*, pp. 279–339.

15. This discussion of the family in Fascist Germany is based on Friedrich and Brzezinski, *Totalitarian Dictatorship*, pp. 290–298.

16. See William L. Shirer, *The Rise and Fall of the Third Reich* (New York: Simon and Schuster, 1960), pp. 234–240.

17. See Carsten, *Rise of Fascism*, p. 156.

18. Considerable damage had been done to German science, particularly to physics and chemistry, before the Fascists realized the harm they could cause themselves by further interference. See Shirer, *Rise and Fall of the Third Reich*, pp. 248–256.

19. This is not to say that in Fascist Germany or anywhere else for that matter, science was or will be free from political demands. For a discussion of the ways in which the structure of science is linked to political systems, see Stuart S. Blume, *Toward a Political Sociology of Science,* (New York: Free Press, 1974).

20. Widely read books on the Holocaust include Lucy Dawidowicz, *The War Against the Jews: 1933–1945.* (New York: Holt, Rinehart and Winston, 1975); Raul Hilberg, *The Destruction of European Jews.* (Chicago: Quadrangle Books, 1961); Nora Levin, *The Holocaust: The Destruction of European Jewry 1933–1945.* (New York: Schocken, 1968). For a vivid account of the conditions to which Russians have been subjected under Communist totalitarianism see Aleksandr Solzhenitsyn, *The Gulag Archipelago, 1918–1956.* (New York: Harper & Row, 1973–1974).

21. "Russian intellectuals, disaffected and critical, were ever eager to slake their thirst for ideas about history and society and to show their disapproval of Russian conditions by adopting the most radical ideas found in the West. The curious consequence was that the first foreign language into which Marx's major work was translated was Russian." Alfred G. Meyer, *Communism*, 3rd ed. (New York: Random House, 1967), p. 59.

22. It is impossible to determine the extent to which this view represents an analysis of the political needs of an economically backward nation if it is to modernize rapidly and the extent to which this view represents a rationalization for Stalin's own desire for unrestricted personal power.

23. See Friedrich and Brzezinski, *Totalitarian Dictatorship*, pp. 205–218. While initially such centralization reduces problems of coordination and control, the long-term effects of its

widespread adoption can produce opposite consequences. Conflict between bureaucracies and the emergence of local autocrats become common.

24. Urie Bronfenbrenner, *Two Worlds of Childhood, U.S. and U.S.S.R.* (New York: Simon and Schuster, Touchstone edition, 1972), p. 47.

25. See "The Church and the Communists," *Newsweek,* October 30, 1978, pp. 84–87. The more recent political history of Communist efforts in Afghanistan and Poland reveals something of the political vitality of the church even in hostile nondemocratic settings.

26. The system of unequal privilege in Russia neither began with Stalin's rule nor ended with his death. However, it was considerably elaborated under his government. For an extensive discussion of social inequality under Communism from the time of Lenin to the present, see Mervyn Matthews, *Privilege in the Soviet Union* (London: George Allen and Unwin, 1978).

27. There was *some* correspondence, however. For example, extremely productive individual workers received special bonuses and consumption perquisites. No doubt this encouraged greater worker effort and had some overall positive effect on economic growth.

28. Theda Skocpol, *States and Social Revolutions* (New York: Cambridge University Press, 1979), p. 230.

29. See David Lane, *The Socialist Industrial State* (London: George Allen and Unwin, 1976), pp. 19–43.

30. Samuel P. Huntington and Joan M. Nelson, *No Easy Choice* (Cambridge, Mass.: Harvard University Press, 1976).

31. A study using a sample of 99 countries at varying levels of economic development (excluding all Communist nations but Yugoslavia) concluded that the greater the state control of the economy, the lower the level of political democracy (defined in terms of the level of popular sovereignty and the presence of various political liberties). See Kenneth A. Bollen, "Political Democracy and the Timing of Development," *American Sociological Review,* 44, no. 4 (August 1979) 572–587.

32. Huntington and Nelson, *No Easy Choice,* p. 117.

33. See Eugene V. Rostow and George W. Ball, "The Genesis of the Multinational Corporation," in *Global Companies: The Political Economy of World Business,* George W. Ball, ed. (Englewood Cliffs, N.J.: Prentice-Hall, Spectrum Books, 1975), pp. 4–10.

34. Ronald Müller, "A Qualifying and Dissenting View of the Multinational Corporation," *Ibid.,* p. 36.

35. Source: Richard G. Braungart, "Transnational Corporate Enterprises: Problems, Theory and Research." Presented at a discussion seminar at the Annual Meetings of the American Sociological Association, Boston, August 1979. Also see Louis Turner, *Invisible Empires* (New York: Harcourt Brace Jovanovich, 1971), pp. 135–136.

36. Ralph Nader, Mark Green, and Joel Seligman, *Taming the Giant Corporation* (New York: W. W. Norton, 1976), p. 28.

37. Braungart, "Transnational Corporate Enterprises," p. 3. The two other "forces" are nation-states and labor unions.

38. See Anthony Sampson, *The Sovereign State of I.T.T.* (New York: Fawcett, 1974).

39. Richard J. Barnet and Ronald E. Müller, *Global Reach* (New York: Simon and Schuster, 1974), p. 151.

40. For detailed examples of the direct intervention of multinational corporations in the internal politics of nations, see "Multinationals at Bay: How Clean Is Business?" *Newsweek,* September 1, 1975, pp. 50–54; "Payoffs, The Growing Scandal," *Newsweek,* February 23, 1976, pp. 26–33.

41. Immanuel Wallerstein, *The Capitalist World Economy* (Cambridge: Cambridge University Press, 1979), p. 53.

42. Immanuel Wallerstein, *The Modern World System: Capitalist Agriculture and the Origins of the European World Economy in the Sixteenth Century* (New York: Academic Press, 1974).

43. See Skocpol, *States and Social Revolutions,* p. 22.

44. Clyde Z. Nunn, Harry J. Crockett, Jr., and J. Allen Williams, Jr., *Tolerance for Nonconformity* (San Francisco: Jossey-Bass, 1978), p. 7.

45. For an illustration of the dilemma presented to political democracies by international terrorism, see Lord Gardiner, *Report of a Committee to Consider, in the Context of Civil Liberties and Human Rights, Measures to Deal with Terrorism in Northern Ireland* (London: Her Majesty's Stationery Office, 1975).

POSTSCRIPT
THE RELEVANCE OF
POLITICAL SOCIOLOGY[1]

On these final few pages I would like to present, very briefly, a view of what value the study of political sociology can have for students. I hope that the materials in this book have had some intrinsic interest, and further that their study has had, or will have, some influence on beliefs, attitudes, and future patterns of political participation.

It has been my experience that most students who choose to explore political sociology have some interest in the bearing on their own everyday lives of the ideas with which they believe they will be presented. Students have often expressed this interest to me as a concern for "relevance." The concern that political sociology be relevant, somehow, to everyday life raises a number of related questions. First, what are some of the explicit expectations of students who want "relevance"? No discussion of this interest can proceed until some of the ambiguities which accompany it have been resolved. If a number of explicit expectations can be identified, a second question arises: with respect to political sociology texts and courses, are all or any of these expectations legitimate? Finally, if a case can be made for the legitimacy of some of these expectations, how well can those who write and teach in the area of political sociology hope to do in attempting to meet them? Discussion of these questions requires some definition of the field of political sociology, a specification of the possible meanings of the "relevance" that the field, so defined, may have, and the development of a set of criteria for determining the legitimacy of the requests for "relevance" in each of the various senses which are identified.

In the first section of this book I attempted to develop an analytically useful definition of political sociology. The definition which emerged specified that "political sociology" is to be understood as the concern with the structure and dynamics of power and authority relations as these are organized and exercised at relatively inclusive levels of social organization and as these influence and are influenced by the social bonds of kinship, religion, and class, by interest groups based on other than purely ascriptive or economic ties, and by socially shared belief and value systems.

A number of meanings of the desire for relevance in political sociology courses and texts can be distinguished. Students may be requesting *analytic* relevance. Here interest is in the explication of theories which are applicable to certain salient, contemporary events. Requests for explanations of the social processes affecting national political decision making in America, the diminishing proportions of Americans who vote in national elections, or the social and cultural conditions under which revolutions are most likely to occur can serve as examples of this variety of interest. Students may also be requesting *practical* relevance. Here the desire is for the presentation of clear strategies for realizing given political goals. Questions about the most efficient means of insuring that the administration of a university will attend to student demands or about methods of containing the influence of the military in the determination of American foreign policy illustrate this type of interest. There may also be a demand for *moral* relevance. Here specific expectations are less clear and a number of claims may be involved. Students may desire discussions in moral terms of what they perceive to be the major, pressing political situations of the day. For example, they might want a consideration of the "justness" of a government's attempts to balance the national budget and increase military spending at the cost of drastically reducing the funding of numerous other programs—particularly those which benefit the poor at home and others benefiting the peoples of economically poor nations. Alternatively, students may be seeking a relatively systematic basis for making moral judgments about political institutions, ideologies, and patterns of behavior. A question exemplifying this variety of ethical concern might be "On what grounds can I judge one political system to be more responsive to its citizens' needs than another?" Two additional interpretations of "moral relevance" can be indicated. Students may want to learn of a way for determining what sort of political commitment they personally should make. Finally, they may simply desire the presentation of data which support an ideological position they already hold and which they assume is or ought to be held by most others.

One way to decide upon the legitimacy of these different requests for relevance is to determine whether or not efforts to meet them would be compatible with a conception of political sociology such as that developed in Chapter 6. There I made a distinction between political sociology and political ideology. While many of the topical areas of political sociology and political ideology correspond, the distinction identified differences in the methodology of theory construction between political ideology and political sociology as well as differences in the objectives of presenting the analyses. Political sociology was characterized as being *empirical, theoretical, cumulative,* and *value-explicit.* Each of these qualities requires some additional discussion here.

One sense in which political sociology is empirical is that its truth claims are based on data derived from observation. Unlike political ideology, political sociology is normatively committed to change its truth claims in the light of new observational data which indicate the inadequacies of existing theoretical explanations of political structures and processes. The amount of empirical data now available on political life is considerably more impressive than the amount available a decade ago. An increase in the number of empirical studies conducted, new computer hardware and software, and the development of data archives such as those of the Inter-University Consortium for Political Research and the Roper Institute at Williams College have enhanced qualitatively and quantitatively the empirical character of political sociology. The work of the Committee on Political Sociology of the International Sociological Association has produced an increasing number of theoretically interrelated comparative studies and has fostered international cooperation and coordination of empirical research programs. Such investigations represent valuable additions to the work of American political sociologists which, until quite recently, primarily has been noncomparative.

Much of the work of political sociologists remains uncodified. However, middle-range theories have been developed in a number of areas of research. These areas include party identification and voting behavior, political participation, public opinion and ideology, community power, political aspects of bureaucratic organization, and political movements. Promising new areas of theoretical development include social revolution and the political economy of the modern world system. The end in view of such theory construction has been that of enhancing empirical understanding of these political structures and processes. The theories primarily have been developed to maximize intellectual clarity rather than to advocate political action.

The thesis that major advances in a science occur in a revolutionary fashion with the replacement of one paradigm by another is not less applicable to political sociology than to any other area of empirical investigation.[2] A case could be made for the contention that insofar as there has been a paradigm guiding research and theory construction in political sociology for the past few decades, it has handicapped the analysis of non-routine political participation and the political change of economically poor nations. Hence, the time is right for revolutionary developments in the field. While this argument may have some merit, the history of political sociology to the present has been one of continuing incremental progress in explanatory abilities. I have taken the position throughout this book that the central approaches, concepts, and hypotheses of political sociology can be traced to the works of Marx, Weber, and Durkheim. The future of political sociology lies in a continued use of these analytic tools—though not in the way in which most American political sociologists typically employed them. Rather, the future should see a return to macroanalytic, historical-comparative studies, many of which focus on change. Such a reinstatement of political sociology's original thrust would not represent a revolution so much as it would represent a kind of cumulative development. On the basis of theoretical and methodological progress, political sociology seems to be ready to deal in an empirically sophisticated manner with the types of questions raised by its theoretical forebears. New developments in the study of social revolution and the political economy of the modern world system, noted above, support this view.

Insofar as they are aware of their value orientations, political sociologists can make them explicit in their writing and in their teaching and can try to locate and correct distortions which such orientations may have introduced. They can also identify those topics which they have cho-sen *not* to discuss, thus indicating that they will consider only a particular set of political phenomena, e.g., routine processes such as voting rather than nonroutine processes such as vehement protest.

Before proceeding to an assessment of the legitimacy of each of the requests for text and course relevance in terms of its compatibility with the view of political sociology as *empirical, theoretical, cumulative,* and *value-explicit,* a number of clarifications are necessary. First, when I contend that a certain topic of discussion is not legitimate I do not wish to suggest that it is unworthy of serious consideration. I merely want to assert that the topic does not fall within the domain of political sociology where that domain is in part delimited by the possession of the qualities noted above. Second, I do not assume that all, or even most, of the work done by those who identify themselves as political sociologists exhibits these qualities. The ap-proach which I have taken here is explicitly normative. Not all will agree with it. While arguments are presented here, and throughout this book, in its support, my purpose in writing this postscript is solely to encourage those with interest in political sociology—authors, researchers, teachers, and students—to make explicit to themselves what they think they legiti-mately can ask of political sociology.

My decision to assess the legitimacy of each of the expectations in terms of its compatibility with the conception of political sociology as pos-sessing the four specified qualities is based upon my belief that the subject matter of political sociology courses should present materials which make the political world which students experience more intelligible to them, and this will enable them to act more effectively within their social environment and act in ways oriented toward the reduction of human suffering.[3] It is also based on my assumption that to the extent that political sociology exhibits each of these four qualities, authors and instructors will be able to achieve these objectives.

In any social system, there will be some debate about what education "is for." While one of the defining characteristics of educational institutions is their concern with the transmission of a body of "knowledge" (as this is culturally defined) seldom will there be total agreement in a social system about what "knowledge" is most important to communicate. Beyond this there is likely to be considerable disagreement on other proper functions of the system's educational institutions.

One function of political sociology texts and courses is the transmission of information concerning a body of empirical research literature. It can be assumed that there will be a number of different interpretations of the empirical quality and theoretical significance of research in the various areas which might be discussed, such as political participation, community power, mass movements, public opinion and ideology, and so on. Beyond this there are a number of positions in the philosophy of education which are taken. My view which I have outlined above represents but one of these.

We have already seen that while the empirical investigation of power and authority relations is a relatively recent intellectual development, discussions of power and authority have a long and rich history. No doubt most with such interests have not had as one of their major aims the development of empirically valid and reliable theory. Nevertheless, such explanations are intimately related to the moral and practical concerns which they did express, concerns quite similar to those felt by students today. Dahl has noted that it would be difficult to explain the extent to which political theorists for the past centuries have been concerned with relations of power and authority were it not for the moral and practical significance of power to any person in political life, whether as observer or activist.[4] Some understanding of power is usually thought to be indispensable for moral and ethical appraisals of political systems. In addition, intelligent action to bring about a result of some kind in a political system, such as a change in a law or a policy, a revolution, or a settlement of an international dispute, requires knowledge of how to produce or cause the results.

In short, an aim of this book, and the aims of political sociology courses as defined here, are in keeping with the desires of those with evaluative and practical interests. Debate over the relative merits of alternative forms of political organizations which utilize some information about the actual operation of these forms are more productive than are discussions which apply only ideal types (this was one reason for the presentation of some detailed description of Fascist Germany and Russia under Stalin in Chapter 8). Plans for political action based on some understanding of the probable outcomes of alternative strategies are more likely to achieve desired results for those who formulate them than are proposed actions based solely on slogans, hopes, and aspirations. Having specified these views, I now want to discuss directly the legitimacy of student expectations that political sociology should be relevant to their intellectual, practical and moral concerns.

Analytic Relevance. It seems to me that student requests for analytically relevant political sociology texts and courses clearly are legitimate. The expectation even facilitates the development of empirical, theoretical, and cumulative qualities insofar as it encourages the codification of findings and reveals theoretical lacunae. However, particular caution must be taken by authors and instructors to insure that meeting such demands does not have the opposite effect, i.e., the presentation of apparently unrelated propositions which are narrowly historical and nonabstractive. Such propositions abound in political sociology, and they will not enable the author or the instructor to meet the requests for analytic relevance.

As I have pointed out many times in this book, historically, the overriding concern of political sociologists has been with factors contributing to the stability of Western polities. Consequently, at present students may not be able to find satisfactory answers to many of their questions which focus on noninstitutionalized political conflict and the political problems of the economically poor nations of the world—and these are the very topics in which they are likely to have considerable interest. While students may have legitimate requests, authors and instructors may not have available sufficiently valid responses. However, as we have seen, there are indicators that in the not too distant future, this situation will no longer be found.

Practical Relevance. I feel that the desire for practical relevance is legitimate if what is being requested is the systematic presentation of widely applicable propositions which increase the ability to calculate the risks, costs, and rewards of alternative political strategies. Such demands are problematic, however, to the degree that they exclude the exposition of the theoretical contexts from which such propositions are taken. To some extent the ability to provide "practically relevant" information is inversely related to the size, cultural heterogeneity, and structural complexity of the social unit about which such information is desired.

Leader-follower relations in small face-to-face groups (both primary and secondary) have interested political sociologists probably since Lippitt and White's classic experiment and certainly since Verba called political analysts' attention to this body of research literature.[5] Information at least implicitly suggesting strategies for increasing control over the manner in which influence is exercised in such contexts is widely available. While discussion of such topics is legitimate, it must be remembered that, in terms of the definition used in this book, such concerns are not central to political sociology, which focuses on power and authority relations at relatively inclusive levels of social organization.

Following Weber, many political sociologists have been interested in the study of bureaucracy. Numerous factors which contribute to or which can inhibit their antidemocratic tendencies have been identified. Students seeking "practically relevant" information concerning industrial, governmental, party, or university bureaucracies should find numerous suggestive propositions in this body of literature.

The ability to provide "practically relevant" information concerning structures more complex than bureaucratic organizations is rather limited. As I pointed out in Chapter 7, there is a lack of consensus among political sociologists as to the feasibility of alternative models for analyzing the distribution and exercise of power in American communities and in the nation as a whole. Discussions between "pluralists" and "elitists" more often have taken the form of debates between supporters of divergent ideologies than the form of a discussion of the relative analytic utility of different models. The development of sets of empirically valid and theoretically relevant statements about authority structures (the kind of statements that are also practically relevant) requires something other than the empirical search for what one hopes to find, i.e., data suggesting the merit of the societal model to which one is committed. It requires, instead, commitment to the methodological canons of empirical research, particularly to the methodological guideline that the approach seek its own potential disconfirmation in observable structures and processes. It also requires commitment to the principle that, insofar as it is possible, one be explicit to oneself and to one's audience about the values which play some role in one's political actions and in one's writing about politics. Progress along these lines was also noted in Chapter 7. Using newer approaches such as "network" analysis, political sociologists should soon be able to provide some "practically relevant" information about community and perhaps even national power structures.

The situation in political sociology with respect to knowledge about non-Western polities needs considerable improvement before political sociologists are able to meet legitimate demands for "practical relevance." However, a new thrust in the direction of macroanalytic historical studies offers considerable hope for future abilities in this broad area.

Moral Relevance. I believe that the request for discussions of major political issues in moral terms is legitimate according to the criteria specified earlier in this postscript if (1) such discussions are to involve the presentation of empirical findings identifying those conditions within a social system which are labeled and reacted to as "political problems" by the political leaders and/or by the other members of the system and (2) these findings are accompanied by systematic, theoretically derived explanations indicating why these conditions are labeled as "political problems" and how and why the political institutions of the social system have dealt or have failed to deal with these "problems." Discussion of the relationship between public wants and government policies should make each student's own political world more intelligible and should suggest some possibilities for, and some limitations to, successful collective political action.

The request for discussions of political issues in moral terms is also legitimate if such discussions are to involve (3) the presentation of empirical findings identifying the differential consequences of a social system's institutional policies and practices on the well-being of the members of its various subgroups.

The request for discussions of political issues in moral terms is not legitimate according to the criteria used here if desired discussions are to focus primarily on labeling certain political policies and practices as "moral" or "immoral," as "just" or "unjust," and the like. To be legitimate such labeling must be accompanied by a clear specification of the empirical conditions under which such labels are to be applied, sets of valid and reliable descriptions of the objects of evaluation, and a theoretically viable explanation for the persistence of those policies and practices which are judged negatively.

The request for a systematic basis for making moral judgments is legitimate if this involves (4) the provision of skills for the conduct of empirical inquiry—i.e., teaching students how to operationalize concepts such as "democratic" or "authoritarian" and how to determine the applicability of such concepts to empirical situations. The request is not legitimate if it requires merely the explication of a set of moral values or the statement of a set of preferences for certain specific political values, beliefs, and practices.

It is my own belief that political sociologists should encourage the development of political orientations consistent with the reduction of human suffering. However, this is not to maintain that those who write about political sociology and teach political sociology courses should act as agents of moral indoctrination. To encourage humane thought and action is not to inculcate rather specific values. A great variety of politically relevant beliefs, norms, values, and practices are consistent with the desire to reduce human suffering.

In response to student requests for general direction concerning the political commitment they should make, authors or instructors can indicate legitimately the situations which various members of their society label "political problems" and can explain how these problems have been dealt with. They can indicate where there are clear gaps between public wants and government policies. In addition they can (5) encourage students to consider the reduction of human suffering as a general value to pursue in political action.

There is yet another legitimate response to the request for political guidance. Authors or instructors can (6) indicate conditions which might well be but generally are not regarded as "problems" in their society— "problems" which might find political solutions.[6] This would involve specification of conditions which have demonstrably negative consequences for certain segments of the population or for society as a whole. In addition, the conditions must be subject to human control and alterable through political action. Hence, another sense in which a text or course in political sociology might be "morally relevant" involves the development of new political concerns. Author or instructors can not only point out and explain gaps between public wants and political policies, but they can also point out public wants that might well exist but do not. (Considerations of the absence of certain public wants could generate testable hypotheses about political phenomena such as relationships between private corporations and government or the manipulation of public opinion.)

Finally, the preceding should make it clear that I feel the request for selective presentation of data which support a given ideological position is not legitimate. Such a demand is incompatible with the conception of political sociology which I have employed throughout this book. The development and presentation of valid empirical theory, which is a precondition for meeting any demands for relevance, requires consideration of data collected in ways specifically designed to reduce bias. The norm that political sociology should be value-explicit is intended to help reveal potential sources of bias in the conduct of political inquiry and in the interpretation and presentation of results.

Conceived of as a body of knowledge, as "knowledge" is defined at present in our culture, political sociology consists of sets of assertions about relations between items of empirically derived information. However, as argued above, this body of knowledge does reflect the value orientations of those who have developed it. The body of knowledge also has extensive practical and moral implications. The more clearly political sociology adheres to the norm of being empirical, theoretical, cumulative, and value-explicit, the more valuable it will be to those who seek a better world.

NOTES

1. This postscript is adapted from my article, "On Teaching Political Sociology," *Journal of Political and Military Sociology*, 2, no. 1 (Spring 1974), 21–32.

2. See Thomas S. Kuhn, *The Structure of Scientific Revolutions* (Chicago: University of Chicago Press, 1962).

3. Moore effectively argues that while people find it difficult to agree upon the meaning and the causes of happiness, they find it much easier to know when they are suffering. We do not need to prove, for example, that they have hardly ever enjoyed starvation and illness, the loss of beloved persons through the acts of others over which they had no control, losing the means of livelihood for the expression of unpopular beliefs, and so on. From the standpoint of social arrangements, in rough-and-ready empirical categories, the causes of human misery have been and continue to be (1) the ravages of war, (2) poverty, hunger and disease, (3) injustice and oppression, (4) persecution for dissident beliefs. See Barrington Moore, Jr., *Reflections on the Causes of Human Misery* (Boston: Beacon Press, 1970).

4. See Robert A. Dahl, "Power," V. 12 in *International Encyclopedia of the Social Sciences*, ed. David L. Sills (New York: Macmillan and The Free Press, 1968), pp. 405–415.

5. See Ronald Lippitt and Ralph White, "An Experimental Study of Leadership and Group Life," in *Readings in Social Psychology*, E. M. Maccoby et al., eds. (New York: Holt, 1958), pp. 496–511; Sidney Verba, *Small Groups and Political Behavior* (Princeton, N.J.: Princeton University Press, 1961).

6. Hamilton distinguishes between "issues," "unformulated issues," and "undeveloped concerns." A concern, which is a felt or sensed need, Hamilton points out, is not necessarily a subject for widespread public discussion. Nor is it necessarily of interest to political parties. An issue, characteristically defined as an object of discussion in political campaigns, nearly always has an underlying concern as its basis, but there are occasions when the issues chosen by political leaders have apparently been of little concern to the mass public. Widespread concerns that are not made the subject of political discussions, because of the choices of political leaders, are unformulated issues. Undeveloped concerns exist in situations where conditions are found which are in some way detrimental to public welfare but which are not sensed as a problem. Hence there are no demands for control of the conditions. See Richard F. Hamilton, *Class and Politics in the United States* (New York: John Wiley & Sons, 1972).

INDEX

369

371

374